*f*P

The Division of Labor in Society

by

Emile Durkheim

With an introduction by **Lewis A. Coser**

Translated by **W. D. Halls**

THE FREE PRESS

THE FREE PRESS
A Division of Simon & Schuster Inc.
1230 Avenue of the Americas
New York, NY 10020

First Paperback Edition 1997
Originally published in Great Britain by Macmillan Education Ltd.

THE FREE PRESS and colophon are trademarks
of Simon & Schuster Inc.

Manufactured in the United States of America

20 19 18 17 16 15 14

Library of Congress Cataloging-in-Publication Data

Durkheim, Emile, 1858–1917.
    The division of labor in society.
    Translation of: De la division du travail social.
    Originally published: Emile Durkheim on the division of labor in society. New
    York: Macmillan, 1933.
    Includes bibliographical references.
    1. Division of labor.   I. Halls, W. D.
II. Title.
HD51.D9613   1984   306'.36   84-10111
ISBN-13: 978-0-684-83638-6
ISBN-10:   0-684-83638-6

Contents

BOOK III   THE ABNORMAL FORMS

Translator's Note

For various reasons it has proved impossible to check every footnote and to supply complete references. Durkheim omitted very frequently details that would have made this possible.

However, most of the direct quotations from English-speaking authors have been found and the original inserted. Where this has not been possible, what are given as direct quotations in Durkheim have been turned into indirect speech.

W.D.H.

Introduction*

Emile Durkheim's *The Division of Labour in Society*, his doctoral dissertation and his first major work, was published in 1893. Though a previous translation into English appeared in 1933, the present volume is the first exact, adequate and satisfying translation of this key work.

The Division of Labour is a highly original treatment of the subject, yet it should be read within the context of earlier attempts to come to grips with the complex division of labour that emerged with the industrial revolution, first in England and then on the Continent. What is novel in Durkheim's thought can best be understood if one refers, even if only sketchily, to previous attempts to define and come to grips with the emergence of an unprecedented system of production and the allocation of both productive and other societal tasks in the late eighteenth century.

Some forms of the division of labour, be it only along sexual lines, have characterised all known types of society from the 'primitive' to the modern. In all of them, certain types of labour, but also of other functions, were allocated to specific groups of people. Even in the smallest known human societies there are some forms of human differentiation in the allocation of tasks and roles.

---

* In the following pages I am deeply in debt to the writings of Anthony Giddens on Durkheim, in particular his *Capitalism and Modern Social Theory* (Cambridge, Cambridge University Press, 1971) and his *Durkheim* (London, Fontana/Collins, 1978). I also owe a great deal to Steven Lukes's *Emile Durkheim: His Life and Work* (London, Allen Lane, 1973). Other, less extensive, debts are acknowledged in textual notes. Philippe Besnard and Anthony Giddens read an earlier version of this introduction and made many helpful suggestions for which I am grateful.

Mediaeval society and its characteristic thinkers were well aware of the diversity of work activities in their midst, and writings on the differences among such 'callings' took prominent place among the Protestant reformers of the sixteenth century and after. But the pre-modern division of labour involved, by and large, either divisions between urban artisans and rural folk who were involved in specific trades and occupations or rough class divisions between the members of the various estates that together made up pre-modern society. Butchers, bakers, and candlestick makers fashioned products of a different nature and were socially visible in the pursuit of these different occupational ways of life. On the other hand, there were sharp divisions between those devoted to military affairs, people who were following a religious calling, and those, the great majority, who laboured in the fields or in urban occupations.

A qualitative sea change in the character of the division of labour – a change from relative simplicity to rapidly advancing complexity – occurred, though adumbrations can be found much earlier, only with the beginning of the industrial revolution, first in the latter part of the eighteenth century in England and soon after in the rest of Europe and in America.

The emerging industrial form of production involved the gradual replacement of an artisanal mode of production, that is, a division of labour in which a particular producer, sometimes with the assistance of a few others, fashioned a whole product, by a mode of production based on a much finer differentiation of tasks and activities than previously. The products of the new industrial system were no longer created by individual craftsmen or by the collaboration of a few, but emerged instead from the co-ordinated activities of a large number of persons who had been assigned specialised tasks. The final product was the result of the integration of the work of a great number of workers who were submitted to overall discipline and co-ordination – be it by the tyranny of the clock, by the constraints of supervisors, or by mechanical rhythms. Moreover, the diversification of economic tasks was paralleled in the modern era by differentiation in many other spheres, in government as well as in the law, in the sciences as well as in legal institutions.

Adam Smith's *The Wealth of Nations* was the first major work that attempted to come to grips with this revolutionary development not only in the productive system but in the general character of social living. What characterised the dawning world of modern industry, so Smith argued, was above all the enormous increase in productivity that the new industrial division of labour brought in its wake. The combined labours of a number of specialised workers could now produce many more products in a specified number of hours than any single worker could have produced under the older system of production. The new division of labour, so Smith argued, could become an enormous boon to humanity by raising living standards to a degree simply unimaginable in previous days. Moreover, if previous barriers to commerce and exchange, both within given countries and in international trade, were removed so that goods could be produced in the economically most favoured locations, the new national and international division of labour would add further gains of productivity to those already achieved in the workplace.

It would be unduly simplifying Smith's thought were one to overlook the fact that although he concentrated attention on the beneficial effects of the new division of labour, he was also concerned about some of its deleterious consequences. What would become of people, Smith asked, who would throughout their lives perform the same number of simple tasks over and over again? Would this not lead to the deterioration of their mental faculties? How could one expect over-specialised workers to develop a sense of citizenship and a devotion to the common weal? Yet, in contrast to many radical as well as conservative thinkers who followed in his wake, Smith remained basically optimistic about the benefits that the new mode of production would bring. Surely the great majority of readers carried from their reading of *The Wealth of Nations* an exhilarating sense of the bounties of the world to come. Vastly increased productive capacities would raise the level of human happiness to previously undreamed of degrees.

However, only a few decades after Smith had published his work, dissenting voices began to be heard in England as well as on the Continent. The underdevelopment of human capacities that Smith had only dealt with as a kind of afterthought became now a mainstay of critical reaction. The critics argued, to quote from the historian J. G. A. Pocock, that 'society as an engine for the production and multiplication of goods was inherently hostile to society as the moral foundation of personality' (*The Machiavellian Moment: Florentine Political Thought and the Atlantic Republican Tradition*, Princeton,

NJ, Princeton University Press, 1975, p. 501). The new division of labour, argued Carlyle as well as many English romantics, when it began to be applied in the 'satanic mills' of the new industrial age, stultified individual human beings and atrophied individual capacities. Human beings became anaesthetised cogs in a vast productive apparatus. Roughly at the same time, German thinkers from Schiller to Hegel or Fichte, though writing in a country that was as yet hardly touched by the industrial revolution, echoed British thinkers and wrathfully castigated the new division of labour that could only lead to the emergence of stunted human beings who would no longer be able to develop full and autonomous personalities.

These critical voices found their culminating expression in the work of Karl Marx who argued that, at least in its capitalist form, the new industrial division of labour alienated human beings from the products of their labour, from their work, as well as from their fellows, and even from themselves. Marx, as well as many other critics, were prepared to agree with Smith that productivity under the new system had enormously increased, but they were intent upon showing that, at least under current conditions, these gains were accompanied by enormous human costs. The new mode of production, they argued, was inhuman in its consequences. A system that Smith had believed to bring great increments in human happiness had in fact resulted perversely in enormous increases in human misery and degradation. The human beings now bound to the Ixion's wheel of the modern factory had become suffering victims instead of happy beneficiaries of the new division of labour.

The debate between the defenders and the antagonists of the new system of industrial production was carried on throughout most of the nineteenth century, and though individual voices can surely be distinguished, the general terms of the debate remained largely unaltered. It was the great merit of Emile Durkheim to renew the debate by largely eschewing the discussions of the past about productivity versus alienation, and putting a largely novel perspective before his audience.

Writing over a century after Adam Smith, Durkheim was no longer concerned with the productive gains made by the new division of labour, nor was he much concerned with what Marx had called alienation, although he was indeed perturbed by what he called the pathological consequences of the 'abnormal' conditions of the contemporary division of labour. What concerned Durkheim above everything else were questions that had hardly been raised by his predecessors, though there are anticipations of his thought among such thinkers as Auguste Comte or Saint-Simon. What were the consequences of a complex and advanced system of the division of labour on the cohesion and solidarity of societies? And, more important still, how could the autonomy of the individual, to which Durkheim was passionately attached, be reconciled with the necessary regulation and discipline that was required to maintain social order in modern differentiated types of societies? How, in other words, could social bonds be maintained and reinforced without submitting individuals to the distasteful guidance of tutelary institutions that would repress human autonomy and individuality?

Durkheim saw himself as a dispassionate scientific student of society. Yet he was also strongly concerned with social reform. As he put it, 'because what we propose to study is above all reality, it does not follow that we should give up the idea of improving it. We would esteem our research not worth the labour of a single hour if its interest were merely speculative' (p. xxvi). At the time of writing *The Division of Labour*, Durkheim placed himself in the tradition of positivism at the same time as he was far removed from the *laissez-faire* positivism of many nineteenth-century English and Continental thinkers. His positivism, just like that of Auguste Comte, was intended to prepare the ground for active social intervention.

Durkheim was a political liberal with pronounced melioristic as well as conservative sentiments. Though beholden to the idea of progress, he was equally concerned with the conditions that made social order possible. In this respect resembling Max Weber, Durkheim wanted to enhance the autonomy of the individual even as he clung to the idea that such autonomy could only be attained upon secure foundations in conditions of social solidarity firmly binding its members to each other. To put the question in his own words:

The question that has been the starting point for our study has been that of the connection between the individual personality and social solidarity. How does it come about that the individual, whilst becoming more autonomous, depends ever more closely upon society? How can he become at the same time more of an individual and yet more linked to society? . . . It has seemed to us that what resolved this apparent antinomy was the transformation of social solidarity which arises from the ever-increasing division of labour (p. xxx).

In order to clarify the dialectical relations between social solidarity in the modern industrial world and personal autonomy, or, as he called it, the 'cult of the individual', Durkheim attempted systematically to distinguish the type of solidarity prevalent in relatively simple societies with that to be found in the modern world. He called the first *mechanical solidarity* and the second *organic solidarity*. This twofold distinction was in tune with much nineteenth-century thought. Spencer's distinction between military and industrial societies, Maine's societies based on status as against those based on contract, and, above all, Tönnies's distinction between *Gemeinschaft* and *Gesellschaft* have obvious similarities with Durkheim's concepts. Yet his divergencies from these thinkers are at least as pronounced as their similarities. To Spencer as well as to Maine the general trend of human evolution was marked by the gradual decline of societal regulation and the emergence of unfettered individualism. On the other hand, as has been seen, Durkheim was convinced that without stable social bonds, without social solidarity, individualism would lead to the decay of society. Yet he felt equally uncongenial to Tönnies and other German thinkers who argued that true solidarity could only exist in village communities of the past and that the breath of modernity undermined what these thinkers conceived to be the only true solidary societal formation, the now decayed or decaying *Gemeinschaft*.

Despite their divergencies, Durkheim and the other thinkers faced a common question: If preindustrial societies were held together by common values, sentiments and norms, equally shared by all, what held modern societies together, given the fact that the modern forms or organisation and production had made people unlike each other and hence no longer susceptible to solidarities and regulations encompassing everyone with equal vigour?

Spencer and Maine believed that freely engaged contracts between individuals were gradually replacing now largely obsolete solidarities and regulations. In one of the main contentions of his work, Durkheim objected that individual contracts could not lay the foundation of a social order and that, to the contrary, contracts could only be engaged in on the basis of an already existing moral order. 'The contract is not sufficient by itself, but is only possible because of the regulation of contracts, which is of social origin' (p. 162). In other words, contracts presuppose social order -- they cannot serve as its foundation. The social order has primacy over individually motivated actions. The individualistic – utilitarian solution to the problem of social order in modern societies leads to an impasse.

Durkheim did not only limit himself to documenting that contracts between individuals could not, as such, form the basis of social cohesion. He went further and asserted that the modern type of individual, far from being an existential given, was in fact a historically emergent, a societal creation. 'In fact, if in lower societies so little place is allowed for the individual personality', he argued, 'it is not that it has been constricted or suppressed artificially, it is quite simply because at that moment in history *it did not exist*' (p. 142). The whole matter is once again put in a nutshell when Durkheim argued in an endnote:

> We believe this is sufficient to answer those who think that they can prove that in social life everything is individual, because society is made up only of individuals. Undoubtedly no other substratum exists. But because individuals form a society, new phenomena occur whose cause is association, and which, reacting upon the consciousness of individuals, for the most part shapes them. This is why, although society is nothing without individuals, each one of them is more a product of society than he is the author (p. 288).

Durkheim was equally opposed to the German train of thought, best exemplified by the work of Tönnies, which claimed that true solidarity could only exist in relatively undifferentiated societies in which the sense of individuality had not yet corroded the social fabric. Tönnies's dyspeptic picture of the present and his glorification of an undivided past, Durkheim argued, was rooted in the assumption that the maintenance of social bonds could only be achieved when social differentiation was at a minimum. Yet it was a fact, Durkheim believed, that while mechanical solidarity could indeed only thrive where human beings were engaged in essentially similar activities, organic solidarity could develop from spontaneously arising consensus between individual actors who, just because they were engaged in different roles and tasks, were dependent on one another. While mechanical solidarity was founded upon likeness, organic solidarity arose because of complementarity between actors engaged in different pursuits.

To summarise: it is not the decay of social solidarity, as both the British and the German thinkers assumed, that marked the transition from relatively simple to relatively complex societies in Durkheim's eyes. Rather there emerged a new type of solidarity in the world of modernity once the relatively simple societies of the past had given way to the complex world of an elaborate division of labour.

What then accounted for the evolutionary transition from the rigid social controls and uniform beliefs and sentiments of societies based on mechanical solidarity to the societies of organic solidarity where each element operates more independently and is not simply a miniature image or an appendage of the collective body? Here Durkheim advanced an essentially Darwinian argument. As in the course of human evolution the density of settlement increases not only because the number of individuals in a given territory increases but also because, partly as a consequence, the number of interactions between individuals increases, there is need for specialisation of activities so as to increase productivity. Specialisation is required if a greater number of interacting individuals are forced to assure their livelihood on a given territory.

Still beholden, as were many of his contemporaries, to biological analogies, Durkheim argued that the shift from mechanical to organic solidarity might profitably be compared to the changes that appeared on the evolutionary scale. Relatively simple organisms showing only minimal degrees of internal differentiation, cede place to more highly differentiated organisms whose functional specialisation allows them to exploit more efficiently the resources of the ecological niche in which they happen to be placed. The more specialised the functions of an organism, the higher its level on the evolutionary scale, and the higher its survival value. In similar ways, the more differentiated a society, the higher its chances to exploit the maximum of available resources, and hence the higher its efficiency in procuring indispensable means of subsistence in a given territory.

Having located the basic differences between modern and

simpler societies in the differing forms of solidarity that they exhibit, Durkheim was then moved to indicate how it was possible to distinguish between mechanical and organic solidarity even though such moral phenomena were evidently not measurable directly. Searching for an indicator of types of solidarity, Durkheim turned to the study of legal codes. He asserted that legal regulations, that is, rules of conduct that are sanctioned, can be roughly divided into two major types: repressive sanctions, which are characteristic of penal law and involve punishment for transgressions and deviance, and restitutory sanctions, which, in contrast, do not rely on punishment but rather on righting of a balance upset by the violation. Repressive laws come into play when deviance is termed a 'crime', while restitutive laws set up the moral obligation to recompense claimants who have been injured. Most civil and commercial law is restitutory in character, whereas most criminal law is based on penal sanctions.

The predominance of penal or restitutory law in given societies, Durkheim argued, could serve as an index of the type of society, or the type of solidarity under consideration. Societies based on mechanical solidarity relied almost exclusively on penal sanctions. What was punished was departure from the collective way of life, the shared values and beliefs of the society. Any action that was perceived as an infringement of the collective consciousness – the shared mental and moral orientations of societies – was conceived as a crime and sanctioned accordingly. In modern societies, on the other hand, in which individuality, and hence the violation of individual rights is central, restitutory rather than penal sanctions predominate.

As has been seen, Durkheim argued that the origin of the modern division of labour had to be looked for in the intensified struggle for existence that came into play once larger numbers of people in given territories engaged in denser forms of interaction and were therefore forced to specialise in order to survive. We have also noted that Durkheim argued, in contrast to his British and German contemporaries, that the modern organic division of labour did not necessarily bring deleterious consequences but could create bonds between autonomous individuals just as enduring and persistent as those that earlier had linked members of societies with mechanical solidarity enveloped by a common consciousness.

This brings us to an important aspect of Durkheim's methodological views, namely that the origin of an institution does not explain its function. Organic social solidarity did not originate in order to enhance solidary bonds between individuals but was brought about by quite different causes. To Durkheim, causal inquiries have to be carried out separately from functional analyses. If today the modern division of labour serves the function of increasing solidarity through complementarity, it did not come into being for such reasons. Or, to take an example from Durkheim's later work on religion, various religious systems may have very different historical causes and reasons for emergence. Yet all of them may serve the common function of drawing people together in devotion to religious symbols and rites that make them aware of their common dependence on the society of which they are a part.

At the time that Durkheim was writing *The Division of Labour*, he was, by and large, beholden to a structural explanation of moral phenomena. Restitutory law replaced penal law, he argued, as societies moved from morphological forms rooted in relationships between people having similar positions in the process of production to morphological forms characterised by higher degrees of dissimilarity. As people now engaged in differentiated societal tasks and work routines they developed new institutional relations and moral ideas. In other words, to use Marxian terminology for just a moment, different economic infrastructures produced different forms of superstructures. The essential differences between types of society were to be sought on the structural or morphological level. The causal arrow in the analysis of social phenomena went largely from productive relations and structural linkages between people to moral or legal systems of thought. The enlargement of the volume and density of a society caused new modes of the division of labour and this in turn found a reflection in legal and moral forms as well as in types of social bonds. In subsequent works, especially in those in which he investigated religious sentiments and practices in instructive detail, Durkheim was to move in a somewhat more 'idealistic' direction by granting more autonomy to such ideational phenomena as religion. But such later shifts in his theoretical and analytical orientation need not obscure the fact that in *The Division of Labour* he is largely a structural analyst not as far removed from Marx as certain commentators have sometimes been inclined to think.

Another shift in Durkheim's analytical approach at the time of writing *The Division of Labour*, and in subsequent works, needs to be mentioned. In the *Division*, the collective consciousness, a conception that Durkheim largely developed in derivation from Rousseau's 'general will' and Comte's 'consensus', is conceived as the major cement that binds people in their mechanical solidarity. Indeed, the common consciousness, with its emphasis on the commonness of beliefs and sentiments, appears almost as the defining characteristic of societies grounded in mechanical solidarity. If this were the case, it would then appear as if in societies based on organic solidarity collective consciousness would inevitably decay. There are indeed several passages in the present work that seem strongly to suggest that Durkheim did believe this to be the case. In such passages he seems to feel that the common consciousness would largely be displaced by the mutual dependence of people engaged in different yet complementary rounds of life. Later works, however, largely correct this view. Such a correction is already presaged in the present pages; Durkheim stresses that although the collective consciousness in the world of modernity can no longer define the specific norms that pertain to the exercise of differentiated tasks, it is still needed so as to assure overall coordination and integration of the society as a whole. Much of Durkheim's later work can be read as a continuing effort to define the basis for a kind of civic religion which, through education and other means, would provide common values to societies otherwise characterised by a great variety of role – and task – specific norms and regulations. As Talcott Parsons has emphasised (see his 'Emile Durkheim' in *International Encyclopedia of the Social Sciences*, New York, Macmillan, 1968), to the mature Durkheim 'the sharing of common values is a constant feature of all systems at whatever level of differentiation'.

I have commented so far exclusively on Books I and II of *The Division of Labour* in which Durkheim argues with admirable logical rigour that in the course of evolutionary development different societies have moved from a basis in mechanical solidarity to one in organic solidarity. The reader is hence likely to react with initial shock when finding that in Book III, entitled 'The Abnormal Forms', Durkheim introduces considerations that seem to fit but poorly into the neat scheme explicated in earlier parts of the work. I shall argue that Durkheim may have lost some logical coherence with Book III, but that this loss of rigour is amply compensated for by an increase in realistic awareness of the blemishes of the social scene as they intruded on his vision when he observed the industrial world of the *fin de siècle*.

This world, Durkheim notes, is marred by a variety of pathological phenomena. Far from the parts of the whole being harmoniously adjusted to each other through complementarity, mutual dependence, and smooth adjustment, the industrial scene is in fact characterised, *inter alia*, by hostility and struggle between labour and capital, by commercial crises and the attending bankruptcies, by normlessness (anomie), lack of regulation, unrestricted play of individual or collective self-interest. Such conditions, far from being exceptional, can generally be found in the modern industrial and social world. Just like in Yeats's great poem 'The Second Coming', the centre does no longer seem to hold. Such an evaluation of the industrial world was, of course, widespread among social commentators towards the end of the nineteenth century. But, initially one is surprised to find it coming from the pen of Emile Durkheim. He had argued insistently and repeatedly in his effort to distinguish normal from pathological phenomena that conditions generally found in a society represent the normal state of affairs. Suddenly it now turns out that what can indeed be found to be widespread general phenomena, such as class struggles and commercial crises, are nevertheless abnormal and pathological.

How then does Durkheim attempt to find a solution to this apparent impasse? How can he avoid the logical conclusion that the bleak picture he paints in Book III is the effect of the modern division of labour itself and hence the root cause of present disorders? Here he has recourse to certain ideas previously found in Saint-Simon as well as Auguste Comte. These authors had argued that in contemplating history one found two different types of societal arrangements. There were indeed 'organic' periods in which the various social forces were harmoniously adjusted to each other, but there were also 'critical' periods of transition that exhibited a variety of disorders in the body social. Critical periods brought a great deal of turmoil and human suffering in their wake but they also already contained new healthy forces that would in the long run right unbalanced conditions and lead to fresh adjustments. Durkheim largely followed this type of reasoning in Book III. He argued that, 'contrary to what has been said, the division of labour does not produce these [deleterious] consequences through some imperative of its own nature, but only in exceptional and abnormal circumstances' (p. 307). If, for example, the modern worker seems to have a sense of being alienated from his work, this is not because alienation is inherent in modern modes of production but only because workers lack at the present time a sense of being engaged in a collective endeavour, a sense of spontaneously derived co-operation with their fellows and superiors. They do not feel at present that they are of some use and therefore feel indeed like cogs in a vast machine. The division of labour as one encounters it in modern industry is an 'abnormal division of labour', a division that springs not from spontaneity but from forceful imposition. When coercive constraints replace spontaneously given consent, the whole human enterprise is weakened.

Durkheim's proposed remedies are in tune with his prognosis of the malady of modern societies. If coercion has primacy over spontaneous adjustments – if the division of economic functions produces a low degree of social cohesion and solidarity, if technical developments have outstripped the growth of an appropriate regulative apparatus – it behoves social scientists to warn decision-makers that only the creation of new institutionalised moral bonds can prevent social decay through strife and the spreading of social disorder.

Though Durkheim was by no means averse to state intervention when it came to the imposition of new regulations to ameliorate the forced division of labour, his major recommendation for overcoming the present crisis did not involve state action. The state might one day move to abolish the hereditary transmission of property as a means to bring about a meritocratic society with equal opportunity for all. But state action was too far removed from the lives of ordinary men and women and from the institutional setting of workplace and factory, to be of much utility in overcoming the contemporary anomic and forced division of labour. What was required here was the re-emergence of 'secondary institutions', – a concept that had already been conceived by Tocqueville. What was meant was those institutions that were placed midway, so to speak, between the remote world of the state's powers and the concrete everyday world of the individual. Taking his clues from his study of

Roman and mediaeval, largely artisainal, 'corporations', Durkheim argued in the preface to the second edition of *The Division of Labour* for a revival of a new corporatism.

Durkheim envisaged that in the various industrial branches throughout the country new types of corporations would be instituted in which both employers and employees of each specific branch would be represented. The administrative council of these corporations would have the power to regulate labour relations, wages and salaries, conditions of work, appointments and promotions, as well as relations with other branches of industry and with governmental authorities. There would be a central administrative council for a given branch of industry as well as local or regional bodies. Durkheim felt that it was not the role of the scientist but rather of the statesman to elaborate on the organisational details that would have to be attended to for a new net of corporate institutions to arise and, at least partly, to replace present administrative structures. But, he had no doubt that the professional corporation was destined in the future to take a key position in the structure of modern societies as a vivifying source of new social norms and new social bonds.

Let me sum up: Durkheim was deeply convinced of the pathology of present-day acquisitive society. Yet he did not believe that the present pathological features could be traced to an inherent flaw in systems built on organic solidarity. Rather, he thought that the present malaise and anomie could be traced to transitional difficulties that could be overcome through the emergence of new norms and values in the institutional setting of a new corporate organisation of industrial affairs. While the radical elements in Durkheim's intellectual make-up had made him sensitive to the flaws in present industrial and class relations, his more conservative strands of thought led him to neglect the possibility that the disorders he witnessed were linked with the structure of capitalist society and not only with transitional phenomena. His liberal conscience, in turn, led him to reform proposals that, though they could perhaps not do away with what the Marxists considered built-in class conflicts, might yet so harmonise relations between employers and employees that adjustment within the framework of a new corporate society would replace the pathological strife of the present. Beholden to none of the political and social orientations of his day, Durkheim always attempted to look for a balanced middle way.

Durkheim was not opposed to the expanding role that the state plays in modern social life. But he was deeply concerned that an excessive growth of state power would eventually lead to the extinction of autonomous individuality that he prized above all. 'A society made up of an extremely large mass of unorganised individuals,' he argued, 'which an overgrown state attempts to limit and restrain, constitutes a veritable sociological monstrosity' (p. liv). Hence his attempt to envisage an institutional structure, equidistant from individuals and the tutelary state, that would allow the emergence of a full-blown 'cult of the individual' while still re-creating partly atrophied bonds of complementarity and solidarity that would assure cohesion in free societies.

This might be the place to move from an attempt to depict the major features of Durkheim's argument to some critical comments. His discussion of the forced division of labour provides a good springboard for such critical commentary. A major flaw in Durkheim's mode of argumentation is his tendency, as Steven Lukes has put it (*Emile Durkheim: His Life and Work*, p. 177), to assume an identity between the 'normal', the ideal, and that which was about to happen. Even though he argued repeatedly that the normal was that found generally in a society, he refused to accept general social phenomena as 'normal' if they went counter to his ideal moral demands and standards. That which he found repellent simply *could* not be normal. This is, perhaps, an admirable human sentiment, but it does no particular credit to Durkheim's logical rigour or scientific stance. It was Renan who once proclaimed that, 'Il se pourrait que la vérité soit triste'. This is a sentiment that Durkheim, with his buoyant, even if mainly rhetorical, optimism about the future, does not seem to have been able to entertain. What was distasteful could only be transitory and would surely be remedied in the none too distant future. In this respect Durkheim, writing in the *fin de siècle* that had for many already dispelled the Enlightenment certainties of their predecessors, still remained a true son of the Enlightenment tradition.

Turning now to a few other critical comments, a brief discussion of his use of anthropological and historical data seems in order. His deficiencies in this respect are glaring to the modern reader. Yet it has to be kept in mind that, especially in regard to simpler societies, scientific knowledge in Durkheim's time was still in its infancy. It will not do to cultivate a sense of our own superiority over what seem to us 'elementary mistakes' in Durkheim's work. We know much more than Durkheim about these matters simply because we live almost a hundred years later. No modern anthropologist or sociologist will concur nowadays with Durkheim's assertion that simpler societies lack restitutive sanctions. We have come to learn from Malinowski and his disciples that pre-modern societies rely to a large extent on reciprocal obligations – be it of individuals or of groups of individuals. Such societies are largely based on restitution whenever the reciprocal balances between the various forces of society are upset. Whether the rule be an eye for an eye or the return of another piece of cattle when one has been wrongfully appropriated, simple societies, contrary to Durkheim, seem in fact to be at least as devoted to the law of restitution as are modern societies.

In similar ways, Durkheim's attempt to distinguish between types of societies along the axis of likeness v. complementarity fails to be satisfying if it is realised at the hand of new anthropological studies that Trobriand Islanders or natives of New Guinea differ in personal characteristic to a highly significant extent. But such a distinction has still much to recommend itself if, instead of making polar distinctions we limit ourselves to relative differences. It may be that the presence or absence of literacy in human groups may be a better distinguishing mark between them than the Durkheimian distinction (see Jack Goody, *Domestication of the Savage Mind*, Cambridge, Cambridge University Press, 1977), yet it remains the case that later typological distinctions were in large part stimulated by Durkheim's earlier effort.

Criticism of Durkheim has become in our days a minor cottage industry, I hence feel no need in this brief introduction unduly to extend my critical objections. To be sure, a variety of Durkheim's findings, some of his major methodological assertions, and above all his frequent polemical exaggerations, need to be rejected by contemporary scholarship. But this is as it should be if it is agreed that continuous attempts at refutation and correction mark the very nature of scientific discourse.

LEWIS COSER

Preface to the First Edition

This book is above all an attempt to treat the facts of moral life according to the methods of the positive sciences. Yet this term 'method' has been employed in a way that distorts its meaning, and it is one to which we do not subscribe. Those moralists who deduce their doctrine not from an *a priori* principle, but from a few propositions borrowed from one or more of the positive sciences such as biology, psychology or sociology, term their morality 'scientific'. This is not the method we propose to follow. We do not wish to deduce morality from science, but to constitute the science of morality, which is very different. Moral facts are phenomena like any others. They consist of rules for action that are recognisable by certain distinctive characteristics. It should thus be possible to observe, describe and classify them, as well as to seek out the laws that explain them. This is what we intend to do for a few of these facts. The objection will be raised regarding the existence of freedom. But if this fact really does imply the negation of any determinate law, it is an insuperable obstacle not only for the psychological and social sciences, but for all the sciences. Since human volition is always linked to some external forces, this renders determinism just as unintelligible for what lies outside us as for what resides within us. Yet none disputes the possibility of the physical and biological sciences. We claim the same right for our own science.[1]

Thus understood, this science is not opposed to any kind of philosophy, because it takes its stand on very different ground. It may be that morality has some transcendental finality that experience cannot attain. This is a matter with which the metaphysician must deal. Yet what above all is certain is that morality develops over the course of history and is dominated by historical causes, fulfilling a role in our life in time. If it is as it is at any given moment, it is because the conditions in which men are living at that time do not permit it to be otherwise. The proof of this is that it changes when these conditions change, and only in that eventuality. Nowadays we can no longer believe that moral evolution consists in the development of one self-same idea, held in a muddled and hesitant way by primitive man, but one that gradually becomes clearer and more precise as enlightenment spontaneously occurs. If the ancient Romans had not the broad conception of humanity that we possess today, it is not because of any defect attributable to their limited intelligence, but because such ideas were incompatible with the nature of the Roman state. Our cosmopolitanism could no more come to the light of day than a plant can germinate on a soil unable to nourish it. What is more, for Rome such a principle could only be fatal. Conversely, if the principle has appeared since, it is not as a result of philosophical discoveries. Nor is it because our minds have become receptive to truths that they failed to acknowledge. It is because changes have occurred in the social structure that have necessitated this change in morals. Thus morality is formed, transformed and maintained for reasons of an experimental kind. It is these reasons alone that the science of morality sets out to determine.

Yet because what we propose to study is above all reality, it does not follow that we should give up the idea of improving it. We would esteem our research not worth the labour of a single hour if its interest were merely speculative. If we distinguish carefully between theoretical and practical problems it is not in order to neglect the latter category. On the contrary, it is in order to put ourselves in a position where we can better resolve them. Yet it is customary to reproach all those who undertake the scientific study of morality with the inability to formulate an ideal. It is alleged that their respect for facts does not allow them to go beyond them, that they can indeed observe what exists, but are not able to provide us with rules for future conduct. We trust that this book will at least serve to weaken that prejudice, because we shall demonstrate in it how science can help in finding the direction in which our conduct ought to go, assisting us to determine the ideal that gropingly we seek. But we shall only be able to raise ourselves up to that ideal after having observed reality, for we shall distil the ideal from it. Indeed, is any other procedure possible? Even the most boundless idealist can follow no other method, for an ideal is stayed upon nothing if its roots are not grounded in reality. All the difference resides in the fact that the idealists study reality in very cursory fashion. Often they merely content themselves with elevating some impulse of their sensibility, a rather sudden aspiration of the heart – *which is nevertheless only a fact* – into a kind of imperative before which their reason bows low, and they ask us to do likewise.

It will be objected that the method of observation lacks any rules by which to assess the facts that have been garnered. But the rule emerges from the facts themselves, as we shall have occasion to demonstrate. Firstly, a state of moral health exists that science alone can competently determine and, as it is nowhere wholly attained, it is already an ideal to strive towards it. Moreover, the conditions of this state change because societies evolve. The most serious practical problems that we have to resolve consist precisely in determining that state afresh, as a function of changes that have been effected in the environment. Science, by providing us with a law for the variations through which that state has already passed, allows us to anticipate those which are in progress and which the new order of things demands. If we know the direction in which the law of property is evolving as societies grow in size, becoming more densely concentrated, and if some increase in volume and density makes further modifications necessary, we shall be able to foresee them and, by foreseeing them, will them in advance. Finally, by comparing internally the normal type – a strictly scientific operation – we shall be able to discover that the latter is not entirely at harmony within itself, that it contains contradictions – imperfections – which we can then seek to eliminate or remedy. This is a new purpose that science proposes to the will. But, it may be argued, if science can foresee, it cannot command. This is true: it can only tell us what is needful for life. Yet how can we fail to see that, *assuming mankind wishes life to continue*, a very simple operation may immediately transform the laws that science has established into rules that are categorical for our behaviour? Doubtless, science then becomes an art. But the transition from one to the other occurs with no break in continuity. It remains to be ascertained whether we ought to wish to continue our existence, but even on this ultimate question we believe that science is not mute.[2]

But if the science of morality does not make us indifferent or resigned spectators of reality, at the same time it teaches us to treat it with the utmost caution. It imparts to us a prudently conservative disposition of mind. Certain theories which claim to be scientific have been rightly reproached with being subversive and revolutionary. But this is because they are scientific in name only. In fact they erect a structure, but fail to observe. They see in morality not a set of acquired facts which must be studied, but a kind of legislation, always liable to be repealed, which every thinker works out afresh. Morality as really practised by men is then considered as a mere bundle of habits and prejudices which are of value only if they conform with the doctrine being put forward. As this doctrine is derived from the study of a principle that has not been induced from the observation of moral facts, but borrowed from sciences that are alien to it, it inevitably runs counter in more than one respect to the existing moral order. We, on the other hand, are less exposed to this danger than anyone, since morality for us is a system of facts that have been realised, linked to the total world system. Now a fact does not change in a trice, even when this may be desirable. Moreover, since it is solidly linked to other facts, it cannot be modified without these also being affected, and it is often very difficult to work out beforehand the end-result of this series of repercussions. Thus upon contemplating such risks, even the boldest spirit becomes more prudent. Finally, and above all, any fact of a vital nature – as moral facts are – cannot survive if it does not serve a purpose or correspond to some need. Thus, so long as the contrary has not been proved, it has a right to our respect. Undoubtedly it may turn out to be not all it should be, and consequently it may be appropriate to intervene, as we ourselves have just demonstrated. But then the intervention is limited: its purpose is not to construct in its entirety another morality alongside or above the predominant one, but to correct the latter, or partially to improve it.

Thus there disappears the antithesis that some have often attempted to establish between science and morality, an impressive argument whereby the mystics of every age have sought to undermine human reason. To regulate relationships with our fellow-men there is no need to resort to any means save those that serve to regulate our relationships with things; reflective thinking, methodically applied, suffices in both cases. What reconciles science and morality is the science of morality, for at the same time as it teaches us to respect moral reality it affords us the means of improving it.

We therefore believe that the study of this book can and must be tackled without lack of confidence or any hidden misgivings. However, the reader must expect to meet with propositions that run counter to certain accepted ideas. Since we feel the need to understand, or to think we understand, the reasons for our behaviour, reflective thinking was applied to morality a considerable while before morality became the object of scientific study. Thus a certain mode in which to represent and explain to ourselves the main facts of moral life has become customary with us, and yet it is in no way scientific. This is because it arose unsystematically by chance, the result of a summary and perfunctory investigation, carried out, so to speak, incidentally. Unless we divest ourselves of these ready-made judgements, clearly we cannot embark upon the considerations that are to follow. Here as elsewhere, science presupposes the entire freedom of the mind. We must rid ourselves of those ways of perceiving and judging that long habit has implanted within us. We must rigorously subject ourselves to the discipline of methodical doubt. Moreover, this doubt entails no risk, for it relates not to moral reality, which is not in question, but to the explanation that incompetent and ill-informed thinking attributes to it.

We must make it incumbent upon us to allow no explanation that does not rely upon genuine proofs. The procedures we have employed to impart the greatest possible rigour to our proofs will be assessed. To submit an order of facts to the scrutiny of science it is not enough carefully to observe, describe and classify them. But – and this is much more difficult – we must also, in Descartes' phrase, discover the perspective from which they become scientific, that is, find in them some objective element which is capable of precise determination and, if possible, measurement. We have attempted to satisfy this, the condition of all science. In particular, it will be seen how we have studied social solidarity through the system of juridical rules, how in the search for causes, we have laid aside everything that too readily lends itself to personal judgements and subjective appraisal – this so as to penetrate certain facts of social structure profound enough to be objects of the understanding, and consequently of science. At the same time we have imposed upon ourselves a rule that obliges us to refrain from the method too often followed by those sociologists who, to prove their thesis, content themselves with citing in no specific order and at random a more or less imposing number of favourable facts without worrying about those that are contradictory. We have been concerned to institute genuine experiments, that is, methodical comparisons. Nevertheless, no matter how numerous the precautions observed, it is absolutely certain that such attempts can remain only very imperfect. But, however defective they may be, we deem it necessary to attempt them. Indeed there is only one way to create a science, and that is to dare to do so, but to do so with method. It is doubtless impossible to undertake the task if all raw data for it is lacking. On the other hand we buoy ourselves up with a vain hope if we believe that the best means of preparing for the coming of a new science is first patiently to accumulate all the data it will use. For we cannot know which it will require unless we have already formed some conception of it and its needs, and consequently whether it exists.

The question that has been the starting point for our study has been that of the connection between the individual personality and social solidarity. How does it come about that the individual, whilst becoming more autonomous, depends ever more closely upon society? How can he become at the same time more of an individual and yet more linked to society? For it is indisputable that these two movements, however contradictory they appear to be, are carried on in tandem. Such is the nature of the problem that we have set ourselves. It has seemed to us that what resolved this apparent antimony was the transformation of social solidarity which arises from the ever-increasing division of labour. This is how we have been led to make this the subject of our study.[3]

Notes

1. The reproach has been made (Beudant, *Le droit individuel et l'Etat*, p. 244) that we have at some stage characterised this question of freedom as 'subtle'. For us, the expression was in no way used scornfully. If we set this question on one side it is solely because the solution given to it, *whatever that may be*, cannot hinder our research.
2. We touch upon it a little later. Cf. *infra*, Book II, Chapter 1, p. 190.
3. We need not recall that the question of social solidarity has already been studied in the second part of Marion, *La Solidarité morale*. But Marion tackled the problem from a different viewpoint, being above all concerned with establishing the reality of the phenomenon of solidarity.

Preface to the Second Edition

Some Remarks on Professional Groups

In republishing this book we have refrained from modifying its original structure. A book possesses an individuality that it ought to retain. It is fitting to leave intact the appearance under which it has become known.[1]

Yet there is one idea that remained somewhat obscure in the first edition which it seems useful to us to bring out more clearly and precisely, for it will throw light on certain parts of the present work and even on what we have published since.[2] It concerns the role that professional groups are called upon to fulfil at the present time in the social organisation of peoples. If originally we only touched obliquely upon this problem,[3] it is because we were intending to take it up again, making it the object of a special study. Since other preoccupations have arisen to divert us from this project, and since we do not see when it will be possible for us to carry it out, we would like to take advantage of this second edition to show how this question is linked to the subject dealt with in the rest of this book, indicating the terms in which it is posed, and attempting especially to dispose of the reasons that still prevent too many minds from comprehending the urgency and importance of the problem. Such is the purpose of this new preface.

I

In the course of this book, on a number of occasions we emphasise the state of legal and moral anomie in which economic life exists at the present time.[4] In fact, in this particular sphere of activity, professional ethics only exist in a very rudimentary state. There are professional ethics for the lawyer and magistrate, the soldier and professor, the doctor and priest, etc. Yet if we attempted to express in somewhat more precise terms contemporary ideas of what should be the relationship between employer and white-collar worker, between the industrial worker and the factory boss, between industrialists in competition with one another or between industrialists and the public, how imprecise would be the statements that we could formulate! Some vague generalities about the loyalty and commitment that employees of every kind owe to those who employ them, or about the moderation that employers should manifest in exercising their economic superiority, a certain condemnation of any competition that is too blatantly unfair, or of any too glaring exploitation of the consumer: this is almost the sum total of what the ethical consciousness of these professions comprises. Moreover, most of these precepts lack any juridical character. They are backed only by public opinion and not by the law – and it is well known how indulgent that opinion shows itself to be about the way in which such vague obligations are fulfilled. Those actions most blameworthy are so often excused by success that the boundary between the permissible and the prohibited, between what is just and what is unjust, is no longer fixed in any way, but seems capable of being shifted by individuals in an almost arbitrary fashion. So vague a morality, one so inconsistent, cannot constitute any kind of discipline. The upshot is that this entire sphere of collective life is for the most part removed from the moderating action of any rules.

It is to this state of anomie that, as we shall show, must be attributed the continually recurring conflicts and disorders of every kind of which the economic world affords so sorry a spectacle. For, since nothing restrains the forces present from reacting together, or prescribes limits for them that they are obliged to respect, they tend to grow beyond all bounds, each clashing with the other, each warding off and weakening the other. To be sure, those forces that are the most vigorous succeed in crushing the weakest or subjecting them to their will. Yet, although the vanquished can for a while resign themselves to an enforced domination, they do not concur in it, and consequently such a state can provide no stable equilibrium.[5] Truces imposed by violence are never anything other than temporary, and pacify no one. Men's passions are only stayed by a moral presence they respect. If all authority of this kind is lacking, it is the law of the strongest that rules, and a state of warfare, either latent or acute, is necessarily endemic.

That such anarchy is an unhealthy phenomenon is clearly very evident, since it runs counter to the very purpose of society, which is to eliminate or at least to moderate warfare among men, by subjecting the physical law of the strongest to a higher law. In vain one may claim to justify this absence of rules by asserting that it is conducive to the individual exercising his liberty freely. Yet nothing is more false than the antimony that people have too often wished to establish between the authority of rules and the freedom of the individual. On the contrary, liberty (by which we mean a just liberty, one for which society is duty bound to enforce respect) is itself the product of a set of rules. I can be free only in so far as the other person is prevented from turning to his own benefit that superiority, whether physical, economic or of any other kind, which he possesses, in order to fetter my liberty. Only a social rule can serve as a barrier against such abuses of power. We are now aware of how complex a set of rules is necessary in order to ensure that economic independence for individuals without which their liberty is purely nominal.

Yet, nowadays in particular, what causes the exceptional gravity of such a state of affairs is the extent, hitherto unrealised, to which economic functions have developed over approximately the past two centuries. Whereas previously they had played only a secondary role, they have now become of prime importance. The time is long past when these functions were contemptuously left to the lower classes. Increasingly we are seeing how military, religious and administrative functions are yielding ground to them. Scientific functions alone are capable of contesting their position. Even so, today science scarcely enjoys any prestige save inasmuch as it can be utilised in practical affairs, which means for the most part in professions relating to the economy. This is why the assertion has been able to be made, not unreasonably, that our societies are, or tend to be, essentially industrial. A form of activity which in this way has acquired such a position in the overall life of society can clearly not remain unregulated without very profound disturbances ensuing. Specifically, this is a source of moral deterioration. Precisely because economic functions today employ the largest number of citizens, thousands of individuals spend their lives almost entirely in an industrial and commercial environment. Hence it follows that, since this environment lacks anything save a slight moral tincture, most of their life is pursued without any moral framework. Yet for the sense of duty to strike deep roots within us, the conditions in which we live should constantly sustain that sense. By nature we are not inclined to curb ourselves and exercise restraint. Thus unless we are continually exhorted to exert that control over ourselves without which there can be no morality, how may we acquire the habit of doing so? If, in activities that almost completely fill our days, we follow no rule save that of our own self-interest, as we understand it, how then can we acquire a taste for altruism, for forgetfulness of self and sacrifice? Thus the lack of any economic discipline cannot fail to produce effects that spill over beyond the economic sphere, bringing with it a decline in public morality.

But, having diagnosed the sickness, what is its cause and what might be the remedy?

In the main body of this work we have been especially concerned to demonstrate that the division of labour can bear no responsibility for this state of affairs, a charge that has sometimes unjustly been levelled against it. Nor does that division necessarily produce fragmentation and lack of coherence. Indeed, when its functions are sufficiently linked together they tend of their own accord to achieve an equilibrium, becoming self-regulatory. Yet such an explanation is incomplete. Although it is true that social functions seek spontaneously to adapt to one another, provided that they are in regular contact, on the other hand this mode of adaptation only becomes a rule of behaviour if a group bestows its authority upon it. Nor indeed is a rule merely a customary manner in which to act: it is above all *an obligatory manner of acting*, that is, one to some extent not subject to individual arbitrariness. Only a duly constituted society enjoys the moral and material supremacy indispensable for prescribing what the law should be for individuals, for the only moral entity which is above that of private individuals is the one constituted by the collectivity. Moreover, it alone has that continuity, and indeed enduring character, necessary to sustain the rule beyond the ephemeral relationships in which it is manifested day by day. What is more, the role of the collectivity is not solely limited to establishing categorical imperatives derived from vague generalities arising from contracts between individuals; it also intervenes actively and positively in the formulation of each rule.

Firstly, it is the arbiter appointed by nature for disentangling conflicting interests and assigning appropriate bounds to each. Next, it has a paramount interest in the maintenance of order and peace. If anomie is an evil it is above all because society suffers through it, since it cannot exist without cohesion and regulation. Thus moral or legal rules essentially express social needs which society alone can identify. They rest upon a climate of opinion, and all opinion is a collective matter, the result of being worked out collectively. To be shot of anomie a group must thus exist or be formed within which can be drawn up the system of rules that is now lacking.

Political society as a whole, or the state, clearly cannot discharge this function. Economic life, because it is very special and is daily becoming increasingly specialised, lies outside their authority and sphere of action.[6] Activity within a profession can only be effectively regulated through a group close enough to that profession to be thoroughly cognisant of how it functions, capable of perceiving all its needs and following every fluctuation in them. The sole group that meets these conditions is that constituted by all those working in the same industry, assembled together and organised in a single body. This is what is termed a corporation, or professional group.

Yet in the economic field the professional group no more exists than does a professional ethic. Since the last century when, *not without reason*, the ancient corporations were dissolved, hardly more than fragmentary and incomplete attempts have been made to reconstitute them on a different basis. Doubtless, individuals who are busy in the same trade are in contact with one another by the very fact that their activities are similar. Competition with one another engenders mutual relationships. But these are in no way regular; depending upon chance meetings, they are very often entirely of an individual nature. One industrialist finds himself in contact with another, but the body of industrialists in some particular speciality do not meet to act in concert. Exceptionally, we do see all members of the same profession come together at a conference to deal with some problem of common interest. But such conferences last only a short while: they do not survive the particular circumstances that gave rise to them. Consequently the collective life for which they provided an opportunity dies more or less entirely with them.

The sole groups that have a certain permanence are what today are called unions, either of employers or workers. There is no doubt that this represents the beginnings of any organisation by occupation, although still in a rudimentary and amorphous form. In the first place, this is because a union is a private association, lacking legal authority and consequently any regulatory power. The number of such unions is theoretically unlimited, even within a particular branch of industry. As each one is independent of the others, unless they federate or unite there is nothing about them that expresses the unity of the profession as a whole. Finally, not only are unions of employers and unions of employees distinct from each other, *which is both legitimate and necessary*, but there are no regular contacts between them. They lack a common organisation to draw them together without causing them to lose their individuality, one within which they might work out a common set of rules and which, fixing their relationship to each other, would bear down with equal authority upon both. Consequently it is always the law of the strongest that decides any disputes, and a state of out and out warfare prevails. Except for actions of theirs that are dependent upon ordinary morality, in their relation to each other employers and workers are in the same situation as two autonomous states, but unequal in strength. They can, as peoples do through their governments, draw up contracts with each other. But these contracts merely express the respective state of the economic forces present, just as the treaties concluded by two belligerents do no more than express the state of their respective military forces. They confirm a state of fact; they cannot make of it a state of law.

For a professional morality and code of law to become established within the various professions in the economy, instead of the corporation remaining a conglomerate body lacking unity, it must become, or rather become once more, a well-defined, organised group – in short, a public institution. But any project of this kind clashes with a certain number of prejudices which it is essential to foresee and dispel.

To begin with, the corporation has the disadvantage of its historic past. It is considered to be closely linked to the *ancien régime* politically, and consequently unable to survive it. Apparently to advocate a corporative organisation for industry and commerce is to attempt to go against the tide of history. Such a step backwards is in fact regarded as either impossible or abnormal.

The argument would have substance if it were proposed to revive artificially the ancient corporation as it existed in the Middle Ages. But this is not the way in which the problem presents itself. It is not a question of knowing whether the mediaeval institution can be suitable in every respect for our present-day societies, but whether the needs that it fulfilled are not those of every age, although for those needs to be met the institution requires transforming to fit the environment.

What does not allow us to view corporations as temporary organisations, appropriate merely in a certain era and a certain civilisation, is both their great antiquity and the manner in which they have developed throughout history. If they went back only to the Middle Ages we could indeed believe that, since they arose within a political system, they were necessarily destined to vanish with it. Yet in reality their origin is much more ancient. Generally they appear as soon as trades do, that is, as soon as industry stops being purely agricultural. If they appear to have been unknown in Greece, at least until the period of the Roman conquest, it is because trades, being disdained there, were almost exclusively carried on by foreigners, and consequently they remained outside the legal organisation of the city.[7] In Rome, however, the corporations go back at least to the early days of the Republic; a tradition even ascribed their creation to King Numa.[8] It is true that for a long while they were obliged to lead a somewhat lowly existence, for historians and records mention them only rarely. Thus we know extremely little about the way they were organised. But from Cicero's time onwards their number became considerable and they were beginning to play a part in society. At that time, as Walzing puts it, 'all classes of workers seemed seized with a desire to increase greatly the number of professional associations'. These continued their upward movement, to reach at the time of the Empire, 'a level which has perhaps never been surpassed since, if economic differences are taken into account'.[9] All the numerous classes of workers, it would seem, ended up by grouping themselves into collegial bodies, and the same was true for those who lived by commerce. At the same time such groupings became modified in their character, finishing up as mere cogs in the administrative machine. They fulfilled official functions, with each corporation being looked upon as a public service for which the corresponding corporation assumed the obligation and responsibility *vis-à-vis* the state.[10]

This was the ruin of the institution, for this dependence *vis-à-vis* the state swiftly degenerated into a state of intolerable servitude, which the emperors could not maintain except by constraint. All sorts of devices were employed to prevent workers from evading the onerous obligations laid upon them by virtue of their profession. The state even went so far as to resort to enforced recruitment and enrolment. Plainly such a system could only survive as long as the political power was strong enough to sustain it. This is why it did not outlive the collapse of the Empire. Furthermore, civil wars and invasions had destroyed commerce and industry. Artisans took advantage of these conditions to flee from the towns, scattering themselves over the countryside. Thus the first centuries AD saw a phenomenon occur which was to be repeated almost identically at the end of the eighteenth century: corporative life was almost completely extinguished. In towns of Roman origin in Gaul and Germany scarcely any traces of it remained. If therefore at that moment some theoretician had been aware of the situation, he would most likely have concluded, as did economists later, that the corporations had no reason to exist, or at least no longer had any reason, that they had vanished beyond recall, and he would doubtless have regarded as retrograde and unrealisable any attempt to reconstitute them. Yet events would soon have belied such a prediction.

Indeed, after having suffered an eclipse for a while, the corporations began a fresh existence in all European societies. They were to rise again about the eleventh and twelfth centuries. From then onwards, states Levasseur, 'artisans began to feel the need to unite and form their first associations'.[11] In any case, by the thirteenth century they were again flourishing, continuing to develop until the day when a new decadence set in once more. So persistent an institution cannot depend upon special contingent and chance circumstances. Even less can we concede that it may have been the product of some collective aberration or another. If, from the origins of the city to the apotheosis of the Empire, from the dawn of Christian societies down to modern times, corporations have been necessary, it is precisely because they correspond to deep and lasting needs. Above all, the very fact that, having disappeared once, they reconstituted themselves in a different form by themselves, robs of all substance the argument which presents their violent disappearance at the end of the last century as proof that they are no longer in harmony with the new conditions of collective existence. Moreover, the need felt nowadays by all great civilised societies to revive them is the surest indication that radical abolition was not a remedy, and that Turgot's reform necessitated another which could not be indefinitely deferred.

II

Yet if any corporative organisation is not necessarily an historical anachronism, can we legitimately believe that it is called upon to play in contemporary societies the considerable part that we attribute to it? For if we deem it indispensable it is not because of the services it might render the economy, but on account of the moral influence it could exercise. What we particularly see in the professional grouping is a moral force capable of curbing individual egoism, nurturing among workers a more envigorated feeling of their common solidarity, and preventing the law of the strongest from being applied too brutally in industrial and commercial relationships. Yet such a grouping is deemed unfit for such a role. Because it springs from temporal interests, it can seemingly only serve utilitarian ends, and the memories that survive of the corporations during the *ancien régime* only confirm this impression. We incline to vizualise them in the future as they were towards the end of their former existence, intent above all on maintaining or increasing their privileges and monopolies. We fail to see how such narrow vocational concerns might have any beneficial effect upon the morality of the corporation or its members.

However, we should refrain from extending to the entire corporative system what may have been true of certain corporations during a very short period in their development. Far from the system having been, because of its very constitution, infected by a kind of moral sickness, during the greater part of its existence it played above all a moral role. This is especially evident with the Roman corporation. 'Among the Romans,' declares Walzing, 'the corporations of artisans were far from having so pronounced a professional character as in the Middle Ages. We come across no regulations concerning methods, no obligatory apprenticeship, and no monopoly. Nor was their purpose to accumulate the capital necessary to exploit an industry.'[12] Doubtless their associating together gave them more power to safeguard the common interest, when the need arose. But this was only one of the useful by-products that the institution engendered. It was not the justification for its existence, nor its main function. Above all else, the corporation was a collegiate religious body. Each one possessed its own particular god, who, when the means were available, was worshipped in a special temple. Just as every family had its *Lar familiaris* and every city its *Genius publicus*, so every collegiate body had its protecting divinity, the *Genius collegii*. Naturally this professional form of worship was not without its festivities, and sacrifices and banquets were celebrated in common together. Moreover, all kinds of circumstances would serve as the occasion for festive gatherings; distribution of food and money was often made at the expense of the community. The question has been raised as to whether the corporation had a mutual assistance fund and whether it regularly came to the help of those of its members who were in need, but views regarding this are divided.[13] Some of the interest and relevance are however taken out of this discussion because these communal banquets, held more or less at intervals, and the distributions that accompanied them, were often substitutes for assistance proper, thus fulfilling the role of an indirect aid. In any case those in need knew that they could rely on this concealed subsidy. A corollary to their religious character was the fact that the *collegium* of artisans was at the same time one for funeral rites. United in common worship during their lifetime, as were the *Gentiles*, members of the corporation wished, as did the *Gentiles*, to share their last sleep together. All corporations rich enough possessed a collective *columbarium*, where, when the *collegium* lacked the means to buy a burial ground, at least it was able to assure for its members honourable funeral rites which were charged to the common fund.

A common cult, shared banquets and festivities, a cemetery in common – are not all these features, when considered together, those distinctive of Roman domestic organisation? Thus it has been said that the Roman corporation was a 'great family'. Waltzing declares: 'No better term characterizes the nature of the relationships which united the members of the confraternity, and there are many signs that prove a great spirit of brotherhood reigned among them.'[14] A commonality of interests replaced ties of blood. 'So much did the members look upon one another as brothers that sometimes they used that term to address one another.' It is true that the commonest term employed was *sodales*, but even this word expresses a spiritual kinship which implies a close fraternity. The patron and patroness of the *collegium* often assumed the title of father and mother. 'One proof of the devotion which members of the confraternity had for their *collegium* is the legacies and gifts they bestowed upon it. A further proof is the funeral monuments on which we read: *Pius in collegio* – "he was pious towards his *collegium*" – just as is said, *pius in suos.*'[15] This family style of existence was so developed that Boissier elevates it to being the main purpose of all Roman corporations. 'Even in corporations of workmen,' he states, 'above all they came together for the pleasure of leading a life in common, to find outside their own home a distraction from their weariness and troubles, to create a less restricted form of intimacy than within the family, yet one less diffuse than that of the city, thus making life easier and more agreeable'.[16]

Just as Christian societies belong to a social type very different from the city, the medieval corporations did not resemble exactly the Roman corporations. Yet they also constituted for their members a moral environment. 'The corporation,' says Levasseur, 'united in close ties people of the same trade. Not infrequently it was instituted in the parish or in a special chapel, and placed itself under the invocation of a saint who became the patron of the whole community. . . . It was there they assembled, there that the confraternity attended solemn masses in great state, the members afterwards rounding off the day together in a joyous banquet: In this regard the medieval corporations strongly resembled those of Roman times.'[17] Moreover, the corporation often devoted to good works a portion of the funds that made up its budget.

Furthermore, precise rules laid down for each trade the respective duties of employers and workmen, as well as the duties of employers to one another.[18] Certainly among these regulations are some that run counter to our present ideas. But they must be judged according to the morality of their time, since this is what they express. What cannot be disputed is that the rules were all inspired by concern not for some individual interest or another, but for the corporate interest, no matter whether this was rightly or wrongly understood. But the subordination of private utility to a common utility, whatever that may be, has always a moral character, for it necessarily implies some spirit of sacrifice and abnegation.

Moreover, many of these prescripts sprang from moral sentiments that we still share. The labourer was protected from the whim of his master, who could not dismiss him at will. Certainly the obligation was a reciprocal one. But beyond the fact that such reciprocity is intrinsically fair, it was the more strongly justified because of the considerable privileges that the workman then enjoyed. Thus it was forbidden for employers to deprive him of his *right to work* by seeking the help of their neighbours or even that of their wives. In short, states Levasseur, 'These regulations for apprentices and workmen should by no means be despised by the historian and the economist. They are not the handiwork of a barbarous era. They bear the stamp of a logical mind and a certain common sense which, without the slightest doubt, deserve attention.'[19] Finally, a whole string of rules was aimed at guaranteeing professional integrity. All kinds of precautions were taken to prevent the merchant or artisan from deceiving the buyer and to oblige them 'to work well and fairly'.[20] Doubtless the time came when the rules became needlessly vexatious, when master tradesmen concerned themselves much more with safeguarding their privileges than watching over the good reputation of their profession and the honesty of its members. However, there is no institution that, at some moment, does not degenerate, either because it is unable to effect change at the appropriate time and therefore stagnates, or because it develops only in one particular way, distorting some of its characteristics. This, then, renders it less skilful in carrying out the services for which it is responsible. This may be grounds for seeking to reform it, but not for declaring it useless for all time, and seeking to destroy it.

Whatever the force of this assertion, the facts cited adequately demonstrate that a professional grouping is not at all incapable of exerting a moral effect. The very important place that religion held in its life, both in Rome and during the Middle Ages, highlights very particularly the true nature of its functions, for in such times every religious community constituted a moral environment, just as every kind of moral discipline necessarily tended to take on a religious form. Moreover, this characteristic of corporative organisation is due to the effect of very general causes which we can see at work in different circumstances. Within a political society, as soon as a certain number of individuals find they hold in common ideas, interests, sentiments and occupations which the rest of the population does not share in, it is inevitable that, under the influence of these similarities, they should be attracted to one another. They will seek one another out, enter into relationships and associate together. Thus a restricted group is gradually formed within society as a whole, with its own special features. Once such a group is formed, a moral life evolves within it which naturally bears the distinguishing mark of the special conditions in which it has developed. It is impossible for men to live together and be in regular contact with one another without their acquiring some feeling for the group which they constitute through having united together, without their becoming attached to it, concerning themselves with its interests and taking it into account in their behaviour. And this attachment to something that transcends the individual, this subordination of the particular to the general interest, is the very well-spring of all moral activity. Let this sentiment only crystallise and grow more determinate, let it be translated into well-defined formulas by being applied to the most common circumstances of life, and we see gradually being constituted a corpus of moral rules.

This outcome is not only effected of its own accord; by the very nature of things it also possesses utility, and this sentiment of its utility contributes to its strength. Moreover, society is not alone in having an interest in these special groups being constituted and regulating their own activities, which otherwise would degenerate into anarchy. For his part the individual finds in them a source of satisfaction, for anarchy is personally harmful to him. He likewise suffers from the conflicts and disorders that ensue every time that relationships between individuals are not subject to some regulatory influence. It is not good for a man to live, so to speak, on a war footing among his immediate companions. The feelings of general hostility and mutual distrust that result, as well as the tensions necessarily caused, become distressing conditions when they are endemic. If we like war, we also like the delights of peace, and the more highly men prize them, the more thoroughly they are socialised, or in other words more thoroughly civilised, for the two terms are synonymous. A life lived in common is attractive, yet at the same time it exerts a coercion. Undoubtedly constraint is necessary to induce man to rise above himself and superimpose upon his physical nature one of a different kind. But, as he learns to savour the charm of this new existence, he develops the need for it; there is no field of activity in which he does not passionately seek after it. This is why, when individuals discover they have interests in common and come together, it is not only to defend those interests, but also so as to associate with one another and not feel isolated in the midst of their adversaries, so as to enjoy the pleasure of communicating with one another, to feel at one with several others, which in the end means to lead the same moral life together.

Domestic morality did not arise any differently. Because of the prestige that the family retains in our eyes, if it appears to us to have been and continue to be a school of altruism and abnegation, the highest seat of morality, it is through the very special characteristics it is privileged to possess, ones that could not be found at any level elsewhere. We like to believe that in blood kinship there exists an extraordinarily powerful reason for moral identification with others. But, as we have often had occasion to show,[21] blood kinship has in no way the extraordinary effectiveness attributed to it. The proof of this is that in a large number of societies relations not linked by the blood tie are very numerous in a family. Thus so-called artificial kinship is entered into very readily and has all the effects of natural kinship. Conversely, very frequently those closely knit by ties of blood are morally and legally strangers to one another. For example, this is true of blood kin in the Roman family. Thus the family does not derive its whole strength from unity of descent. Quite simply, it is a group of individuals who have drawn close to one another within the body politic through a very specially close community of ideas, feelings and interests. Blood kinship was able to make such a concentration of individuals easier, for it naturally tends to have the effect of bringing different consciousnesses together. Yet many other factors have also intervened: physical proximity, solidarity of interest, the need to unite to fight a common danger, or simply to unite, have been causes of a different kind which have made people come together.

Such causes are not peculiar to the family but are to be found, although in different forms, within the corporation. Thus if the former group has played so important a role in the moral history of humanity, why should not also the latter be capable of so doing? Undoubtedly one difference will always exist between them, inasmuch as family members share in common their entire existence, whereas the members of a corporation share only their professional concerns. The family is a kind of complete society whose influence extends to economic activity as well as to that of religion, politics, and science, etc. Everything of any importance that we do, even outside the home, has repercussions upon it and sparks off an appropriate reaction. In one sense the corporation's sphere of influence is more limited. Yet we must not forget the ever more important place that our profession assumes in our lives as work becomes increasingly segmented. The field of each individual's activity tends to be restricted by the limits prescribed by the functions especially entrusted to each individual. Moreover, if the influence of the family extends to everything, this can only be very generally so. Thus the detail escapes it. Finally, and above all, the family, by losing its former unity and indivisibility, has lost at the same time much of its effectiveness. Since nowadays the family is dispersed with each generation, man spends a not inconsiderable part of his existence far removed from any domestic influence.[22] The corporation does not experience any such interruptions: it is as continuous as life itself. Thus the inferior position it may evince as compared with the family is in certain respects not uncompensated.

If we have thought it necessary to compare the family and the corporation in this way, it is not merely to establish between them an instructive parallel, but it is because the two institutions are not wholly unconnected. This is particularly illustrated in the history of the Roman corporations. We saw in fact that they were modelled on domestic society, of which at first they were merely a new and enlarged form. A professional grouping would not to this extent recall to mind the family grouping unless there was something akin about them. Indeed in one sense the corporation was heir to the family. So long as the economy remains exclusively agricultural, it possesses in the family and in the village (which itself is only a kind of large family) its direct organ, and it needs no other. As exchange is not at all, or only slightly developed, the peasant's life does not draw him beyond the family circle. Since economic activity has no repercussions outside the home, the family suffices to regulate it, thus itself serving as the professional grouping. But this is no longer so when trades develop, for to live off a trade one must have customers, and go outside the home to find them. One has also to go outside it in order to come into contact with one's competitors, to vie with them, and to reach an understanding with them. Moreover, directly or indirectly trades imply towns, and towns have always been created and in the main peopled by migrants, that is, individuals who have left their birthplace. Thus in this way a new form of activity was constituted, one that went beyond the primitive family organisation. For the activity not to remain in a state without any organisation, a new framework had to be created, one particular to it. In other words, a secondary group of a new kind had to be constituted. Thus the corporation was born. Exercising a function that had first been domestic, but that could no longer remain so, it replaced the family. Yet these origins do not justify our attributing to it that kind of constitutionally amoral state with which we gratuitously credit it. Just as the family had been the environment within which domestic morality and law had been worked out, so the corporation was the natural environment within which professional morality and law had to be elaborated.

III

However, in order to dispel all preconceptions and to demonstrate beyond doubt that the corporative system is not solely an institution of the past, we would have to show what changes it ought and could undergo so as to adapt itself to modern societies, for it is plain that it could not be today what it was in the Middle Ages.

In order to deal with this question methodically we would first have to establish beforehand the way in which the system of corporations evolved in the past, and the causes determining the main variations it has undergone. We might then be able to make with some assurance a judgement about what it is destined to become, given the conditions at present prevailing in European societies. Yet in order to do this comparative studies that have not yet been carried out would be required, and these cannot be undertaken as we go along. Yet perhaps it is not impossible, even now, to catch a glimpse, although in only its most general traits, of what that development has been.

From what has been stated above it has already emerged that the corporation in Rome was not what it later became in Christian societies. It differs not only through its more religious and less professional character, but in the place that it occupied in society. At least in its origins it was, in fact, an institution standing outside society. An historian undertaking to break down the Roman political organisation into its constituent elements encounters in the course of his analysis not a single fact which might alert him to the existence of corporations. As well-defined, recognised bodies they did not figure in the Roman constitution. In not one elective or military assembly did artisans form up in their respective *collegia*. Nowhere did the professional group participate as such in public life, either as a body or through its regular representatives. At the very most the question could arise in connection with the three or four *collegia* which we believe we can identify with certain centuries constituted by Servus Tullius (*tignarii*, *aerarii*, *libicines*, *cornicines*), but even this is not a well-established fact.[23] As for the other corporations, they certainly stood outside the official organisation of the Roman people.[24]

Their position outside society is in some way explicable by the very conditions in which they had been formed. They make an appearance at the moment when trades begin to develop. But for a long while trades were only an ancillary and secondary form of Roman social activity. Rome was essentially an agricultural and warrior society. As an agricultural society it was divided into *gentes* and *curiae*; assemblies in centuries reflected rather the military organisation. As for industrial functions, these were too rudimentary to affect the political structure of the city.[25] Moreover, up to a very advanced stage in the history of Rome, trades were tainted by moral disapproval, and this did not permit them to occupy a regular position within the state. Doubtless the time came when their social status improved. But the manner in which this improvement was effected is itself significant. To succeed in achieving respect for their interests and in playing a part in public life, the artisans had to resort to irregular procedures outside the law. They only overcame the scorn to which they were subjected by means of plots, conspiracies and secret agitation.[26] This is the best proof that Roman society did not open up to them of its own accord. If later they ended up by being integrated into the state, becoming cogs in the administrative machine, this position was for them not one of glorious conquest, but of irksome dependence. If they then came within the ambit of the state it was not to occupy the place to which their services to society might have entitled them, but merely so that they might be more skilfully supervised by the government authorities. 'The corporation,' writes Levasseur, 'became the chain which bound them prisoner, one which the hand of empire pulled ever tighter the more arduous their work was, or the more necessary to the State'.[27]

Their position in mediaeval societies was wholly different. As soon as the corporation makes an appearance, from the outset it shows itself to be the normal organisation for a segment of the population called upon to play such an important role within the state: the bourgeoisie, or the Third Estate. Indeed for a long time bourgeoisie and tradesmen formed a single body. 'In the thirteenth century,' says Levasseur, 'the bourgeoisie was made up entirely of tradesmen. A class of magistrates and lawyers was hardly beginning to emerge; scholars still belonged to the clergy; the number of rentiers was very limited, because land ownership was then almost entirely in the hands of the nobles. For commoners there remained only the tasks of the workshop or counting-house, and it was through industry or commerce that they gained a status in the kingdom.'[28] The same was true in Germany. Bourgeois and city-dweller were synonymous terms. What is more, we know that the German towns grew up around permanent markets, opened by a lord on a site on his estate.[29] The population that came to settle round these markets, which developed into the town-dwellers, was therefore made up almost exclusively of artisans and merchants. Thus the terms *forenses* or *mercatores* were used indiscriminately to designate the inhabitants of towns, and the *jus civile*, or urban law, is very often called *jus fori*, or market law. The organisation of trades and commerce thus seems to have represented the primitive organisation of the European bourgeoisie.

Moreover, when the towns had freed themselves of the nobles' yoke and the commune was formed, the craft guilds, which had preceded and paved the way for this development, became the foundation of the communal constitution. Indeed, 'in almost all communes the political system and the election of magistrates are based upon the division of the citizens into craft guilds'.[30] Frequently the vote was taken by trades, and the heads of the corporation and of the commune were chosen at the same time:

> At Amiens, for example, the artisans met every year to elect the 'mayors' of each corporation or 'banner'. The elected 'mayors' then appointed twelve aldermen, who appointed a further twelve, and the body of aldermen in its turn presented to the 'mayors' of the 'banners' three people from whom they chose the mayor of the commune. . . . In some cities the election procedure was even more complicated, but in every case political and municipal organisation was closely linked to the organisation of labour.[31]

Conversely, just as the commune consisted of all the craft guilds, the latter were each a commune in miniature, by the very fact that they had been the model of which the institution of the commune was the enlarged and developed form.

We know what the commune has been in the history of our societies, and how in the course of time it has become their very cornerstone. Consequently, since it was a union of corporations and modelled itself upon the corporation, it was in the last analysis the latter that served as the foundation for the entire political system which emerged from the movement to communes. As it progressed we can see its extraordinary growth in importance and dignity. Whereas in Rome it started by being almost completely outside the normal social framework, it has, by contrast, served as the elementary framework for present-day societies. This is yet another reason for us to reject the view that it is a type of archaic institution, destined to vanish from history. In the past the role that it played became increasingly vital with the development of commerce and industry. Thus it is entirely unlikely that further economic progress could have the effect of depriving it of the reason for its existence. The opposite hypothesis would appear more justified.[32]

But other lessons can be drawn from the brief picture just outlined.

Firstly, it permits us to conjecture how the corporation fell into temporary disrepute for some two centuries and, as a result, what it must become in order to regain its status among our public institutions. We have in fact just seen how the form that it assumed in the Middle Ages was closely linked to the organisation of the commune. Their solidarity was not disadvantageous, so long as the trades themselves were of a communal character. In principle, so long as artisans and merchants drew their custom more or less exclusively from the town-dwellers or the immediate neighbourhood alone, that is, so long as the market was mainly a local one, the guild, with its municipal organisation, sufficed for every need. But it was no longer the case once large-scale industry had sprung up. Not being particularly urban in any way, it could not conform to a system that had not been designed for it. In the first place its locus was not necessarily the town. It can even be installed far from any existing population settlement, whether rural or urban. It merely seeks the spot where it can be best supplied and from where it can spread out as easily as possible. Next, its field of activity is not confined to any particular region and it draws its customers from anywhere. An institution so wholly involved in the commune as was the old corporation could not therefore serve to embody and regulate a form of collective activity so utterly alien to communal life.

In fact, as soon as large-scale industry appeared it quite naturally lay outside the regime of the corporations. This was also why craft guilds strove by every means to prevent it developing. Yet large-scale industry was by no means exempt from every form of control; in its early days the state performed for it a role similar to that played by the corporation for small businesses and town-based trades. While the royal authority granted manufactories certain privileges, in return it subordinated them to its control, as is shown by the very title of 'royal manufactory' granted them. However, we know just how unsuitable the state is to fulfil this function. This condition of direct tutelage therefore inevitably became oppressive. It even became almost impossible as soon as large-scale industry had reached a certain level of development and diversification. This is why classical economists rightly demanded that this control be abolished. But if the corporation, as it then was, could not adapt itself to this new form of industry, and if the state could be no substitute for the former corporative discipline, it did not follow that in future every kind of discipline would be useless. What remained was that the old-style corporation would have to change if it were to continue to play its part in the new conditions of economic life. Unfortunately it lacked sufficient flexibility to reform itself in time, and this is why it broke up. Not being able to assimilate the new life that was emerging, life receded from it, and the corporation became what it was on the eve of the Revolution, a kind of lifeless substance, a foreign body that could no longer be sustained within the social organism save by the weight of its own inertia. Thus, not surprisingly, the time came when it was brutally cast out by society. But to destroy it was not the way to meet the needs that it had been unable to satisfy. Thus we are still faced with the problem, only in a more acute form, after a century of groping after solutions and of fruitless experiments.

The sociologist's task is not that of the statesman. Accordingly we do not have to set out in detail what that reform should be. We need only indicate its general principles as they appear to emerge from the facts just stated.

What past experience demonstrates above all is that the organisational framework of the professional group should always be related to that of economic life. It is because this condition was not fulfilled that the system of corporations disappeared. Thus, since the market, from being municipal as it once was, has become national and international, the corporation should assume the same dimensions. Instead of being restricted exclusively to the artisans of one town, it must grow so as to include all the members of one profession scattered over the whole country,[33] for in whatever region they may be, whether they live in town or countryside, they are all linked to one another and share a common life. Since this common life is in certain respects independent of any territorial boundaries, a suitable organism must be created to give expression to this life and to regulate its functions. Because of the dimensions that it assumes, such an organism should necessarily be closely in contact and directly linked with the central organism of the life of the collectivity. Events important enough to affect a whole category of industrial enterprises within a country necessarily have wide repercussions of which the state cannot fail to be aware. This impels it to intervene. Thus for good reason the royal power tended instinctively not to leave large-scale industry outside its ambit as soon as it appeared. It could not fail to take an interest in a form of activity which by its very nature is always liable to affect society as a whole. Yet such regulatory action, although necessary, should not degenerate into utter subordination, as happened in the seventeenth and eighteenth centuries. The two organisms, although in contact with each other, should remain distinct and autonomous; each has functions that it alone can perform. If it falls to political assemblies to lay down the general principles for industrial legislation, they are not capable of diversifying them according to the various types of industry. It is this diversification that is the corporation's proper task.[34] A unitary organisation over a whole country also in no way precludes the formation of secondary organisations which include similar workers in the same region or locality. Their role could be to spell out even more specifically, in accordance with local or regional needs, the regulations for a profession. Thus economic activity could be regulated and demarcated without losing any of its diversity.

By so doing the corporative system would be shielded against that tendency to inertia with which it has so often been justly reproached in the past. This defect stemmed from the closely communal character of the corporation. So long as it was limited to the confines of one town it inevitably fell a prisoner to tradition, as did the town itself. Within so confined a group, since living conditions almost invariably remain unchanged, habit exerts over both people and things a sway that lacks any countervailing force, with the result that innovations come even to be feared. The traditionalism of corporations was therefore only a facet of communal traditionalism, having the same rationale behind it. Then, once it had become rooted in custom, it outlived the causes which had occasioned its creation and which had originally been its justification. A material and moral concentration within the country, and the large-scale industry ensuing from this, had stirred people's minds to wish to satisfy new wants, had stimulated new needs, and had introduced into taste and fashion a variability hitherto unknown. This is why the corporation, stubbornly clinging to its old customs, was incapable of responding to these novel demands. National corporations, however, through their very size and complexity, would not be exposed to this danger. Too many different minds would be stimulated to activity for any static uniformity to be established. Within any body composed of many diverse elements regroupings constantly occur, and these in themselves are each a source of innovation.[35] There would therefore be no fixed equilibrium in such an organisation, and in consequence it would naturally be attuned to a variable equilibrium of needs and ideas.

Moreover, we must reject the belief that the corporation's sole role should consist in laying down and applying rules. It is undoubtedly true that wherever a group is formed, a moral discipline is also formed. But the institution of that discipline is only one of the numerous ways in which any collective activity manifests itself. A group is not only a moral authority regulating the life of its members, but also a source of life *sui generis*. From it there arises a warmth that quickens or gives fresh life to each individual, which makes him disposed to empathise, causing selfishness to melt away. Thus in the past the family has been responsible for legislating a code of law and morality whose severity has often been carried to an extreme of harshness. But it has also been the environment where, for the first time, men have learnt to appreciate the outpouring of feeling. We have likewise seen how the corporation, both in Rome and during the Middle Ages, created these same needs and sought to satisfy them. The corporations of the future will be assigned even greater and more complex functions, because of their increased scope. Around their purely professional functions will be grouped others which at present are exercised by the communes and private associations. Among these are functions of mutual assistance which, in order to be entirely fulfilled, assume between helpers and helped feelings of solidarity as well as a certain homogeneity of intellect and morals, such as that readily engendered by the exercise of the same profession. Many educational activities (technical education, adult education, etc.) should also, it seems, find in the corporation their natural habitat. The same is also true for a certain type of artistic activity. It would seem in accordance with the nature of things that such a noble form of diversion and recreation should develop alongside the more serious aspects of life, acting as a balancing and restorative influence. In fact we now already see trade unions acting at the same time as friendly societies, and others are setting up communal centres where courses are organised, and concerts and dramatic performances held. Hence the activity of a corporation can take on the most varied forms.

We may even reasonably suppose that the corporation will be called upon to become the foundation, or one of the essential foundations, of our political organisation. We have seen that, although it first began outside the social system, it tended to become more and more closely involved in it as economic life developed. We have therefore every reason to anticipate that, if progress continues on the same lines, the corporation is destined to assume an ever more central and preponderant place in society. It was once the elementary division of communal organisation. Now that the commune, from being the autonomous unit that it once was, has been absorbed into the state just as the municipal market was absorbed into the national market, may we not legitimately think that the corporation should also undergo a corresponding transformation and become the elementary division of the state, the basic political unit? Society, instead of remaining what it is today – a conglomerate of land masses juxtaposed together – would become a vast system of national corporations. The demand is raised in various quarters for electoral colleges to be constituted by professions and not by territorial constituencies. Certainly in this way political assemblies would more accurately reflect the diversity of social interests and their interconnections. They would more exactly epitomise social life as a whole. Yet if we state that the country, in order to become conscious of itself, should be grouped by professions, is not this to acknowledge that the organised profession or the corporation should become the essential organ of public life?

In this way a serious gap in the structure of European societies, and in our own in particular, the nature of which we shall indicate later, would be filled.[36] We shall see how, as history unfolds, an organisation based on territorial groupings (village, town, district or province, etc.) becomes progressively weaker. There is no doubt that we each belong to a commune or a *département*, but the ties binding us to them become daily more loose' and tenuous. These geographical divisions are in the main artificial, and no longer arouse deep emotions within us. The provincial spirit has vanished beyond recall. 'Parish pump' patriotism has become an anachronism that cannot be restored at will. Strictly local or *département* matters hardly affect or enthrall us either any longer, save in so far as they go hand in hand with matters relating to our profession. Our activity extends much beyond these groups, which are too narrow for it; moreover, much of what happens within them leaves us indifferent. Thus what might be described as the spontaneous collapse of the old social structure has occurred. But this internal organisation cannot disappear without something taking its place. A society made up of an extremely large mass of unorganised individuals, which an overgrown state attempts to limit and restrain, constitutes a veritable sociological monstrosity. For collective activity is always too complex to be capable of finding expression in the one single organ of the state. Moreover, the state is too remote from individuals, its connections with them too superficial and irregular, to be able to penetrate the depths of their consciousness and socialise them from within. This is why, when the state constitutes the sole environment in which men can fit themselves for the business of living in common, they inevitably 'contract out', detaching themselves from one another, and thus society disintegrates to a corresponding extent. A nation cannot be maintained unless, between the state and individuals, a whole range of secondary groups are interposed. These must be close enough to the individual to attract him strongly to their activities and, in so doing, to absorb him into the mainstream of social life. We have just demonstrated how professional groupings are fitted to perform this role, and how indeed everything marks them out for it. Hence we can comprehend how important it is, particularly in the economic sphere, that they should emerge from that inchoate and disorgan-ised state in which they have lain for a century, since professions of this kind today absorb the greater part of the energies of society.[37]

We shall perhaps now be in a better position to explain the conclusions we reached at the end of our book, *Le Suicide.*[38] We proposed in it already a strong corporative organisation as a means of curing the malaise whose existence is demonstrated by the increase in suicide, linked as well to many other symptoms. Certain critics have considered that the remedy we propounded did not match up to the extent of the evil. But this is because they have misunderstood the true nature of the corporation, the place where it rightfully belongs in our collective life as a whole, and the serious anomaly arising from its abolition. They have regarded it only as a utilitarian body whose entire effect would be to improve the way in which we organise our economic interests, whereas in reality it should constitute the essential element in our social structure. The absence of any corporative institution therefore creates, in the organisation of a people such as ours, a vacuum the significance of which it is difficult to overestimate. We therefore lack a whole system of organs necessary to the normal functioning of social life. Such a structural defect is plainly not some local affliction limited to one segment of society: it is a sickness *totius substantiae*, one that affects the entire organism. Consequently any venture whose purpose is to effect a cure cannot fail to have the most far-reaching consequences. The general health of the body social is at stake.

Yet this is not to say that the corporation is a kind of cure-all which can serve any purpose. The crisis from which we are suffering does not stem from one single, unique cause. For it to be dispelled, it is not enough to establish some kind of regulatory system wherever necessary: the system should also be fair, as is fitting. But, as we shall state later on, 'So long as there are rich and poor from birth, there can exist no just contract,' nor any just distribution of social status.[39] Yet if corporative reform does not remove the need for other reforms, it is the *sine qua non* of their effectiveness. Let us suppose that the overriding consideration of ideal justice has been finally realised, that men begin their lives in a state of perfect economic equality, that is, that wealth has completely ceased to be hereditary. The problems with which we are now grappling would not thereby have been resolved. In fact, the economic mechanism will always continue to exist, as will the various actors who co-operate in its workings. Thus their rights and duties will have to be determined, and indeed for every type of industry. For each profession a set of rules will have to be drawn up, fixing the amount of labour required, the just reward for the various people engaged in it, and their duties towards the community and towards one another, etc. Thus, just as at the present time, we shall be faced with a clean sweep. Merely because wealth will not be handed down according to the same principles as at the present time, the state of anarchy will not have disappeared. That state does not only depend upon the fact that things are located here rather than there, or in the hands of this person rather than in another's, but will depend upon the fact that the activity for which these matters are the occasion, or the instrument, remains unregulated. Nor will it become regulated as if by magic as soon as it becomes useful to do so, unless the forces needed to institute that regulatory system have been mobilised and organised beforehand.

Something else must be added: new difficulties would then arise which would remain insoluble without a corporative organisation. Up to now it has been the family which, either by the institution of property held in common or by that of inheritance, has maintained the continuity of economic life. Either it possessed and exploited wealth on an indivisible basis or, as soon as this ancient family form of communism was upset, it was the family which received the wealth bequeathed – the family represented by the closest relatives, upon the death of the owner.[40] In the first case no change was even wrought through death, and the relationship of things to persons remained as they were, with no modification even through the accession of new generations. In the second case the change was effected automatically and there was no perceptible time when the wealth remained idle, with no one available to utilise it. But if domestic society is no longer to play this role, another social organ must indeed replace it in order to exercise this most necessary function. For there is only one means by which to prevent the functioning of affairs from being interrupted from time to time. This is if a group – such as the family – which is an enduring entity, either owns or exploits possessions itself, or receives them as deaths occur, in order to hand them on, where appropriate, to someone else to whom they are entrusted for development. But we have stated, and repeat, that the state is ill-suited for these economic tasks, which are too specialised for it. Hence there remains only the professional grouping which can usefully perform them. It does indeed meet the two necessary conditions: it is too closely bound up with economic life not to be conscious of the economy's every need, and at the same time is at least as equally enduring as the family. But in order to fulfil that office, it must first exist, and indeed have achieved sufficient consistency and maturity to be equal to the new and complex role that may befall it. .

Thus, although the problem of the corporation is not the only one which imposes itself upon public attention, there is certainly none more pressing, for other problems can only be tackled when this one has been resolved. No notable innovation of a legal kind can be introduced unless we begin by creating the body needed for the creation of the new law. This is why it is otiose to waste time in working out in too precise detail what that law should be. In the present state of scientific knowledge we cannot foresee what it should be, except in ever approximate and uncertain terms. How much more important it is to set to work immediately on constituting the moral forces which alone can give that law substance and shape!

Notes

1. We have confined ourselves to eliminating from the original Introduction some thirty pages, which now appear to us to be of no value. We also explain the reasons for this omission at the place where it occurs.
2. Cf. The conclusion of *Le Suicide*.
3. Cf. *infra*, pp. 132–9, 165.
4. Cf. *infra*, pp. 164–5, 292.
5. Cf. Book III, Chapter I, § III.
6. Cf. We return to this point later. Cf. pp. 296 ff.
7. Cf. Hermann, *Lehrbuch der griechischen Antiquitäten*, 3rd edn, vol. IV, p. 398. Sometimes the artisan, by virtue of his occupation, was even deprived of his citizenship (ibid., p. 392). We do not know whether, although no legal and official organisation existed, a clandestine one did. What is beyond doubt is that there were corporations of tradesmen. (Cf. Francotte, *L'Industrie dans la Grèce antique*, vol. II, pp. 204 ff.)
8. Plutarch, *Numa*, vol. XVII; Pliny, *Natural History*, vol. XXXIV. This is doubtless only a legend but it proves that the Romans esteemed their corporations to be one of their oldest institutions.
9. Waltzing, *Etude historique sur les corporations professionnelles chez les Romains*, vol. I, pp. 56–7.

10. Certain historians believe that from the beginning the corporations had links with the state. But in any case it is absolutely certain that their official character evolved differently under the Empire.
11. Levasseur, *Les classes ouvrières en France jusqu'à la Révolution*, vol. I, p. 194.
12. Waltzing, *Etude historique*, vol. I, p. 194.
13. The majority of historians esteem that certain *collegia* were, at the very least, mutual assistance societies.
14. Waltzing, *Etude historique*, vol. I, p. 330.
15. Ibid., vol. I, p. 331.
16. Boissier, *La religion romaine*, vol. II, pp. 287–8.
17. Levasseur, *Les classes*, pp. 217–18.
18. Levasseur, *Les classes*, vol. I, p. 221. Cf., for the same moral character of the corporation in Germany, Gierke, *Das deutsche Genossenschaftswesen*, vol. I, p. 384; and in England, Ashley, *Histoire des doctrines économiques*, vol. I, p. 101.
19. Levasseur, *Les classes*, p. 238.
20. Ibid., pp. 240–61.
21. Cf. especially *Année sociologique*, vol. I, pp. 313 ff.
22. We have enlarged upon this idea in *Le Suicide*, p. 433.
23. It appears more likely that the centuries with these names did not contain all the carpenters or smiths, but only those who made or repaired weapons and war equipment. Denis of Halicarnassus informs us categorically that the workmen grouped in this way exercised a purely military function, $\epsilon\iota\delta\ \tau\grave{o}\nu\ \pi o\lambda\epsilon\mu\grave{o}\nu$. Thus they were not real 'colleges' but divisions within the army.
24. All we are saying about the position of the corporations leaves entirely open the controversial question of knowing whether the state, from the beginning, intervened in their formation. Even if in the beginning they might have been dependent on the state, which does not appear likely, the fact remains that they did not affect the political structure. It is this that is important for us.
25. If we go one stage further back in their evolution, their situation is even more one of being outside the official organisation. In Athens they are not only outside society, but almost outside the law.
26. Waltzing, *Etude historique*, vol. I, pp. 85 ff.
27. Levasseur, *Les classes*, vol. I, p. 31.
28. Ibid., vol. I, p. 191.
29. Cf. Rietschel, *Markt und Stadt in ihrem rechtlichen Verhältnis* (Leipzig, 1897) *passim*, and all the works of Sohm on this point.
30. Rietschel, *Markt und Stadt*, vol. I, p. 193.
31. Ibid., vol. I, p. 183.
32. It is true that when occupations organise themselves on caste lines, they happen to assume very early on a visible position in the social constitution. This is the case in Indian societies. But a caste is not a corporation. It is essentially a family and religious group; and not an occupational one. Each caste has it own particular level of religious feeling. And, as society is organised on religious lines, this religiosity, which depends on various causes, assigns to each caste its determinate

rank within the social system as a whole. But its economic role has no influence over this official position. (Cf. C. Bouglé, 'Remarques sur le régime des castes', *Année sociologique*, vol. IV.)

33. We need not discuss the international organisation which, because of the international character of the market, would necessarily develop at a level above that of the national organisation. For at present the latter alone can constitute a legal entity. In the present state of European law the former can only result from arrangements freely concluded between national corporations.

34. This specialisation could not occur without the help of elected assemblies charged with representing the corporation. In the present state of industry, these assemblies, as well as those tribunals entrusted with the task of applying the regulations of an occupation, should clearly include representatives of employees and employers, as is already the case with the industrial arbitration tribunals. The proportion of each should correspond to the respective importance attributed by public opinion to these two factors of production. But if it is necessary for both sides to meet on the governing councils of the corporation it is no less indispensable for them to constitute distinct and independent groups at the lower level of corporative organisation, because too often their interests vie with one another and are opposing. To feel that they exist freely, they must be aware of their separate existence. The two bodies so constituted can then appoint their representatives to the common assemblies.

35. Cf. *infra*, Book II, Chapter III, § IV.

36. Cf. *infra*, p. 165.

37. Moreover, we do not mean that territorial constituencies are destined to disappear completely, but only that they will fade into the background. Old institutions never vanish in the face of new ones to such an extent that they leave no trace of themselves. They persist not only by the mere fact of survival, but also because there persists some trace of the needs to which they corresponded. Material proximity will always constitute a link between men. Consequently the political and social organisation based on territory will certainly subsist. But it will no longer enjoy its present predominance, precisely because that link is losing some of its force. What is more, we have shown above that, even at the base of the corporation will still be found geographical divisions. Moreover, between the various corporations from a same locality or region there will necessarily be special relationships of solidarity which will, from time to time, demand an appropriate organisation.

38. *Le Suicide*, pp. 434 ff.

39. Cf. *infra*, Book III, Chapter II.

40. It is true that where a system of wills exists, the owner can himself determine to whom his wealth is to be passed on. But a will merely represents the means of dispensing with the rule of the right of succession. It is this rule that is the norm for determining how these legacies are handed on. Moreover, these dispensations are restricted very generally and are always the exception.

Introduction

The Problem

Although the division of labour is not of recent origin, it was only at the end of the last century that societies began to become aware of this law, to which up to then they had submitted almost unwittingly. Undoubtedly even from antiquity several thinkers had perceived its importance.[1] Yet Adam Smith was the first to attempt to elaborate the theory of it. Moreover, it was he who first coined the term, which social science later lent to biology.

Nowadays the phenomenon has become so widespread that it catches everyone's attention. We can no longer be under any illusion about the trends in modern industry. It involves increasingly powerful mechanisms, large-scale groupings of power and capital, and consequently an extreme division of labour. Inside factories, not only are jobs demarcated, becoming extremely specialised, but each product is itself a speciality entailing the existence of others. Adam Smith and John Stuart Mill persisted in hoping that agriculture at least would prove an exception to the rule, seeing in it the last refuge of small-scale ownership. Although in such a matter we must guard against generalising unduly, nowadays it appears difficult to deny that the main branches of the agricultural industry are increasingly swept along in the general trend.[2] Finally, commerce itself contrives ways to follow and reflect, in all their distinctive nuances, the boundless diversity of industrial undertakings. Although this evolution occurs spontaneously and unthinkingly, those economists who study its causes and evaluate its results, far from condemning such diversification or attacking it, proclaim its necessity. They perceive in it the higher law of human societies and the condition for progress.

1

Yet the division of labour is not peculiar to economic life. We can observe its increasing influence in the most diverse sectors of society. Functions, whether political, administrative or judicial, are becoming more and more specialised. The same is true in the arts and sciences. The time lies far behind us when philosophy constituted the sole science. It has become fragmented into a host of special disciplines, each having its purpose, method and ethos. 'From one half-century to another the men who have left their mark upon the sciences have become more specialized.'[3]

Having to pinpoint the nature of the studies which for over two centuries had engaged the most celebrated scientists, de Candolle noted that in the age of Leibnitz and Newton he would have had to write down:

> two or three descriptions almost always for each scientist: for example, astronomer and physicist, or mathematician, astronomer and physicist, or alternatively, to use only such general terms as philosopher or naturalist. Even that would not have been enough. Mathematicians and naturalists were sometimes scholars or poets. Even at the end of the eighteenth century, a number of designations would have been needed to indicate precisely what was remarkable about men such as Wolff, Haller or Charles Bonnet in several different branches of science and letters. In the nineteenth century this difficulty no longer exists or at least occurs very infrequently.[4]

Not only is the scientist no longer immersed in different sciences at the same time, but he can no longer encompass the whole field of one science. The range of his research is limited to a finite category of problems or even to a single one of them. Likewise, the functions of the scientist which formerly were almost always exercised alongside another more lucrative one, such as that of doctor, priest, magistrate or soldier, are increasingly sufficient by themselves. De Candolle even predicts that one day not too far distant the profession of scientist and that of teacher, at present still so closely linked, will be irrevocably separated.

The recent philosophical speculations in biology have finally caused us to realise that the division of labour is a fact of a generality that the economists, who were the first to speak of it, had been incapable of suspecting. Indeed, since the work of Wolff, von Baer and Milne-Edwards we know that the law of the division of labour applies to organisms as well as to societies. It may even be stated that an organism occupies the more exalted a place in the animal hierarchy the more specialised its functions are. This discovery has had the result of not only enlarging enormously the field of action of the divison of labour, but also of setting its origins back into an infinitely distant past, since it becomes almost contemporaneous with the coming of life upon earth. It is no longer a mere social institution whose roots lie in the intelligence and the will of men, but a general biological phenomenon, the conditions for which must seemingly be sought in the essential properties of organised matter. The division of labour in society appears no more than a special form of this general development. In conforming to this law societies apparently yield to a movement that arose long before they existed and which sweeps along in the same direction the whole of the living world.

Such a fact clearly cannot manifest itself without affecting profoundly our moral constitution, for the evolution of mankind will develop in two utterly opposing directions, depending on whether we abandon ourselves to this tendency or whether we resist it. Yet, then, one question poses itself urgently: of these two directions, which one should we choose? Is it our duty to seek to become a rounded, complete creature, a whole sufficient unto itself or, on the contrary, to be only a part of the whole, the organ of an organism? In short, whilst the division of labour is a law of nature, is it also a moral rule for human conduct and, if it possesses this last characteristic, through what causes and to what extent? There is no need to demonstrate the serious nature of this practical problem: whatever assessment we make of the division of labour, we all sense that it is, and increasingly so, one of the fundamental bases of the social order.

The problem is one that the moral consciousness of nations has often posed, but in a muddled fashion, and without being able to resolve it. Two opposing tendencies confront one another, and neither has succeeded in gaining entirely the upper hand.

It seems undoubtedly clear that the view is gaining ground that the division of labour should become a categorical rule of behaviour, one that should be imposed as a duty. It is true that those who infringe it are not meted out any precise punishment laid down by law, but they do suffer rebuke. The time is past when the perfect man seemed to us the one who, capable of being interested in everything but attaching himself exclusively to nothing, able to savour everything and understand everything, found the means to combine and epitomise within himself the finest aspects of civilisation. Today that general culture, once so highly extolled, no longer impresses us save as a flabby, lax form of discipline.[5] To struggle against nature we need to possess more vigorous faculties, deploy more productive energies. We desire our activity to be concentrated, instead of being scattered over a wide area, gaining in intensity what it has lost in breadth. We are wary of those too volatile men of talent, who, lending themselves equally to all forms of employment, refuse to choose for themselves a special role and to adhere to it. We feel a coolness towards those men whose sole preoccupation is to organise their faculties, limbering them up, but without putting them to any special use or sacrificing a single one, as if each man among them ought to be self-sufficient, constituting his own independent world. It appears to us that such a state of detachment and indeterminateness is somewhat antisocial. The man of parts, as he once was, is for us no more than a dilettante, and we accord no moral value to dilettantism. Rather, do we perceive perfection in the competent man, one who seeks not to be complete but to be productive, one who has a well-defined job to which he devotes himself, and carries out his task, ploughing his single furrow. 'To perfect oneself,' says Secrétant, 'is to learn one's role, to make oneself fit to fulfil one's function. . . . The yardstick for our perfection is no longer to be found in satisfaction with ourselves, in the plaudits of the crowd or the approving smile of an affected dilettantism, but in the sum total of services rendered, and in our ability to continue to render them.'[6] Thus the moral ideal, from being the sole one, simple and impersonal, has become increasingly diversified. We no longer think that the exclusive duty of man is to realise within himself the qualities of man in general, but we believe that he is no less obliged to have those qualities that relate to his employment. One fact, among others, reflects this view: this is the increasingly specialist character assumed by education. More and more we deem it necessary not to subject all children to a uniform culture, as if all were destined to lead the same life, but to train them differently according to the varying functions they will be called upon to fulfil. In short, in one of its aspects the categorical imperative of the moral consciousness is coming to assume the following form: *Equip yourself to fulfil usefully a specific function.*

Yet, confronted with these facts, we can cite others that contradict them. If public opinion recognises the rule of the division of labour, it is not without some anxiety and hesitation. Whilst commanding men to specialise, it has always seemingly the fear that they will do so to excess. Side by side with maxims extolling intensive labour are others, no less widely current, which alert us to its dangers. 'It is,' declares Jean-Baptiste Say, 'sad to have to confess that one has never produced more than the eighteenth part of a pin; and do not let us imagine that it is solely the workman who all his life wields a file and hammer, who demeans the dignity of his nature in this way. It is also the man who, through his status, exercises the most subtle faculties of his mind.'[7] At the very beginning of the century Lemontey,[8] comparing the existence of the modern worker to the free and easy life of the savage, found the latter more favoured than the former. Nor is de Tocqueville any less severe. 'As the principle of the division of labour is ever increasingly applied,' he states, 'art makes progress but the artisan regresses.'[9] Generally speaking, the maxim that decrees that we should specialise is as if refuted everywhere by its opposite, which bids us all realise the same ideal, one that is far from having lost all authority. In principle this conflict of ideas is certainly not surprising. Moral life, like that of body and mind, responds to different needs which may even be contradictory. Thus it is natural for it to be made up in part of opposing elements, which have a mutually limiting and balancing effect. Nevertheless, there is truly something about so marked an antimony which should trouble the moral consciousness of nations. It needs indeed to be able to explain how such a contradiction can arise.

To end this state of indecision we shall not resort to the normal method of the moralists who, wishing to decide upon the moral worth of a precept, start by laying down a general formula for morality, and then measure the disputed maxim up against it. Nowadays we know how little value may be attached to such summary generalisations.[10] Set out at the beginning of a study, before any observation of the facts, their purpose is not to account for them, but to enunciate the abstract principle for an ideal legislative code to be created out of nothing. Thus these generalisations do not summarise for us the essential characteristics which moral rules really represent in a particular society or in a determinate social type. They merely express the manner in which the moralist himself conceives morality. In this respect they assuredly do not cease to be instructive, for they inform us of the trends in morality that are emerging at the moment in question. But they merely possess the interest appertaining to one fact, not that of a scientific view. We are in no way justified in seeing in the personal aspirations that a thinker feels, however real these may be, an adequate expression of moral reality. They interpret needs that are never more than a part of the whole. They correspond to some special, determined desideratum that the consciousness, by an illusion customary to it, elevates to one ultimate single goal. How often do such aspirations even turn out to be of a morbid nature! We cannot therefore refer to them as objective criteria enabling us to assess the morality of the practices that occur.

We must lay on one side such deductions, which are usually employed only to give the semblance of an argument and to justify, after the event, preconceived sentiments and personal impressions. The sole means of successfully evaluating objectively the division of labour is first to study it in itself, in an entirely speculative fashion, investigating its utility and on what it is contingent – in short, to form for ourselves as adequate an idea of it as possible. When this has been accomplished, we are in a position to compare it with other moral phenomena and perceive what relationship it entertains with them. If we find that it plays a role similar to some other practice whose moral and normal character is unquestionable; that if in certain cases it does not fulfil that role it is because of abnormal deviations; and that if the causes that determine it are also the determining conditions for other moral rules, then we shall be able to conclude that it may be classified with those rules. Thus, without seeking to substitute ourselves for the moral consciousness of societies, without claiming to legislate in its place, we shall be able to bring some enlightenment to that consciousness and reduce its perplexities.

Our study will therefore be divided into three main sections.

We shall first investigate the function of the division of labour, that is, the social need to which it corresponds.

Next, we shall determine the causes and conditions upon which it depends.

Finally, as it would not have been the subject of such serious charges against it did it not in reality deviate more or less frequently from the normal state, we shall aim to classify the principal abnormal forms that it assumes, in order to avoid confusing them with the rest. In addition, the study will be of interest because, as in biology, the pathological here will enable us to understand better the physiological.

Moreover, if there has been so much argument about the moral value of the division of labour it is much less because agreement is lacking upon a general formula for morality than because the questions of fact we propose to tackle have been unduly neglected. Reasoning about these has always been as if they were self-evident – as if, in order to know the nature, role and causes of the division of labour, it was enough to analyse the conception of them that each one of us possesses. Such a method does not lead to any scientific conclusions. Thus since Adam Smith the theory of the division of labour has made very little progress. 'His successors,' declares Schmoller,[11] 'with a notable poverty of ideas, clung stubbornly to his examples and observations, until the time when the socialists broadened their perspective and contrasted the division of labour in factories today with that in the workshops of the eighteenth century. Even so, the theory has not been developed in any systematic and profound way. The technological considerations and the true but banal observations by some economists could not, furthermore, particularly favour the development of these ideas.' To understand objectively the division of labour it is not enough to develop the substance of the conception we have of it. We should rather treat it as an objective fact, to be observed and comparisons made. As we shall see, the result of these observations is often different from what the intimate meaning suggests to us.[12]

Notes

1. Οὐ γάρ εχ δύο ἰατρων γιγνεται χοινωία, αλλ' εξ ἰατρου χαὶ δεωργου χαὶ δλωζ ξ τέρων οὐχ ισων, *Nichomachean Ethics*, E. 1133a, 16.
2. *Journal des économistes* (November 1884) p. 211.
3. De Candolle, *Histoire des Sciences et des Savants*, 2nd edn, p. 263.
4. Ibid.
5. This passage has occasionally been construed as implying a root and branch condemnation of any kind of general culture. In reality, as the context makes plain, we are speaking here only of humanist culture, which is indeed a general culture, but not the only possible one.
6. Secrétant, *Le principe de la morale*, p. 189.

7.   J.-B. Say, *Traité d'économie politique*, book I, ch. 8.
8.   Lemontey, *Raison ou folie*: chapter on the influence of the division of labour.
9.   De Tocqueville, *La démocratie en Amérique*.
10. In the first edition of this book, we developed at length the reasons which, in our view, prove the sterility of this method. Today we believe that we can be more brief. There are arguments that should not be indefinitely prolonged.
11. 'La division du travail étudiée au point de vue historique', *Revue d'économie politique* (1889) p. 567.
12. Since 1893 two works have appeared, or about which we have come to hear, which concern the question treated in our book. First, there is Simmel's *Soziale Differenzierung* (Leipzig, pp. vii and 147), which does not deal especially with the division of labour but with the process of individual specialisation in general. Next, there is the work by Bücher, *Die Entstehung der Volkswirtschaft*, recently translated into French as *Etudes d'histoire d'économie politique* (Alcan, Paris, 1901), several chapters of which are given over to the economic division of labour.

Book I

The Function of the Division of Labour

Chapter I

The Method of Determining This Function

The word *function* is used in two somewhat different ways. Sometimes it designates a system of living movements, divorced from their effects. At other times it expresses the corresponding relationship existing between these movements and certain needs of the organism. Thus we speak of the digestive or respiratory functions, etc. But we also say that the digestion fulfils the function of controlling the absorption into the organism of fluid or solid substances intended to make good its losses. We likewise say that the respiration fulfils the function of introducing into animal tissues the gases necessary for sustaining life, etc. It is in this second connotation that we intend the term. Thus to ask what is the function of the division of labour is to investigate the need to which it corresponds. Once this question has been resolved we shall be able to see if that need is of the same kind as those to which correspond other rules of behaviour whose moral character is undisputed.

If we have chosen this term, it is because any other would be inexact or ambiguous. We cannot use 'aim' or 'purpose', and speak of the goal of the division of labour, because that would suppose that the division of labour exists *for the sake of results* that we shall determine. To use 'results' or 'effects' cannot satisfy us either, because no idea of correspondence is evoked. On the other hand, the term 'role' or 'function' has the great advantage of implying that idea, but in no way prejudges the question of knowing how that correspondence has been established, or whether it arises from some intended and preconceived adaptation or from some adjustment after the event. What is important for us is to know whether this correspondence exists, and in what it consists, and not whether

11

it has been vaguely foreseen beforehand, or even whether it has been realised later.

I

At first sight nothing appears easier than to determine the role of the division of labour. Are not its efforts known to everybody? Since it increases both the productive capacity and skill of the workman, it is the necessary condition for the intellectual and material development of societies; it is the source of civilisation. Moreover, since we ascribe somewhat glibly an absolute value to civilisation, it does not even occur to us to seek out any different function for the division of labour.

We cannot conceive it necessary to argue that it does in reality have such a result. But if it had no other result and served no other purpose, there would be no reason for attributing any moral character to it.

Indeed the services that it renders in this way are almost entirely divorced from moral life, or at most have with it merely a very indirect and distant relationship. Although it is somewhat customary nowadays to reply to Rousseau's diatribes by dithyrambs of the opposing kind, it is by no means demonstrated that civilisation is a moral matter. To resolve the question we cannot rely on the analysis of concepts that are necessarily subjective. Rather we should pick out some fact that might serve to measure the average level of morality and then observe its variations as civilisation progresses. Unfortunately we lack this unit of measurement, although we do possess one for collective immorality. The average number of suicides and crimes of every description may serve to indicate the level of immorality in any given society. Now, if such an operation is carried out, it hardly redounds to the credit of civilisation, for the number of such morbid phenomena seems to increase as the arts, science and industry progress.[1] It would doubtless be somewhat rash to conclude from this fact that civilisation is immoral, but at the very least we may rest assured that, if civilisation exerts any positive and favourable influence upon moral life, that influence is somewhat weak.

If, moreover, we analyse that ill-defined conglomerate dubbed 'civilisation', we find that the elements of which it is made up lack any moral character.

This particularly holds good for the economic activity that always accompanies civilisation. Far from it assisting the progress of morality, it is in the great industrial centres that crime and suicide are most frequent. In any case civilisation does not exhibit those external indicators from which moral facts can be discerned. We have replaced the stage coach by the railway, sailing ships by ocean liners, and small workshops by factories. All this expansion of activity is generally acknowledged to be useful, but there is nothing obligatorily moral about it. The artisan or small-scale industrialist who resists this general trend and stubbornly perseveres in carrying on his modest business fulfils his duty as much as the great manufacturer who covers the country with factories and assembles under his orders a whole army of workmen. The moral consciousness of nations is not deceived: it prefers a modicum of justice to all the industrial improvements in the world. Assuredly such industrial activities have a reason for their existence; they correspond to needs, but these needs are not moral ones.

This is even more true of art, which remains entirely resistant to anything resembling an obligation, since its domain is one where freedom reigns. It is a luxury and an ornament that it may well be fine to possess, but that one cannot be compelled to acquire: what is a superfluity cannot be imposed upon people. By contrast, morality is the indispensable minimum, that which is strictly necessary, the daily bread without which societies cannot live. Art corresponds to the need we have to widen those of our activities that lack purpose, for the pleasure of doing so, whilst morality constrains us to follow a path laid down, one which leads towards a definite goal. He who speaks of obligation speaks at the same time of constraint. Thus, although art can draw inspiration from moral ideas or is to be found intermingled with the evolution of strictly moral phenomena, it is not moral in itself. Observation might even establish perhaps that, with individuals as with societies, from the moral viewpoint the inordinate development of the aesthetic faculties is a grave symptom.

Among all the elements of civilisation science is the sole one to assume, under certain conditions, a moral character. Indeed societies are increasingly tending to regard it as a duty of the individual to develop his intelligence by absorbing those scientific truths already established. Already nowadays there are certain areas of knowledge that we should all possess. We are not forced to throw ourselves into the hurly-burly of industry, or to become an artist, but we are now all expected not to remain ignorant. So keenly felt is this obligation that, in certain societies, it is not only hallowed by general opinion, but by the law. Moreover, we can indeed perceive how this special privilege of science arises. It is because science is none other than consciousness raised to the acme of clarity. For societies to be able to live in the conditions of existence now available to them the sphere of consciousness, whether individual or social, must be extended and clarified. Indeed, as the environment in which societies live becomes increasingly complex, and consequently more fluctuating, they must change frequently in order to survive. Furthermore, the more the consciousness remains unenlightened, the more averse it is to change, because it does not perceive rapidly enough either the need for change or the direction change should take. On the contrary, the enlightened consciousness has learnt how to prepare itself beforehand for the way in which it has to adapt. This is why intelligence, guided by science, requires to assume a greater role in the processes of collective life.

However, the science that everybody is called upon to possess in this way hardly deserves that name. It is not science; or at the very most it is the most common and general part of it. It is indeed limited to a few indispensable elements of knowledge which are only required of everyone because they are within everyone's grasp. Science proper soars infinitely beyond this vulgar level. It includes not only what one would blush at not knowing, but all that it is possible to know. It presumes among those who are its adepts not only those average faculties possessed by all men, but special aptitudes. In consequence, since it is accessible only to an elite, it is not obligatory. Although something fine and useful, it is not so utterly indispensable that society categorically requires it. There is advantage in being equipped with it, but nothing immoral about not acquiring it. It is a field of activity open to everyone on their own initiative, but one which no one is compelled to enter. One is no more required to be a scientist than an artist. Thus science, like art and industry, lies outside the realm of ethics.[2]

If so much controversy has centred round the moral character of civilisation, it is because too often moralists have lacked any objective criterion by which to distinguish moral facts from those that are not. It is customary to categorise as moral everything that has something noble or valuable about it, everything that is the object of no mean aspirations. It is because of this exaggerated extension of the meaning of the term that civilisation has been included within the moral domain. But the field of ethics is far from being so indeterminate. It comprises all the rules of action that are imposed categorically upon behaviour and to which a punishment is attached, but goes no further than this. Consequently, since civilisation comprises nothing that displays this criterion of morality, it is morally neutral. Thus if the role of the division of labour were solely to make civilisation possible, it would share this same moral neutrality.

It is because we have generally perceived no other function for the division of labour, that the theories that have been put forward regarding it are to this extent inconsistent. In fact, even supposing a neutral area could exist in the field of morality, it would be impossible for the division of labour to be sited within it.[3] If the division of labour is not good, it must be bad; if it is not moral, then it must represent a falling away from morality. Thus if it serves no other purpose we fall into unresolvable contradictions, for the economic advantages it affords are set against moral disadvantages. As we cannot subtract these two heterogeneous and uncomparable quantities from each other, we cannot tell which one takes precedence over the other. Nor, consequently, can we arrive at a decision. The primacy of morality will be invoked in an out-and-out condemnation of the division of labour. But, besides the fact that this *ultima ratio* always represents a scientific *coup d'état*, the evident need for specialisation makes such a position impossible to sustain.

Something else must be said: if the division of labour fulfils no other role, not only does it posses no moral character, but no reason for its existence can be perceived. Indeed we shall see that of itself civilisation has no intrinsic and absolute value. What confers value upon it is the fact that it meets certain needs. Later the proposition[4] will be demonstrated that these needs are themselves consequences of the division of labour. It is because the division of labour is accompanied by an increase in fatigue that man is constrained to seek after, as a compensatory increase, those goods of civilisation that otherwise would present no interest for him. Thus if the division of labour corresponded to no other needs than these, its sole function would be to mitigate the effects that it produces itself, one of binding up the wounds that it inflicts. In such circumstances it might be necessary to submit to it, but there would be no reason to desire it, since the services it would render would reduce themselves to repairing the damage that itself caused.

Everything therefore impels us to search for some other function for the division of labour. A few commonly observed facts will set us on the path to a solution.

II

Everybody knows that we like what resembles us, those who think and feel as we do. But the opposite phenomenon is no less frequently encountered. Very often we happen to feel drawn to people who do not resemble us, precisely because they do *not* do so. These facts are seemingly so much at odds that in every age moralists have hesitated about the true nature of friendship and have traced it now to the one cause, now to the other. The Greeks had already posed the question. 'Friendship,' says Aristotle, 'gives rise to much argument. For some it consists in a certain resemblance, and those who resemble each other like each other: hence the proverbs, "like goes with like", and "birds of a feather flock together", and other similar sayings. But on the contrary, according to others, all those who resemble one another grate upon one another. Other explanations are sought at a higher level which are taken from a consideration of nature. Thus Euripides says that the parched earth is in love with the rain, and that the overcast sky heavy with rain pours down upon the earth in a fury of love. Heraclitus claims that one only accommodates to what one opposes, that the finest harmony is born from differences, and that discord is the law of all becoming.'[5]

What demonstrates these opposing doctrines is the fact that both forms of friendship exist in nature. Dissimilarity, just like resemblance, can be a cause of mutual attraction. However, not every kind of dissimilarity is sufficient to bring this about. We find no pleasure in meeting others whose nature is merely different from our own. Prodigals do not seek the company of the miserly, nor upright and frank characters that of the hypocritical and underhand. Kind and gentle spirits feel no attraction for those of harsh and evil disposition. Thus only differences of a certain kind incline us towards one another. These are those which, instead of mutually opposing and excluding one another, complement one another. Bain says, 'There is a kind of disparity that repels and a kind that attracts; a kind that tends to rivalry, and a kind that tends to friendship . . . if what the one has, the other has not, but desires, there is a basis of positive attraction.'[6]

Thus the theorist with a reasoning and subtle mind has often a very special sympathy for practical men who are direct and whose intuition is swift. The fearful are attracted to those who are decisive and resolute, the weak to the strong, and vice versa. However richly endowed we may be, we always lack something, and the best among us feel our own inadequacy. This is why we seek in our friends those qualities we lack, because in uniting with them we share in some way in their nature, feeling ourselves then less incomplete. In this way small groups of friends grow up in which each individual plays a role in keeping with his character, in which a veritable exchange of services occurs. The one protects, the other consoles; one advises, the other executes, and it is this distribution of functions or, to use the common expression, this division of labour, that determines these relations of friendship.

We are therefore led to consider the division of labour in a new light. In this case, indeed, the economic services that it can render are insignificant compared with the moral effect that it produces, and its true function is to create between two or more people a feeling of solidarity. However this result is accomplished, it is this that gives rise to these associations of friends and sets its mark upon them.

The history of marital relationships affords an even more striking example of the same phenomenon.

Doubtless, sexual attraction is never felt save between individuals of the same species, and fairly generally love presumes a certain harmony of thought and feeling. It is nevertheless true that what imparts its specific character to this tendency and generates its specific force is not the similarity but the dissimilarity of the natures that it links together. It is because men and women differ from one another that they seek out one another with such passion. However, as in the previous case, it is not purely and simply contrast that causes reciprocal feelings to arise: only those differences that are assumed and that complement one another possess this power. In fact, men and women in isolation from each other are only different parts of the same concrete whole, which they reconstitute by uniting with each other. In other words, it is the sexual division of labour which is the source of conjugal solidarity, and this is why psychologists have very aptly remarked that the separation of the sexes was an event of prime importance in the evolution of the sentiments. This is because it has made possible perhaps the strongest of all disinterested tendencies.

There is something else. The division of labour between the sexes is capable of being more, and capable of being less. It can relate only to the sexual organs and some secondary traits that depend on them, or, on the contrary, can extend to all organic and social functions. It can be seen historically as having developed precisely along the same lines and in the same way as marital solidarity.

The further we go back into the past, the more we see that the division of labour between the sexes is reduced to very little. In those distant times woman was not at all the weak creature that she has become as morality has progressed. Prehistoric bone remains attest to the fact that the difference between the strength of a man and a woman was relatively much less than it is today.[7] Even nowadays, in infancy and up to puberty, the skeletal frame of the two sexes is not appreciably different: its characteristics are principally female. If one accepts that the development of the individual reproduces in abridged form that of the species, we may justifiably conjecture that the same homogeneity was to be found at the beginnings of human evolution, and see in the female form a close image of what was originally that single, common type from which the male sex has gradually become distinct. Moreover, travellers report that among a certain number of South American tribes man and woman show in their general build and appearance a similarity greater than that found elsewhere.[8] Finally, Dr Lebon has been able to establish directly, with mathematical precision, this original resemblance between the sexes, in regard to the pre-eminent organ of physical and mental life, the brain. By comparing a large number of skulls selected from among different races and societies, he arrived at the following conclusion:

> The volume of the skull of a man or woman, even when subjects of the same age, size and weight are being compared, presents considerable differences in favour of the man, and this disparity likewise increases with the advance of civilization, so that, as regards the mass of the brain, and consequently of the intellig-

ence, woman tends increasingly to become different from man. For example, the difference which exists between the average size of the brain between present-day Parisian men and women is almost double that observed betwen male and female skulls in ancient Egypt.[9]

A German anthropologist, Bischoff, has arrived at the same result in this respect.[10]

These anatomical similarities are concomitant with functional ones. In fact, in these same societies the female functions are not very clearly distinguished from the masculine ones, but the two sexes lead roughly the same kind of existence. Even now there is still a very large number of savage peoples where the woman takes part in political life. This has been observed especially among the Indian tribes of America, such as the Iroquois and the Natchez,[11] in Hawaii where she shares in the life of the man in countless ways,[12] in New Zealand and Samoa. Similarly we see very frequently the women going off to war with the men, stimulating them to fight, and even participating very actively in the fighting. In Cuba and Dahomey they are as warlike as the men, fighting side by side with them.[13] One of the distinctive attributes of a woman today, that of gentleness, does not originally appear to have been characteristic of her. Already among certain animal species the female is, on the contrary, noted for the opposite characteristic.

Among these same peoples marriage exists only in a very rudimentary state. Even if not yet demonstrated with certainty, it is even very likely that there was an era in the history of the family when marriage did not exist. Sexual relationships were made and unmade at will, the partners being bound by no legal tie. In any case we know of a family type relatively close to us[14] in which marriage is still only in a distinctly embryonic state, that is, the matriarchal family. The relationships between mother and children are very clearly defined, but those between the two partners are very lax. They can cease as soon as the parties wish, or indeed may be entered into only for a limited period.[15] Marital fidelity is still not required. Marriage, or what is so termed, comprises solely obligations of a strictly limited nature, and these are very often of short duration, linking the husband to the wife's relations. Thus it amounts to very little. In any given society the set of legal rules that constitute marriage only symbolises the state of conjugal solidarity. If this is very strong, the bonds uniting husband and wife are numerous and complex, and consequently the marriage rules, whose purpose is to define them, are themselves very elaborate. If, on the other hand, the marital state lacks cohesiveness, if the relations between the man and the woman are unstable and sporadic, they cannot assume a very fixed form. Consequently marriage comes down to a small number of rules lacking rigour and preciseness. The state of marriage in societies where the two sexes are only slightly differentiated thus bears witness to the fact that conjugal solidarity is itself very weak.

On the other hand, as we approach modern times, we see marriage developing. The network of ties that it creates becomes ever more extensive, the obligations that it imposes increase. The conditions on which it may be entered into, and those on which it may be dissolved are stipulated with increasing precision, as are the consequences of such a dissolution. The duty of fidelity takes on an organised form; at first laid upon the wife alone, it later becomes reciprocal. When the institution of the dowry makes its appearance, very complex rules emerge fixing the respective rights of each partner regarding their individual fortunes. Moreover, we need only cast a glance through our legal codes to see how important is the place of marriage. The union of the two spouses has ceased to be ephemeral; no longer is it an external, temporary and partial contact, but an intimate association, one that is lasting, often even indissoluble, between two lives throughout their whole existence.

Beyond question, over the same period of time labour became increasingly divided up as between the sexes. At first limited to the sexual functions alone, it gradually extended to many other functions. The woman had long withdrawn from warfare and public affairs, and had centred her existence entirely round the family. Since then her role has become even more specialised. Nowadays, among civilised peoples the woman leads an existence entirely different from the man's. It might be said that the two great functions of psychological life had become as if dissociated from each other, one sex having taken over the affective, the other the intellectual function. Noticing how, among certain social classes the women are taken up with art and literature, just as are the men, one might, it is true, believe that the activities of both sexes are tending once more to become homogeneous. But even in this sphere of activity, the woman brings to bear her own nature, and her role remains very special, one very different from that of the man. What is more, if art and letters are beginning to become matters that occupy women, the other sex appears to be abandoning them so as to devote itself more especially to science. Thus it might well happen that this apparent reversion to a primeval homogeneity is no more than the beginning of a fresh differentiation. Moreover, these functional differences are made perceptible physically by the morphological differences they have brought about. Not only are size, weight and general shape very dissimilar as between a man and a woman, but Dr Lebon has shown, as we have seen, that with the advance of civilisation the brain of the two sexes has increasingly developed differently. According to this observer, this progressive gap between the two may be due both to the considerable development of the male skull and to a cessation and even a regression in the growth of the female skull. He states: 'Whilst the average size of the skulls of male Parisians places them among the largest known skulls, the average size of those of female Parisians places them among the smallest skulls observed, very much below those of Chinese women and scarcely above those of the women of New Caledonia.'[16]

In all these examples the most notable effect of the division of labour is not that it increases the productivity of the functions that are divided in this way, but that it links them very closely together. In all these cases its role is not simply to embellish or improve existing societies, but to make possible societies which, without these functions, would not exist. If we reduce the division of labour between the sexes beyond a certain point marital life disappears, leaving only sexual relationships that are predominantly ephemeral. If indeed the sexes had not separated off from each other at all, a whole style of social living would not have arisen. It is possible that the economic usefulness of the division of labour has had some bearing upon the outcome. In any case, however, it goes very considerably beyond the sphere of purely economic interests, for it constitutes the establishment of a social and moral order *sui generis*. Individuals are linked to one another who would otherwise be independent; instead of developing separately, they concert their efforts. They are solidly tied to one another and the links between them function not only in the brief moments when they engage in an exchange of services, but extend considerably beyond. For example, marital solidarity as it exists today among the most cultured peoples – does it not make its effect felt at every moment and in every detail of life? Moreover, those societies established by the division of labour cannot fail to bear its mark. Since they have this special origin, they cannot resemble those that are determined by the attraction of like for like. They must be constituted differently, rest upon a different foundation, and appeal to different sentiments.

If exchange alone has often been held to constitute the social relationships that arise from the division of labour, it is because we have failed to recognise what exchange implies and what results from it. It presumes that two beings are mutually dependent upon each other because they are both incomplete, and it does no more than interpret externally this mutual dependence. Thus it is only the superficial expression of an internal and deeper condition. Precisely because this condition remains constant, it gives rise to a whole system of images which function with a continuity that is lacking in exchange. The image of the one who complements us becomes inseparable within us from our own, not only because of the frequency with which it is associated with it, but above all because it is its natural complement. Thus it becomes an integral, permanent part of our consciousness to such a degree that we can no longer do without it. We seek out everything that can increase the image's strength. This is why we like the company of the one the image represents, because the presence of the object whose expression it is, by causing it to pass to the state of perception here and now, gives it greater vividness. By contrast, we suffer in any circumstance where, such as in absence or death, the effect can be to prevent its return or to lessen its intensity.

Despite the brevity of this analysis, it is sufficient to show that this mechanism is not identical to the one on which are founded those feelings of empathy that spring from similarity. There can certainly never be solidarity between ourselves and another person unless the image of the other person is united with our own. But when union derives from the similarity between two images, it consists in an agglutination. The two representations become solidly bonded together because, being indistinct from each other either wholly or in part, they fuse completely, becoming one. They are only solid with one another in so far as they are fused in this way. On the contrary, in the case of the division of labour, they remain outside each other and are linked only because they are distinct. The feelings that arise cannot therefore be the same in both cases, nor can the social relationships that derive from them.

Thus we are led to ask whether the division of labour might not play the same role in more extensive groupings – whether, in contemporary societies where it has developed in the way that we know, it might not fulfil the function of integrating the body social and of ensuring its unity. It is perfectly legitimate to suppose that the facts we have just observed are replicated here also, but on a broader scale; that these great political societies also cannot sustain their equilibrium save by the specialisation of tasks; and that the division of labour is the source – if not the sole, at least the main one – of social solidarity. Comte had already taken this view. Among all the sociologists, so far as we are aware, he was the first to point out that in the division of labour there was something other than a purely economic phenomenon. He saw in it 'the most essential condition of social life', provided that it were conceived of 'in all its rational extent, namely, as being applied to the whole range of our various activities of all kinds, instead of being limited, as is only too common, to mere material uses'. Considered from this viewpoint, he said:

> it leads one immediately to look not only at individuals and classes but also, in many respects, at different peoples, as participating at one and the same time, each following in its own fashion and to its own special, determined degree, in a vast common enterprise. It is one whose inevitable and gradual development links, moreover, those co-operating together at the present time with the line of their predecessors, whoever these may have been, and even to the line of their various successors. Thus it is the continuous distribution of different human tasks which constitutes the principal element in social solidarity and which becomes the primary cause of the scale and growing complexity of the social organism.[17]

If this hypothesis were proved, the division of labour may play a much more important role than is normally attached to it. It would serve not only to endow societies with luxury, perhaps enviable but nevertheless superfluous. It would be a condition for their existence. It is through the division of labour, or at least mainly through it, that the cohesion of societies would be ensured. It would determine the essential characteristics that constitute them. By this very fact, although we are not yet in a position to resolve the question with any rigour, already we can nevertheless vaguely perceive that, if this is the real function of the division of labour, it must possess a moral character, since needs for order, harmony and social solidarity are generally reckoned to be moral ones.

Yet before examining whether this hypothesis is well founded, we must verify the hypothesis we have just enunciated regarding the role of the division of labour. Let us see whether, in fact, in the societies in which we live today, it is from this that social solidarity essentially derives.

III

Yet how does one proceed to this verification?

We have not merely to investigate whether, in these kinds of societies, there exists a social solidarity arising from the division of labour. This is a self-evident truth, since in them the division of labour is highly developed and it engenders solidarity. But above all we must determine the degree to which the solidarity it produces contributes generally to the integration of society. Only then shall we learn to what extent it is necessary, whether it is an essential factor in social cohesion, or whether, on the contrary, it is only an ancillary and secondary condition for it. To answer this question we must therefore compare this social bond to others, in order to measure what share in the total effect must be attributed to it. To do this it is indispensable to begin by classifying the different species of social solidarity.

However, social solidarity is a wholly moral phenomenon which by itself is not amenable to exact observation and especially not to measurement. To arrive at this classification, as well as this comparison, we must therefore substitute for this internal datum, which escapes us, an external one which symbolises it, and then study the former through the latter.

That visible symbol is the law. Indeed where social solidarity exists, in spite of its non-material nature, it does not remain in a state of pure potentiality, but shows its presence through perceptible effects. Where it is strong it attracts men strongly to one another, ensures frequent contacts between them, and multiplies the opportunities available to them to enter into mutual relationships. To state the position precisely, at the point we have now reached it is not easy to say whether it is social solidarity that produces these phenomena or, on the contrary, whether it is the result of them. Likewise it is a moot point whether men draw closer to one another because of the strong effects of social solidarity, or whether it is strong because men *have* come closer together. However, for the moment we need not concern ourselves with clarifying this question. It is enough to state that these two orders of facts are linked, varying with each other simultaneously and directly. The more closely knit the members of a society, the more they maintain various relationships either with one another or with the group collectively. For if they met together rarely, they would not be mutually dependent, except sporadically and somewhat weakly. Moreover, the number of these relationships is necessarily proportional to that of the legal rules that determine them. In fact, social life, wherever it becomes lasting, inevitably tends to assume a definite form and become organised. Law is nothing more than this very organisation in its most stable and precise form.[18] Life in general within a society cannot enlarge in scope without legal activity simultaneously increasing in proportion. Thus we may be sure to find reflected in the law all the essential varieties of social solidarity.

It may certainly be objected that social relationships can be forged without necessarily taking on a legal form. Some do exist where the process of regulation does not attain such a level of consolidation and precision. This does not mean that they remain indeterminate; instead of being regulated by law they are merely regulated by custom. Thus law mirrors only a part of social life and consequently provides us with only incomplete data with which to resolve the problem. What is more, it is often the case that custom is out of step with the law. It is repeatedly stated that custom tempers the harshness of the law, corrects the excesses that arise from its formal nature, and is even occasionally inspired with a very different ethos. Might then custom display other kinds of social solidarity than those expressed in positive law?

But such an antithesis only occurs in wholly exceptional circumstances. For it to occur law must have ceased to correspond to the present state of society and yet, although lacking any reason to exist, is sustained through force of habit. In that event, the new relationships that are established in spite of it will become organised, for they cannot subsist without seeking to consolidate themselves. Yet, being at odds with the old law, which persists, and not succeeding in penetrating the legal domain proper, they do not rise beyond the level of custom. Thus opposition breaks out. But this can only happen in rare, pathological cases, and cannot even continue without becoming dangerous. Normally custom is not opposed to law; on the contrary, it forms the basis for it. It is true that sometimes nothing further is built upon this basis. There may exist social relationships governed only by that diffuse form of regulation arising from custom. But this is because they lack importance and continuity, excepting naturally those abnormal cases just mentioned. Thus if types of social solidarity chance to exist which custom alone renders apparent, these are assuredly of a very secondary order. On the other hand the law reproduces all those types that are essential, and it is about these alone that we need to know.

Should we go further and assert that social solidarity does not consist entirely in its visible manifestations; that these express it only partially and imperfectly; that beyond law and custom there exists an inner state from which solidarity derives; and that to know it in reality we must penetrate to its heart, without any intermediary? But in science we can know causes only through the effects that they produce. In order to determine the nature of these causes more precisely science selects only those results that are the most objective and that best lend themselves to quantification. Science studies heat through the variations in volume that changes in temperature cause in bodies, electricity through its physical and chemical effects, and force through movement. Why should social solidarity prove an exception?

Moreover, what remains of social solidarity once it is divested of its social forms? What imparts to it its specific characteristics is the nature of the group whose unity it ensures, and this is why it varies according to the types of society. It is not the same within the family as within political societies. We are not attached to our native land in the same way as the Roman was to his city or the German to his tribe. But since such differences spring from social causes, we can only grasp them through the differences that the social effects of solidarity present to us. Thus if we neglect the differences, all varieties become indistinguishable, and we can perceive no more than that which is common to all varieties, that is, the general tendency to sociability, a tendency that is always and everywhere the same and is not linked to any particular social type. But this residual element is only an abstraction, for sociability *per se* is met with nowhere. What exists and what is really alive are the special forms of solidarity – domestic, professional, national, that of the past and that of today, etc. Each has its own special nature. Hence generalities can in any case only furnish a very incomplete explanation of the phenomenon, since they necessarily allow to escape what is concrete and living about it.

Thus the study of solidarity lies within the domain of sociology. It is a social fact that can only be thoroughly known through its social effects. If so many moralists and psychologists have been able to deal with this question without following this method, it is because they have avoided the difficulty. They have divested the phenomenon of everything that is more specifically social about it, retaining only the psychological core from which it develops. It is certain that solidarity, whilst being pre-eminently a social fact, is dependent upon our individual organism. In order to be capable of existing it must fit our physical and psychological constitution. Thus, at the very least, we can content ourselves with studying it from this viewpoint. But in that case we shall perceive only that aspect of it which is the most indistinct and the least special. Strictly speaking, this is not even solidarity itself, but only what makes it possible.

Even so, such an abstract study cannot yield very fruitful results. For, so long as it remains in the state of a mere predisposition of our psychological nature, solidarity is something too indefinite to be easily understood. It remains an intangible virtuality too elusive to observe. To take on a form that we can grasp, social outcomes must provide an external interpretation of it. Moreover, even in such an indeterminate state, it depends on social conditions that explain it, and cannot consequently be detached from them. This is why some sociological perspectives are not infrequently to be found mixed up with these purely psychological analyses. For example, some mention is made of the influence of the *gregarious state* on the formation of social feeling in general;[19] or the main social relationships on which sociability most obviously depends are rapidly sketched out.[20] Undoubtedly such additional considerations, introduced unsystematically as examples and at random as they suggest themselves, cannot suffice to cast much light on the social nature of solidarity. Yet at least they demonstrate that the sociological viewpoint must weigh even with the psychologists.

Thus our method is clearly traced out for us. Since law reproduces the main forms of social solidarity, we have only to classify the different types of law in order to be able to investigate which types of social solidarity correspond to them. It is already likely that one species of law exists which symbolises the special solidarity engendered by the division of labour. Once we have made this investigation, in order to judge what part the division of labour plays it will be enough to compare the number of legal rules which give it expression with the total volume of law.

To undertake this study we cannot use the habitual distinctions made by jurisprudents. Conceived for the practice of law, from this viewpoint they can be very convenient, but science cannot be satisfied with such empirical classifications and approximations. The most widespread classification is that which divides law into public and private law. Public law is held to regulate the relationships of the individual with the state, private law those of individuals with one another. Yet when we attempt to define these terms closely, the dividing line, which appeared at first sight to be so clear-cut, disappears. All law is private, in the sense that always and everywhere individuals are concerned and are its actors. Above all, however, all law is public, in the sense that it is a social function, and all individuals are, although in different respects, functionaries of society. The functions of marriage and parenthood, etc. are not spelt out or organised any differently from those of ministers or legislators. Not without reason did Roman law term guardianship a *munus publicum*. Moreover, what is the state? Where does it begin, where does it end? The controversial nature of this question is well known. It is unscientific to base such a fundamental classification on such an obscure and inadequately analysed idea.

In order to proceed methodically, we have to discover some characteristic which, whilst essential to juridical phenomena, is capable of varying as they vary. Now, every legal precept may be defined as a rule of behaviour to which sanctions apply. Moreover, it is clear that the sanctions change according to the degree of seriousness attached to the precepts, the place they occupy in the public consciousness, and the role they play in society. Thus it is appropriate to classify legal rules according to the different sanctions that are attached to them.

These are of two kinds. The first consist essentially in some injury, or at least some disadvantage imposed upon the perpetrator of a crime. Their purpose is to do harm to him through his fortune, his honour, his life, his liberty, or to deprive him of some object whose possession he enjoys. These are said to be repressive sanctions, such as those laid down in the penal code. It is true that those that appertain to purely moral rules are of the same character. Yet such sanctions are administered in a diffuse way by everybody without distinction, whilst those of the penal code are applied only through the mediation of a definite body – they are organised. As for the other kind of sanctions, they do not necessarily imply any suffering on the part of the perpetrator, but merely consist in *restoring the previous state of affairs*, re-establishing relationships that have been disturbed from their normal form. This is done either by forcibly redressing the action impugned, restoring it to the type from which it has deviated, or by annulling it, that is depriving it of all social value. Thus legal rules must be divided into two main species, according to whether they relate to repressive, organised sanctions, or to ones that are purely restitutory. The first group covers all penal law; the second, civil law, commercial law, procedural law, administrative and constitutional law, when any penal rules which may be attached to them have been removed.

Let us now investigate what kind of social solidarity corresponds to each of these species.

Notes

1. Cf. Alexander von Oettingen, *Moralstatistik* (Erlangen, 1882) p. 37ff.; also Tarde, *Criminalité comparée* (Alcan, Paris),ch. II. For suicides, cf. *infra*, Book II, Chapter I, § II.
2. 'The essential characteristic of the good, as compared with the true, is therefore to be obligatory. Taken by itself, the true does not possess this characteristic' (Janet, *Morale*, p. 139).
3. For it is in opposition to a moral rule (cf. p. 5).
4. Cf. *infra*, Book II, Chapters I and V.
5. *Nichomachean Ethics*, vol. VIII, no. 1, 1155a, 32.
6. A. Bain, *The Emotions and the Will* (London, 1889).
7. Topinard, *Anthropologie*, p. 146.
8. H. Spencer, *Essays: Scientific, Political, and Speculative* (London, 1858). Waitz, in his *Anthropologie der Naturvölker*, vol. I, p. 76, reports many facts of the same kind.

9.   Lebon, *L'homme et les sociétés*, vol. II, p. 154.
10. Bischoff, *Das Herngewicht der Menschen. Eine Studie* (Bonn, 1880).
11. Waitz, *Anthropologie*, vol. III, pp. 101–2.
12. Ibid., vol. VI, p. 121.
13. H. Spencer, *The Principles of Sociology* (London, 1876) vol. I, pp. 753–4.
14. The matriarchal family certainly existed among the Germanic tribes. Cf. Dargun, *Mutterrecht und Raubehe im germanischen Rechte* (Breslau, 1883).
15. W. Robertson Smith, *Marriage and Kinship in Early Arabia* (Cambridge, 1885) p. 67.
16. Lebon, *L'homme*, p. 154.
17. A. Comte, *Cours de philosophie positive*, vol. IV, p. 425. Analogous ideas are to be found in Schaeffle, *Bau und Leben des sozialen Körpers*, vol. II, *passim*, and Clément, *Science sociale*, vol. I, pp. 235 ff.
18. Cf. *infra*, Book III, Chapter I.
19. Bain, *Emotions and The Will*.
20. H. Spencer, *The Principles of Psychology* (London, 1881) vol. I, pp. 558–77.

Chapter II

Mechanical Solidarity, or Solidarity by Similarities

The bond of social solidarity to which repressive law corresponds is one the breaking of which constitutes the crime. We use the term 'crime' to designate any act which, regardless of degree, provokes against the perpetrator the characteristic reaction known as punishment. To investigate the nature of this bond is therefore to ask what is the cause of the punishment or, more precisely, what in essence the crime consists of.

Assuredly crimes of different species exist. But it is no less certain that all these species of crime have something in common. This is proved by the reaction that they provoke from society: the fact that punishment, except for differences in degree, always and everywhere exists. The oneness of the effect reveals the oneness of the cause. Undoubtedly essential resemblances exist not only among all crimes provided for in the legislation of a single society, but among all crimes recognised as such and punished in different types of society. No matter how different these acts termed crimes may appear to be at first sight, they cannot fail to have some common basis. Universally they strike the moral consciousness of nations in the same way and universally produce the same consequence. All are crimes, that is, acts repressed by prescribed punishments. Now the essential properties of a thing lie in those observed wherever it exists and which are peculiar to it. Thus if we wish to learn in what crime essentially consists, we must distinguish those traits identical in all the varieties of crime in different types of society. Not a single one of these types may be omitted. Legal conceptions in the lowest forms of society are as worthy of consideration as those in the highest forms. They are facts that prove no less instructive. To rule them out of court would be to run the risk of perceiving the essence of crime where it is not. It would be like the biologist whose definition of living phenomena would be very inexact if he had scorned to observe single-cell entities. If he had looked at organisms alone – and particularly the higher organisms – he would have wrongly concluded that life consists essentially in the organisation of cells.

The way to discover this permanent, general element is clearly not to go through all those acts which have been designated as crimes at all times and in all places, in order to note the characteristics they present. For, despite what has been stated, if there are acts that have been universally regarded as criminal, these constitute a tiny minority. Thus such a method would provide us with only a singularly distorted notion of the phenomenon, because it would apply only to exceptions.[1] The variations in repressive law at the same time prove that this unchanging character is not to be found in the intrinsic properties of acts imposed or prohibited by penal rules, because these display so great a diversity, but in the relationship they entertain with some condition outside themselves.

This relationship was believed to lie in the kind of antagonism existing between these acts and the larger interests of society. It has been claimed that penal rules have expressed for each type of society the basic conditions for collective life. Their authority thus sprang from necessity. Moreover, since these needs vary according to societies, one could in this way explain the variations in repressive law. We have already given our views on this point. Such a theory ascribes much too large a part to deliberate calculation and reflection in directing social evolution. There are a whole host of acts which have been, and still are, regarded as criminal, without in themselves being harmful to society. The act of touching an object that is taboo, or an animal or man who is impure or consecrated, of letting the sacred fire die out, of eating certain kinds of meat, of not offering the traditional sacrifice on one's parents' grave, of not pronouncing the precise ritual formula, or of not celebrating certain feasts, etc. – how have any of these ever constituted a danger to society? Yet we know the prominent position occupied in the repressive law of a large number of peoples by such a regulation of ritual, etiquette, ceremonial and religious practices. We need only open the Pentateuch to be convinced of it. Moreover, as these facts are found normally in certain social species, we cannot regard them as mere anomalies or pathological cases which we may legitimately dismiss.

Even where the criminal act is certainly harmful to society, the degree of damage it causes is far from being regularly in proportion to the intensity of repression it incurs. In the penal law of most civilised peoples murder is universally regarded as the greatest of crimes. Yet an economic crisis, a crash on the stock market, even a bankruptcy, can disorganise the body social much more seriously than the isolated case of homicide. Assuredly murder is always an evil, but nothing proves that it is the greatest evil. What does one human being the less matter to society? Or one cell fewer in the organism? It is said that public safety would be endangered in the future if the act remained unpunished. But if we compare the degree of danger, however real it may be, to the penalty, there is a striking disproportion. All in all, the instances just cited show that an act can be disastrous for society without suffering the slightest repression. On any score, therefore, this definition of crime is inadequate.

Modifying the definition, can it be asserted that criminal acts are those that *seem* harmful to the society that represses them? Can we also say that penal rules express, not the conditions essential to social life, but those that *appear* to be so to the group observing the rules? Yet such an explanation explains nothing: it does not allow us to understand why, in so many cases, societies have mistakenly enforced practices which in themselves were not even useful. In the end this alleged solution to the problem really amounts to a truism. If societies therefore force every individual to obey these rules it is plainly because, rightly or wrongly, they esteem this systematic and exact obedience to be indispensable, insisting strongly upon it. This therefore comes down to our saying that societies deem the rules necessary because they deem them necessary! What we should be saying is why they judge them necessary. If the view held by societies was based upon the objective necessity for prescriptive punishments, or at least upon their utility, this would be an explanation. But this goes against the facts, so the entire problem remains unsolved.

However, this latter theory is not without some foundation. It is correct in seeking the conditions that constitute criminality in certain states of the individual. Indeed, the only feature common to all crimes is that, saving some apparent exceptions to be examined later, they comprise acts universally condemned by the members of each society. Nowadays the question is raised as to whether such condemnation is rational and whether it would not be wiser to look upon crime as a mere sickness or error. But we need not launch into such discussions, for we are seeking to determine what is or has been, not what should be. The real nature of the fact we have just established cannot be disputed, viz., that crime disturbs those feelings that in any one type of society are to be found in every healthy consciousness.

We can determine in no other way the nature of these sentiments nor define them in relation to their special purposes, for these purposes have varied infinitely, and can vary again.[2] Nowadays it is altruistic sentiments that manifest this characteristic most markedly. But at one time, not at all distant, religious or domestic sentiments, and a host of other traditional sentiments, had precisely the same effect. Even now, despite what Garofalo says, a mere negative sympathy for others is by no means the only condition for bringing about such an effect. Even in peacetime do we not feel as much aversion for the man who betrays his country as for the robber and swindler? In countries where feeling for the monarchy is still alive, do not crimes of *lèse-majesté* arouse the general indignation? In democratic countries do not insults levelled at the people unleash the same anger? Thus we cannot draw up a catalogue of those sentiments the violation of which constitutes the criminal act. Such feelings are indistinguishable from others, save for one characteristic: they are shared by most average individuals in the same society. Thus the rules forbidding those acts for which the penal law provides sanctions are the sole ones to which the celebrated legal axiom, 'No man is presumed ignorant of the law', can be applied without exaggeration. Since the rules are inscribed upon everyone's consciousness, all are aware of them and feel they are founded upon right. At least this is true for the normal condition. If adults are encountered who are ignorant of these basic rules or refuse to recognise their authority, such ignorance or refusal to submit are irrefutably symptoms of a pathological aversion. Or if by chance a penal rule persists for some time although disputed by everyone, it is because of a conjunction of exceptional circumstances, which are consequently abnormal – and such a state of affairs can never endure.

This explains the special manner in which penal law becomes codified. All written law serves a dual purpose: to prescribe certain obligations, and to define the sanctions attached to them. In civil law, and more generally in every kind of law where sanctions are restitutory, the legislator approaches and resolves these two problems separately. Firstly, he determines the nature of the obligation as exactly as possible; only then does he state the manner in which a sanction should be applied. For example, in the chapter of the French civil code devoted to the respective duties of husband and wife, these rights and duties are spelt out in a positive way, but nothing is said as to what happens when these duties are not fulfilled by one or the other party. The sanction must be sought elsewhere in the Code. Occasionally the sanction is even taken totally for granted. Thus Article 214 of the civil code prescribes that the wife must live with her husband; one may deduce that the husband can oblige her to return to the marital home, but this sanction is nowhere formally laid down. By contrast, penal law prescribes only sanctions and says nothing about the obligations to which they relate. It does not ordain that the life of another person must be respected, but ordains the death of the murderer. It does not first state, as does civil law: This is the duty; but states immediately: This is the punishment. Undoubtedly if an act is punished, it is because it is contrary to a mandatory rule, but this rule is not expressly spelt out. There can be only one reason for this: it is because the rule is known and accepted by everybody. When a customary law acquires the status of a written law and is codified, it is because litigious questions require a solution more closely defined. If the custom continued quietly to function, provoking no argument or difficulty, there would be no reason for it to undergo this transformation. Since penal law is only codified so as to establish a sliding scale of penalties, it is therefore because a custom by itself can give rise to doubt. Conversely, if rules whose violation entails punishment need no juridical expression it is because they are not at all a subject of dispute, and because everyone feels their authority.[3]

It is true that sometimes the Pentateuch does not lay down sanctions, although, as we shall see, it contains little else than penal rules. This is the case for the Ten Commandments, as they are formulated in Exodus 20 and Deuteronomy 5. But this is because the Pentateuch, although it fulfilled the function of a code, is not properly one. Its purpose is not to gather together into a single system, and to detail with a view to their application, the penal rules followed by the Jewish people. So far short does it fall of forming a codification that the various sections comprising it do not even seem to have been drawn up at the same time. It is above all a summary of the traditions of all kinds through which the Jews explained to themselves, and in their own way, the origins of the world, of their society and of their main social practices. Thus if the Pentateuch enunciates certain duties to which punishments were certainly attached, this is not because they were unknown or failed to be acknowledged by the Jews, or because it was necessary to reveal them to them. On the contrary, since the book is merely a compilation of national legends, we may be sure that all it contained was graven on everyone's consciousness. Nevertheless it was essential to recapitulate in a set form the popular beliefs about the origins of these precepts, the historical circumstances in which it was assumed that they had been promulgated, and the sources of their authority. From this viewpoint, therefore, the determination of punishments becomes something incidental.[4]

For the same reason the operation of repressive justice always tends to some extent to remain diffuse. In very different types of society it is not exercised through a special magistrate, but society as a whole shares in it to a greater or lesser degree. In primitive societies where, as we shall see, law is wholly penal in character, it is the people assembled together who mete out justice. This was the case for the primitive Germans.[5] In Rome, whereas civil matters fell to the praetor, criminal ones were judged by the people, at first by the *comices curiates*, and then, from the law of the Twelve Tables onwards, by the *comices centuriates*. Until the end of the Republic, although in fact the people had delegated its powers to standing commissions, they remained the supreme judges in these kinds of cases.[6] In Athens, under the legislation of Solon, criminal jurisdiction fell in part to the Ηλίαια, a huge collegial body which nominally included all citizens over the age of thirty.[7] Lastly, in Germano-Roman nations society intervened in the exercise of these same functions in the form of the jury. Thus the diffuse state that pervades this sphere of judicial power would be inexplicable if the rules whose observance it ensures, and in consequence the sentiments these rules reflect, were not immanent in everyone's consciousness. It is true that in other cases the power was held by a privileged class or by special magistrates. Yet these facts do not detract from the value as proof of the other ones mentioned. Although the feelings of the collectivity are no longer expressed save through certain intermediaries, it does not follow that these feelings are no longer of a collective nature just because they are restricted to the consciousnesses of a limited number of people. Their delegation to these people may be due either to an ever-increasing growth in cases necessitating the appointment of special officials, or to the extreme importance assumed by certain personages or classes in society, which authorises them to be the interpreters of its collective sentiments.

Yet crime has not been defined when we have stated that it consists of an injury done to the collective sentiments, since some of these may be wounded without any crime having been committed. Thus incest is fairly generally an object of aversion, and yet it is a purely immoral act. The same holds good for breaches of sexual honour committed by a woman outside marriage, either by yielding her liberty utterly to another or by receiving the surrender of his liberty. Thus the collective sentiments to which a crime corresponds must be distinguished from other sentiments by some striking characteristic: they must be of a certain average intensity. Not only are they written upon the consciousness of everyone, but they are deeply written. They are in no way mere halting, superficial caprices of the will, but emotions and dispositions strongly rooted within us. The extreme slowness with which the penal law evolves demonstrates this. It is not only less easily modified than custom, but is the one sector of positive law least amenable to change. For instance, if we observe what the law-givers have accomplished since the beginning of the century in the different spheres of the law, innovations in penal law have been extremely rare and limited in scope. By contrast, new rules have proliferated in other branches of the law – civil, commercial, administrative or constitutional. If we compare penal law as laid down in Rome by the Law of the Twelve Tables with its condition in the classical era, the changes we note are minimal beside those that civil law underwent over the same period. Mainz states that from the Twelve Tables onwards the main crimes and offences were fixed: 'For ten generations the calendar of public crimes was not added to save by a few laws which punished embezzlement of public funds, conspiracy and perhaps *plagium*.'[8] As for private offences, only two new ones were recognised: plundering (*actio bonorum vi raptorum*) and malicious damage (*damnum injuria datum*). Such is the position everywhere. In the lower forms of society, as will be seen, law is almost exclusively of a penal kind, and consequently remains unchanged. Generally religious law is always repressive: it is essentially conservative. This unchangeable character of penal law demonstrates the strength of resistance exerted by the collective sentiments to which it corresponds. Conversely, the greater malleability of purely moral laws and the relative swiftness with which they evolve demonstrates the lesser strength of the sentiments underlying them. They have either developed more recently and have not yet had time to penetrate deeply the individual consciousness, or their roots are in a state of decay and are floating to the surface.

A last addition is needed for our definition to be accurate. If, in general, the sentiments that purely moral sanctions protect, that is, ones that are diffuse, are less intense and less solidly organised than those protected by punishments proper, exceptions still remain. Thus there is no reason to concede that normal filial piety or even the elementary forms of compassion for the most blatant forms of misery are nowadays more superficial sentiments than is the respect for property or public authority. Yet the wayward son and even the most arrant egoist are not treated as criminals. Consequently it is not enough for these sentiments to be strongly held; they must be precise. Indeed, every single one relates to a very clearly defined practice. Such a practice may be simple or complex, positive or negative, that is, consisting in an action undertaken or avoided; but it is always determinate. It is a question of doing or not doing this or that, of not killing or wounding, or uttering a particular formula, or accomplishing a particular rite, etc. By contrast, sentiments such as filial love or charity are vague aspirations to very general objects. Thus penal rules are notable for their clarity and precision, whilst purely moral rules are generally somewhat fluid in character. Their indeterminate nature not infrequently makes it hard to formulate any clear definition of them. We may state very generally that people should work, or have compassion for others, etc., but we cannot determine precisely the manner or extent to which they should do so. Consequently there is room here for variations and shades of meaning. By contrast, because the sentiments embodied in penal rules are determinate, they possess a much greater uniformity. As they cannot be interpreted in different ways, they are everywhere the same.

We are now in a position to conclude.

The totality of beliefs and sentiments common to the average members of a society forms a determinate system with a life of its own. It can be termed the collective or common consciousness. Undoubtedly the substratum of this consciousness does not consist of a single organ. By definition it is diffused over society as a whole, but nonetheless possesses specific characteristics that make it a distinctive reality. In fact it is independent of the particular conditions in which individuals find themselves. Individuals pass on, but it abides. It is the same in north and south, in large towns and in small, and in different professions. Likewise it does not change with every generation but, on the contrary, links successive generations to one another. Thus it is something totally different from the consciousnesses of individuals, although it is only realised in individuals. It is the psychological type of society, one which has its properties, conditions for existence and mode of development, just as individual types do, but in a different fashion. For this reason it has the right to be designated by a special term. It is true that the one we have employed above is not without ambiguity. Since the terms 'collective' and 'social' are often taken as synonyms, one is inclined to believe that the collective consciousness is the entire social consciousness, that is, co-terminous with the psychological life of society, whereas, particularly in higher societies, it constitutes only a very limited part of it. Those functions that are judicial, governmental, scientific or industrial – in short, all the specific functions – appertain to the psychological order, since they consist of systems of representation and action. However, they clearly lie outside the common consciousness. To avoid a confusion[9] that has occurred it would perhaps be best to invent a technical expression which would specifically designate the sum total of social similarities. However, since the use of a new term, when it is not absolutely necessary, is not without its disadvantages, we shall retain the more generally used expression, 'collective (or common) consciousness', but always keeping in mind the restricted sense in which we are employing it.

Thus, summing up the above analysis, we may state that an act is criminal when it offends the strong, well-defined states of the collective consciousness.[10]

This proposition, taken literally, is scarcely disputed, although usually we give it a meaning very different from the one it should have. It is taken as if it expressed, not the essential characteristics of the crime, but one of its repercussions. We well know that crime

offends very general sentiments, but ones that are strongly held. But
it is believed that their generality and strength spring from the
criminal nature of the act, which consequently still remains wholly
to be defined. It is not disputed that any criminal act excites
universal disapproval, but it is taken for granted that this results
from its criminal nature. Yet one is then hard put to it to state what is
the nature of this criminality. Is it in a particularly serious form of
immorality? I would concur, but this is to answer a question by
posing another, by substituting one term for another. For what *is*
immorality is precisely what we want to know – and particularly that
special form of immorality which society represses by an organised
system of punishments, and which constitutes criminality. Clearly it
can only derive from one or several characteristics common to all
varieties of crime. Now the only characteristic to satisfy that
condition refers to the opposition that exists between crime of any
kind and certain collective sentiments. It is thus this opposition
which, far from deriving from the crime, constitutes the crime. In
other words, we should not say that an act offends the common
consciousness because it is criminal, but that it is criminal because it
offends that consciousness. We do not condemn it because it is a
crime, but it is a crime because we condemn it. As regards the
intrinsic nature of these feelings, we cannot specify what that is.
They have very diverse objects, so that they cannot be encompassed
within a single formula. They cannot be said to relate to the vital
interests of society or to a minimum of justice. All such definitions
are inadequate. But by the mere fact that a sentiment, whatever
may be its origin and purpose, is found in every consciousness and
endowed with a certain degree of strength and precision, every act
that disturbs it is a crime. Present-day psychology is increasingly
turning back to Spinoza's idea that things are good because we like
them, rather than that we like them because they are good. What is
primary is the tendency and disposition: pleasure and pain are only
facts derived from this. The same holds good for social life. An act is
socially evil because it is rejected by society. But, it will be
contended, are there no collective sentiments that arise from the
pleasure or pain that society feels when it comes into contact with
their objects? This is doubtless so, but all such sentiments do not
originate in this way. Many, if not the majority, derive from utterly
different causes. Anything that obliges our activity to take on a
definite form can give rise to habits that result in dispositions which

then have to be satisfied. Moreover, these dispositions alone are truly fundamental. The others are only special forms of them and are more determinate. Thus to find charm in a particular object, collective sensibility must already have been constituted in such a way as to be able to appreciate it. If the corresponding sentiments are abolished, an act most disastrous for society will not only be capable of being tolerated, but honoured and held up as an example. Pleasure cannot create a disposition out of nothing; it can only link to a particular end those dispositions that already exist, provided that end is in accordance with their original nature.

Yet there are cases where the above explanation does not appear to apply. There are acts that are repressed with greater severity than the strength of their condemnation by public opinion. Thus combinations between officials, the encroachment by judicial authorities on the administrative powers, or by religious upon secular functions are the object of a repression which is disproportionate to the indignation they arouse in the individual consciousness. The misappropriation of public property leaves us fairly indifferent, and yet for it fairly stiff punishments are meted out. It may even happen that an act that is punished does not directly offend any collective sentiment. We feel no urge to protest against fishing or hunting in the close season, or against overloaded vehicles on the public highway. Yet we have no grounds for distinguishing these offences completely from others. Any radical distinction[11] would be arbitrary, since all exhibit in varying degree the same external criterion. Doubtless in none of these examples does the punishment appear unjust. If the punishment is not rejected by public opinion, such opinion, if left to its own devices, would either not insist upon it at all or would show itself less demanding. Thus in all cases of this kind the criminality does not derive – or at least not entirely so – from the degree of sensitivity of the collective sentiments which are offended, but may be traced to another cause.

It is undoubtedly the case that once some governmental authority is instituted it possesses enough power of itself to attach penal sanctions on its own initiative to certain rules of conduct. By its own action it has the ability to create certain crimes or to attach greater seriousness to the criminal character of certain others. Thus all the acts we have just instanced have one characteristic in common, that is, they are directed against one or other of the bodies that control the life of society. Should we then concede that they are two types of crime springing from two different causes? Such an hypothesis cannot be considered for a moment. However numerous its varieties, crime is essentially the same everywhere, since everywhere it entails the same consequence, that is, punishment. Although this may vary in severity, it does not thereby change in nature. Now the same fact cannot have two causes, unless this duality is only apparent and fundamentally the causes are one. That power to react peculiar to the state must be of the same nature as that spread throughout society as a whole.

Where, in fact, might it originate? From the serious nature of the interests that the state directs, interests that require protecting in a very special way? But we know that the harm alone done to these interests, weighty though they may be, is not enough to determine the reaction of punishment. The harm must also be perceived in a certain manner. Moreover, how does it come about that the slightest injury done to the organ of government is punished, whilst other injuries of a much more fearsome kind inflicted on other bodies within society are redressed only by recourse to civil law? The slightest infringement of the regulations relating to the highways and waterways is penalised by a fine. But even the repeated breaching of contracts, or persistently unscrupulous conduct in economic relationships, merely necessitates the apportionment of damages. The machinery of government certainly plays an outstanding role in social life, but there are other bodies in society whose interests continue to be vital and yet whose functioning is not underpinned in the same manner. If the brain is of importance, the stomach is likewise an essential organ, and the latter's ailments may be threatening to life, just as are the former's. Why is this privileged position accorded to what is occasionally called the 'brain' of society?

The problem is easily solved when we perceive that wherever an authority with power to govern is established its first and foremost function is to ensure respect for beliefs, traditions and collective practices – namely, to defend the common consciousness from all its enemies, from within as well as without. It thus becomes the symbol of that consciousness, in everybody's eyes its living expression. Consequently the energy immanent within the consciousness is communicated to that authority, just as affinities of ideas are transmitted to the words they represent. This is how the authority assumes a character that renders it unrivalled. It is no longer a social function of greater or lesser importance, it is the embodiment of the collectivity. Thus it partakes of the authority that the collectivity exercises over the consciousness of individuals, and from this stems its strength. Yet once this strength has arisen, not breaking free from the source from which it derives and on which it continues to feed, it nevertheless becomes a factor of social life which is autonomous, capable of producing its own spontaneous actions. Precisely because of the hegemony this strength has acquired, these actions are totally independent of any external impulsion. On the other hand, since it is merely derived from the power immanent in the common consciousness, it necessarily possesses the same properties and reacts in similar fashion, even when the common consciousness does not react entirely in unison. It thus wards off any hostile force, just as would the diffused consciousness of society, even if the latter does not feel that hostility or feels it less strongly; that is, a governing authority categorises as crimes those acts that are harmful to it, even when the sentiments of the collectivity are not affected to the same extent. Nevertheless, it is from these latter sentiments that it receives the whole power allowing it to create crimes and offences. As well as the certainty that the power cannot come from elsewhere and yet cannot come from nothing, the following facts (on which we shall expand fully in the rest of this volume) confirm this explanation. The scope of the action that governmental authority exerts over the number of criminal acts, and the designation of what is criminal, depend upon the power it possesses. This power in turn may be measured either by the degree of authority that it exercises over its citizens or by the degree of seriousness attributed to the crimes directed against it. We shall see that it is in lower societies that this authority is greatest and where this seriousness weighs most heavily, and moreover, that it is in these self-same types of society that the collective consciousness possesses most power.[12]

Thus it is always to the collective consciousness that we must return. From it, directly or indirectly, all criminality flows. Crime is not only injury done to interests which may be serious; it is also an offence against an authority which is in some way transcendent. Experientially speaking, there exists no moral force superior to that of the individual, save that of the collectivity.

Moreover, there exists a means of verifying the conclusion at which we have just arrived. What characterises a crime is that it determines the punishment. Thus if our own definition of crime is exact it must account for all the characteristics of the punishment. We shall proceed to verify this.

Firstly, however, we must establish what those characteristics are.

II

In the first place, punishment constitutes an emotional reaction. This characteristic is all the more apparent the less cultured societies are. Indeed primitive peoples punish for the sake of punishing, causing the guilty person to suffer solely for the sake of suffering and without expecting any advantage for themselves from the suffering they inflict upon him. The proof of this is that they do not aim to punish fairly or usefully, but only for the sake of punishing. Thus they punish animals that have committed the act that is stigmatised,[13] or even inanimate things which have been its passive instrument.[14] When the punishment is applied solely to people, it often extends well beyond the guilty person and strikes even the innocent – his wife, children or neighbours, etc.[15] This is because the passionate feeling that lies at the heart of punishment dies down only when it is spent. Thus if, after having destroyed the one who was its most immediate cause, some strength of feeling still remains, quite automatically it reaches out further. Even when it is sufficiently moderate in intensity to attack only the guilty person it manifests its presence by its tendency to exceed in seriousness the act against which it is reacting. From this there arose refinements of pain that were added to capital punishment. In Rome the thief had not only to give back the object stolen but also to pay a fine of double or even quadruple its value.[16] Moreover, is not the aim of the very widespread punishment of talion to assuage the passion for vengeance?

Nowadays, however, it is said that punishment has changed in nature. Society no longer punishes to avenge, but to defend itself. In its hands the pain it inflicts is only a systematic instrument for its protection. Society punishes, not because the punishment of itself affords some satisfaction, but in order that the fear of punishment may give pause to the evilly inclined. It is no longer wrath that governs repression, but well premeditated foresight. Thus the preceding remarks cannot be generally applied: they may only concern the primitive form of punishment and cannot be extended to cover its present-day form.

Yet, in order to justify legitimately so radical a distinction between these two sorts of punishment it is not enough to demonstrate that they are employed for different ends. The nature of a practice does not necessarily alter because the conscious intentions of those implementing it are modified. Indeed it could already have fulfilled the same role in former times without this having been perceived. In that case why should it be transformed by the mere fact that we realise more fully the effects that it produces? It adapts itself to the new conditions of existence created for it without thus undergoing any essential changes. This is what happened in the case of punishment.

It would indeed be mistaken to believe that vengeance is mere wanton cruelty. It may very possibly constitute by itself an automatic, purposeless reaction, an emotional and senseless impulse, and an unreasoned compulsion to destroy. But in fact what it tends to destroy was a threat to us. Therefore in reality it constitutes a veritable act of defence, albeit instinctive and unreflecting. We wreak vengeance only upon what has done us harm, and what has done us harm is always dangerous. The instinct for revenge is, after all, merely a heightened instinct of self-preservation in the face of danger. Thus it is far from true that vengeance has played in human history the negative and sterile role attributed to it. It is a weapon of defence, which has its own value – only it is a rough and ready weapon. As it has no conception of the services that it automatically renders it cannot consequently be regulated. It strikes somewhat at random, a prey to the unseeing forces that urge it on, and with nothing to curb its accesses of rage. Nowadays, since we are better aware of the purpose to be achieved, we also know better how to use the means at our disposal. We protect ourselves more systematically, and consequently more effectively. But from the very beginning this result was achieved, although less perfectly. Thus between the punishment of today and yesterday there is no great gulf, and consequently it had no need to change to accommodate itself to the role that it plays in our civilised societies. The whole difference lies in the fact that punishment now produces its effects with a greater awareness of what it is about.

Now, although the individual or social consciousness does not fail to influence the reality it highlights, it has no power to change the nature of that reality. The internal structure of the phenomena remains unchanged, whether these are conscious or not. We may therefore expect the essential elements of punishment to be the same as before.

And indeed punishment has remained an act of vengeance, at least in part. It is claimed that we do not make the guilty person suffer for the sake of suffering. It is nevertheless true that we deem it fair that he should suffer. We may be wrong, but this is not what is at issue. We are seeking for the present to define punishment as it is or has been, and not how it should be. Certainly the term 'public vindication', which recurs incessantly in the language of the law-courts, is no vain expression. If we suppose that punishment can really serve to shield us in the future, we esteem that above all it should be an *expiation* for the past. What proves this are the meticulous precautions we take to make the punishment fit the seriousness of the crime as exactly as possible. These precautions would be inexplicable unless we believed that the guilty person must suffer because it is he who has done the injury, and indeed must suffer in equal measure. In fact this gradation is unnecessary if punishment is only a defence mechanism. It would undoubtedly be dangerous for society if the gravest criminal undertakings were placed on the same level as mere minor offences. Yet in most cases there could only be advantage in placing the minor ones on the same level as the serious ones. One cannot take too many precautions against one's enemy. Can we say that the perpetrators of the most trivial offences possess natures any less perverse and that, to counteract their evil instincts, less onerous punishments will suffice? But although their tendencies may be less tainted with vice, they are not thereby less intense. Thieves are as strongly disposed to thieving as murderers to homicide. The resistance shown by the former category is in no way weaker than that of the latter. Thus, to overcome it, we should have recourse to the same means. If, as has been said, it was solely a matter of repelling a harmful force by an opposing one, the latter's intensity should be merely commensurate with that of the former, without the quality of the harmful force being taken into consideration. The scale of punishments should therefore comprise only very few gradations. The punishment should vary only according to whether the subject is more or less hardened a criminal, and not according to the nature of the criminal act. An incorrigible thief should be treated like an incorrigible murderer. But in fact, even when it had been shown that the guilty person is definitely incurable, we would still not feel bound to mete out excessive punishment to him. This demonstrates that we have remained true to the principle of talion, although we conceive of it in a more lofty sense than once we did. We no longer measure in so material and rough terms either the gravity of the fault or the degree of punishment. But we still consider that there should be an equilibrium between the two elements, whether we derive any advantage or not in striking such a balance. Thus punishment has remained for us what it was for our predecessors. It is still an act of vengeance, since it is an expiation. What we are avenging, and what the criminal is expiating, is the outrage to morality.

There is above all one form of punishment where this passionate character is more apparent than elsewhere: it is shame that doubles most punishments, and that increases with them. Very often it serves no purpose. What good does it do to disgrace a man who is no longer to live in the society of his peers and who has more than abundantly proved by his behaviour that more fearful threats have failed to deter him? To disgrace him is understandable when there is no other punishment available, or as a supplement to some comparatively trivial material penalty. Where this is not the case punishment does the same task twice over. One may even say that society only resorts to legal punishments when others are inadequate. If this is so, why continue with the latter? They are a form of additional tribulation that serves no purpose, or one whose sole reason is the need to repay evil with evil. They are so much the result of instinctive, irresistible feelings that they often spread to innocent objects. Thus the scene of the crime, the tools used in it, the relatives of the guilty person – all sometimes share in the opprobium that we heap upon him. The causes that give rise to this diffused repression are also those of the organised repression that accompanies it. Moreover, we need only observe how punishment operates in the law-courts to acknowledge that its motivating force is entirely emotional. For it is to the emotions that both prosecuting and defending counsel address themselves. The latter seeks to arouse sympathy for the guilty person, the former to stir up the social sentiments that have been offended by the criminal act, and it is under the influence of these opposing passions that the judge delivers sentence.

Thus the nature of punishment has remained essentially unchanged. All that can be said is that the necessity for vengeance is better directed nowadays than in the past. The spirit of foresight that has been awakened no longer leaves the field so clear for the blind play of passion; it contains it within set limits, opposing absurd acts of violence and damage inflicted wantonly. Being more enlightened, such passionate action spreads itself less at random. We no longer see it turn upon the innocent, in order to have satisfaction come what may. Nevertheless it lies at the very heart of the penal system. We can therefore state that punishment consists of a passionate reaction graduated in intensity.[17]

From where, however, does this reaction spring? Is it from the individual or from society?

We all know that it is society that punishes. But it might be that it does not do so on its own behalf. Yet what places beyond doubt the social character of punishment is that once it is pronounced, it cannot be revoked save by government, in the name of society. If it were a satisfaction granted to individuals, they would always be the ones to decide whether to commute it: one cannot conceive of a privilege that is imposed and which the beneficiary cannot renounce. If it is society alone that exerts repression, it is because it is harmed even when the harm done is to individuals, and it is the attack upon society that is repressed by punishment.

Yet we can cite cases where the carrying out of the punishment depends upon the will of individuals. In Rome certain offences were punished by a fine that went to the injured party, who would waive it or make it the subject of bargaining: such was the case for covert theft, rapine, slander and malicious damage.[18] These offences, termed private offences (*delicta privata*), were contrasted with crimes proper, repression of which was carried out in the name of the city. The same distinction is found in Greece and among the Jews.[19] Among more primitive peoples punishment seems occasionally to be a matter even more completely private, as the practice of the vendetta tends to show. Such societies are made up of elementary aggregates, almost of a family nature, which may conveniently be designated *clans*. When an attack is committed by one or several members of a clan against another clan, it is the latter that itself punishes the offence committed against it.[20] What at least apparently gives even more importance to these facts, from the theoretical viewpoint, is that it has been frequently maintained that the vendetta was originally the sole form of punishment. Thus at first punishment may have consisted of private acts of vengeance. But then, if today society is armed with the right to punish, it seems that this can only be by virtue of some sort of delegation by individuals. Society is only their agent. It is their interests that it looks after in their stead, probably because it looks after them better. But they are not properly those of society itself. In the beginning individuals took vengeance themselves; now it is society that avenges them. Yet since the penal law cannot have changed its nature through this simple transfer, there is thus nothing peculiarly social about it. If society appears to play a predominant role it is only as a substitute for individuals.

Yet however widely held this theory may be, it runs counter to the best established facts. We cannot instance a single society where the vendetta was the primitive form of punishment. On the contrary, it is certain that penal law was essentially religious in origin. This is clearly the case of India and Judaea, since the law practised there was considered to be one of revelation.[21] In Egypt the ten books of Hermes, which contained the criminal law and all other laws relating to the governance of the state, were called sacerdotal, and Élien asserts that from earliest times the Egyptian priests exercised judicial power.[22] The same holds true for ancient Germany.[23] In Greece justice was considered to be an emanation from Zeus, and the passion as a vengeance from the god.[24] In Rome the religious origins of the penal law are made clear by ancient traditions,[25] by archaic practices which subsisted until a late date, and by legal terminology itself.[26] But religion is something essentially social. Far from pursuing only individual ends, it exercises constraint over the individual at every moment. It obliges him to observe practices that are irksome to him and sacrifices, whether great or small, which cost him something. He must give from his possessions the offerings which he is constrained to present to the divinity. He must take from his work or leisure time the necessary moments for the performance of rites. He must impose upon himself every kind of privation that is commanded of him, and even renounce life itself if the gods so decree. The religious life is made up entirely of abnegation and altruism. Thus if criminal law was originally religious law, we may be sure that the interests it served were social. It is offences against themselves that the gods avenge by punishment, and not those of individuals. But the offences against the gods are offences against society.

Thus in lower societies the most numerous offences are those that are injurious to the public interest: offences against religion, customs, authority, etc. We have only to see in the Bible, the laws of Manou, and the records surviving of ancient Egyptian law, how slight in comparison is the importance given to prescripts that protect individuals. This is in contrast to the abundant growth of repressive legislation concerning the various forms of sacrilege, failure to observe the various religious obligations, and the requirements of ceremonial, etc.[27] At the same time these crimes are those most severely punished. Among the Jews the most abominable crimes are those committed against religion.[28] Among the ancient Germans two crimes alone were punished by death, according to Tacitus: treason and desertion.[29] According to Confucius and Meng Tseu, impiety is a more grievous transgression than assassination.[30] In Egypt the slightest act of sacrilege was punished by death.[31] In Rome, at the top of the scale of criminality was to be found the *crimen perduellionis*.[32]

But what then are these private punishments, instances of which we have noted earlier? They are of a mixed nature, partaking of both a repressive and a restitutory sanction. Thus the private offence in Roman law represents a kind of intermediate stage between real crime and the purely civil offence. It has features of both and hovers on the bounds of both domains. It is an offence, in the sense that the sanction prescribed by the law does not consist merely in putting matters to rights; the offender is not only obliged to make good the damage he has caused, but he owes something else in addition, an act of expiation. However, it is not entirely a crime since, although it is society that pronounces the sentence, it is not society that is empowered to apply it. This is a right that society confers upon the injured party, who alone can exercise it freely.[33] Likewise, the *vendetta* is clearly a punishment that society recognises as legitimate, but leaves to individuals the task of carrying out. Thus these facts merely confirm what we have stated regarding the nature of the penal system. If this kind of intermediate sanction is partly a private matter, to a corresponding extent it is not a punishment. Its penal nature is proportionately less pronounced when its social character is less evident, and vice versa. Private vengeance is therefore far from being the prototype of punishment; on the contrary, it is only an incomplete punishment. Far from crimes against the person being the first to be repressed, in the beginning they are merely situated on the threshold of the penal law. They only moved up in the scale of criminality as society correspondingly assumed control of them more completely. This process, which we need not describe, was certainly not effected by a mere act of transferral. On the contrary, the history of this penal system is nothing but a progressive succession of encroachments by society upon the individual, or rather upon the primary groupings that it comprises. The effect of these encroachments was increasingly to substitute for the law relating to individuals that relating to society.[34]

But the characteristics outlined above belong just as much to that diffused repression which follows acts that are merely immoral as to legal repression. What distinguishes the latter, as we have said, is that it is organised. But in what does this organisation consist?

When we reflect upon the penal law as it functions in present-day societies we represent it as a code in which very precise punishments are attached to crimes equally precisely defined. It is true that the judge enjoys a certain latitude in applying to each particular case these general dispositions. But in its essentials the punishment is predetermined for each category of criminal acts. This elaborate organisation is not, however, an essential element in punishment, because many societies exist in which punishments are not prescribed in advance. In the Bible there are numerous prohibitions which are utterly categoric but which are nevertheless not sanctioned by an expressly formulated punishment. Their penal character, however, is not in dispute, for, although the texts remain silent regarding the punishment, at the same time they express so great an abhorrence for the forbidden act that one cannot suspect for a moment that it will remain unpunished.[35] Thus there is every reason to believe that this silence on the part of the law simply relates to the fact that how a crime was to be repressed was not determined. Indeed many of the stories in the Pentateuch teach us that there were criminal acts whose criminality was undisputed, but where the punishment was determined only by the judge who applied it. Society was well aware that it was faced with a crime, but the penal sanction that was to be attached to it was not yet defined.[36]

Moreover, even among those punishments laid down by the legislator there are many that are not precisely specified. Thus we know that there were different forms of capital punishment which were not all on the same footing. Yet in a great number of cases the texts speak only generally of the death penalty, without stating what manner of death should be inflicted. According to Sumner Maine the same was true of early Rome; the *crimina* were tried before the assembly of the people which, acting in a sovereign capacity, decreed what the punishment was to be by a law, at the same time as establishing the truth of the charge.[37] Moreover, even until the sixteenth century the general principle of the penal system 'was that its application was left to the discretion of the judge, *arbitrio et officio judicis.* . . . Only the judge was not allowed to devise punishments other than those that were customary.'[38] Another consequence of this judicial power was to make dependent upon the judge's discretion even the nature of the criminal act, which was thus itself indeterminate.[39]

So it is not the regulation of punishment that constitutes the distinctive organisation of this kind of repression. Nor is it the institution of a criminal procedure. The facts we have just cited suffice to show that for a long time this was lacking. The only organisation met with everywhere that punishment proper existed is thus reduced to the establishment of a court of law. In whatever way this was constituted, whether it comprised the people as a whole or only an elite, whether or not it followed a regular procedure both in investigating the case and in applying the punishment, by the mere fact that the offence, instead of being judged by an individual, was submitted for consideration to a properly constituted body and that the reaction of society was expressed through the intermediary of a well-defined organism, it ceased to be diffuse: it was organised. The organisation might have been more complete, but henceforth it existed.

Thus punishment constitutes essentially a reaction of passionate feeling, graduated in intensity, which society exerts through the mediation of an organised body over those of its members who have violated certain rules of conduct.

Now the definition of crime we have given quite easily accounts for all these characteristics of punishment.

III

Every strong state of the consciousness is a source of life; it is an essential factor in our general vitality. Consequently all that tends to weaken it diminishes and depresses us. The result is an impression of being disturbed and upset, one similar to what we feel when an important function is halted or slows down. It is therefore inevitable that we should react vigorously against the cause of what threatens such a lowering of the consciousness, that we should attempt to throw it off, so as to maintain our consciousness in its entirety.

Among the most outstanding causes that produce this effect must be ranged the representation we have of the opposing state. In fact a representation is not a simple image of reality, a motionless shadow projected into us by things. It is rather a force that stirs up around us a whole whirlwind of organic and psychological phenomena. Not only does the nervous current that accompanies the formation of ideas flow within the cortical centres around the point where it originated, passing from one plexus to another, but it also vibrates within the motor centres, where it determines our movements, and within the sensorial centres where it evokes images. It occasionally sparks off the beginnings of illusions and may even affect the maturative functions.[40] This vibration is the stronger the more intense the representation itself, and the more the emotional element in it is developed. Thus the representation of a feeling in contradiction to our own acts within us, moving in the same direction and in the same fashion as the feeling for which it has become the substitute. It is as if itself it had entered our consciousness. Indeed it has the same affinities, although these are less strong; it tends to arouse the same ideas, the same impulsions, the same emotions. Thus it offers resistance to the free play of our personal feeling, and so weakens it, whilst attracting in an opposite direction an entire part of our energy. It is as if a foreign force had penetrated us, one of a kind capable of upsetting the free functioning of our psychological life. This is why a conviction opposed to our own cannot manifest itself before us without disturbing us. It is because at the same time as it penetrates into us, being antagonistic to all that it encounters, it provokes a veritable disorder. Undoubtedly, so long as the conflict breaks out only between abstract ideas there is nothing very painful about it, because there is nothing very profound. The locus of such ideas is at one and the same time the most elevated and yet the most superficial area of the consciousness. The changes that occur within it, not having widespread repercussions, do not affect us strongly. Yet when some cherished belief of ours is at stake we do not allow, and cannot allow, violence to be done to it with impunity. Any assault upon it provokes an emotional reaction of a more or less violent nature, which is turned upon the assailant. We lose our temper, wax indignant against it, inveigh against it, and the sentiments stirred up in this way cannot fail to be translated into action. We flee from it, keep it at a distance, and banish it from our society, etc.

Certainly we do not claim that any strong conviction is necessarily intolerant; common observation is enough to prove the contrary. But this is because external causes neutralise those whose effects we have just analysed. For instance, there may exist between two adversaries some general sympathy which keeps their antagonism within bounds, tempering it. But this sympathy needs to be stronger than the antagonism, or else it does not survive. Or indeed the two elements confronting each other will abandon the contest when it becomes evident that it will be indecisive; each will content itself with maintaining its respective position. Not being able to destroy each other, they are mutually tolerant. The reciprocal toleration that sometimes marks the end of wars of religion is often of this nature. In all such cases, if the clash of feelings does not produce its natural consequences, it is not because it does not contain them, but because it is prevented from producing them.

Nevertheless such consequences are useful at the same time as being necessary. Apart from the fact that they inevitably flow from the causes that produce them, they assist in maintaining those causes. All such violent emotions really constitute an appeal to additional forces to restore to the sentiment under attack the energy drained from it by opposition. It has sometimes been asserted that anger is useless because it is a mere destructive passion, but this is to regard it from only one viewpoint. In fact it consists in the over-stimulation of the latent forces available, which come to the aid of our personal feeling, enabling it to stand up to the dangers facing it by stiffening those forces. In a state of peace, if we may express it in this way, that feeling is not adequately equipped for the struggle. It would be in danger of succumbing if reserves of passion were not marshalled to enter the fight at the requisite time. Anger is no more than the mobilisation of such reserves. It may even turn out that, since the support summoned up in this way goes beyond what is necessary, argument, far from shaking our convictions, has the effect on us of strengthening them even more.

We are aware of how much force a belief or sentiment may acquire merely because they are experienced within a single community of people in contact with one another. Nowadays the causes of this phenomenon are well known.[41] Just as opposing states of consciousness are mutually enfeebling to one another, identical states of consciousness, intermingling with one another, strengthen one another. Whilst the former take something away from one another, the latter add something. If someone expresses to us an idea that was already one we had, the representation we evoke of it is added to our own idea; it superimposes itself upon it, intermingles with it, and transmits to it its own vitality. From this act of fusion burgeons a new idea that absorbs the former ones and which in consequence is more filled with vitality than each idea taken separately. This is why in large gatherings of people an emotion can assume such violence. It is because the strength with which it is produced in each individual consciousness is reciprocated in every other consciousness. To acquire such an intensity for us, a collective sentiment need not even be felt already by us, by virtue of our own individual nature, for what we add to it, all in all, is very little. It suffices for us not to prove too impervious for the collective sentiment to impose itself upon us, penetrating us from the outside with a strength it draws from its origins. Therefore since the sentiments that crime offends within a single society are the most universally collective ones of all, since they represent especially powerful states of the common consciousness, they cannot possibly brook any opposition. Above all, if this opposition is not purely theoretical, if it asserts itself not only in words but deeds, since it then rises to a peak, we cannot fail to react against it passionately. A mere re-establishment of the order that has been disturbed cannot suffice. We need a more violent form of satisfaction. The force that the crime has come up against is too intense for it to react with so much moderation. Indeed it could not do so without becoming weakened, for it is thanks to the intensity of its reaction that it recovers, maintaining the same level of vitality.

In this way we can explain one characteristic of this reaction which has often been pointed out as irrational. It is certain that behind the notion of expiation there is the idea of a satisfaction rendered to some power, real or ideal, which is superior to ourselves. When we demand the repression of crime it is not because we are seeking a personal vengeance, but rather vengeance for something sacred which we vaguely feel is more or less outside and above us. Depending upon time and place, we conceive of this object in different ways. Occasionally it is a simple idea, such as morality or duty. Very often we represent it to ourselves in the form of one or several concrete beings: ancestors, or a divinity. This is why penal law is not only of essentially religious origin, but continues always to bear a certain stamp of religiosity. This is because the acts that it punishes always appear as attacks upon something which is transcendent, whether this is a being or a concept. It is for this same reason that we explain to ourselves how such attacks appear to require from us a higher sanction than the mere reparation we content ourselves with in the sphere of purely human interests.

Such a representation is assuredly an illusion. In one sense it is indeed ourselves that we are avenging, and ourselves to whom we afford satisfaction, since it is within us, and within us alone, that are to be found the feelings that have been offended. But this illusion is necessary. Since these sentiments, because of their collective origin, their universality, their permanence over time, and their intrinsic intensity, are exceptionally strong, they stand radically apart from the rest of our consciousness, where other states are much weaker. They dominate us, they possess, so to speak, something superhuman about them. At the same time they bind us to objects that lie outside our existence in time. Thus they appear to us to be an echo resounding within ourselves of a force that is alien, one moreover superior to that which we are ourselves. We are therefore forced to project them outside ourselves, relating what concerns them to some external object. Today we know how these partial alienations of personality occur. Such a mirage is so inevitable that it will occur in one form or another so long as a repressive system exists. For, were it otherwise, we would need to nurture within us only collective sentiments of moderate intensity, and in that case punishment would no longer exist. It will be asserted that the error will disappear of its own accord as soon as men have become aware of it. Yet in vain do we know that the sun is an immense sphere: we see it always as a disc a few inches across. Our understanding may well teach us to interpret our sensations, but it cannot change them. Moreover, the error is only in part. Since these sentiments are collective, it is not us that they represent in us, but society. Thus by taking vengeance for them it is indeed society and not ourselves that we are avenging. Moreover, it is something that is superior to the individual. We are therefore wrong to impugn this quasi-religious characteristic of expiation, making it some kind of unnecessary, parasitical trait. On the contrary, it is an integrating element in punishment. Certainly it only expresses its nature metaphorically, but the metaphor is not without truth.

Moreover, it is understandable that the reaction of punishment is not in every case uniform, since the emotions that determine it are not always the same. In fact they vary in intensity according to the strength of the feeling that has suffered injury, as well as according to the gravity of the offence it has sustained. A strong state of feeling reacts more than does a weak one, and two states of equal intensity react unequally according to the degree to which they have been violently attacked. Such variations must necessarily occur and are useful, moreover, for it is important that the strength invoked should be proportionate to the extent of the danger. If too weak, it would be insufficient; if too violent, it would represent a useless dissipation of energy. Since the gravity of the criminal act varies according to the same factors, the proportionality everywhere observed between crime and punishment is therefore established with a kind of mechanical spontaneity, without any necessity to make elaborate computations in order to calculate it. What brings about a gradation in crimes is also what brings about a gradation in punishments; consequently the two measures cannot fail to correspond, and such correspondence, since it is necessary, is at the same time constantly useful.

As for the social character of the reaction, this derives from the social nature of the sentiments offended. Because these are to be found in every individual consciousness the wrong done arouses among all who witness it or who know of its existence the same indignation. All are affected by it; consequently everyone stiffens himself against the attack. Not only is reaction general, but it is collective – which is not the same thing. It does not occur in each individual in isolation but all together and in unison, moreover varying according to each case. In fact, just as opposing sentiments repel each other, like sentiments attract, and this occurs the more strongly the more intense they are. As opposition is a danger that exacerbates them, this strengthens their power of attraction. Never does one feel so great the need to see once more one's fellow countrymen as when one is abroad. Never does the believer feel himself so strongly drawn towards his co-religionists as in time of persecution. Undoubtedly the company of those who think and feel as we do is agreeable at any time. But we seek it out, not only with pleasure but passionately, after arguments have taken place in which the beliefs we share have been hotly disputed. Crime therefore draws honest consciousnesses together, concentrating them. We have only to observe what happens, particularly in a small town, when some scandal involving morality has just taken place. People stop each other in the street, call upon one another, meet in their customary places to talk about what has happened. A common indignation is expressed. From all the similar impressions exchanged and all the different expressions of wrath there rises up a single fount of anger, more or less clear-cut according to the particular case, anger which is that of everybody without being that of anybody in particular. It is public anger.

Moreover, this can prove to be of use by itself. The sentiments brought into play draw their entire strength from the fact that they are common to everybody: they are strongly felt because they are not contested. The reason for the particular respect given them is the fact that they are universally respected. Now crime is only possible if this respect is not truly universal. It consequently implies that the sentiments are not absolutely collective, and it attacks that unanimity, the source of their authority. If therefore when this occurs the individual consciousnesses that the crime offends did not unite together to demonstrate to one another that they were still at one, that the particular case was an anomaly, in the long run they could not fail to be weakened. But they need to strengthen one another by giving mutual assurance that they are still in unison. Their sole means of doing so is to react in common. In short, since it is the common consciousness that is wounded, it must also be this that resists; consequently, resistance must be collective.

Why this resistance is organised remains to be expounded.

This trait can be explained if we note that an organised repression is not in opposition to a diffuse repression, but is distinguished from it by a mere difference in degree: the reaction is more united. The greater intensity of the sentiments, and their more definite nature, which punishment proper avenges, easily account for this more complete state of unity. If the feeling that has been denied is weak, or is only weakly offended, it can only provoke a weak concentration of those consciousnesses that have been outraged. However, quite the contrary occurs if the state of feeling is strongly offended and if the offence is grave: the entire group attacked closes ranks in the face of danger and, in a manner of speaking, clings closer together. One is no longer content to exchange impressions when the occasion presents itself, nor draw closer together when the chance occurs or when meeting is convenient. On the contrary, the anxiety that has spread from one person to another impels forcibly together all those who resemble one another, causing them to assemble in one place. This physical concentration of the whole group, bringing the interpenetration of minds ever closer, also facilitates every concerted action. Emotional reactions enacted within each individual consciousness are thus afforded the most favourable conditions in which to coalesce together. Yet if they were too diverse in quantity or quality a complete fusion would not be possible between those elements which were partially heterogeneous and irreducible. But we know that the sentiments that determine these reactions are very definite and in consequence very uniform. Thus, partaking of the same uniformity, as a result they merge very naturally with one another, blending into a single amalgam, which serves as a surrogate for each one, a surrogate that is utilised, not by each individual in isolation, but by the body social constituted in this way.

Historically many facts go to prove that this was the genesis of punishment. Indeed we know that in the beginning it was the gathering of the whole people which fulfilled the functions of a court of law. And if we refer again to the examples we quoted recently from the Pentateuch,[42] it will be seen that things happened as we have just described. As soon as the news of a crime became widely known, the people gathered together and, although the punishment was not predetermined, their reaction was unanimous. In certain cases it was even the people who carried out the sentence collectively as soon as it had been pronounced.[43] Then, when the assembly became embodied in the person of a leader, the latter became wholly or in part the organ of punitive reaction and the system developed in conformity with the general laws for any organic development.

Thus it is certainly the nature of the collective sentiments that accounts for punishment, and consequently for crime. Moreover, we can again see that the power to react, which is available to the functions of government, once these have emerged, is only an emanation of the power diffused throughout society, since it springs from it. The one power is no more than the reflection of the other; the extent of the one varies with the extent of the other. Moreover, we must add that the institution of this power serves to sustain the common consciousness itself. For that consciousness would grow weaker if the organ that represented it did not share the respect that it inspires and the special authority that it wields. But that organ cannot partake of that respect unless every action that offends it is combated and repulsed, just as are those actions that offend the collective consciousness, even indeed when that consciousness is not directly affected.

IV

Thus our analysis of punishment has substantiated our definition of crime. We began by establishing inductively that crime consisted essentially in an act contrary to strong, well-defined states of the common consciousness. We have just seen that in effect all the characteristics of punishment derive from the nature of crime. Thus the rules sanctioned by punishment are the expression of the most essential social similarities.

We can therefore see what kind of solidarity the penal law symbolises. In fact we all know that a social cohesion exists whose cause can be traced to a certain conformity of each individual consciousness to a common type, which is none other than the psychological type of society. Indeed under these conditions all members of the group are not only individually attracted to one another because they resemble one another, but they are also linked to what is the condition for the existence of this collective type, that is, to the society that they form by coming together. Not only do fellow-citizens like one another, seeking one another out in preference to foreigners, but they love their country. They wish for it what they would wish for themselves, they care that it should be lasting and prosperous, because without it a whole area of their psychological life would fail to function smoothly. Conversely, society insists upon its citizens displaying all these basic resemblances because it is a condition for its own cohesion. Two consciousnesses exist within us: the one comprises only states that are personal to each one of us, characteristic of us as individuals, whilst the other comprises states that are common to the whole of society.[44] The former represents only our individual personality, which it constitutes; the latter represents the collective type and consequently the society without which it would not exist. When it is an element of the latter determining our behaviour, we do not act with an eye to our own personal interest, but are pursuing collective ends. Now, although distinct, these two consciousnesses are linked to each other, since in the end they constitute only one entity, for both have one and the same organic basis. Thus they are solidly joined together. This gives rise to a solidarity *sui generis* which, deriving from resemblances, binds the individual directly to society. In the next chapter we shall be better able to demonstrate why we propose to term this solidarity mechanical. It does not consist merely in a general, indeterminate attachment of the individual to the group, but is also one that concerts their detailed actions. Indeed, since such collective motives are the same everywhere, they produce everywhere the same effects. Consequently, whenever they are brought into play all wills spontaneously move as one in the same direction

It is this solidarity that repressive law expresses, at least in regard to what is vital to it. Indeed the acts which such law forbids and stigmatises as crimes are of two kinds: either they manifest directly a too violent dissimilarity between the one who commits them and the collective type; or they offend the organ of the common consciousness. In both cases the force shocked by the crime and that rejects it is thus the same. It is a result of the most vital social similarities, and its effect is to maintain the social cohesion that arises from these similarities. It is that force which the penal law guards against being weakened in any way. At the same time it does this by insisting upon a minimum number of similarities from each one of us, without which the individual would be a threat to the unity of the body social, and by enforcing respect for the symbol which expresses and epitomises these resemblances, whilst simultaneously guaranteeing them.

By this is explained why some acts have so frequently been held to be criminal, and punished as such, without in themselves being harmful to society. Indeed, just like the individual type, the collective type has been fashioned under the influence of very diverse causes, and even of random events. A product of historical development, it bears the mark of those circumstances of every kind through which society has lived during its history. It would therefore be a miracle if everything to be found in it were geared to some useful end. Some elements, more or less numerous, cannot fail to have been introduced into it which are unrelated to social utility. Among the dispositions and tendencies the individual has received from his ancestors or has developed over time there are certainly many that serve no purpose, or that cost more than the benefits they bring. Undoubtedly most of these are not harmful, for if they were, in such conditions the individual could not live. But there are some that persist although lacking in all utility. Even those that do undisputedly render a service are frequently of an intensity disproportionate to their usefulness, because that intensity derives in part from other causes. The same holds good for collective emotions. Every act that disturbs them is not dangerous in itself, or at least is not so perilous as the condemnation it earns. However, the reprobation such acts incur is not without reason. For, whatever the origin of these sentiments, once they constitute a part of the collective type, and particularly if they are essential elements in it, everything that serves to undermine them at the same time undermines social cohesion and is prejudicial to society. In their origin they had no usefulness but, having survived, it becomes necessary for them to continue despite their irrationality. This is generally why it is good that acts that offend these sentiments should not be tolerated. Doubtless, by reasoning in the abstract it can indeed be shown that there are no grounds for a society to prohibit the eating of a particular kind of meat, an action inoffensive in itself. But once an abhorrence of this food has become an integral part of the common consciousness it cannot disappear without social bonds becoming loosened, and of this the healthy individual consciousness is vaguely aware.[45]

The same is true of punishment. Although it proceeds from an entirely mechanical reaction and from an access of passionate emotion, for the most part unthinking, it continues to play a useful role. But that role is not the one commonly perceived. It does not serve, or serves only very incidentally, to correct the guilty person or to scare off any possible imitators. From this dual viewpoint its effectiveness may rightly be questioned; in any case it is mediocre. Its real function is to maintain inviolate the cohesion of society by sustaining the common consciousness in all its vigour. If that consciousness were thwarted so categorically, it would necessarily lose some of its power, were an emotional reaction from the community not forthcoming to make good that loss. Thus there would result a relaxation in the bonds of social solidarity. The consciousness must therefore be conspicuously reinforced the moment it meets with opposition. The sole means of doing so is to give voice to the unanimous aversion that the crime continues to evoke, and this by an official act, which can only mean suffering inflicted upon the wrongdoer. Thus, although a necessary outcome of the causes that give rise to it, this suffering is not a gratuitous act of cruelty. It is a sign indicating that the sentiments of the collectivity are still unchanged, that the communion of minds sharing the same beliefs remains absolute, and in this way the injury that the crime has inflicted upon society is made good. This is why it is right to maintain that the criminal should suffer in proportion to his crime, and why theories that deny to punishment any expiatory character appear, in the minds of many, to subvert the social order. In fact such theories could only be put into practice in a society from which almost every trace of the common consciousness has been expunged. Without this necessary act of satisfaction what is called the moral consciousness could not be preserved. Thus, without being paradoxical, we may state that punishment is above all intended to have its effect upon honest people. Since it serves to heal the wounds inflicted upon the collective sentiments, it can only fulfil this role where such sentiments exist, and in so far as they are active. Undoubtedly, by forestalling in minds already distressed any further weakening of the collective psyche, punishment can indeed prevent such attacks from multiplying. But such a result, useful though it is, is merely a particular side-effect. In short, to visualise an exact idea of punishment, the two opposing theories that have been advanced must be reconciled: the one sees in punishment an expiation, the other conceives it as a weapon for the defence of society. Certainly it does fulfil the function of protecting society, but this is because of its expiatory nature. Moreover, if it must be expiatory, this is not because suffering redeems error by virtue of some mystic strength or another, but because it cannot produce its socially useful effect save on this one condition.[46]

From this chapter it can be seen that a social solidarity exists which arises because a certain number of states of consciousness are common to all members of the same society. It is this solidarity that repressive law materially embodies, at least in its most essential elements. The share it has in the general integration of society plainly depends upon the extent, whether great or small, of social life included in the common consciousness and regulated by it. The more varied the relationships on which that consciousness makes its action felt, the more also it creates ties that bind the individual to the group; the more, consequently, social cohesion derives entirely from this cause and bears this imprint. Yet on the other hand the number of these relationships is itself proportionate to the number of repressive rules. In determining what part of the judicial apparatus is represented by penal law, we shall at the same time measure the relative importance of this solidarity. It is true that by proceeding in this way we shall leave out of account certain elements of the collective consciousness which, because of their lesser intensity or their indeterminate nature, remain outside the scope of repressive law whilst contributing to the maintenance of social harmony. It is these elements that are protected by punishments of a mere diffuse kind. Yet the same holds good for the other sectors of the law. None exists that is not supplemented by custom and, as there is no reason to suppose that the relationship between law and custom is not the same in these different domains, this omission will not jeopardise the results of our comparison.

Notes

1. Yet this is the method that Garofalo followed. Undoubtedly he appears to abandon it when he acknowledges the impossibility of drawing up a list of actions that are universally punished (*Criminologie*, p. 5), which moreover is exaggerated. Yet in the end he comes back to this method since, all in all, the natural crime for him is one that disturbs those sentiments everywhere fundamental to the penal law, viz., a fixed element in the moral sense, and that alone. But why should a crime which disturbs a sentiment peculiar only to certain types of society be less of a crime than the others? Thus Garofalo is led to deny the character of crime to acts that have been universally acknowledged to be criminal among certain social species, and in consequence is led to limit artificially the bounds of criminality. The result is that his notion of crime is singularly incomplete. It is also very

fluctuating, for the author does not include in his comparisons all types of society, but excludes a large number that he characterises as abnormal. A social fact may be stated to be abnormal in relation to the type of species, but a species itself cannot be abnormal. The two words are a contradiction in terms. However interesting Garofalo's attempt to arrive at a scientific notion of crime may be, it is not carried out using a sufficiently exact and accurate method. This is clearly shown in his use of the expression 'natural crime'. Are not all crimes natural? We are probably seeing here a reversion to Spencer's doctrine, in which social life is only really natural in industrial societies. Unfortunately, nothing can be more untrue.

2. We do not see what scientific grounds Garofalo has for saying that the moral sentiments at present possessed by the civilised portion of humanity constitute a morality 'not capable of being lost, but whose development is continually growing' (ibid., p. 9). What grounds are there for setting bounds to the changes that may occur, whether in one direction, or the other?

3. Binding, *Die Normen und ihre Übertretung* (Leipzig, 1872) vol. I, pp. 6 ff.

4. The only real exceptions to this peculiarity of the penal code occur when it is an official act of authority that creates the offence. In that case the duty is generally defined independently of its sanction. Later we shall explain the reason for his exception.

5. Tacitus, *Germania*, ch. XII.

6. Cf. Walter, *Histoire de la procédure civile et du droit criminel chez les Romains* (Fr. trans.) § 829; Rein, *Kriminalrecht der Römer*, p. 63.

7. Cf. Gilbert, *Handbuch der Griechischen Staatsalterthümer* (Leipzig, 1881) vol. I, p 138.

8. 'Esquisse historique du droit criminel de l'ancienne Rome', *Nouvelle Revue historique du droit français et étranger* (1882) pp. 24 and 27.

9. Such a confusion is not without its dangers. Thus it is occasionally asked whether the individual consciousness varies with the collective consciousness. Everything depends on the meaning assigned to the term. If it represents social similarities, the variation, as will be seen, is one of inverse relationship. If it designates the entire psychological life of society, the relationship is direct. Hence the need to draw a distinction.

10. We shall not go into the question as to whether the collective consciousness is like that of the individual. For us this term merely designates the sum total of social similarities, without prejudice to the category by which this system of phenomena must be defined.

11. One has only to see how Garofalo distinguishes what he calls true crimes from others (*Criminologie*, p. 45). This is based upon a personal appraisal, which relies upon no objective characteristic.

12. Moreover, when the punishment is made up entirely of a fine, since it is merely a reparation, whose amount is fixed, the action lies on the boundary between penal and restitutory law.

13. Cf. Exodus 21:28; Leviticus 20:16.

14. For example, the knife used to commit a murder. Cf. Post, *Bausteine für eine allgemeine Rechtswissenschaft*, vol. I, pp. 230–1.
15. Cf. Exodus 20:4 and 5; Deuteronomy 12:12–18; Thonissen, *Etudes sur l'histoire du droit criminel*, vol. I, pp. 70 and 178 ff.
16. Walter, *Histoire de la procédure civile et du droit criminel chez les Romains*, (Fr. trans.), § 793.
17. Moreover, this is recognised even by those who find the idea of expiation incomprehensible. Their conclusion is that, to be congruent with their doctrine, the traditional conception of punishment should be utterly transformed, and reformed from top to bottom. This is because the conception rests, as it has always done, on the principle that they oppose (cf. Fouillée, *Science sociale*, pp. 307 ff.).
18. Rein, *Kriminalrecht der Römer*, p. 111.
19. Among the Jews theft, violation of trusteeship, abuse of confidence, were treated as private offences.
20. Cf. L. H. Morgan, *Ancient Society* (London, 1870) p. 76.
21. In Judaea the judges were not priests, but every judge was the representative of God, the man of God (Deuteronomy, chapter I, verse 17; Exodus, chapter XXII, verse 28). In India it was the king who passed judgement, but this function was regarded as essentially religious (*Manou*, VIII, V, pp. 303–11).
22. Thonissen, *Etudes sur l'histoire du droit criminel*, vol. I, p. 107.
23. Zöpfl, *Deutsche Rechtsgeschichte*, p. 909.
24. Hesiod says: 'It is the son of Saturn who gave men justice' (*Travaux et jours*, vol. V, 279 and 280, ed. Didot). 'When mortals give themselves over . . . to wrong actions, far-sighted Zeus inflicts prompt punishment upon them' (ibid., p. 266; cf. *Iliad*, vol. XVI, pp. 384 ff.).
25. Walter, *Histoire de la procédure*, p. 788.
26. Rein, *Kriminalrecht*, pp. 27–36.
27. Cf. Thonissen, *Etudes*, *passim*.
28. Munck, *Palestine*, p. 216.
29. Tacitus, *Germania*, ch. XII.
30. Plath, *Gesetz und Recht im alten China* (1865) pp. 69 and 70.
31. Thonissen, *Etudes*, vol. I, p. 145.
32. Walter, *Histoire de la procédure*, ss. 803.
33. However, what accentuated the penal character of the private offence was that it entailed infamy, a real public punishment. (Cf. Rein, *Kriminalrecht*, p. 916, and Bouvy, *De l'infamie en droit romain* (Paris, 1884) p. 35.)
34. In any case it is important to note that the *vendetta* is a matter which is eminently of a collective nature. It is not the individual who takes revenge, but his clan; later it is the clan or family which is paid restitution.
35. Deuteronomy 6:25.
36. A man was found gathering wood on the Sabbath day: 'Those who had caught him in the act brought him to Moses and Aaron and all the community, and they kept him in custody, *because it was not clearly known what was to be done with him*' (Numbers 15:32–34). Elsewhere

the case concerns a man who had taken God's name in vain. Those present arrested him but did not know how he should be dealt with. Moses himself did not know, and went away to consult God's will (Leviticus 24:12–16). (The Biblical quotation is given in the translation of the New English Bible.)

37. H. Sumner Maine, *Ancient Law* (London, 1861) pp. 372–3.
38. Du Boys, *Histoire du droit criminel des peuples modernes*, vol. VI, p. 11.
39. Ibid., p. 14.
40. H. Maudsley, *The Physiology of Mind* (London, 1876) p. 271.
41. Cf. Espinas, *Sociétés animales* (Alcan, Paris) *passim*.
42. Cf. *supra*, note 3b.
43. Cf. Thonissen, *Etudes*, vol. I, pp. 30 and 232. Witnesses to a crime sometimes played a predominant role in carrying out the sentence.
44. In order to simplify our exposition we assume that the individual belongs to only one society. In fact we form a part of several groups and there exist in us several collective consciousnesses; but this complication does not in any way change the relationship we are establishing.
45. This does not mean that a penal rule should nonetheless be retained because at some given moment it corresponded to a particular collective feeling. The rule has no justification unless the feeling is still alive and active. If it has disappeared or grown weak nothing is so vain or even counter-productive as to attempt to preserve it artificially by force. It may even happen to become necessary to fight against a practice that was common once, but is no longer so, one that militates against the establishment of new and essential practices. But we need not enter into this problem of a casuistic nature.
46. In saying that punishment, as it is, has a reason for its existence we do not mean that it is perfect and cannot be improved upon. On the contrary, it is only too plain that, since it is produced by purely mechanical causes, it can only be very imperfectly attuned to its role. The justification can only be a rough and ready one.

Chapter III

Solidarity Arising from the Division of Labour, or Organic Solidarity

I

The very nature of the restitutory sanction is sufficient to show that the social solidarity to which that law corresponds is of a completely different kind.

The distinguishing mark of this sanction is that it is not expiatory, but comes down to a mere *restoration of the 'status quo ante'*. Suffering in proportion to the offence is not inflicted upon the one who has broken the law or failed to acknowledge it; he is merely condemned to submit to it. If certain acts have already been performed, the judge restores them to what they should be. He pronounces what the law is, but does not talk of punishment. Damages awarded have no penal character: they are simply a means of putting back the clock so as to restore the past, so far as possible, to its normal state. It is true that Tarde believed that he had discovered a kind of civil penal law in the awarding of costs, which are always borne by the losing party.[1] Yet taken in this sense the term has no more than a metaphorical value. For there to be punishment there should at least be some proportionality between the punishment and the wrong, and for this one would have to establish exactly the degree of seriousness of the wrong. In fact the loser of the case pays its costs even when his intentions were innocent and he is guilty of nothing more than ignorance. The reasons for this rule therefore seem to be entirely different. Since justice is not administered free, it seems equitable that the costs should be borne by the one who has occasioned them. Moreover, although it is possible that the prospect of such costs may stop the overhasty litigant, this is not enough for them to be considered a punishment. The fear of ruin that is normally consequent upon idleness and neglect may cause the businessman to be energetic and diligent. Yet ruin, in the exact connotation of the term, is not the penal sanction for his shortcomings.

Failure to observe these rules is not even sanctioned by a diffused form of punishment. The plaintiff who has lost his case is not disgraced, nor is his honour impugned. We can even envisage these rules being different from what they are without any feeling of repugnance. The idea that murder can be tolerated sets us up in arms, but we very readily accept that the law of inheritance might be modified, and many even conceive that it could be abolished. At least it is a question that we are not unwilling to discuss. Likewise, we agree without difficulty that the laws regarding easements or usufruct might be framed differently, or that the mutual obligations of buyer and vendor might be determined in another way, and that administrative functions might be allocated according to different principles. Since these prescriptions do not correspond to any feeling within us, and as generally we do not know their scientific justification, since this science does not yet exist, they have no deep roots in most of us. Doubtless there are exceptions. We do not tolerate the idea that an undertaking entered into that is contrary to morals or obtained either by violence or fraud can bind the contracting parties. Thus when public opinion is faced with cases of this kind it shows itself less indifferent than we have just asserted, and it adds its disapprobation to the legal sanction, causing it to weigh more heavily. This is because there are no clear-cut partitions between the various domains of moral life. On the contrary, they form a continuum, and consequently adjacent areas exist where different characteristics may be found at one and the same time. Nevertheless the proposition we have enunciated remains true in the overwhelming majority of cases. It demonstrates that rules where sanctions are restitutory either constitute no part at all of the collective consciousness, or subsist in it in only a weak state. Repressive law corresponds to what is the heart and centre of the common consciousness. Purely moral rules are already a less central part of it. Lastly, restitutory law springs from the farthest zones of consciousness and extends well beyond them. The more it becomes truly itself, the more it takes its distance.

This characteristic is moreover evinced in the way that it functions. Whereas repressive law tends to stay diffused throughout society, restitutory law sets up for itself ever more specialized bodies: consular courts, and industrial and administrative tribunals of every kind. Even in its most general sector, that of civil law, it is brought into use only by special officials – magistrates, lawyers, etc., who have been equipped for their role by a very special kind of training.

But although these rules are more or less outside the collective consciousness, they do not merely concern private individuals. If this were the case, restitutory law would have nothing in common with social solidarity, for the relationships it regulates would join individuals to one another without their being linked to society. They would be mere events of private life, as are, for instance, relationships of friendship. Yet it is far from the case that society is absent from this sphere of legal activity. Generally it is true that it does not intervene by itself and of its own volition: it must be solicited to do so by the parties concerned. Yet although it has to be invoked, its intervention is none the less the essential cog in the mechanism, since it alone causes that mechanism to function. It is society that declares what the law is, through its body of representatives.

However, it has been maintained that this role is in no way an especially social one, but comes down to being that of a conciliator of private interests. Consequently it has been held that any private individual could fulfil it, and that if society adopted it, this was solely for reasons of convenience. Yet it is wholly inaccurate to make society a kind of third-party arbitrator between the other parties. When it is induced to intervene it is not to reconcile the interests of individuals. It does not investigate what may be the most advantageous solution for the protagonists, nor does it suggest a compromise. But it does apply to the particular case submitted to it the general and traditional rules of the law. Yet the law is pre-eminently a social matter, whose object is absolutely different from the interests of the litigants. The judge who examines a divorce petition is not concerned to know whether this form of separation is really desirable for the husband and wife, but whether the causes invoked for it fall into one of the categories stipulated by law.

Yet to assess accurately the importance of the intervention by society it must be observed not only at the moment when the sanction is applied, or when the relationship that has been upset is restored, but also when it is instituted.

Social action is in fact necessary either to lay a foundation for, or to modify, a number of legal relationships regulated by this form of law, and which the assent of the interested parties is not adequate enough either to institute or alter. Of this nature are those relationships in particular that concern personal status. Although marriage is a contract, the partners can neither draw it up nor rescind it at will. The same holds good for all other domestic relationships, and *a fortiori* for all those regulated by administrative law. It is true that obligations that are properly contractual can be entered into or abrogated by the mere will to agreement of the parties. Yet we must bear in mind that, if a contract has binding force, it is society which confers that force. Let us assume that it does not give its blessing to the obligations that have been contracted; these then become pure promises possessing only moral authority.[2] Every contract therefore assumes that behind the parties who bind each other, society is there, quite prepared to intervene and to enforce respect for any undertakings entered into. Thus it only bestows this obligatory force upon contracts that have a social value in themselves, that is, those that are in conformity with the rules of law. We shall even occasionally see that its intervention is still more positive. It is therefore present in every relationship determined by restitutory law, even in ones that appear the most completely private, and its presence, although not felt, at least under normal conditions, is no less essential.[3]

Since the rules where sanctions are restitutory do not involve the common consciousness, the relationships that they determine are not of the sort that affect everyone indiscriminately. This means that they are instituted directly, not between the individual and society, but between limited and particular elements in society, which they link to one another. Yet on the other hand, since society is not absent it must necessarily indeed be concerned to some extent, and feel some repercussions. Then, depending upon the intensity with which it feels them, it intervenes at a greater or lesser distance, and more or less actively, through the mediation of special bodies whose task it is to represent it. These relationships are therefore very different from those regulated by repressive law, for the latter join directly, without any intermediary, the individual consciousness to that of society, that is, the individual himself to society.

But these relationships can assume two very different forms.

Sometimes they are negative and come down to a mere abstention; at other times they are positive, or ones affording co-operation. To the two categories of rules that determine either kind of relationship correspond two kinds of social solidarity between which a distinction must be drawn.

II

The negative relationship that may serve as a model for the others is that which joins a thing to a person.

Things in fact are a part of society, just as persons are, and play a specific part in it. Thus their relationship to the body social needs to be determined. So we may say that there exists a solidarity of things whose nature is special enough to be outwardly interpreted in legal consequences of a very particular character.

Jurisconsults in fact distinguish between two kinds of rights: they term one kind 'real', the other 'personal'. The right of property and mortgage belongs to the first kind, the right to credit to the second kind. What characterises 'real' rights is that they alone give rise to a right of preference and succession. In this case the right that I possess over something is exclusive of any other that might be established after mine. If, for example, a property has been successively mortgaged to two creditors, the second mortgage cannot in any way restrict the rights acquired under the first. Moreover, if my debtor disposes of the thing over which I possess a mortgage right, this is in no way affected, but the third party acquiring it is obliged to pay me or to surrender what he has acquired. Now, for this to be the case, the legal bond must link directly, without the mediation of any third person, the thing specific to me in my legal status. This privileged situation is thus the consequence of the solidarity peculiar to things. When, on the contrary, the right is personal, the person under an obligation to me can, by contracting new obligations, give me co-creditors whose right is equal to mine and, although I possess as surety all my debtor's goods, if he disposes of them they are removed from my surety by being no longer part of his estate. This is because no special relationship exists between these goods and myself, but one between the person of their owner and myself.[4]

We can thus see what this 'real' form of solidarity consists of: it links things directly to persons, but not persons with one another. In an extreme case someone, believing himself to be alone in the world, may exercise a 'real' right, leaving other persons out of account. Consequently, since it is only through the mediation of persons that things are integrated into society, the solidarity that arises from this integration is wholly negative. It does not cause individual wills to move towards common ends, but only causes things to gravitate around those individual wills in an orderly fashion. Because 'real' rights are limited in this way, they do not come into conflicts; disputes are forestalled, but there is no active co-operation, no *consensus*. Let us envisage such agreement to be as complete as possible; the society where it obtains, if it does so alone, will resemble a huge constellation in which each star moves in its orbit without disturbing the motion of neighbouring stars. Such a solidarity thus does not shape from the elements drawn together an entity capable of acting in unison. It contributes nothing to the unity of the body social.

From the above, it is easy to determine to what part of restitutory law this form of solidarity corresponds: it is the corpus of 'real' rights. Now, from the very definition that has been given of these, it follows that the law of property is its most perfect exemplar. Indeed the most perfect relationship that can exist between a thing and a person is one that wholly subordinates the former to the latter. Yet this relationship is itself very complex, and the various elements that form it can become the object of as many 'real' secondary rights, such as usufruct, easements, usage and habitation. All in all we may say that 'real' rights comprise property law in its various forms (literary, artistic, industrial, personal estate, real estate) and its different modes, such as those regulated by the second book of the Civil Code. As well as this book, French law recognises four other 'real' rights, but which are only ancillaries to or possible substitutes for personal rights: surety, property usufruct, preferential right and mortgage (arts. 2071–2203). It is appropriate to add to these all matters relating to the law of inheritance, the law of testacy, and consequently, of intestacy, since the latter creates, when it has been declared, a sort of provisional succession. Indeed inheritance is a thing, or a set of things, over which heirs and legatees have a 'real' right, whether this is acquired *ipso facto* by the decease of the former owner, or whether it is only opened up as the result of a judicial act, as happens for indirect heirs and legatees with a particular title. In all these cases the legal relationship is directly established, not between one person and another, but between a person and a thing. The same is true for gifts made by will, which is no more than the exercise of the 'real' right that the owner disposes of over his possessions, or at least over the portion of which he is free to dispose.

But there are relationships between one person and another which, although in no way 'real', are nevertheless as negative as those just mentioned, and express a solidarity of the same kind.

Firstly, there are relationships that bring into play the exercise of 'real' rights proper. In fact, inevitably the functioning of these sometimes brings up against one another holders of those rights themselves. For example, when one thing is added on to another, the owner of the thing deemed to be the principal one becomes at the same time the owner of the other one; only 'he must pay the other person the value of the thing joined to his' (art. 566). This obligation is clearly a personal one. Likewise any owner of a party wall who wishes to raise its height is obliged to pay the co-proprietor an indemnity for the obligation imposed (art. 658). A legatee with a particular title to an article must address himself to the main legatee to obtain the release to him of the thing bequeathed, although he acquires a right to it immediately upon the decease of the testator (art. 1014). But the solidarity that these relationships express does not differ from those we have just discussed: in fact they are established only to make good or forestall any damage occasioned. If the holder of a 'real' right could always exercise it without ever going beyond bounds, with each person remaining in his own domain, there would be no reason for any legal relationship. But in fact such overlapping is constantly occurring between these different rights, so that one cannot realise the value of one right without encroaching upon the other rights that limit it. In one case the thing over which I enjoy a right is in the hands of another; this is what happens with a legacy. In another, I cannot enjoy my right without harming that of another; this is what occurs for certain easements charges. Relationships are therefore needful to repair the damage if it has already been done, or to prevent it happening. But there is nothing positive about these relationships. They do not cause the persons whom they bring into contact to co-operate together; they do not imply any such co-operation. But they merely restore or maintain, in the new conditions that have been brought about, that negative solidarity which has been disturbed in its functioning by circumstances. Far from uniting people, they only arise in order to unravel more efficiently what has been united by force of circumstance, to re-establish boundaries that have been violated and to reinstate each individual in his own domain..These relationships are so closely identical to those of a thing with a person that those who drew up the civil Code have not dealt with them separately, but have treated them at the same time as 'real' rights.

Finally, the obligations that arise from an offence or a quasi-offence are of exactly the same character.[5] Indeed they constrain each individual to repair the damage he has wrongfully caused to the legitimate interests of another. Thus they are personal, but the solidarity to which they correspond is clearly entirely negative, since they consist not in rendering a service, but in refraining from harm. The tie the breaking of which they penalise is wholly external. The only difference between these relationships and the previous ones is that, in the one case, the break arises from a misdeed and in the other, from circumstances determined and foreseen by the law. But the system of order disturbed is the same one; it arises, not from competition, but purely from abstention.[6] Moreover the rights whose infringement gives rise to these obligations are themselves 'real', for I am the owner of my body, my health, my honour and my reputation by the same right and in the same way as the material things controlled by me.

To sum up: the rules relating to 'real' rights and personal relationships that are established by virtue of them form a definite system whose function is not to link together the different parts of society, but on the contrary to detach them from one another, and mark out clearly the barriers separating them. Thus they do not correspond to any positive social tie. The very expression 'negative solidarity' that we have employed is not absolutely exact. It is not a true solidarity, having its own life and being of a special nature, but rather the negative aspects of every type of solidarity. The first condition for an entity to become coherent is for the parts that form it not to clash discordantly. But such an external harmony does not bring about cohesion. On the contrary, it presumes it. Negative solidarity is only possible where another kind is present, positive in nature, of which it is both the result and the condition.

Indeed the rights that individuals possess both over themselves and things can only be determined by means of compromise and mutual concessions, for everything that is granted to some is necessarily given up by others. It is sometimes stated that the level of normal development in an individual could be deduced either from the concept of human personality (Kant), or from the idea of the individual organism (Spencer). This is possible, although the rigour in this reasoning is very questionable. In any case what is certain is that, in historical reality, it is not upon these abstract considerations that the moral order was founded. In fact, for a man to acknowledge that others have rights, not only as a matter of logic, but as one of daily living, he must have agreed to limit his own. Consequently this mutual limitation was only realisable in a spirit of understanding and harmony. Now if we assume a host of individuals with no previous ties binding them to one another, what reason might have impelled them to make these reciprocal sacrifices? The need to live in peace? But peace in itself is no more desirable than war. The latter has its drawbacks and advantages. Have there not been peoples and individuals whose passion has at all times been war? The instincts to which it corresponds are no less powerful than those that peace satisfies. No doubt sheer weariness of hostilities can for a while put an end to them, but this simple truce can be no more lasting than the temporary lassitude that brought it about. This is all the more true of outcomes due merely to the triumph of force. They are as provisional and precarious as the treaties that terminate wars between nations. Men need peace only in so far as they are already united by some bond of sociability. In this case the feelings that cause them to turn towards one another modify entirely naturally promptings of egoism. From another viewpoint the society that encloses them, unable to exist save when not shaken at every instant by some upheaval, bears down upon them with all its weight to force them to make the necessary concessions to one another. It is true that we sometimes see independent societies reach agreement to determine the extent of their respective rights over things, that is, over their territory. But the extreme instability of these relationships is precisely the best proof that negative solidarity alone is not sufficient. If today, among cultured peoples, it seems to be stronger, if that portion of international law that determines what might be called the 'real' rights of European societies perhaps possesses more authority than once it did, it is because the different nations of Europe are also much less independent of one another. This is because in certain respects they are all part of the same society, still incohesive, it is true, but one becoming increasingly conscious of itself. What has been termed the balance of power in Europe marks the beginning of the organisation of that society.

It is customary to distinguish carefully between justice and charity, that is, the mere respect of others' rights, from every act that goes beyond that purely negative virtue. In both these kinds of practices may be seen two independent strata of ethics: justice, by itself, might constitute its basic foundation; charity might be its crowning glory. The distinction is such a radical one that, according to the protagonists of a certain kind of ethics, justice alone is needful for the smooth functioning of social life. Altruism is scarcely more than a private virtue, which it is laudable for the individual to pursue, but which society can very well do without. Many even view its intervention in public life with some disquiet. From what was stated previously we can see just how far this conception is from according with the facts. In reality, for men to acknowledge and mutually guarantee the rights of one another, they must first have a mutual liking, and have some reason that makes them cling to one another and to the single society of which they form a part. Justice is filled with charity, or to employ once more our expression, negative solidarity is only the emanation of another solidarity that is positive in nature: it is the repercussion of social feelings in the sphere of 'real' rights which come from a different source. Thus there is nothing specific about justice, but it is the necessary accompaniment to every kind of solidarity. It is necessarily encountered everywhere men live a life in common, whether this results from the social division of labour or from the attraction of like to like.

III

If the rules just discussed are separated from restitutory law, what remains constitutes a system that is no less well defined, and includes domestic law, contractual law, commercial law, procedural law, and administrative and constitutional law. The relationships that are regulated by these laws are of a nature entirely different from the preceding ones; they express a positive contribution, a co-operation deriving essentially from the division of labour.

The questions resolved by domestic law may be reduced to the following two types:
(1) Who is entrusted with the different domestic functions? Who is the spouse, who the father, who the legitimate child, who the guardian, etc.?
(2) What is the normal type of these functions and their relationships?
The stipulations laid down to meet the first of these questions are those that determine the status and conditions required to contract a marriage, the necessary formalities for the marriage to be a valid one, the conditions regarding legitimate, illegitimate and adoptive children, the mode of selecting a guardian, etc.

On the other hand, it is the second question that is settled by the section on the respective laws and duties relating to husband and wife, on the state of their relationship in case of divorce, nullity or separation (including division of property), on the powers of the father, on the legal consequences of adoption, on administration by a guardian and on his relationship with his ward, on the role of the family council *vis-à-vis* guardian and ward, on the role of parents in the case of suspension of civil rights, and on the constitution of a board of guardians.

This section of civil law has therefore as its purpose the determination of how the various family functions are allocated and what should be the relationship of each function to the others. Their significance is that they express the special solidarity that unites the members of a family as the result of the domestic division of labour. It is true that we are scarcely accustomed to conceiving the family in this light. It is very often believed that what brings about this cohesion is exclusively a commonality of sentiments and beliefs. Indeed there are so many matters shared in common between the members of the family group that the special character of the tasks incumbent upon each member easily eludes us. This prompted Comte to declare that domestic union excludes 'any thought of direct and common co-operation towards any common goal'.[7] But the legal organisation of the family whose essential traits we have just briefly recalled, demonstrates the reality of these functional differences and their importance. The history of the family from its origins shows in fact a mere uninterrupted movement towards dissociation, in the course of which these various functions, at first undivided and overlapping, have gradually separated out and been constituted independently, being distributed among the various relatives according to sex, age and dependent relationships, so as to make each relative a specialised functionary in domestic society.[8] Far from being only an ancillary and secondary phenomenon, this family division of labour, on the contrary, dominates the whole of the development of the family.

The relationship of the division of labour to contractual law is no less marked.

The contract is indeed the supreme legal expression of co-operation. It is true that there exist so-called 'benevolent' contracts that bind only one of the parties. If I make an unconditional gift to another person, if I assume voluntarily the trusteeship of some object, or a power of attorney, there ensue for me precise, clear-cut obligations. Yet no real co-operation between the contracting parties exists since burdens are laid upon one of them alone. Yet co-operation is not entirely absent from the phenomenon; it is merely gratuitous or unilateral. For instance, what is a gift if not an exchange without reciprocal obligations? These kinds of contract are therefore merely a variation of contracts of a truly co-operative nature.

Moreover, they are very rare, for it is only exceptionally that gratuitous acts fall under legal regulation. As for the other contracts, which comprise the overwhelming majority, the obligations to which they give rise are correlative, either through reciprocal obligations or through services previously rendered. The undertaking entered into by the one party stems either from that entered into by the other, or from a service already performed by the latter.[9] Now such reciprocity is only possible where co-operation exists and this in turn does not occur without the division of labour. To co-operate, in fact, is to share with one another a common task. If this task is subdivided into tasks qualitatively similar, although indispensable to one another, there is a simple or first-level division of labour. If they are different in kind, there is composite division of labour, or specialisation proper.

This latter form of co-operation is moreover the one that the contract by far the most usually expresses. The only one of different significance is the contract of association, and also perhaps the marriage contract, in so far as it determines the share in household expenses to be contributed by husband and wife. Even for this to be the case, the contract of association must place all associates on the same level, with identical contributions and functions. But this is a case which never exactly occurs in matrimonial relations, because of the division of labour between husband and wife. Against these rare kinds of contract let us contrast the innumerable contracts whose purpose is to harmonise functions that are special and different: contracts between buyer and seller, exchange contracts, contracts between employers and workers, between hirer and person hiring, between lender and borrower, between the repository and the depositor, between innkeeper and traveller, between one enjoying a power of attorney and his mandatory, between the creditor and the pledge given by the debtor, etc. In general, the contract is the symbol of exchange. Thus not unjustifiably Spencer was able to term a contract physiological, one like that which at every moment occurs in the exchange of substances between the different organs of the living body.[10] Now it is plain that exchange always assumes some more or less developed division of labour. It is true that the contracts we have just mentioned are still of a somewhat general character. But we must not forget that law only draws the general contours, the main features of social relationships, those that are to be found identical in the different spheres of collective life. Thus each one of these types of contract assumes a host of others, more specialised, of which it is, as it were, the common blueprint, but which at the same time regulates the others, those in which relationships are established between more specialised functions. Thus despite the relative simplicity of this scheme, it is enough to demonstrate the extreme complexity of the facts that it epitomises.

Moreover, this specialisation of functions is directly manifest in the commercial code, which especially regulates contracts specific to commerce: contracts between agent and principal, between carrier and consignor, between the bearer of a bill of exchange and the drawer, between shipowner and creditors, or shipowner and captain and crew, between the freighting agency and the charterer, between lender and borrower in a contract duly legally engrossed, between insurer and insured. Yet here again a great gap exists between the comparatively general nature of the legal prescriptions and the diversity of special functions whose relationships are regulated by these, as is shown by the important position accorded in commercial law to custom.

Where the commercial code does not regulate contracts proper, it determines what certain special functions must be, such as those of the stockbroker, the dealer, the ship's captain, the receiver in a case of bankruptcy, so as to ensure solidarity in all the various parts of the commercial system.

Procedural law, whether this be criminal, civil or commercial, plays the same role in the legal system. The sanctions of legal rules of all kinds can only be applied through a certain number of ancillary functions, such as those of magistrates, defence lawyers, solicitors, jurors, plaintiffs and defendants. Procedures decide the manner in which the functions must be applied and relate to one another. It states what they should be and what is the role of each one in the general life of the corpus of the law.

It seems to us that, in a rational classification of legal rules, procedural law should be considered merely as a variety of administrative law: we do not see what rational difference separates the administration of justice from the rest of administration. Whatever the rights or wrongs of this viewpoint, administrative law proper regulates ill-defined functions that are termed administrative,[11] just as procedural law does judicial functions. It determines what their normal type is, and their relationships either with one another or with the diffused functions of society. One would only need to except a certain number of rules which are generally classified under this heading, although they are penal in character.[12] Finally, constitutional law performs the same role for governmental functions.

It may well be surprising to see classified under the same heading administrative and political law with what is usually termed private law. Yet firstly, such a connection is needed if the nature of the sanctions is taken as the basis for classification. Nor does it seem possible for us to adopt any other system if we wish to proceed scientifically. Moreover, to separate completely these two kinds of law we would have to admit that private law really exists, whereas we believe that all law is public, because all law is social. All the functions of society are social, just as all the functions of an organism are organic. The economic functions, just like the others, are also of this character. Moreover, even among the most diffuse functions there are none that are not to some extent subject to the effects of the machinery of government. Thus from this viewpoint between them there is no more than a difference in degree.

To sum up: the relationships that are regulated by co-operative law, with its restitutory sanctions, and the solidarity these relationships express, result from the social division of labour. Moreover, it is explicable that, in general, co-operative relationships do not carry with them any other form of sanctions. Indeed, special tasks, by their very nature, are exempt from the effects of the collective consciousness. This is because if something is to be the object of shared sentiments, the first condition is that it should be shared, that is, present in every consciousness, and that each individual may be able to conceive of it from a single, identical viewpoint. Doubtless, so long as functions are of a certain general nature, everyone can have some feeling for them. Yet the more specific they become the more also the number is restricted of those who are aware of each and every function. Consequently the more they overflow beyond the common consciousness. The rules that determine them cannot therefore possess that superior force and transcendent authority which, when it suffers harm, exacts expiation. It is indeed also from public opinion that their authority springs, just as do penal rules, but from an opinion that is specific to certain sectors of society.

Moreover, even in those special circles where the rules are applied, and where consequently they are evoked in the minds of people, they do not reflect any very acute feelings, nor even in most cases any kind of emotional state. For, since they determine the manner in which the different functions should work together in the various combinations of circumstances that may arise, the objects to which they relate are not ever-present in the consciousness. We are not always having to administer a guardianship or a trusteeship,[13] nor having to exercise our rights as creditor or buyer, etc. Above all, we do not have to exercise them in particular conditions. But the states of consciousness are strong only in so far as they are permanent. The infringement of these rules does not therefore touch to the quick the common spirit of society, nor, at least usually, that of these special groups. Consequently the infringement cannot provoke more than a very moderate reaction. All that we require is for the functions to work together in a regular fashion. Thus if this regularity is disturbed, we are satisfied if it is re-established. This is most certainly not to say that the development of the division of labour cannot have repercussions in the penal law. There are, as we already know, administrative and governmental functions where certain relationships are regulated by repressive law, because of the special character marking the organ of the common consciousness and everything appertaining to it. In yet other cases, the bonds of solidarity linking certain social functions may be such that once they are broken repercussions occur that are sufficiently general to provoke a reaction of punishment. But for reasons we have already stated, these consequences are exceptional.

In the end this law plays a part analogous in society to that of the nervous system in the organism. That system, in effect, has the task of regulating the various bodily functions in such a way that they work harmoniously together. Thus it expresses in a very natural way the degree of concentration that the organism has reached as a result of the physiological division of labour. Therefore we can at the different levels of the animal scale ascertain the measure of that concentration according to the development of the nervous system. Likewise this means that we can ascertain the measure of concentration that a society has reached through the social division of labour, according to the development of co-operative law with its restitutory sanctions. One can foresee that such a criterion will be of great utility to us.

IV

Since negative solidarity on its own brings about no integration, and since, moreover, there is nothing specific in it, we shall identify only two kinds of positive solidarity, distinguished by the following characteristics:

(1) The first kind links the individual directly to society without any intermediary. With the second kind he depends upon society because he depends upon the parts that go to constitute it.

(2) In the two cases, society is not viewed from the same perspective. In the first, the term is used to denote a more or less organised society composed of beliefs and sentiments common to all the members of the group: this is the collective type. On the contrary, in the second case the society to which we are solidly joined is a system of different and special functions united by definite relationships. Moreover, these two societies are really one. They are two facets of one and the same reality, but which none the less need to be distinguished from each other.

(3) From this second difference there arises another which will serve to allow us to characterise and delineate the features of these two kinds of solidarity.

The first kind can only be strong to the extent that the ideas and tendencies common to all members of the society exceed in number and intensity those that appertain personally to each one of those members. The greater this excess, the more active this kind of society is. Now what constitutes our personality is that which each one of us possesses that is peculiar and characteristic, what distinguishes it from others. This solidarity can therefore only increase in inverse relationship to the personality. As we have said, there is in the consciousness of each one of us two consciousnesses: one that we share in common with our group in its entirety, which is consequently not ourselves, but society living and acting within us; the other that, on the contrary, represents us alone in what is personal and distinctive about us, what makes us an individual.[14] The solidarity that derives from similarities is at its *maximum* when the collective consciousness completely envelops our total consciousness, coinciding with it at every point. At that moment our individuality is zero. That individuality cannot arise until the community fills us less completely. Here there are two opposing forces, the one centripetal, the other centrifugal, which cannot increase at the same time. We cannot ourselves develop simultaneously in two so opposing directions. If we have a strong inclination to think and act for ourselves we cannot be strongly inclined to think and act like other people. If the ideal is to create for ourselves a special, personal image, this cannot mean to be like everyone else. Moreover, at the very moment when this solidarity exerts its effect, our personality, it may be said by definition, disappears, for we are no longer ourselves, but a collective being.

The social molecules that can only cohere in this one manner cannot therefore move as a unit save in so far as they lack any movement of their own, as do the molecules of inorganic bodies. This is why we suggest that this kind of solidarity should be called mechanical. The word does not mean that the solidarity is produced by mechanical and artificial means. We only use this term for it by analogy with the cohesion that links together the elements of raw materials, in contrast to that which encompasses the unity of living organisms. What finally justifies the use of this term is the fact that the bond that thus unites the individual with society is completely analogous to that which links the thing to the person. The individual consciousness, considered from this viewpoint, is simply a dependency of the collective type, and follows all its motions, just as the object possessed follows those which its owner imposes upon it. In societies where this solidarity is highly developed the individual, as we shall see later, does not belong to himself; he is literally a thing at the disposal of society. Thus, in these same social types, personal rights are still not yet distinguished from 'real' rights.

The situation is entirely different in the case of solidarity that brings about the division of labour. Whereas the other solidarity implies that individuals resemble one another, the latter assumes that they are different from one another. The former type is only possible in so far as the individual personality is absorbed into the collective personality; the latter is only possible if each one of us has a sphere of action that is peculiarly our own, and consequently a personality. Thus the collective consciousness leaves uncovered a part of the individual consciousness, so that there may be established in it those special functions that it cannot regulate. The more extensive this free area is, the stronger the cohesion that arises from this solidarity. Indeed, on the one hand each one of us depends more intimately upon society the more labour is divided up, and on the other, the activity of each one of us is correspondingly more specialised, the more personal it is. Doubtless, however circumscribed that activity may be, it is never completely original. Even in the exercise of our profession we conform to usages and practices that are common to us all within our corporation. Yet even in this case, the burden that we bear is in a different way less heavy than when the whole of society bears down upon us, and this leaves much more room for the free play of our initiative. Here, then, the individuality of the whole grows at the same time as that of the parts. Society becomes more effective in moving in concert, at the same time as each of its elements has more movements that are peculiarly its own. This solidarity resembles that observed in the higher animals. In fact each organ has its own special characteristics and autonomy, yet the greater the unity of the organism, the more marked the individualisation of the parts. Using this analogy, we propose to call 'organic' the solidarity that is due to the division of labour.

At the same time this chapter and the preceding one provide us with the means of estimating the part played by each one of these two social links in the overall, common result which by different ways they contribute in producing. In fact we know under what external forms these two kinds of solidarity are symbolised, that is, what is the corpus of legal rules corresponding to each one. Consequently to know their respective importance within a given social type, it is enough to compare the respective extent of the two kinds of law that express them, since the law always varies with the social relationships that it regulates.[15]

Notes

1. Tarde, *Criminalité comparée* (Alcan, Paris) p. 113.
2. Even that moral authority derives from custom, and hence from society.
3. We must confine ourselves here to these general remarks, common to every form of restitutory law. Numerous demonstrations of this truth will be found later (Chapter VII) for that part of law that corresponds to the solidarity engendered by the division of labour.
4. It has sometimes been stated that the status of father or son, etc. was the object of 'real' rights (cf. Ortolan, *Instituts*, vol. I, p. 660). But such forms of status are only abstract symbols of various rights, some 'real' (for example, a father's right over the fortune of his under-age children), others personal.
5. Arts 1382–1386 of the Civil Code. To these might be linked the articles concerning the reclaiming of a debt.
6. A contracting party who fails to fulfil his undertakings is also obliged to indemnify the other party. But in that case the damages awarded serve as a sanction for a positive bond. It is not because he has committed any harm that the breaker of a contract pays, but for not having carried out his obligation.
7. A. Comte, *Cours de philosophie positive*, vol. IV, p. 419.
8. For further development of this point, cf. Chapter VII.
9. For instance, in the case of a loan with interest.
10. H. Spencer, *Principles of Ethics* (London, 1893).
11. We have retained the expression normally used. But it would require to be defined, and this we are not able to do. All in all, it seems to us that these functions are those placed directly under the influence of governmental authorities. But many distinctions would have to be made.
12. Also, those that concern the 'real' rights of legally constituted bodies ('*personnes morales*') of an administrative kind, for the relationships that they determine are negative ones.
13. This is why the law that regulates the relationships of domestic functions is not penal in character, although its functions are fairly general.
14. Nevertheless these two consciousnesses are not regions of ourselves that are 'geographically' distinct, for they interpenetrate each other at every point.

15. To clarify ideas, in the table that follows we develop the classification of legal rules that is implicit in this chapter and the preceding one:

I. *Rules with an organised, repressive sanction.*
(A classification will be found in the next chapter.)

II. *Rules with a restitutory sanction determining different relationships.*

Negative or abstaining relationships

- Of a thing to a person
  - Right to property in its various forms (personal estate, real estate, etc.)
  - Various procedures of the right of property (estate charges, usufruct, etc.)
- Of persons to one another
  - Determined by the normal exercise of 'real' rights
  - Determined by the illegal violation of 'real' rights.

Between domestic functions

Positive or co-operative relationships

- Between diffused economic functions
  - Contractual relationships in general.
  - Special contracts.
- Administrative functions
  - One to another.
  - With governmental functions.
  - With functions diffused throughout society.
- Governmental functions
  - One to another.
  - With administrative functions.
  - With diffused political functions.

Chapter IV

Another Proof of the Preceding Theory

However, because of the importance of the results just set out, it is wise, before proceeding further, to confirm them once more. This fresh verification is all the more useful because it will provide us with an opportunity for establishing a law that, whilst it will serve to prove the results, will also serve to make clear everything that is to follow.

If the two kinds of solidarity that we have just distinguished indeed assume the legal expression we have stated, the preponderance of repressive law over co-operative law must be all the greater when the collective type is more pronounced and the division of labour more rudimentary. Conversely, to the degree that individual types develop and tasks become specialised, the balance between the extent of these two kinds of law must tend to be upset. Now the reality of this relationship can be demonstrated experimentally.

I

The more primitive societies are, the more resemblances there are between the individuals from which they have been formed. Already Hippocrates, in his *De Aere et Locis*, had said that Scythians were an ethnic type and had no personal types. Humboldt notes in his *Neuspanien*[1] that among barbarian peoples is to be found a physiognomy more characteristic of the horde rather than individual physiognomies, and this fact has been confirmed by a large number of observers:

Just as the Romans found among the ancient Germans very great similarities, so do the so-called savages produce the same effect upon the civilized European. To tell the truth, lack of practice can often be the main cause which induces the traveller to form such a judgement. . . . Yet this inexperience could hardly produce this consequence if the differences to which the civilized man is accustomed in his native environment were not in reality more considerable than those he encounters among primitive peoples. This saying of Ulloa is well known and often quoted: that he who has seen one native of America has seen them all.[2]

By contrast, among civilised peoples two individuals can be distinguished from one another at a first glance, and without any prior initiation being necessary.

Dr Lebon was able to establish objectively this homogeneity, which increases as one goes further back in time towards the origins. He compared skulls belonging to different races and societies and found 'that the differences in cranial capacity existing between individuals of the same race are much greater according to how advanced the race is on the ladder of civilisation. After having grouped together the capacity of the craniums of each race in a progressive series, taking care to establish comparisons only for series numerous enough for the individual examples to be linked in a graduated way, [I recognised,] he states 'that the difference in volume between the largest adult male craniums and the smallest amounts in round figures to 200 cubic centimetres for the gorilla, 280 for the untouchables in India, 310 for the Australian aborigine, 350 for the ancient Egyptian, 470 for the twelfth-century Parisian, 600 for the modern Parisian, 700 for the German.'[3] There are even some tribes where the difference is non-existent. 'The Andaman Islanders and the Todas are all alike. The same may also almost be said of the inhabitants of Greenland. Five craniums of Patagonians owned by M. Broca's laboratory are identical.'[4]

There is no doubt that these organic similarities correspond to psychological similarities. 'It is certain,' states Waitz, 'that this great physical resemblance among natives arises essentially from the absence of any strong psychological individuality and from the inferior state of intellectual culture in general. The homogeneity of characters (*Gemütseigenschaften*) within a Negro tribe is indisputable. In Upper Egypt the slave dealer only inquires in detail about the place of origin of the slave and not about his individual character, for long experience has taught him that the differences between individuals of the same tribe are insignificant beside those that derive from race. Thus the Nubas and the Gallus are reputed to be very loyal, the Northern Abyssinians treacherous and perfidious, and most of the others are deemed to be good domestic slaves, but hardly usable for physical labour. Those of Fertit are held to be savage and swift to seek vengeance.'[5] Thus originality is not only rare; there is, so to speak, no room for it. Everybody then accepts and practises without argument the same religion; different sects and quarrels are unknown: they would not be tolerated. At this time religion includes everything, extends to everything. It embraces, although in a very confused state, besides religious beliefs proper, ethics, law, the principles of political organisation, and even science, or at least what passes for it. It regulates even the minutiae of private life. Thus to state that religious consciousnesses are then identical, and that this identity is absolute, is implicitly to assert that, except for those sensations that relate to the organism and states of the organism, every individual consciousness is roughly made up of the same elements. Even sensory impressions themselves need not display great diversity, because of the physical resemblances displayed by individuals.

Yet the idea is still fairly widespread that civilisation, on the contrary, has the effect of increasing social similarities. 'To the extent that human settlements spread,' states Tarde, 'the diffusion of ideas, which follows a regular geometrical progression, becomes more marked.'[6] According to Hale,[7] it is a mistake to attribute to primitive peoples a certain uniformity of character, and he cites as proof the fact that the yellow and black races of the Pacific Ocean, who live side by side, are more strongly distinguishable from each other than two European peoples. Likewise, are not the differences that separate the Frenchman from the Englishman or the German less today than they were formerly? In almost all European societies law, ethics, customs, even the basic political institutions, are roughly identical. It has also been noted that within the same country today the contrasts that were once encountered are no longer to be found. Social life no longer varies, or not as much, from one province to another; in unified countries such as France, it is almost the same in every region, and this process of evening out is greater among the cultured classes.[8]

But these facts in no way invalidate our proposition. Certainly the different societies tend to resemble one another more closely, but this is not true for the individuals that they comprise. There is now less of a gap than formerly between the Frenchman and the Englishman in general, but this does not prevent Frenchmen today from being much more different from one another than they were once. Likewise, it is indeed the case that each province is tending to lose its distinctive appearance, but this does not prevent each individual from assuming increasingly an appearance personal to him. The Norman is less different from the Gascon, and the Gascon from the Lorrainer or the Provençal: all share hardly more than the characteristics common to all Frenchmen. But the diversity that Frenchmen exhibit as a whole has continually increased. For, if the few provincial types that once existed tend to blend in with each other and disappear, in their place there is a multitude of individual types, important in a different way. There are no longer as many differences as there are large regions, but there are almost as many differences as there are individuals. Conversely, whereas each province has its own personality, this is not true of individuals. These can be very heterogeneous as compared with one another, and yet be formed only from similar elements. This is also what occurs in political societies. In the same way, in the world of biology the protozoans are distinct from one another to such an extent that it is impossible to classify them into species.[9] Yet each one is made up of matter that is perfectly homogeneous.

This view therefore rests upon a confusion between individual and collective types, whether these are provincial or national. It is beyond question that civilisation tends to level out differences between collective types, but it has been wrongly concluded that it has the same effect upon individual types and that uniformity is becoming general. Far from these two kinds of types both varying, we shall see that the disappearance of the first is the necessary cause for the appearance of the other.[10] But there is never more than a limited number of collective types within the same society, for it can only include a small number of races and regions that are different enough to produce such dissimilarities. On the other hand, individuals are capable of infinite diversity. The diversity is therefore all the greater as types become more developed.

The foregoing applies identically to professional types. We have reason to suppose that they are losing something of their former contours, that the gulf that once separated professions, and particularly certain ones, is in the process of being filled up. But what is sure is that within each profession differences have grown. Each individual has more his own ways of thinking and acting, and is less subject to the general view of the corporation. Moreover, if from one profession to another the differences are less clear-cut, they are in any case more numerous, for occupational types have themselves multiplied as the work becomes more shared out. If they are no longer distinguishable from one another save in some small respects, at least these have become more and more varied. The diversity has therefore not lessened, even from this viewpoint, although it no longer manifests itself in the form of violent and striking contrasts.

Thus we may rest assured that the farther we go back in history, the greater the homogeneity. Moreover, the more we reach the highest social types, the more developed the division of labour. Let us now see how the two forms of law we have distinguished themselves vary, at diverse levels in the social scale.

II

So far as we can judge the state of the law in the very lowest societies, it seems to be wholly repressive. Lubbock states: 'No savage is free. All over the world his daily life is regulated by a complicated and apparently most inconvenient set of customs (as forcible as laws), of quaint prohibitions and privileges' (p. 303). 'Nay, every action of their lives is regulated by numerous rules, none the less stringent because unwritten' (p. 302).[11]

Indeed we know with what ease the ways of acting among primitive peoples become consolidated into traditional practices, and moreover how great the strength of tradition is among them. The customs of their ancestors are shrouded in so much respect that they cannot depart from them without being punished.

Yet such observations are necessarily imprecise, for nothing is more difficult to grasp than customs that are so vague. For our demonstration to be conducted methodically, we must bring it to bear as much as possible upon written law.

The four final books of the Pentateuch – Exodus, Leviticus, Numbers and Deuteronomy – represent the most ancient record of this nature that we possess.[12] Of the 4,000–5,000 verses there is only a relatively tiny number in which are expressed rules that might conceivably pass as not being repressive. They are concerned with the following objects:

Law of property: right of withdrawal; jubilee; property of Levites (Leviticus 15:14–25, 29–34 and 27:1–34).

Domestic law: marriage (Deuteronomy 21:11–14; 23:5; 25:5–10; Leviticus 21:7, 13, 14); law of succession (Numbers 27:8–11 and 26:8; Deuteronomy 21:15–17); slavery of native-born and foreigners (Deuteronomy 15:12–17; Exodus 21:2–11; Leviticus 19:20; 25:39–44; 36:44–54).

Loans and wages: (Deuteronomy 15:7–9; 23:19–20; 24:6 and 10–13; 25:15).

Quasi-offences: (Exodus 21:18–33 and 33–35; 22:6 and 10–17).[13]

Organisation of public functions: functions of priests (Numbers 10); of Levites (Numbers 3 and 4); of elders (Deuteronomy 21:19; 22:15; 25:7; 21:1; Leviticus 4:15); of judges (Exodus 18:25; Deuteronomy 1:15–17).

Thus restitutory law and co-operative law in particular amount to very little. Nor is this all. Among the rules we have just mentioned many are not so far remote from the penal law as at first sight one might believe, for they are all marked with a religious character. They all likewise emanate from the Godhead; to violate them is to offend him, and such offences are sins that must be expiated. The Book does not distinguish between this kind of commandment and another, for they are all divine words that cannot be disobeyed with impunity. 'If you do not observe and fulfil all the law written down in this book, if you do not revere this honoured and dreaded name, this name "the Lord your God," then the Lord will strike you and your descendants . . .' (Deuteronomy 28:58–9, NEB). The failure, even by a mistake, to observe any precept whatsoever constitutes a sin and demands expiation. Threats of this kind, whose penal character is beyond dispute, even sanction directly some of those rules that we have attributed to restitutory law. Having decided that a divorced wife cannot be taken back by her first husband, if after having married again she divorces once more, the text adds: 'This is abominable to the Lord; *you must not bring sin upon the land* which the Lord your God is giving you as your patrimony' (Deuteronomy 24:4). Likewise, the verse that follows prescribes the manner in which wages are to be paid: 'Pay him [the hired man] his wages on the same day before sunset, for he is poor and his heart is set on them: *he may appeal to the Lord against you and you will be guilty of sin'* (Deuteronomy 24:15). The restitutions that arise from quasi-offences seem also to be presented as veritable expiatory acts. Thus we read in Leviticus: 'When one man strikes another and kills him he shall be put to death. Whosoever strikes a beast and kills it shall make restitution, life for life . . . fracture for fracture, eye for eye, tooth for tooth.'[14] Redress for the damage suffered has every appearance of being assimilated to the punishment for murder and considered to be an application of the law of talion.

It is true that there are a certain number of precepts for which a sanction is not particularly specified, but we already know that it will certainly be of a penal character. The nature of the expressions used is sufficient to prove it. Moreover, tradition informs us that a physical punishment was inflicted upon anyone who violated a negative precept, when the law formally prescribed no specific punishment.[15] In short, at various levels the whole of Hebrew law revealed to us in the Pentateuch bears essentially the stamp of repression. This is more apparent in certain places, more concealed in others, but we feel it to be always present. Because all the expressions contained in the Pentateuch are the commandments of God, sealed, so to speak, with his direct guarantee, from this origin they all derive an extraordinary prestige that renders them sacrosanct. Thus when they are violated the public conscience is not content with mere reparation, but insists upon an expiation, one of vengeance. Since what is peculiar to the nature of the penal law is the extraordinary authority of the rules that it sanctions, and since men have never known or imagined any higher authority than that which the believer attributes to his God, a law deemed to be the word of God Himself cannot fail to be essentially repressive. We could even say that every penal law is more or less religious, for what lies at its heart is the feeling of respect for a force superior to that of the individual, for a power in some way transcendental, regardless of the particular symbol whereby it impinges upon the consciousness, and this sentiment is at the basis of all religious feeling. This is why, in a general fashion, repression dominates the entire corpus of law in lower societies: it is because religion permeates all legal activity, just as, moreover, it does all social life.

Thus this characteristic is still very marked in the laws of Manou. We have only to see the prominent place that the laws assign to criminal justice among national institutions as a whole: 'To help the king in his functions,' states Manou, 'the Lord produced from the very beginning the genius of punishment, protector of all beings, the executant of justice, his own son, and whose essence is wholly divine. It is the fear of punishment which allows all creatures, whether they move or are immovable, to enjoy what is their own, and which prevents them from straying from their duties. ... Punishment governs the human race, punishment protects it; punishment remains on watch whilst all else is sleeping; punishment is justice, say the wise. ... All classes would become corrupt, all barriers would be overtoppled, the universe would be mere chaos, if punishment no longer performed its duty.'[16]

The Law of the Twelve Tables already relates to a society much more advanced[17] and closer to us than was the Hebrew people. What proves this is that Roman society did not arrive at the type of the city until it had passed through the type in which Jewish society had remained static, and had gone beyond it. We shall have proof of this later.[18] Other facts also bear witness to this lesser distance from us. Firstly, in the Law of the Twelve Tables we find in embryonic form the main elements of our present body of law, whereas there is nothing in common, so to speak, between Hebraic law and our own.[19] Secondly, the Law of the Twelve Tables is completely secular. If in primitive Rome lawgivers such as Numa Pompilius were held to receive their inspiration from the divinity, and if in consequence law and religion were then closely intermingled, at the time when the Twelve Tables were drawn up this alliance had certainly ceased, for this legal monument was presented from the beginning as an entirely human edifice intended to cover only human relationships. We find in it only a few clauses relating to religious ceremonies, and even these seem to have been admitted because they were sumptuary laws. Now a more or less complete state of dissociation existing between legal and religious elements is one of the best indicators for discovering whether one society is more, or less, developed than another.[20]

Thus criminal law no longer arrogates to itself the whole field. Rules reinforced by punishments and those that carry only restitutory sanctions are by this time clearly distinguished from each other. Restitutory law has disentangled itself from repressive law, which in the beginning subsumed it completely. It now possesses its own characteristics, its particular constitution and individuality. It exists as a distinct legal species, equipped with its own special bodies and procedures. Co-operative law itself makes its appearance: in the Twelve Tables are to be found both domestic and contractual law.

Yet if penal law has lost its original preponderancy, its share of the whole remains large. Of the 115 fragments of that law that Voigt succeeded in reconstituting, only 66 can be attributed to restitutory law, and 49 are strongly penal in nature.[21] Consequently penal law is not far from representing half of that Code as it has come down to us. Yet what remains of it can only provide us with a very incomplete picture of the importance of repressive law at the time when it was drawn up, for it is those parts that concerned this kind of law which have probably been most easily lost. It is to the jurisconsults of the classical era that, almost exclusively, we owe the fragments that have been preserved for us. Yet the jurisconsults were much more interested in problems of civil law than in questions relating to the criminal law. The latter hardly lends itself to the splendid controversies that in every age have stirred the passions of lawyers. The general indifference shown towards it must have had the effect of consigning to oblivion a large part of the ancient penal law of Rome. Moreover, even the authentic, complete text of the Law of the Twelve Tables certainly did not wholly comprise all that law. Thus it did not speak of religious and domestic crimes, which were both tried in special courts, nor of offences against morals. Finally, we must allow for the reluctance, so to say, of the penal law, in becoming codified. Since it is engraved on the consciousness of each one, no need is felt to write it down in order to make it known. For all such reasons, we may rightly presume that, even in fourth-century Rome, penal law still represented the larger part of juridical rules.

This preponderance is even much more certain and much more marked if it is compared not to the whole of restitutory law, but only to that part of the law that corresponds to organic solidarity. Indeed at that time there existed hardly anything other than domestic law, the organisation of which was already fairly advanced. Procedure, although irksome, is not varied or complicated. Contractual law is only just beginning: 'The small number of contracts recognized in ancient law,' says Voigt, 'is in striking contrast to the host of obligations that arise from criminal offences.'[22] As for public law, besides the fact that it is still fairly simple, it has for the most part a penal character, because it has retained its religious character.

From this time on repressive law did not cease to diminish in relative importance. On the one hand, even presuming that it had not regressed on a great number of points, and that many acts originally regarded as criminal had not gradually ceased to be repressed, and the contrary is certainly the case for religious offences, at least repressive law did not perceptibly increase. We know that from the era of the Twelve Tables the principal criminological types of Roman law were constituted. On the other hand, contractual law, procedure and public law did not cease increasingly to expand. As time passes, we see the rare and scrappy formulas concerning these different points, which were contained in the Twelve Tables, continually developing and multiplying until they become the gigantic systems of the classical era. Domestic law itself grows more complex and diverse, as praetorian law is gradually added to the primitive form of civil law.

This history of Christian societies affords yet another example of the same phenomenon. Already Sumner Maine had conjectured that by comparing with one another the different laws of the barbarians one would discover that the prominence given to penal law would be the greater the more ancient it was.[23] The facts bear out this proposition.

Salic law relates to a society less developed than fourth-century Rome. For if, like the latter, it had already gone beyond the social type at which the Hebrew people had stopped, it was, however, less completely separated from it. As we shall show later, its traces are much more apparent. Thus penal law was of much greater importance in it. Of the 293 articles that make up the text of the Salic law, as published by Waitz,[24] there are scarcely 25 (roughly 9 per cent) that are not repressive in nature. These are those that relate to the constitution of the Frankish family.[25] Contractual is not entirely separated from penal law, for a refusal to honour an agreement entered into on the appointed day gives rise to a fine. But the Salic law comprises only part of the penal law of the Franks, since it concerns solely crimes and offences in which settlements can be made. Now there were certainly some of these that could not be redeemed in this way. If one reflects that the *Lex* contains not a word about crimes against the state, nor about military crimes, or those against religion, then the preponderance of repressive law will appear even more considerable.[26]

It is already less in Burgundian law, which is more recent. Of 311 articles, we have counted 98 – roughly one-third – that present no penal character. But any increase relates solely to domestic law, which has become more complicated, both in the law concerning things and that concerning persons. Contractual law is not much more developed than it was in Salic law.

Finally, the law of the Visigoths, of even more recent date, that relates to an even more cultured people, attests to further progress in the same direction. Although penal law is still predominant, restitutory law has almost equal importance. Indeed we find an entire code of procedure (Books I and II), a matrimonial law and a domestic law, which are already very advanced (Book III, titles I and VI; Book IV). Lastly, for the first time a whole book, the fifth, is devoted to transactions.

The lack of codification does not permit us to observe with the same accuracy this dual development as it proceeds over the whole of our history. But it is indisputable that it continued in the same direction. Indeed, from this time onwards the legal calendar of crimes and offences is already very comprehensive. By contrast, domestic law, contractual law, procedural and public law have continued to develop uninterruptedly, and it is in this way that finally the two parts of the law that we are comparing are found to have been reversed.

Repressive and co-operative law thus vary exactly as was predicted in the theory, which is therefore confirmed. It is true that this predominance of penal law in lower societies has sometimes been attributed to a different cause. It has been explained, 'by the violence habitual to the communities which for the first time reduced their laws to writing. The legislator, it is said, proportioned the divisions of his work to the frequency of a certain class of incidents in barbarian life.'[27] Sumner Maine, who reports this explanation, finds it incomplete; in reality it is not only incomplete, it is false. First of all, it makes law out to be an artificial creation of the lawgiver, since it is deemed to have been instituted to counter public morals and react against them. Such a conception is today no longer tenable. Law is the expression of morals, and if it reacts against them it is with a strength that has been borrowed from them. Where acts of violence are frequent, they are tolerated. Their criminal character is in inverse proportion to their frequency. Thus with the lower peoples, crimes against the person are more usual than in our civilised societies. Accordingly, they are placed on the lowest rung of the penal ladder. It may almost be stated that physical attacks are the more severely punished the rarer they are. Moreover, what causes such a plethora of primitive penal laws is not because today our crimes are subject to more extensive regulation, but because there existed an abundant growth of crime peculiar to those societies, and which cannot be accounted for by their alleged violence: offences against religious faith, against ritual and ceremonial, against traditions of every kind, etc. The real reason for the development of repressive measures is therefore that at that time the evolution of the collective consciousness was both widespread and strong, whilst the division of labour had not yet taken place.

Now that we have laid down these principles, the conclusion will appear self-evident.

Notes

1. Von Humboldt, *Neuspanien*, vol. I, p. 116.
2. Waitz, *Anthropologie der Naturvölker*, vol. I, pp. 75–6.
3. G. Lebon, *Les sociétés*, p. 193.
4. Topinard, *Anthropologie*, p. 393.
5. Waitz, *Anthropologie*, p. 77. Cf. also p. 446.
6. Tarde, *Lois de l'imitation*, p. 19.
7. Hale, *Ethnography and Philology of the United States* (Philadelphia, 1846) p. 13.
8. This is the cause of Tarde's statement: 'The traveller who crosses several European countries observes more dissimilarities between the common people who have remained faithful to their old customs than between persons of the upper classes' (*Lois de l'imitation*, p. 59).
9. Perrier, *Transformisme*, p. 235.
10. Cf. *infra*, Book II, Chapters II and III. What we say there may serve both to explain and confirm the facts we are establishing here.
11. J. Lubbock, *The Origin of Civilization* (London, 1870) pp. 302–3. Cf. also H. Spencer, *Principles of Sociology* (London, 1855) p. 435.
12. We need not make a judgement about the real antiquity of these works – it is sufficient for us that they relate to a society of a much lower type – nor about the relative age of each section of them, since, from the viewpoint with which we are at present concerned, they are all appreciably of the same character. Thus we are considering them as a whole.
13. The total number of these verses is 135, which excludes those that deal with official functions.
14. Leviticus 24: 17, 18, 20 (NEB).

15. Cf. Munck, *Palestine*, p. 216. Selden, *De Sunedriis*, pp. 809–903, following Maïmonides, lists all the precepts that fall into this category.
16. *Lois de Manou*, trans. by Loiseleur, Vol. VII, pp. 14–24.
17. In stating that one social type is more advanced than another, we do not mean that the different types of society are set out in gradations according to the same ascending linear series, in variable steepness depending upon the historical period. On the contrary, it is certain that if it were possible to draw up the complete genealogical table of social types, it would have rather the shape of a bushy tree, doubtless with a single trunk, but with diverging branches. Yet, despite such a configuration, the distance between two types is measurable, because of their varying height. We are especially justified in asserting that one type is superior to another if it began by taking on the form of the latter but then overtaking it. It is certainly the case that it belongs to a branch or a bough that is higher.
18. Cf. *infra*, Chapter VI, § II.
19. The laws relating to contracts, wills, guardianship, adoption, etc. are unknown in the Pentateuch.
20. Cf. Walter, § 1 and 2; Voigt, *Die XII Tafeln*, vol. I, p. 43.
21. Ten sumptuary laws do not expressly mention any sanction, but their penal character is beyond question.
22. Voigt, vol. II, p. 448.
23. Sumner Maine, p. 347.
24. Waitz, *Das alte Recht der Salischen Franken* (Kiel, 1846).
25. Ibid., titles XLIV, XLV, XLVI, LIX, LX, LXII.
26. Cf. Thonissen, *Procédure de la loi salique*, p. 244.
27. Sumner Maine, p. 348.

Chapter V

The Increasing Preponderance of Organic Solidarity and its Consequences

One needs only cast an eye over our legal codes to confirm the much diminished position occupied in them by repressive law in comparison with co-operative law. What price the former beside that vast system made up of domestic law, contractual law, commercial law, etc.? All of those relationships that are subject to penal measures thus represent only the merest fraction of social life in general. Consequently the ties binding us to society, which spring from a commonality of beliefs and sentiments, are much fewer than those that result from the division of labour.

As we have already remarked, it is true that the common consciousness and the solidarity it engenders do not reach their fullest expression in penal law. The common consciousness creates bonds other than those whose breaking it represses. There are weaker or less precise states of the common consciousness that make their effect felt through morals and public opinion, without any legal sanction being attached to them, and which nevertheless contribute to ensuring social cohesion. Yet co-operative law does not fully express either all the ties forged by the division of labour, for it affords us also only a sketchy representation of this entire area of social life. In a host of cases, the relationships of mutual interdependence that unite functions that are divided are merely regulated by usage, and these unwritten rules certainly exceed in number those serving as an extension of repressive law, for they must be as diverse as the social functions themselves. The relationship between both is thus the same as that of the two types of law that they supplement. Consequently we can leave them out of the reckoning without the sum total being changed.

However, if we had only discovered this relationship in our present-day societies, at the exact moment in their history at which we have now arrived, we might ask whether it could not be ascribed to temporary causes that perhaps were even pathological. Yet we have just seen that the more a social type is comparable to our own, the more co-operative law predominates. On the other hand, penal law looms correspondingly larger the farther we get away from our present social organisation. Thus this phenomenon is linked not to some accidental cause which is more or less pathological, but to what is most vital in the structure of our societies, since it becomes ever more prominent as social structure becomes more marked. So the law we established in the preceding chapter proves doubly useful to us. Besides confirming the principles on which our conclusion is based, it enables us to establish its universality.

Nevertheless, from this one comparison alone we can still not deduce what is the contribution of that organic solidarity to the general cohesiveness of society. In fact, what causes the individual to be more or less closely linked to his group is not only the larger or smaller number of ties that bind him to it, but also the varying intensity of the forces that attach him. It may then be that the bonds resulting from the division of labour, although more numerous, are weaker than the rest, and that the greater strength of the latter makes up for their numerical inferiority. But it is the opposite that is true.

In fact, the measure of the relative strength of two social ties is the different ease with which they may be broken. The less resistant is plainly the one that snaps under the slightest pressure. Now it is in lower societies, where solidarity through similarities is the only, or almost the only one, where these breaks are the most frequent and the easiest. Spencer says that:

> At first, however, though it is necessary to join some group, it is not necessary to continue in the same group. When oppressed by their chief, Kalmucks and Mongols desert him and go over to other chiefs. Of the Abipones Dobrizhoffer says: 'Without leave asked on their part, or displeasure evinced on his, they remove with their families whithersoever it suits them, and join some other cacique.'[1]

In Southern Africa the Balondas are continually moving from one part of the country to another. MacCulloch has noted the same phenomenon with the Koukis. With the Teutons any man who had a liking for war could become a soldier under the chief of his choice. Nothing, he notes, was more common or seemed more legitimate. A man would stand up in the midst of an assembly and announce that he was going to mount an expedition to such and such a place, against such and such an enemy. Those who gave him their confidence and who were after booty acclaimed him as their chief and followed him. The social bond was too weak to hold men back in spite of themselves, weighed against the temptations of the nomadic life and of gain.[2] Waitz says generally about lower societies that even where the power of a leader is established, every individual preserves enough independence to part company with his chief at any moment, 'and to rise up against him, if he is powerful enough to do so, without such an action being held criminal.'[3] Even when the form of government is despotic, the same author declares, everyone is always free to secede from it with his family. Might not the rule whereby the Roman, made prisoner by his enemies, ceased to be part of the city, also be explained by the ease with which the social tie could then be broken?

Things are entirely different as labour becomes divided up. The different parts of the aggregate, since they fulfil different functions, cannot be easily separated. Spencer says that:

> Middlesex separated from its surroundings would in a few days have all its social processes stopped by lack of supplies. Cut off the cotton-district from Liverpool and other ports, and there would come arrest of its industry followed by mortality of its people. Let a division be made between the coal-mining popula-tions and adjacent populations which smelt metals or make broadcloth by machinery, and both, forthwith dying socially by arrest of their actions, would begin to die individually. Though when a civilized society is so divided that part of it is left without a central controlling agency, it may presently evolve one; yet there is meanwhile much risk of dissolution, and before re-organisation is tolerably efficient, a long period of disorder and weakness must be passed through.[4]

This is why violent annexations, formerly so frequent, become increasingly delicate operations, of doubtful success. It is because nowadays the tearing away of a province from a country is to cut away one or several organs from the organism. Life in the annexed region is deeply disturbed, separated as it is from the essential organs on which it depended. Such acts of mutilation and such disturbance necessarily provoke lasting wounds whose memory does not fade. Even for the isolated individual it is no easy matter to change nationality, despite the greater similarity between different civilisations.[5]

The converse experience would be equally conclusive. The weaker solidarity is, that is, the slacker the thread that links society together, the easier it must be for foreign elements to be incorporated into societies. Now, with the lower peoples naturalisation is the easiest thing in the world. Among North American Indians every member of the clan has the right to introduce new members into it by the process of adoption. 'Captives taken in war were either put to death, or adopted into some *gens*. Women and children taken prisoners usually experienced clemency in this form. Adoption not only conferred gentile rights, but also the nationality of the tribe.'[6] We know how easily Rome originally granted citizenship to those lacking any place of refuge and to the peoples that it conquered.[7] Moreover, it was by incorporations of this kind that primitive societies increased in number. To be so easily penetrated, they had not to possess too strong a feeling of their unity and personality.[8] The opposite phenomenon can be observed where functions have become specialised. Undoubtedly the foreigner can temporarily insert himself into a society, but the process by which he is assimilated, that is, that of naturalisation, becomes long drawn-out and complex. It is no longer possible without the assent of the group, made manifest with due solemnity, and subjected to special conditions.[9]

It may seem astonishing that a tie which binds the individual to the community to the extent that it absorbs him within it can be broken or forged with such ease. But what causes the solidity of the social link is not what makes it a force of resistance. Despite the fact that the parts of the whole, when united, act only in concert, it does not follow that they must either remain united or perish. The exact opposite is the case, since they do not need one another, and since each one contains within itself the whole of social life, it may remove itself elsewhere, the more easily because such acts of secession are generally made in groups. The individual is so constituted that he can only move as a group, even when separating himself from the original group. Society, for its part, certainly requires from each of its members, so long as they remain part of it, a uniformity of beliefs and practices. Yet, since it can lose a certain number of those subjected to it without its internal functioning being disturbed, because labour in society is not greatly divided up, it does not come out strongly against such reductions in its number. Likewise, where solidarity merely arises from similarities, the person who does not deviate unduly from the collective type is incorporated without resistance into the whole. There are no grounds for rejecting him and, if there is room, there are even reasons to attract him. But where society constitutes a system of differentiated parts complementary to one another, new elements cannot be grafted on to the old ones without disturbing their harmony and changing these relationships. Consequently the organism resists intrusions that cannot occur without upsetting its balance.

II

Not only does mechanical solidarity generally bind men together less strongly than does organic solidarity, but, as we mount the scale of social evolution, it becomes increasingly looser.

In fact the strength of the social bonds that derive from this origin varies in accordance with the following three conditions:

(1) The relationship between the extent of the common consciousness and that of the individual consciousness. The social bonds are stronger the more completely the former overlaps with the latter.

(2) The average intensity of the states of collective consciousness. The relationship between the extent of the common and individual consciousness assumed to be equal, the degree of intensity has more effect upon the individual the more energy it possesses. If, on the other hand, that intensity radiates only feebly, its capacity to steer the individual in a collective direction can only be feeble. Thus the more easily will he be able to go his own way, and solidarity will be less strong.

(3) The degree of determinateness of these same states. Indeed the more beliefs and practices are clear-cut, the less room they allow for individual divergences. They act as uniform moulds in which we all cast, in a uniform fashion, our ideas and actions. *Consensus* is

therefore as perfect as possible; every consciousness beats as one. Conversely, the more general and indeterminate the rules of conduct and thought, the more individual reflection must intervene in applying the rules to particular cases. But such reflective thinking cannot be aroused without disagreements breaking out. As it varies in quality and quantity from one man to another, all that it generates is of this character. Centrifugal tendencies thus continue to multiply at the expense of social cohesion and harmony in the workings of society.

On the other hand, strong, well-defined states of the common consciousness are at the root of penal law. We shall see that such states are fewer today than in the past, and the number progressively decreases the more societies approximate to our present type. Thus this is because the average intensity and degree of determinateness of the collective states have themselves diminished. To be sure, we cannot conclude from this fact that the overall area of the common consciousness has grown smaller in size, for it may be that the sector to which penal law corresponds has diminished and that the rest, on the contrary, has swollen in size. There can be less strong, well-defined states, and on the other hand, a greater number of others. But this growth, if it is real, is at the very most the equivalent of what has occurred in the individual consciousness, for at least this has grown, in the same proportion, correspondingly bigger. If there are more matters common to all, there are also many more that are personal to each individual. Indeed there are even grounds for believing that the latter have increased more than the others, for the dissimilarities among men have become more pronounced the more cultured they have become. We have just seen that specialised activities have developed more than the common consciousness. Thus it is at least probable that within each individual consciousness the personal sphere has become much larger than the other. In any case, the relationship between them has at the very most remained the same. As a result, from this viewpoint mechanical solidarity has gained nothing, even supposing that it has lost nothing either. On the other hand, if we therefore establish that the collective consciousness has become weaker and vaguer, we can rest assured that a weakening in this solidarity has occurred, since, of the three conditions on which its power of action depends, at least two lose some of their force, whilst the third remains unchanged.

TABLE V.1   *Rules forbidding acts contrary to the sentiments of the collectivity*

I
Serving general purposes

Religious sentiments	Positive (stipulating the practice of religion)
	Negative[10] – relating to beliefs concerning
	    the divine
	    concerning worship
	    concerning the instruments of
	    worship (sanctuary, priests)

National sentiments	Positive (affirmative civil obligations) Negative (treason, civil war, etc.)
Domestic sentiments	Positive: (a) paternal and filial (b) conjugal (c) relating to kinship in general Negative: the same as above
Sentiments concerning sexual relationships	forbidden unions: { incest – sodomy – improper alliances prostitution public decency decency of behaviour towards minors
Sentiments concerning work	mendicancy vagrancy drunkenness[11] penal rules for work

Various traditional sentiments	relating to: certain vocational practices
	          burial
	          food
	          dress
	          ceremonial
	          practices of all kinds

Sentiments relating to the organ of the common consciousness	In so far as they are directly offended { high treason plots against legitimate authority flagrant insults offering violence to authority – rebellion Indirectly[12] { encroachment by individuals upon official functions – usurpation – public falsification abuse of authority by officials and various offences relating to a profession frauds against the state acts of disobedience of every kind (administrative breaches of regulations)

		II

Serving individual purposes

Sentiments concerning the person of the individual	murder – wounding – suicide	
	individual freedom	physical / moral (pressure exerted through exercise of civil rights)
	honour	insults, slander, libel / false witness
Sentiments concerning individual possessions		theft – swindling, breach of confidence / various types of fraud
Sentiments concerning individuals in general, either in relation to their persons or their possessions		counterfeiting – bankruptcy / fire / brigandage – pillage / public health

To demonstrate this it would be no use for us to compare the number of rules entailing repressive sanctions in the different social types, for the number does not vary in exact proportion to the number of sentiments that the rules represent. Indeed the same sentiment can be offended in several different ways, and thus give rise to several different rules without becoming diversified as a result. Because there are now more ways in which property may be acquired, there are likewise more categories of theft. But the sentiment of respect for the property of others has not grown in consequence. Because the individual personality has developed and comprises more facets, there are more possible assaults that can be made upon it. But the sentiment that these offend remains unchanged. Thus we need, not to count the number of rules, but to group them into classes and sub-classes, depending on whether they relate to the same sentiment or to different ones, or to different varieties of the same sentiment. In this way we shall build up criminological types and their essential variations, the number of which is necessarily equal to the strong, well-defined states of the common consciousness. The more numerous the latter, the more also the number of species of crime and, as a result, the variations of the one reflect exactly those of the others. To crystallise these ideas we have incorporated in the table above [Table V.1] the main types and the main varieties which have been identified in the different kinds of societies. Very clearly such a classification cannot be very complete, nor perfectly rigorous. Yet for the conclusions we are seeking to draw, it is more than sufficient and precise. Indeed it certainly includes all the present criminological types; we run the risk only of having omitted some of those that have disappeared. However, since we do in fact wish to show that their number has decreased, these omissions would provide merely one more argument in support of our proposition.

III

It suffices to cast a glance over this table to recognise that a large number of criminological types have gradually disappeared.

Nowadays the regulation of domestic life has almost entirely lost every trace of its penal character. We have only to except the prohibitions on adultery and bigamy. Even so, in the list of modern crimes adultery occupies a very exceptional place, since a husband has the right to remit the punishment from a wife who has been sentenced for it. As for the duties of other members of the family, no longer does any repressive sanction attach to them. Formerly this was not the case. The Ten Commandments impose a social obligation upon filial piety. Thus to strike one's parents,[13] to curse them,[14] or to disobey one's father[15] was punished by death.

In the Athenian city which, although belonging to the same type as the Roman city, nevertheless represents a more primitive variety of it, legislation upon this matter possessed the same character. Failure to observe family duties gave rise to a special charge, the γραφή παχώσεωζ: 'Those who misused or insulted their parents or those of their lineage, and who did not provide them with the means of subsistence they required, nor obtain for them funeral rites consonant with the dignity of their families . . . might be prosecuted on a charge of γραφή παχώσεωζ.'[16] The duties of relatives towards an orphan child, whether boy or girl, had attached to them actions of the same kind. However, the appreciably less severe punishments applied to these crimes demonstrate that the sentiments to which they corresponded had not the same force or specificity in Athens as they had in Judea.[17]

Finally, in Rome there is apparent a further, even more marked deterioration. The sole family obligations written into the penal law are those that bind the freed client slave to his master and vice versa.[18] As for other domestic misdemeanours, they are punished only by disciplinary measures taken by the father in the household. Certainly the authority he commands allows him to punish them severely. Yet when he exercises his power in this way it is not as a public official or magistrate entrusted with the task of enforcing respect among his household for the general law of the state, but rather does he act as an individual.[19] These kinds of breaches of the law thus tend to become purely private matters, ones in which society has no interest. Thus domestic sentiments gradually move out of the central domain of the common consciousness.[20]

Sentiments dealing with the relationships between the sexes have also evolved in the same way. In the Pentateuch breaches of morals occupy a prominent place. A large number of acts that our legislation today no longer represses are treated as crimes: the debauching of the betrothed of another (Deuteronomy 22:23–7), sexual relations with a slave (Leviticus 19:20–2), the girl who upon marriage fraudulently passes herself off as a virgin (Deuteronomy 22:13–21), sodomy (Leviticus 18:22), bestiality (Exodus 22:19), prostitution (Leviticus 19:29) and more particularly the prostitution of the daughters of priests (Leviticus 21:19), incest – and Leviticus (Chapter 17) records no less than seventeen cases of incest. In addition, all these crimes are subject to very severe punishments – in most cases death. Already in Athenian law they are fewer in number: it merely visits punishment upon pederasty for gain, pimping, relations with an honourable female citizen outside marriage and, finally, incest, although we are poorly informed as to what constitutes an incestuous act. The punishments, moreover, were generally less harsh. In the Roman city the position is roughly the same, although the whole scope of this legislation is more vague. It may be said to have lost its prominence. 'Pederasty in the primitive city,' says Rein, 'without being specified in the law, was punished by the people, the censors of morals or the head of the family, by death, by a fine, or by public disgrace.'[21] The same was roughly the case also for the crime of 'stuprum', or an illicit relationship with a married woman. A father had the right to punish his daughter. The people punished by a fine or exile the same crime when the charge was brought by the municipal magistrates.[22] It certainly appears that the repression of these offences was already partly a domestic and private matter. Finally, nowadays these sentiments are no longer reflected in the penal law save in two cases: when they are publicly outraged or in the person of a minor who is incapable of defending himself.[23]

The category of penal rules we have designated under the heading *various traditions* really represents a host of different criminological types, corresponding to different collective sentiments. Progressively these have all, or almost all, disappeared. In simple societies, where tradition is all-powerful and where almost everything is held in common, the most puerile customs become categorical duties from force of habit. In Tonkin there are a very large number of breaches of convention that are more seriously punished than grave attacks upon society.[24] In China the doctor who has not written out his prescription in the set manner is punished.[25] The Pentateuch is full of rules of the same kind. This is to leave out a very large number of semi-religious practices whose origin is clearly historical and whose whole strength derives from tradition: food,[26] dress,[27] and a host of details relating to economic life are subject in the Book to very extensive regulation.[28] Up to a certain point the same held good for the Greek cities. 'The State,' declares Fustel de Coulanges, 'exercised its tyranny even in most minor matters. At Locres the law prohibited men from drinking unadulterated wine. It was usual for dress invariably to be prescribed by the laws of each city. Spartan legislation regulated the coiffure of females, and that of Athens forbade them to take more than three dresses when going on a journey. In Rhodes the law forbade the shaving off of the beard. In Byzantium it punished by a fine anyone who possessed a razor in his home. On the other hand, in Sparta it required the moustache to be shaved off.'[29] But the number of all such offences is already much diminished. In Rome hardly any are cited save some relating to a few sumptuary regulations regarding women. Nowadays it would be difficult, I believe, to discover any at all in our law.

But the most considerable loss from the penal code is the one due to the total – or almost total – disappearance of religious crimes. Thus here is a whole host of sentiments that have ceased to be counted among the strong and well-defined states of the common consciousness. Certainly, if we content ourselves with comparing our legislation under this heading with that of lower types of society taken as a whole, this regression appears so marked that we may well doubt whether it is normal and lasting. Yet when we follow closely the development of the facts, we perceive that this elimination has occurred regularly and progressively. We see it becoming ever more absolute as one social type evolves into another, and consequently it cannot be due to a temporary or random occurrence.

It would be impossible to list all the religious crimes that the Pentateuch delineates and represses. The Jews had to obey all the commandments of the law under threat of annihilation. 'He shall be cut off from his people because he has brought the word of the Lord into contempt and violated his command.'[30] In this matter he was not only obliged to do nothing that was forbidden, but also to do all that was prescribed, to submit himself and his family to circumcision, to keep the Sabbath and feast-days, etc. There is no need for us to recall how numerous such prescriptions were and with what terrible punishments they were invested.

In Athens, the place occupied by religious crimes was still very prominent. There was a special charge, the γραφὴ ασεδείας, designed to prosecute attacks upon the national religion. Its scope was certainly very extensive. 'According to all appearances, Attic law had not precisely defined the crimes and offences which were to be qualified as ασέδεία, with the result that much was left to the judge's discretion.'[31] However, the list of such crimes was certainly less lengthy than in Hebrew law. Moreover, they were all, or almost all, crimes of commission, rather than of refraining from action. The main ones cited are in fact the following: the denial of beliefs concerning the gods, their existence, and their role in human affairs; the profanation of festivals, sacrifices, games, temples and altars; the violation of the right of asylum, the failure to observe duties towards the dead, the omission or modification of ritual practices by the priest, the act of initiating lay persons into the secret of the mysteries, or of uprooting the sacred olive-trees, the entering of temples by those to whom access was prohibited.[32] Thus crime consisted not in failure to celebrate the cult, but in disturbing it by positive actions or words.[33] Finally, it has not been proved that the introduction of new divinities regularly required authorisation or was treated as impiety, although this charge could be so stretched naturally that it could occasionally have been brought in this case.[34] Moreover, it is clear that the religious consciousness was destined to be less intolerant in the homeland of the Sophists and Socrates than in a theocratic society such as that of the Jews. For philosophy to take root there and develop, traditional beliefs had not to be so strong as to prevent it from flourishing.

At Rome such beliefs weigh even less heavily upon the consciousness of individuals. Fustel de Coulanges has in point of fact emphasised the religious character of Roman society. Yet, compared with earlier peoples, the Roman state was much less imbued with religious feeling.[35] Political functions, which were separated very early on from religious functions, made these subordinate to them. 'Thanks to this preponderance of the political principle and the political character of the Roman religion the State only lent its support to religion in so far as the attacks against religion were indirectly a threat to itself. The religious beliefs of foreign states or of foreigners living within the Roman empire were tolerated, if they were kept within bounds and did not impinge too closely upon the State.'[36] But the state intervened if its citizens turned to foreign gods and consequently harmed the national religion. 'However, this matter was treated less as a question of law than as a concern of higher administration. One intervened against these acts as circumstances required, by edicts warning against or prohibiting them, or by punishments which could even extend to the death penalty.'[37] Religious trials certainly did not have so much importance in the criminal justice of Rome as of Athens. We do not find any juridical institution analogous to that of the γραφή ασεδείαζ.

Not only are crimes against religion more clearly determined and less numerous, but many of them have been downgraded by one or several degrees. In fact the Romans did not place them all on the same level, but distinguished *scelera expiabilia* from *scelera inexpiabilia*. The former only required an expiation consisting of a sacrifice offered to the gods.[38] Doubtless this sacrifice was a punishment, in the sense that the state could insist upon it being performed, since the taint that had blemished the guilty party contaminated society and ran the risk of drawing down upon it the wrath of the gods. However, it was a punishment of an entirely different nature than the death penalty, confiscation of property, or exile, etc. Such errors, which were so easily purged, were the same as those that the law of Athens had repressed with the greatest severity. They were:

(1) The profaning of any *locus sacer*.
(2) The profaning of any *locus religiosus*.
(3) Divorce, in the case of marriage *per confarreationem*.
(4) The sale of a son by such a marriage.

(5) The exposure of a dead person to the sun's rays.

(6) The commission, even with no evil intent, of any one of the *scelera inexpiabilia.*

In Athens the profaning of temples, the slightest disturbance of religious ceremonies, occasionally even the smallest infringement of ritual,[39] were subject to the supreme punishment.

In Rome there were no real punishments save those meted out for offences that were both grave and intentional. The sole *scelera inexpiabilia* were in fact the following:

(1) Any intentional failure by public officials in their duty to consult the auguries or to perform the *sacra*, or indeed the profanation of the *sacra*.

(2) Action by a magistrate to carry out a *legis actio* on a forbidden day, and this intentionally.

(3) the intentional profaning of the *feriae* by actions that were prohibited in such cases.

(4) Incest committed by a vestal virgin or with another vestal virgin.[40]

Christianity has often been reproached for its intolerance. However, in this respect it made a considerable advance over earlier religions. The religious consciousness in Christian societies, even when faith was at its zenith, only incited a penal reaction when a revolt against it consisted of some striking action, or when it was denied or attacked head-on. Separated from temporal existence much more completely than it was even in Rome, it could no longer impose its will with the same authority and had to confine itself much more to a defensive attitude. It no longer demanded repression for infringement of minutiae such as those just alluded to, but only when it was threatened on one of its basic principles. The number of these is not very great, for faith, as it became more spiritual, general and abstract, at the same time became more simple. Sacrilege, of which blasphemy is only one variation, heresy in its different forms – these are henceforth the sole religious crimes.[41] Thus the list continues to grow shorter, thereby attesting to the fact that the strong, well-defined sentiments are becoming fewer. Moreover, how could it be otherwise? Everyone would acknowledge that the Christian religion is the most idealistic that has ever existed. Thus it is made up of very broad and very general articles of faith much more than of special beliefs and well-determined practices. This explains how it came about that the birth of free thinking within the Christian religion took place relatively early on. From its origins different schools of thought and even opposing sects were established. Christian societies had hardly begun to organise in the Middle Ages when scholasticism made its appearance, the first methodical attempt at reflective thinking, the first source of dissent. The rights of discussion are acknowledged in principle. We need not demonstrate that since then this movement has continued to grow stronger. Thus religious criminality ended up by disengaging itself completely, or almost completely, from the penal law.

IV

Thus there are a number of varieties of crime that have progressively disappeared, without any compensating factor, for no varieties that are absolutely new have arisen. We may forbid begging,[42] but Athens punished idleness. There exist no societies where assaults upon national sentiments or national institutions have ever been tolerated. Indeed repression of such attacks seems formerly to have been even harsher, and consequently there is reason to believe that the corresponding sentiments have grown weaker. The crime of *lèse-majesté*, which once could be interpreted in so many differing ways, is increasingly tending to die out.

However, it has occasionally been alleged that crimes against the person of an individual were not recognised among less-civilised peoples and that theft and murder were even honoured among them. Lombroso has recently attempted to revive this thesis. He maintains 'that crime among savages is not an exception, but the general rule . . . that nobody considers them [theft and murder] as a crime'.[43] But in support of this statement he cites only a few sparse and equivocal facts which he interprets uncritically. Thus he is reduced to identifying theft with the practice of communism or international brigandry.[44] Now, although property may not be shared out among all the members of the group, it does not follow at all that the right to theft is acknowledged. There cannot eyen be thieving save to the extent that the institution of property exists.[45] Likewise, because a society does not find pillaging at the expense of neighbouring nations to be abhorrent, we cannot conclude that it tolerates the same practice in its internal relations and does not protect its citizens from one another. So it is the absence of punishment for internal brigandry that must be established. It is true that there is a text of Diodorus and another of Aulus Gellus[46] that might lead us to believe that such licence was permitted in ancient Egypt. But these texts are contradicted by everything that we know about Egyptian civilisation. Thonissen states very aptly, 'How can tolerance of theft be allowed in a country where . . . laws imposed the death penalty upon the person who lived upon his illicit gains, and where the mere alteration of weights and measures was punished by the cutting off of both hands?'[47] By a series of conjectures[48] we can seek to reconstitute the facts, which writers have reported inaccurately, although the inexactness of their account is unquestionable.

As for the acts of homicide that Lombroso refers to, these are always perpetrated in exceptional circumstances. Sometimes they are acts of war, sometimes religious sacrifices, or the result of the absolute power exercised either by a barbaric despot over his subjects, or by a father over his children. What would require to be demonstrated is the complete lack of any rules that in principle proscribe murder. Among these particularly exceptional examples not one bears out such a conclusion. The fact that, under special conditions, exceptions are allowed to this rule does not prove that the rule does not exist. Moreover, are not similar exceptions met with even in our contemporary societies? Is the general who dispatches a regiment to certain death in order to save the remainder of his army acting any differently from the priest who offers a victim up in sacrifice in order to assuage the national god? Does not killing take place in war? Does the husband who inflicts death upon his adulterous wife not enjoy, in certain cases, a relative immunity from punishment, even although such immunity is not absolute? The sympathy occasionally manifested towards murderers and thieves is no less instructive. Individuals can admire the bravery of a man without his action being tolerated in principle.

Moreover, the conception that serves as the foundation for this doctrine is a contradiction in terms. It assumes, in fact, that primitive peoples are bereft of all morality. Now, from the first moment when men form together in a society, however rudimentary it may be, there are necessarily rules that govern their relationships, and consequently a morality which, although not resembling our own, nevertheless exists. In addition, if there is a rule common to all these moral codes, it is certainly the one that forbids attacks against the person, for men who are similar to one another cannot live together without each feeling for his fellows a sympathy that revolts against acts of any kind that will bring suffering upon them.[49]

All that is true about the theory is firstly the fact that the laws that protected the person of the individual formerly excluded from their application a part of the population, viz., children and slaves. Secondly, it is legitimate to believe that such protection is now afforded more zealously, and consequently that the collective sentiments that correspond to it have become stronger. But there is nothing in these two facts that invalidates our conclusion. If all the individuals who, in any capacity whatsoever, make up society are today protected to an equal extent, this greater mildness in morality is due, not to the emergence of a penal rule that is really new, but to the extension of the scope of an ancient rule. From the beginning there was a prohibition on attempts to take the life of any member of the group, but children and slaves were excluded from this category. Now that we no longer make such distinctions actions have become punishable that once were not criminal. But this is merely because there are more persons in society, and not because collective sentiments have increased in number. These have not grown, but the object to which they relate has done so. If however there are grounds for conceding that the respect of society for the individual has become stronger, it does not follow that the central area of the common consciousness has grown in size. No new elements have been brought into play, since this sentiment has existed from earliest times and has always been of sufficient strength not to suffer being harmed in any way. The only change that has occurred is that a primitive element has attained greater intensity. But this mere reinforcement cannot compensate for the numerous and severe losses that we have indicated.

Thus on the whole the common consciousness comprises ever fewer strong and well-defined sentiments. This is therefore the case because the average intensity and degree of determinateness of the collective states of feeling continue still to diminish, as we have just stated. Even the very limited increase that we have just observed only confirms this result. Indeed it is very remarkable that the sole collective sentiments that have gained in intensity are those that relate, not to social matters, but to the individual. For this to be so

the individual personality must have become a much more important factor in the life of society. For it to have been able to acquire
such importance it is not enough for the personal consciousness of
each individual to have increased in absolute terms; it must have
increased more than the common consciousness. The personal
consciousness must have thrown off the yoke of the common
consciousness, and consequently the latter must have lost its power
to dominate and that determining action that it exerted from the
beginning. If indeed the relationship between these two elements
had remained unchanged, if both had developed in extent and
vitality in the same proportion, the collective sentiments that relate
to the individual would likewise have remained unchanged. Above
all, they would not have been the sole sentiments to have grown.
This is because they depend solely on the social value of the
individual factor, which in turn is determined not by any absolute
development of that factor, but by the relative size of the share that
falls to him within the totality of social phenomena.

V

This proposition could be verified by utilising a method that we shall
only sketch out briefly.
    At the present time we do not possess any scientific conception of
what religion is. In order to do so we would need to have dealt with
the problem using the same comparative method that we have
applied to the question of crime, and such an attempt has not yet
been made. It has often been stated that at any moment in history
religion has consisted of the set of beliefs and sentiments of every
kind concerning man's links with a being or beings whose nature he
regards as superior to his own. But such a definition is manifestly
inadequate. In fact there are a host of rules of conduct or ways of
thinking that are certainly religious and that, however, apply to
relationships of a totally different kind. Religion prohibits the Jew
from eating certain kinds of meat and lays down that he must dress
in a prescribed fashion. It imposes upon him this or that view
regarding the nature of men and things, and regarding the origin of
the world. Often it regulates legal, moral and economic relationships. Its sphere of action thus extends far beyond man's communication with the divine. We are assured, moreover, that there exists

at least one religion without a god.[50] This single fact alone, were it firmly established, would suffice to demonstrate that we have no right to define religion as a function of the notion of God. Finally, if the extraordinary authority that the believer attributes to the divinity can account for the special prestige attached to everything that is religious, it remains to be explained how men have been led to ascribe such an authority to a being who, on the admission of everybody, is in many, if not all cases, a figment of their imagination. Nothing proceeds from nothing. Thus the force that the being possesses must come from somewhere, and consequently the above formula does not inform us about the essence of the phenomenon.

Yet, setting this element on one side, the sole characteristic that is apparently shared equally by all religious ideas and sentiments is that they are common to a certain number of individuals living together. Moreover, their average intensity is fairly high. Indeed it is invariably the fact that when a somewhat strong conviction is shared by a single community of people it inevitably assumes a religious character. It inspires in the individual consciousness the same reverential respect as religious beliefs proper. Thus it is extremely probable – but this brief outline doubtless cannot constitute a rigorous proof – that likewise religion corresponds to a very central domain of the common consciousness. It is true that such a domain would have to be mapped out, distinguishing it from the area that corresponds to penal law, with which, moreover, it frequently wholly or partly overlaps. These are problems that have to be studied, but whose solution is not directly relevant to the very feasible conjecture we have just made.

Yet if there is one truth that history has incontrovertibly settled, it is that religion extends over an ever diminishing area of social life. Originally, it extended to everything; everything social was religious – the two words were synonymous. Then gradually political, economic and scientific functions broke free from the religious function, becoming separate entities and taking on more and more a markedly temporal character. God, if we may express it in such a way, from being at first present in every human relationship, has progressively withdrawn. He leaves the world to men and their quarrels. At least, if He continues to rule it, it is from on high and afar off, and the effect that He exercises, becoming more general and indeterminate, leaves freer rein for human forces. The individual thus feels, and he is in reality, much less *acted upon*; he becomes more a source of spontaneous activity. In short, not only is the sphere of religion not increasing at the same time as that of the temporal world, nor in the same proportion, but it is continually diminishing. This regression did not begin at any precise moment in history, but one can follow the phases of its development from the very origins of social evolution. It is therefore bound up with the basic conditions for the development of societies and thus demonstrates that there is a constantly decreasing number of beliefs and collective sentiments that are both sufficiently collective and strong enough to assume a religious character. This means that the average intensity of the common consciousness is itself weakening.

This demonstration has one advantage over the previous one: it allows it to be established that the same law of regression applies to the representative element in the common consciousness as it does to the affective element. Through the penal law we can reach only phenomena that relate to the sensibility, whereas religion embraces not only feelings but also ideas and doctrines.

The decrease in the number of proverbs, adages and sayings as societies develop is still further proof that the collective representations are also becoming less determinate.

Among primitive peoples, in fact, maxims of this kind are very numerous. According to Ellis, 'The Ewe-speaking peoples like most races of West Africa, have a large collection of proverbs, one, at least, being provided for almost every circumstance in life; a peculiarity which is common to most peoples who have made but little progress in civilization.'[51]

More advanced societies are only slightly fertile in this way during the preliminary phases of their existence. Later not only are no new proverbs coined, but the old ones gradually fade away, lose their proper meaning, and end up by not being understood at all. This clearly shows that it is above all in lower societies that they are most favoured, and that today they only succeed in maintaining their currency among the lower classes.[52] But a proverb is the concentrated expression of a collective idea or feeling, relating to a determinate class of objects. Beliefs and feelings of this kind cannot even exist without their crystallising in this form. As every thought tends to find the expression that is most adequate for it, if it is common to a certain number of individuals it necessarily ends up by being encapsulated in a formula that is equally common to them all. Any lasting function fashions an organ for itself in its own image.

Thus it is wrong to have adduced our inclination for realism and our scientific outlook to explain the decline in proverbs. In conversational language we do not pay much attention to precision nor so disdain imagery. On the contrary, we relish greatly the old proverbs that we have preserved. Moreover, the image is not an element inherent in a proverb. It is one of the ways – yet not the only one – in which the thought of the collectivity is epitomised. Yet these brief formulas end up by being too constricting to contain the diversity of individual sentiments. Their unity no longer chimes with the divergences that have occurred. Thus they only sustain their existence successfully by taking on a more general meaning, and gradually die out. The organ becomes atrophied because the function is no longer exercised, that is, because there are fewer collective representations sufficiently well-defined to be enclosed within any determinate form.

Thus everything goes to prove that the evolution of the common consciousness proceeds along the lines we have indicated. Very possibly it progresses less than does the individual consciousness. In any case it becomes weaker and vaguer as a whole. The collective type loses some of its prominence, its forms become more abstract and imprecise. Undoubtedly, if this decline were, as we are often inclined to believe, an original product of our most recent civilisation and a unique event in the history of societies, we might ask whether it would last. But in fact it has continued uninterruptedly from earliest times. This is what we set out to demonstrate. Individualism and free thinking are of no recent date, neither from 1789, the Reformation, scholasticism, the collapse of Graeco-Latin polytheism, nor the fall of oriental theocracies. They are a phenomenon that has no fixed starting point but one that has developed unceasingly throughout history. Their development is undoubtedly not linear. The new societies that replace extinct social types never embark on their course at the very spot where the others came to a halt. How could that be possible? What the child continues is not the old age or the years of maturity of his parents, but their own childhood. Thus if we wish to take stock of the course that has been run we must consider successive societies only at the same stage of their existence. We must, for example, compare the Christian societies of the Middle Ages with primitive Rome, and the latter with the original Greek cities, etc. We then find that this progress or, if you like, this regression, has been accomplished, so to speak, without any break in continuity. Thus an iron law exists against which it would be absurd to revolt.

Moreover, this is not to say that the common consciousness is threatened with total disappearance. But it increasingly comprises modes of thinking and feeling of a very general, indeterminate nature, which leave room for an increasing multitude of individual acts of dissent. There is indeed one area in which the common consciousness has grown stronger, becoming more clearly delineated, viz., in its view of the individual. As all the other beliefs and practices assume less and less religious a character, the individual becomes the object of a sort of religion. We carry on the worship of the dignity of the human person, which, like all strong acts of worship, has already acquired its superstitions. If you like, therefore it is indeed a common faith. Yet first of all, it is only possible because of the collapse of other faiths and consequently it cannot engender the same results as that multiplicity of extinct beliefs. There is no compensation. Moreover, if the faith is common because it is shared among the community, it is individual in its object. If it impels every will towards the same end, that end is not a social one. Thus it holds a wholly exceptional position within the collective consciousness. It is indeed from society that it draws all this strength, but it is not to society that it binds us: it is to ourselves. Thus it does not constitute a truly social link. This is why theorists have been justly reproached with effecting the dissolution of society, because they have made this sentiment the exclusive basis for their moral doctrine. We may therefore conclude by affirming that all those social links resulting from similarity are growing progressively weaker.

This law alone suffices to demonstrate the absolute grandeur of the part played by the division of labour. Indeed, since mechanical solidarity is growing ever weaker, social life proper must either diminish or another form of solidarity must emerge gradually to take the place of the one that is disappearing. We have to choose. In vain is it maintained that the collective consciousness is growing and becoming stronger with that of individuals. We have just proved that these two factors vary in inverse proportion to each other. Yet social progress does not consist in a process of continual dissolution – quite the opposite: the more we evolve, the more societies develop a profound feeling of themselves and their unity. Thus there must indeed be some other social link to bring about this result. And there can be no other save that which derives from the division of labour.

If, moreover, we recall that even where it is most resistant, mechanical solidarity does not bind men together with the same strength as does the division of labour, and also that its sphere of action does not embrace most of present-day social phenomena, it will become even more evident that social solidarity is tending to become exclusively organic. It is the division of labour that is increasingly fulfilling the role that once fell to the common consciousness. This is mainly what holds together social entities in the higher types of society.

This is a function of the division of labour that is important, but in a different way from that normally acknowledged by economists.

Notes

1. H. Spencer, *Principles of Sociology* (London) vol. II, p. 282.
2. Fustel de Coulanges, *Histoire des institutions politiques de l'ancienne France*, pt. 1, p. 352.
3. Waitz, *Anthropologie der Naturvölker*, vol. I, pp. 359–60.
4. Spencer, *Principles of Sociology*, vol. I, pp 505–6.
5. In the same way we shall see in Chapter VII that the bond that joins the individual to his family is the stronger and the more difficult to break, the more domestic labour is divided up.
6. L. H. Morgan, *Ancient Society* (London, 1870) p. 80.
7. Denys of Halicarnassus, vol. I, p. 9. Cf. Accarias, *Précis de droit romain*, vol. I, § 51.
8. This fact is in no way irreconcilable with another one, viz., that in these societies the foreigner is an object of repulsion. He causes these feelings so long as he remains a foreigner. What we are saying is that he easily loses this status of being a foreigner once he is naturalised.
9. In the same way we shall see in Chapter VII that the intrusion of foreigners into the society of the family is the more easy the less domestic labour is divided up.
10. We term positive those sentiments that impose positive actions, such as the practice of religion. Negative sentiments merely entail abstention. Thus between them there are only differences in degree. Such differences are, however, important, for they indicate two points in development.
11. It is likely that other motives come into play in our condemnation of drunkenness, in particular the disgust inspired by the state of degradation in which the drunken person naturally finds himself.
12. Under this heading we place those acts that owe their criminal character to the power of reaction inhering in the organ of consciousness, common at least in part. An exact separation between these two sub-classes is, moreover, difficult to make.

13. Exodus 21:17. Cf. Deuteronomy 27:16.
14. Exodus 21:15.
15. Exodus 21:18–21.
16. Thonissen, *Droit pénal de la République athénienne*, p. 288.
17. The punishment was not prescribed, but appears to have consisted in degradation (ibid., p. 291).
18. *Patronus, si clienti fraudem fecerit, sacer esto*, says the Law of the Twelve Tables. At the origins of the city penal law was less alien in domestic life. A *lex regia*, which tradition traces back to Romulus, cursed the child who had shown brutality to his parents (Festus, p. 230; s.v. *Plorare*).
19. Cf. Voigt, *XII Tafeln*, vol. II, p. 273.
20. It may perhaps be astonishing to be able to speak of a regression in domestic sentiments in Rome, the chosen spot for the patriarchal family. We can only state the facts. What explains them is that the formation of the patriarchal family had had the effect of removing from public life a whole number of elements, setting up a sphere of private action and constituting a kind of inner consciousness. Thus a source of variations was opened up that had hitherto not existed. From the day when family life became removed from social effects by shutting itself within the home, it varied from one household to another, and the domestic sentiments lost their uniformity, becoming less determinate.
21. Rein, *Kriminalrecht der Römer*, p. 865.
22. Ibid., p. 869.
23. We do not group under this heading the kidnapping or rape of a female, into which other elements enter. These are acts of violence rather than of shameful conduct.
24. Post, *Bausteine*, vol. I, p. 226.
25. Ibid. The same was true in ancient Egypt. (Cf. Thonissen, *Etudes sur l'histoire du droit criminel des peuples anciens*, vol. I, p. 149.)
26. Deuteronomy 14:3 ff.
27. Ibid., 22:5, 11, 12; and 14:1.
28. Deuteronomy 22:9 and 10: 'You shall not sow your vineyard with a second crop.' 'You shall not plough with an ox and an ass yoked together.' (NEB.)
29. Fustel de Coulanges, *La Cité antique*, p. 266.
30. Numbers 15:30.
31. Meier and Schömann, *Der attische Prozess*, 2nd edn (Berlin, 1863) p. 367.
32. We reproduce this list from Meier and Schömann, *Der attische Prozess*, p. 368. Cf. Thonissen, *Droit pénal*, ch. 2.
33. It is true that Fustel de Coulanges states that, according to a text of Pollux (vol. VIII, 46) the celebration of feast days was obligatory. But the text quoted speaks of a positive act of profanation and not of abstention.
34. Meier and Schömann, *Der attische Prozess*, p. 369. Cf. *Dictionnaire des antiquités*, article: 'Asebeia'.

35. Fustel de Coulanges himself acknowledges that this feature was much more marked in the Athenian city (cf. *La Cité antique*, ch. 18, last few lines).

36. Rein, *Kriminalrecht*, pp. 887–8.

37. Walter, p. 804.

38. Marquardt, *Römische Staatsverfassung*, 2nd edn, vol. III, p. 185.

39. Cf. the supporting facts in Thonissen, *Droit pénal*, p. 187.

40. According to Voigt, *XII Tafeln*, vol. I, pp. 450–5. Cf. Marquardt, *Römische Alterthümer*, vol. VI, p. 248. We omit one or two *scelera* which had a secular as well as a religious character, and we only count as such those that are directly offences against the things of the gods.

41. Du Boys, vol. VI, pp. 62 ff. Yet we must note that severity for religious crimes was a very late phenomenon. In the ninth century sacrilege was still redeemed by payment of thirty pounds of silver (Du Boys, vol. V, p. 231). It was an ordinance of 1226 which for the first time prescribed the death penalty for heretics. Thus we can believe that the reinforcement of punishments for these crimes is an abnormal phenomenon, due to exceptional circumstances and one that did not enter into the normal development of Christianity.

42. Thonissen, *Droit pénal*, p. 363.

43. Lombroso, *L'homme criminel*, Fr. trans., p. 36.

44. 'Even among civilized peoples,' says Lombroso in support of his statement, 'private property was a long time in establishing itself' (ibid., p. 36).

45. This is something that must not be forgotten in judging certain ideas of primitive peoples regarding theft. Where communism was still recent, the link between a person and a thing was still weak, that is, the right of the individual over a thing was not so strong as it is today, nor in consequence were attacks against this right so serious. This does not signify that for this reason theft was tolerated. It does not exist, in so far as private property does not exist.

46. Diodorus, vol. I, p. 39; Aulus Gellus, *Noctes Atticae*, vol. XI, p. 18.

47. Thonissen, *Etudes*, etc., vol. I, p. 168.

48. Conjectures are easy (cf. Thonissen, and Tarde, *Criminalité*, p. 40).

49. This proposition does not contradict the other which is often enunciated in the course of this study, viz., at that moment in evolution individual personality did not exist. What is lacking then was the psychological personality, and above all the higher psychological personality. But individuals have always a distinct organic life, and this is sufficient to give rise to this sympathy, although it becomes stronger when the personality is more highly developed.

50. Buddhism (cf. article on Buddhism in the *Encyclopédie des sciences religieuses*).

51. Ellis, *The Ewe-Speaking* [sic] *Peoples of the Slave Coast* (London, 1890) p. 258.

52. Wilhelm Borchardt, *Die sprichwörtlichen Redensarten* (Leipzig, 1888) vol. XII. Cf. Wyss, *Die Sprichwörter bei den römischen Komikern* (Zurich, 1889).

Chapter VI

The Increasing Preponderance of Organic Solidarity and its Consequences (cont.)

I

Thus it is a law of history that mechanical solidarity, which at first is isolated, or almost so, should progressively lose ground, and organic solidarity gradually become preponderant. But when the way in which men are solidly linked to one another is modified, it is inevitable that the structure of societies should change. The shape of a body must needs be transformed, when the molecular affinities within are no longer the same. Consequently, if the foregoing proposition is accurate, there must be two social types, corresponding to these two kinds of solidarity.

If, by a process of thought, we attempt to constitute the ideal type of a society whose cohesion would result exclusively from resemblances, we would have to conceive of it as consisting of an absolutely homogeneous mass whose parts would not be distinguishable from one another and consequently not be arranged in any order in relation to one another. In short, the mass would be devoid of any definite form or articulation. This would be the real social protoplasm, the germ from which all social types would have emerged. The aggregate we have characterised in this way we propose to call a *horde*.

It is true that we have not yet observed, with complete authentication, societies that correspond in every respect to this description. Yet what gives us the right to postulate their existence is the fact that lower societies, those that in consequence are the most akin to this

126

primordial stage, are formed by a mere replication of aggregates of this kind. We find an almost wholly pure model of this social organisation among the Indians of North America. For example, each Iroquois tribe is made up of a number of incomplete societies (the most extensive includes eight of them) which present all the features we have just pointed out. Adults of both sexes are equal to one another. The sachems and chiefs at the head of each one of these groups, who form the council administering the common affairs of the tribe, enjoy no superior status. Kinship itself is not organised, for the term cannot be applied to the fact that the mass of the people is distributed in various generation layers. At the late stage when these peoples were observed there were certainly some special ties of obligation joining the child to his maternal relatives. But these relationships were confined to being very few in number and did not appreciably differ from those he maintained with the other members of society. In principle all individuals of the same age were linked to one another in the same degree of kinship.[1] In other cases we are even closer to the horde: Fison and Howitt describe Australian tribes that include only two such divisions.[2]

We shall give the term 'clan' to a horde that has ceased to be independent and has become an element in a more extensive group, and that of *segmentary societies based upon clans* to those peoples that have been constituted from an association of clans. We term such societies 'segmentary' to denote that they are formed from the replication of aggregates that are like one another, analogous to the rings of annelida worms. We also term this elementary aggregate a clan because this word aptly expresses its mixed nature, relating both to the family and to the body politic. It is a family in the sense that all the members who go to make it up consider themselves kin to one another, and indeed it is true that for the most part they share a blood relationship. The affinities produced by sharing a blood kinship are mainly what keeps them united. What is more, they sustain mutual relationships that might be termed domestic, since these are to be found elsewhere in societies whose family character is undisputed: I mean collective revenge, collective responsibility and, as soon as individual property makes an appearance, mutual heredity. Yet on the other hand it is not a family in the true sense of the word, for in order to form part of it, there is no need to have a clear-cut blood relationship with the other clan members. It is enough to exhibit some external criterion, which usually consists in bearing the same name. Although this sign is esteemed to denote a common origin, such an official status really constitutes very ineffective proof, one that is very easy to copy. Thus the clan comprises a large number of strangers, which allows it to attain a size that the family proper never reaches: very often it numbers several thousand people. Moreover, it is the basic political unit; the clan chiefs are the sole authorities in society.[3]

Thus this organisation might also be termed politico-familial. Not only has the clan blood-kinship as its basis, but different clans within the same people very often consider themselves related to one another. Among the Iroquois, according to the circumstances they treat one another as brothers or cousins.[4] Among the Jews who, as we shall see, manifest the most characteristic features of the same social organisation, the ancestor of each one of the clans making up the tribe is deemed to have descended from the founder of the tribe, who is himself regarded as one of the sons of the father of the race. But this designation has one disadvantage as compared with the former one: it does not bring out what constitutes the real structure of these societies.

Yet, whatever term we assign to it, this organisation, just like that of the horde, whose extension it merely is, plainly does not possess any other solidarity save that which derives from similarities. This is because the society is made up of similar segments and these in turn comprise only homogeneous elements. Doubtless each clan has its own peculiar features and is consequently distinct from the others. But their solidarity is the weaker the more heterogeneous they are, and vice versa. For a segmentary organisation to be possible, the segments must both resemble one another (or else they would not be united) and yet be different from one another. Otherwise they would become so lost in one another as to vanish. Depending upon the society, these two opposing necessities are met in different proportions, but the social type remains the same.

This time we have emerged from the sphere of prehistory and conjecture. Not only is this social type far from hypothetical: it is almost the most widespread of all among lower societies. And we know that these are the most numerous. We have already seen that the type was general in America and Australia. Post reports that it is very common among the African negroes.[5] The Jews remained in this same state until a very late stage; the Kabyles have never got beyond it.[6] Thus Waitz, wishing to characterise generally the structure of these peoples, whom he calls *Naturvölker*, depicts them as follows, where is to be found the general pattern of organisation we have just described:

> As a general rule families live side by side in a state of great independence and develop gradually, so as to form small societies (viz. *clans*)[7] which have no definite constitution so long as internal struggles or an external danger – such as war – does not lead to one or several men distinguishing themselves from the mass of society and placing themselves at its head. Their influence, which relies solely on personal attributes, is extended and lasts only when confined within the bounds laid down by the trust and patience of others. Every adult remains in a state of complete independence *vis-à-vis* such a chieftain. This is why we see such peoples, lacking any other internal organisation, can only hold together through the action of external circumstances and through the habit of living their life in common.[8]

The arrangement of clans within society and thus the overall shape of the latter can, it is true, vary. Sometimes they are simply juxtaposed so as to form a kind of linear series: this is the case for many Indian tribes in North America.[9] In other instances – and this is the distinguishing mark of a higher organisation – each one is embedded within a larger group which, having been formed by the coming together of several clans, has its own life and special name. Each one of these groups in turn may be embedded with several other groups in an even more extensive aggregate, and it is from the successive series formed by the embedding process that results the unity of the whole society. Thus among the Kabyle the political unit is the clan, fixed in the form of a village (*djemmaa* or *thaddart*); several *djemmaa* form a tribe (*arch'*), and several tribes form the confederation (*thak'ebilt*), the highest form of political society known to the Kabyles. Likewise, among the Jews the clan is what translators somewhat inaccurately call the *family*, a huge society that included thousands of people descended, according to tradition, from a single ancestor.[10] A certain number of *families* made up of the tribe and the union of twelve tribes made up the whole of the Jewish people.

These societies are the home *par excellence* of mechanical solidarity, so much so that it is from this form of solidarity that they derive their main physiological characteristics.

We know that in them religion pervades the whole of social life. This is because social life is made up almost entirely of common beliefs and practices that draw from their unanimous acceptance a very special kind of intensity. Using the analysis of classical texts alone to go back to an era exactly similar to the one we are discussing, Fustel de Coulanges discovered that the primitive organisation of societies was of the family type and that, moreover, the constitution of the primitive family was based upon religion. Only he mistook cause for effect. After having postulated the religious idea, without tracing its derivation from anything, he deduced from it the social arrangements which he noted,[11] whilst, on the contrary, it is these arrangements that explain the power and nature of the religious idea. Since all such social masses were formed from homogeneous elements, that is to say, since the collective type is very highly developed in them whereas individual types are rudimentary, it was inevitable that the entire psychological life of society should assume a religious character.

From this also springs the notion of communism, which has often been noted among these peoples. In fact, communism is the necessary product of that special cohesion that swallows up the individual within the group, the part into the whole. In the end property is merely the extension of the idea of the person to things. Thus where the collective personality is the sole existing one, property itself is inevitably collective. It can only become individual when the individual, freeing himself from the mass of the people, has also become a personal, distinctive being, not only as an organism, but as a factor in social life.[12]

This type can even be modified without the nature of social solidarity suddenly changing on this account. Indeed not all primitive peoples display that lack of centralisation we have just observed. On the contrary, some of them are subject to an absolute power. The division of labour has therefore appeared in them. However, the link which in this case binds the individual to the chief is identical to that which joins things to persons. The relationships of the barbaric despot to his subjects, like those of the master to his slaves or the father of the Roman family to his descendants, are indistinguishable from those of the owner to the object he possesses. There is nothing about them which corresponds to that reciprocity which brings about the division of labour. It has been rightly stated that they are unilateral.[13] Thus the solidarity they express remains mechanical. The difference lies entirely in the fact that it links the individual no longer directly to the group, but to the one who is its image. But the unity of the whole rules out as before any individuality in the parts.

If this first form of the division of labour, however important it may nevertheless be, has not the effect of making social solidarity more flexible, as might be expected, it is because of the special conditions in which it takes place. It is in fact a general law that the most pre-eminent organ in any society partakes of the nature of the collective entity that it represents. Thus where society possesses this religious character, one that is, so to speak, suprahuman, whose source, as we have shown, lies in the constitution of the common consciousness, it is necessarily transmitted to the chief who directs it and who in consequence finds himself very greatly elevated above all other men. Where individuals are merely dependants of the collective type, they quite naturally become dependent on the central authority that embodies them. Again, in the same way the undivided property right that the community exercised over things passes wholly to the superior personality constituted in this way. The peculiarly professional services that he renders therefore count for little in the extraordinary power with which he is invested. If, in these kinds of societies, the power that is directing has so much authority, it is not because, as has been said, these societies particularly need a more energetic leadership. But this authority is wholly a manifestation of the common consciousness, an authority that is vast, because the common consciousness itself is highly developed. Even if the common consciousness were weaker or only included a smaller section of social life, the need for some supreme regulating function would be no less. However, the rest of society would no longer be in the same state of inferiority *vis-à-vis* the one to whom that function has been entrusted. This is why solidarity remains mechanical so long as the division of labour has not developed further. It is in such conditions that it even attains its *maximum* energy: for the effect of the common consciousness is stronger when it is no longer exerted diffusely, but through the mediation of some clearly defined organ.

Thus there is a social structure of a determinate nature to which mechanical solidarity corresponds. What characterises it is that it comprises a system of homogeneous segments similar to one another.

II

But the structure of societies where organic solidarity is preponderant is entirely different.

These are constituted, not by the replication of similar homogeneous elements, but by a system of different organs, each one of which has a special role and which themselves are formed from differentiated parts. The elements in society are not of the same nature, nor are they arranged in the same manner. They are neither placed together end-on, as are the rings of an annelida worm, nor embedded in one another, but co-ordinated and subordinated to one another around the same central organ, which exerts over the rest of the organism a moderating effect. This organ itself is no longer of the same character as outlined above, for, if the others depend upon it, in turn it depends upon them. Undoubtedly it still enjoys a special place and, one may say, a privileged one. But this is due to the nature of the role that it fulfils and not to some cause external to its functions or to some force imparted to it from outside. Thus it has nothing more than what is temporal and human about it; between the other organs and itself there is no longer any difference save in degree. Thus, with an animal, the priority of the nervous system over the other systems comes down to the right, if it may be so expressed, of receiving a choicer form of sustenance and of taking its share first. But it has need of the other organs, just as they have need of it.

This social type relies upon principles so utterly different from the preceding type that it can only develop to the extent that the latter has vanished. Indeed individuals are distributed within it in groups that are no longer formed in terms of any ancestral relationship, but according to the special nature of the social activity to which they devote themselves. Their natural and necessary environment is no longer that in which they were born, but that of their profession. It is no longer blood relationship, whether real or fictitious, that determines the place of each one, but the functions he fulfils. Undoubtedly, when this new organisation begins to appear, it attempts to use the existing one and to assimilate it to itself. The way in which functions are distributed is therefore modelled as closely as possible upon the way in which society is already divided up. The segments, or at least groups of segments linked by particular affinities, become organs. Thus the clans which as an entity constitute the tribe of the Levites, appropriate for themselves the priestly functions among the Jewish people. Generally it may be said that classes and castes have probably no other origin or nature: they spring from the mixing of the professional organisation, which is just emerging, with a pre-existent family organisation. But this mixed arrangement cannot last for long because, between the two elements that it takes upon itself to reconcile, there is an hostility that must in the end break out. Only a very rudimentary division of labour can fit into these rigid, well-defined moulds, which were not fashioned for it. The division of labour can only increase in so far as it frees itself from the frame that hedges it in. Once it has gone beyond a certain stage of development no longer is there any connection between the fixed number of segments and the ever-increasing number of functions that become specialised, nor between the hereditarily determined properties of the former and the new aptitudes that the latter demand.[14] Thus the social substance must enter into entirely new combinations in order to be organised on completely different foundations. Now the old structure, so long as it subsists, is hostile to this. This is why it must disappear.

The history of these two types indeed shows that the one has only made progress in the proportion to which the other has regressed.

Among the Iroquois, the social constitution based on clans exists in its pure state. The same is true of the Jews, as the Pentateuch shows us, except for the slight deviation that we have just pointed out. Thus the organised social type exists in neither, although we may perhaps perceive its first beginnings in Jewish society.

The same no longer holds good for the Franks of the Salic law: this time it appears with its own special characteristics, free from any compromise. In fact among this people we find, besides a regular, stable, central authority, a whole network of administrative and judicial functions. On the other hand, the existence of contract law, still, it is true, very little developed, bears witness to the fact that economic functions are themselves beginning to separate out and become organised. Thus the politico-family constitution is gravely undermined. Doubtless the last social molecule, the village, is indeed still merely a clan transformed. What proves this is the fact that among the inhabitants of a single village relationships of a clearly domestic nature exist, which are in any case characteristic of the clan. All the members of the village have the right to inherit from one another, in the absence of any relatives proper.[15] A text to be found in the *Capita extravagantia legis salicae* (art. 9) informs us that even in the case of a murder committed in the village neighbours maintained their collective solidarity. Moreover, the village is a system much more hermetically closed to the outside world, concentrated in on itself, than would be a mere territorial constituency, because none can settle in it without the unanimous consent, expressly or tacitly given, of all the inhabitants.[16] But in this form the clan has lost some of its essential characteristics: not only has all memory of a common origin disappeared, but it has been almost completely divested of any political importance. The political unit is the *hundred*. 'The population,' declares Waitz, 'lives in the villages, but both people and land are spread out over the *hundred*, which for all matters of war and peace forms the unit which serves as a basis for all relationships.'[17]

In Rome this dual movement of progression and regression is continued. The Roman clan is the *gens*, and it is indeed certain that the *gens* was the basis for the ancient Roman constitution. But from the time of the foundation of the republic it ceased almost completely to be a public institution. It was no longer a definite territorial unit, like the Frankish village, nor a political unit. It is to be found neither in the territorial arrangement, nor in the structure of the people's assemblies. The *comitia curiata*, in which it used to play a social role,[18] are replaced either by the *comita centuriata* or the *comitia tributa*, which were organised on entirely different principles. It is no longer more than a private association sustained by force of habit, yet one that is destined to disappear because it no longer corresponds to any facet of Roman life. But in addition, from the time of the Twelve Tables onwards, the division of labour was much more advanced in Rome than among earlier peoples, and its organised structure was more developed. Already to be found there are important corporations of public officials (senators, knights, the college of priests, etc.), trade guilds,[19] and at the same time the concept of the secular state begins to arise.

Thus the hierarchy that we have established is justified, according to other criteria of a less methodical nature, between the social types we have compared previously. If we were able to say that the Jews of the Pentateuch belong to a less exalted social type than do the Franks of the Salic law, and that the latter, in their turn, were below the Romans of the Twelve Tables, it is because, as a general rule, the more visible and strong the segmentary organisation based on clans is with a people, the more does that people belong to a lower species. Indeed it cannot rise higher until it has gone beyond this first stage. For this same reason the Athenian city, whilst belonging to the same type as the Roman city is nevertheless a more primitive form of it. This is because the politico-family type of organisation has disappeared from it much more slowly. It survived almost right up to the eve of its decadence.[20]

But it is far from true that the organised type subsists alone, in its pristine state, once the clan has disappeared. The organisation based upon clans is in fact only one species of a more extensive *genus*, the segmentary organisation. The distribution of society into similar compartments corresponds to needs that persist even in new societies where social life is established, needs that nevertheless produce their effects in another form. The mass of the population is no longer divided up according to blood relationships, whether real or fictitious, but according to land divisions. The segments are no longer family aggregates but territorial constituencies.

Moreover, it was through a slow process of evolution that the passage from one state to another took place when the memory of the common origin had faded. When the domestic relationships that sprang from it, but as we have seen often outlive it, have themselves vanished, the clan has no longer any consciousness of itself save as a group of individuals who occupy the same parcel of territory. It becomes the village proper. Thus all those peoples who have passed beyond the stage of the clan are made up from territorial districts (the mark, the commune, etc.) which, just as the Roman *gens* had become implicated in the *curia*, are inserted in other districts of the same kind, but larger in size, termed in one place *hundred*, elsewhere *Kreis* or *arrondisssement*, which in turn are often swallowed up in other entities, even more extensive (county, province, *département*) which unite to form a society.[21] This process of insertion can moreover be more or less an hermetical sealing-off. Likewise the links that join together the most general kind of districts can either be very close, as with the centralised countries of present-day Europe, or more relaxed, as in simple confederations. But the principle behind the structure remains the same, and this is why mechanical solidarity persists even in the highest societies.

Nevertheless, in the same way as mechanical solidarity is no longer preponderant, the arrangement in the form of segments is no longer, as previously, the sole anatomical structure or even the essential structure of society. Firstly, the territorial divisions have necessarily something artificial about them. The ties that arise from living together have not their source so deeply in men's hearts as those arising from blood-relationship. Thus they have a much weaker power of resistance. When one is born into a clan, one cannot change anything more, so to speak, than one's relatives. The same reasons do not prevent one's changing one's town or province. Doubtless, geographical distribution corresponds roughly to a certain moral distribution of the population. For example, each province, each territorial division, has its own special morality and customs, a life peculiarly its own. Thus it exerts over individuals imbued with its spirit an attraction that tends to keep them on the spot and, moreover, to repel others. But within a single country such differences cannot be very numerous or clear-cut. The segments are therefore more open to one another. Indeed, from the Middle Ages onwards 'after the formation of towns, foreign artisans travelled as freely and as far and wide as did goods'.[22] Segmentary organisation had lost its contours.

It is increasingly losing them as societies develop. It is indeed a general law that the partial aggregates that make up a more extensive aggregate see their individuality as growing less and less distinctive. At the same time as the family organisation, local religions have disappeared for ever, yet local customs continue to exist. Gradually these merge into one another and unify, at the same time as dialects and patois dissolve into a single national language and regional administration loses its autonomy. In this fact a simple consequence of the law of imitation has been discerned.[23] However, it seems as if it is rather a levelling-out analogous to that which occurs between two liquids which intermingle together. The partitions that separate the various cells of social life, being less thick, are breached more often. Their permeability increases the more they are penetrated. Consequently they lose their consistency and gradually collapse, and to the same extent environments become mingled together. Now local diversity can only be maintained in so far as a diversity of environments subsists. Territorial divisions are therefore less and less based upon the nature of things, and consequently lose their significance. One might almost say that a people is the more advanced the more superficial its character.

On the other hand, as segmentary organisation vanishes organisation by professions covers it ever more completely with its network. It is true that at the beginning it establishes itself only within the boundaries of the more simple segments, without extending beyond. Every town, with its immediate neighbourhood, forms a group within which work is divided up, but that strives to be self-sufficient. 'The town,' states Schmoller, 'becomes as far as possible the ecclesiastical, political and military centre of the surrounding villages. It aspires to develop every kind of industry to supply the countryside, just as it seeks to concentrate commerce and transport in its area.'[24] At the same time within the town inhabitants are grouped according to their occupation; each trade guild is like a town, living a life of its own.[25] This is the state in which the cities of antiquity remained until a comparatively late era, and from which Christian societies sprang. But the latter went beyond this stage very early on. From the fourteenth century onwards division of labour develops between regions: 'Each town had originally as many cloth-merchants as necessary. But the manufacturers of grey cloth in Basle succumbed already before 1362 in the face of competition from the Alsatians; at Strasburg, Frankfurt and Leipzig the weaving of wool was ruined about 1500. . . . The character of industrial universality of towns of former times was irrevocably destroyed.'

Since then the movement has continued unceasingly to spread:

In the capital are concentrated today, more than in former times, the active forces of the central government, the arts, literature and large-scale credit operations. In the large ports are concentrated more than before all exports and imports. Hundreds of small commercial centres dealing in corn and cattle are prospering and growing in size. Whereas each town had once its ramparts and moat, now a few great fortresses are entrusted with the task of protecting the whole country. Like the capital, the chief towns in the provinces are growing because of the concentration of provincial administration, provincial institutions, collections and schools. The mentally deranged and the sick of a certain category, who were once scattered around the area, are gathered up together, for a whole province or *département*, in a single place. The different towns tend increasingly to develop certain specializations, so that today we distinguish between university towns, civil service towns, factory towns, commercial towns, watering-places, and rentier towns. At certain spots or in certain areas are concentrated the large-scale industries: machine construction, spinning, cloth manufacture, tanning, blast furnaces, the sugar industry, all working for the whole country. Special schools have been established for them, the population of industrial workers adapts to them, the construction of machines is concentrated in them, whilst communications and the organisation of credit adapt themselves also to the special circumstances.[26]

Doubtless to a certain extent this professional organisation attempts to adapt itself to the one that existed before it, as it had originally done for the organisation of the family. This is what emerges from the very description given above. Moreover, it is a very general fact that new institutions are shaped initially in the mould of previous institutions. The territorial regions therefore tend to be specialised in relation to their complexion, organs and different mechanisms, just as was the clan in former times. But just like the latter, they are really incapable of maintaining this role. In fact a town always includes either different organs or parts of organs. Conversely there are hardly any organs that are wholly included within the limits of a particular district, whatever its size. Almost always the district extends beyond them. Likewise, although fairly frequently those organs which are most closely linked to one another tend to draw together, yet in general their physical proximity reflects only very imperfectly the degree of closeness of their relationships. Some are very distant, although depending directly upon one another. Others are physically very close, although their relationships are indirect and distant. The way in which men are grouped together as a result of the division of labour is thus very different from the way the spatial distribution of the population occurs. The professional environment no more coincides with the territorial environment than it does with the family environment. It is a new framework that is substituted for the others. Thus the substitution is only possible to the extent that the others have vanished.

If therefore this social type is nowhere to be observed in a state of absolute purity, likewise nowhere is organic solidarity to be met with in isolation. But at least it frees itself increasingly from any amalgam, just as it becomes increasingly preponderant. Such predominance is all the more rapid and complete because at the very moment when its structure becomes more prominent, the other becomes more indistinct. The segment formed by the clan, so well-defined, is replaced by the territorial district. At least originally, the latter corresponded, although in somewhat vague and approximate fashion, to the real and moral division of the population. But it gradually loses this character, to become no more than an arbitrary combination, one that is a mere convention. As these barriers are lowered, they are covered over by systems of organs which are more and more developed. If therefore social evolution remains subject to the effect of the same determining causes – and we shall see later that this is the sole feasible hypothesis – we may predict that this dual movement will continue in the same direction, and the day will come when the whole of our social and political organisation will have an exclusively, or almost exclusively, professional basis.

Moreover, the studies that follow will establish[27] that this professional organisation is not even today all that it is destined to become; that abnormal causes have prevented it from reaching the stage of development that our present social state requires. From this we may judge the importance that it is destined to assume in the future.

III

The same law governs biological development.

Nowadays we know that the lower animals are made up of similar segments, arranged either in irregular masses or in a linear series. Even at the very lowest point on the scale these elements are not only similar to one another but are even homogeneous in composition. They are usually given the name of *colonies*. But this expression – which incidentally is not without ambiguity – does not signify that these associations are not individual organisms. For 'every colony whose members are made up of continuous tissues is in reality an individual'.[28] Indeed what is characteristic of the individuality of any kind of aggregate is the existence of operations carried out in common by all its parts. Between the members of a colony there is pooling of nutriments and an inability to move save by movements of the whole, so long as the colony is not split up. There is something more: the egg, having emerged from one of the segments that are associated together, reproduces not this segment, but the whole colony of which it formed part: 'Between these colonies of polyps and the higher animal forms, from this viewpoint there is no difference.'[29] Moreover, what makes any radical separation impossible is the fact that there are no organisms at all, however 'centralised' they may be, which to a varying degree do not present the structure of a colony. We find traces of this even in the vertebrates, in the constitution of their skeleton and their uro-genital mechanism, etc. Above all their embryonic development gives indisputable proof that they are nothing more than modified colonies.[30]

Thus there exists in the animal world an individuality 'which is produced outside any combination of organs'.[31] Now this is identical to that of societies that we have termed segmentary. Not only is the structural plan clearly the same, but solidarity is of the same kind. Indeed, since the parts that make up an animal colony are mechanically intertwined with one another, they can only act as a whole, at least so long as they remain joined together. Their activity is collective. In a community of polyps, as each stomach communicates with the others, one individual unit cannot eat unless all the others do so as well. It is, states Perrier, communism in the fullest sense of the word.[32] A member of the colony, particularly when floating, cannot contract without also causing the polyps to which it is joined to move as well, and the movement is passed from each succeeding member to the next.[33] In a worm each ring depends rigidly upon the others – this despite the fact that it can detach itself from them without danger to itself.

But just as the segmentary type vanishes as we advance up the scale of social evolution, the colony type disappears as we move higher up in the scale of organisms. Already started with the annelida, although it is still very visible, it becomes almost imperceptible with the molluscs, and in the end only scientific analysis can succeed in discovering traces of it in vertebrates. We need not point out the analogies that exist between the type that replaces the preceding one and that of organic societies. In both cases, the structure, like the solidarity, derives from the division of labour. Each part of the animal, once it has become an organ, has its own sphere of action, in which it moves independently, without impinging upon the others. Yet from another viewpoint these parts depend much more closely upon one another than in a colony, since they cannot separate from one another without perishing. Finally, in organic as in social evolution, the division of labour begins by using the framework of segmentary organisation, but only eventually to free itself and to develop in an autonomous way. If in fact the organ is sometimes only a transformed segment, this is, however, the exception.[34]

To sum up: we have distinguished between two types of solidarity. We have just discerned that there exist two social types that correspond to them. Just as the first kinds of solidarity develop in inverse relationship to one another, with the two corresponding social types one regresses regularly as the other progresses, and the latter is the one that is defined by the social division of labour. Besides the fact that it confirms the preceding results, this result ends up by demonstrating to us all the importance of the division of labour. Just as it is this which, for the most part, gives cohesion to the societies in which we live, it is also this that determines the characteristics which go to make up their structure and everything leads us to predict that in the future its role, from this viewpoint, can only increase.

IV

The law we have established in the last two chapters in one characteristic, but in one characteristic alone, may have reminded us of the one that dominates the sociology of Spencer. Like him, we have stated that the place of the individual in society, from being originally nothing at all, has grown with civilisation. But this indisputable fact has presented itself in a completely different light than to the English philosopher, so much so that in the end our conclusions are in contradiction to his, more than echoing them.

Firstly, according to him, this absorption of the individual into the group is allegedly the result of a constraint and an artificial organisation necessitated by the state of warfare that is endemic in lower societies. Indeed it is especially in war that union is necessary for success. A group cannot defend itself against another group or subdue it save on condition that it acts as one unit. Thus all individual forces must be clustered together in a concentration that cannot be broken up. Now the only means of ensuring this concentration uninterruptedly is to institute a very powerful authority to which individuals are subjected absolutely. It is necessary that 'As the soldier's will is so suspended that he becomes in everything the agent of his officer's will; so is the will of the citizen in all transactions, private and public, overruled by that of the government.'[35] It therefore is an organised despotism that could annihilate the individual and, since this organisation is essentially a military one, it is by militarism that Spencer defines this kind of society.

We have seen, on the contrary, that this effacement of the individual has its origin in a social type characterised by a complete absence of any centralisation. It is the product of a state of homogeneity that is the distinguishing mark of primitive societies. If the individual is not distinct from the group, it is because the individual consciousness is almost indistinct from the collective consciousness. Spencer, and other sociologists with him, seem to have interpreted these facts of the remote past by means of very modern ideas. The very pronounced sentiment that each one of us today possesses of our own individuality has caused them to believe that personal rights could not be restricted to such a degree save by an organisation that exercised coercion. We cling so much to these rights that it seemed to them that man could not have abandoned them of his own free will. In fact, if in lower societies so little place is allowed for the individual personality, it is not that it has been constricted or suppressed artificially, it is quite simply because at that moment in history *it did not exist.*

Moreover, Spencer recognises himself that among these societies many possess a constitution that is so little military and authoritarian that he himself terms them democratic.[36] But he seeks to view them as the first prelude to those societies of the future which he calls industrial. Yet to do so he must fail to acknowledge one fact: in these societies, just as in those that are subject to despotic government, the individual has no sphere of action that is peculiarly his own, as is proved by the general institution of communism. Likewise traditions, prejudices and collective customs of every kind weigh down upon him no less heavily than would a constituted authority. Therefore they cannot be treated as democratic unless one twists the usual meaning of the word. Moreover, if they were really marked by the precocious individualism attributed to them, we would arrive at the strange conclusion that social evolution has attempted, from the very outset, to produce the most perfect types, since 'no governmental force exists at first save that of the common will expressed by the assembled horde'.[37] Is therefore history circular in its motion and is progress only a step backwards?

In a general way one can easily understand that individuals can be subjected only to a collective despotism, for the members of a society can only be dominated by a force that is superior to themselves, and there is only one of these that possesses this quality: that of the group. Any personality, however powerful it might be, could do nothing alone against a whole society. The latter cannot therefore be enslaved in spite of itself. This is why, as we have seen, the strength of authoritarian governments does not spring from themselves, but derives from the very constitution of society. If, moreover, individualism was to such an extent congenital in humanity, one cannot see how primitive tribes were able so easily to subject themselves to the despotic authority of a chief, wherever it was necessary to do so. Ideas, customs, institutions themselves ought to have risen up against so radical a transformation. On the other hand, all is explained once we have fully realised the nature of these societies, for then this change is no longer so profound as it appears. Individuals, instead of subordinating themselves to the group, subordinated themselves to the one who represented it. As collective authority, when it was diffused, was absolute, the authority of the chief, which was only a way of organising collective authority, naturally assumed the same character.

Far from being able to date the effacement of the individual from the institution of some despotic power, we ought on the contrary to see in it the first step taken along the road to individualism. In fact, the chiefs are the first individual personalities who have risen from the mass of society. Their exceptional position, which makes them unrivalled, imparts to them a distinctive presence and in consequence confers an individuality upon them. Dominating society, they are no longer constrained to follow its every movement. Doubtless it is from the group that they draw their strength. Yet once their strength is organised, it becomes autonomous and renders them capable of personal action. Thus a source for initiative is opened up which until then did not exist. Henceforth there is someone who can engender something new, and even depart from collective customs. The balance is upset.[38]

If we have insisted upon this point it is in order to establish two important propositions.

In the first place, each time that we find ourselves faced with a mechanism of government endowed with great authority we must seek the reason not in the particular situation of those governing, but in the nature of the societies that they govern. We must observe what are the common beliefs, the common sentiments that, in embodying themselves in a person or a family, have bestowed such power. As for the personal superiority of the chief, in this process it plays only a secondary role. It explains why the strength of the collectivity, not without intensity, is concentrated in these hands rather than in those of another. As soon as this force, instead of remaining diffused, is obliged to delegate, this can only be to the benefit of those individuals who have manifested their superiority in other ways. But if this superiority denotes the direction in which the current is moving, it does not create that current. If the father of the family, in Rome, enjoys absolute power, it is not because he is the oldest, the wisest or the most experienced, but because, through the circumstances in which the Roman family finds itself, he embodies the old family communism. Despotism, at least when it is neither a pathological phenomenon nor one of decadence, is nothing more than transformed communism.

In the second place, we see from the above how false is the theory that places egoism as the point of departure for humanity and makes altruism, on the other hand, a recent phenomenon.

What imparts authority to this hypothesis for certain minds is that it appears to be a logical consequence of Darwinian principles. In the name of the dogma of competition to survive, and of natural selection, there is depicted for us in the gloomiest colours that primitive humanity for whom hunger and thirst, both moreover largely unassuaged, were allegedly the sole passions. They were the dark ages, when men seemingly had no other thought or preoccupation than to quarrel amongst one another over their piteous food. In order to react against the retrospective reveries of eighteenth-century philosophy, and also against certain religious doctrines, and to show more strikingly that paradise lost is not behind us and that there is nothing that we ought to regret about our past, it was held necessary to make it appear sombre and systematically to denigrate it. There is nothing more unscientific than this inverted prejudice. If the hypotheses of Darwin are usable in moral matters, it is still with more reservations and moderation than in the other sciences. In fact they remove the essential element of moral life, viz., the moderating influence that society exerts over its members, which tempers and neutralises the brutal effect of the struggle for existence and of selection. Everywhere that societies exist there is altruism, because there is solidarity.

Thus we find altruism at the very dawn of humanity and even in a form that exceeds all bounds, for the hardships that the savage imposes upon himself in order to obey the religious tradition, the abnegation with which he offers up his life as soon as society demands its sacrifice, the irresistible impulsion that drives the widow in India to follow her husband in death, the Gaul not to survive the chief of his clan, the ancient Celt to rid his fellows of a useless mouth to feed by bringing about his own voluntary end – is all that not altruism? Shall we treat these practices as superstitions? No matter, provide that they attest an ability to give oneself. And, moreover, where do superstitions begin and end? We would find ourselves extremely embarrassed to give a reply and to provide a scientific definition for the fact. Is it not also superstition, that attachment we feel towards the places where we have lived, for people with whom we have had a lasting relationship? And yet this power to attach ourselves to something, is it not the mark of a healthy moral constitution? Precisely speaking, the whole life of the sensibility is made up only of superstitions, since it precedes and rules the judgement, rather than depends upon it.

Scientifically conduct is egotistical in so far as it is determined by sentiments and representations that are wholly personal to ourselves. If therefore we recall to what extent in lower societies the consciousness of the individual is assailed by the collective consciousness, we shall be even tempted to believe that it is something wholly other than itself, that it is made up entirely of altruism, as Condillac would say. Yet this conclusion would be an exaggeration, for there is a sphere of psychological life which, no matter how developed the collective type may be, varies from one person to another and belongs by right to each individual. It is that part which is made up of representations, feelings and tendencies that relate to the organism and states of the organism; it is the world of internal and external sensations and those movements directly linked to them. This primal basis of all individuality is inalienable and does not depend upon the social condition. Thus we should not state that altruism is born of egoism, for such a derivation would only be possible if it were a creation *ex nihilo*. But strictly speaking these two springs of behaviour have been present from the very beginning in every human consciousness, for there cannot be one that does not reflect both the things that relate to the individual alone, and things that are not personal to him.

All that can be said is that with the savage that lower part of ourselves represents a more considerable proportion of the total human being, because his being is lesser in extent, the higher reaches of psychological life in him being less developed. Thus it has relatively more importance and in consequence more power over the will. Yet, on the other hand, for everything that goes beyond this domain of physical needs, the primitive consciousness, according to the strongly couched expression of Espinas, is absolutely and entirely outside of itself. For the civilised person the very opposite is true; egoism insinuates itself even to the very centre of the higher representations. Each one of us has his own opinions, beliefs and aspirations, and clings to them. He even comes to be involved in altruism, because it so happens that we have a way of being altruistic that depends upon our personal character, our cast of mind, from which we refuse to depart. Doubtless we should not conclude that the share of egoism has increased for the whole of life, for we must take into account the fact that the whole of consciousness has been extended. It is nevertheless the case that individualism has developed, in terms of absolute value, by penetrating areas that in the beginning were closed to it.

Yet this individualism, the fruit of historical development, is not, however, the one that Spencer described. The societies that he terms industrial no more represent organised societies than military societies resemble segmentary societies based on the family. We shall see this in the next chapter.

Notes

1. L. H. Morgan, *Ancient Society* (London, 1877) pp. 62–122.
2. *Kamilaroi and Kurnai.* This state has moreover been the one through which passed at the outset the societies of American Indians (cf. Morgan, *Ancient Society*).
3. If, in its pure state, as we at least believe, the clan forms an undivided, conglomerate family, later individual families, distinct from one another, appear against this background, which was originally homogeneous. But their appearance does not change the essential characteristics of the social organisation we are describing. This is why

we have no need to dwell upon them. The clan remains the political unit and, since these families are similar and equal among one another, society continues to be made up of similar, homogeneous segments, although within the primitive segments there begin to appear the shapes of fresh segmentations, which however are of the same kind.

4. Morgan, *Ancient Society*, p. 90.

5. Post, *Afrikanische Jurisprudenz*, vol. I.

6. Cf. Hanoteau and Letourneux, *La Kabylie et les coutumes kabyles*, vol. II; and Masqueray, *Formation des cités chez les populations sédentaires d'Algérie* (Paris, 1886) ch. 5.

7. Waitz erroneously presents the clan as deriving from the family. It is the opposite that is the truth. Moreover, although this description is important because of the authority of the author, it is somewhat lacking in precision.

8. Waitz, *Anthropologie*, vol. I, p. 359.

9. Cf. Morgan, *Ancient Society*, p. 153 ff.

10. Thus the tribe of Reuben, which in all included four *families*, counted, according to the book of Numbers (26:7), more than 43,000 adults over the age of twenty. (Cf. Numbers 3:15 ff.; Joshua 7:14.) Cf. Munck, *Palestine*, pp. 116, 125, 191.

11. 'We have set out the history of a belief. It is established: human society is constituted. It is modified: society goes through a series of revolutions. It disappears: society changes its aspect.' (*La Cité antique*, end.)

12. Spencer has already stated that social evolution, moreover like universal evolution, began by a phase of more or less perfect homogeneity. But this proposition, as he understands it, in no way resembles the one we have just developed. For Spencer, in fact, a society that might be perfectly homogeneous would not really be a society. What is homogeneous is unstable by nature, and society is essentially a coherent whole. The social role of homogeneity is entirely secondary; it can trace out a path for later co-operation (*Principles of Sociology* (London, 1855), vol. II, pp. 311–21) but it is not a specific source of social life. At certain times Spencer seems to see in the societies we have just described only an ephemeral juxtaposition of individuals who are independent, a nullity as regards social life (ibid.). On the contrary, we have just seen that societies have a very strong collective life, although it is *sui generis*, which is manifested not by exchanges and contracts, but by a great abundance of beliefs and common practices. These aggregates are coherent, not only although they are homogeneous, but to the extent that they are homogeneous. The community they embody is not only by no means too weak, but we may say that it exists on its own. Moreover, the societies are of a definite type, which springs from their homogeneity. They therefore cannot be treated as a negligible quantity.

13. Cf. Tarde, *Lois de l'imitation*, pp. 404–12.

14. The reasons will be seen below (cf. Book II, Chapter IV).
15. Cf. Glasson, *Le droit de succession dans les lois barbares*, p. 19. It is true that the fact is disputed by Fustel de Coulanges, however categorical the text on which Glasson relies may appear to be.
16. Cf. the title in the Salic law headed *De Migrantibus.*
17. Waitz, *Deutsche Verfassungsgeschichte*, 2nd edn, vol. II, p. 317.
18. In these *comitiae* the vote took place by *curia*, viz. by groups of *gentes*. One text appears even to state that within each *curia* the voting was by *gentes*. (Aulus Gellus, vol. XV, pp. 27 and 4.)
19. Cf. Marquardt, *Privatleben der Römer*, vol. II, p. 4.
20. Up to Clisthenes. Two centuries later Athens lost its independence. Moreover, even after Clisthenes, the Athenian clan, the γένοζ, whilst it had lost all political character, preserved a moderately strong organisation. (G. Gilbert, *Handbuch der Griechischen Staatsalterthümer* (Leipzig, 1881).)
21. We do not mean that these territorial districts were a mere reproduction of former family arrangements. This new mode of grouping, on the other hand, resulted at least in part from new causes that disturbed the old way. The main cause was the formation of towns, which became centres for the concentration of population (cf. *infra*, Book II, Chapter II, § I). Yet, whatever the origins of this arrangement, it is a segmentary one.
22. Schmoller, 'La division du travail étudiée au point de vue historique', *Revue d'économie politique* (1890) p. 145.
23. Cf. Tarde, *Lois de l'imitation*, *passim.*
24. Schmoller, 'La division du travail', p. 144.
25. Cf. Levasseur, *Le classes ouvrières en France jusqu'à la Révolution*, vol. I, p. 195.
26. Schmoller, 'La division du travail', pp. 145–8.
27. Cf. *infra*, Book I, Chapter VII, § II, and Book III, Chapter I.
28. Perrier, *Le Transformisme*, p. 159.
29. Perrier, *Colonies animales*, p. 778.
30. Ibid., book II, chs 5, 6 and 7.
31. Ibid., p. 779.
32. Perrier, *Le Transformisme*, p. 167.
33. Perrier, *Colonies animales*, p. 771.
34. Ibid., pp. 763 ff.
35. Spencer, *Principles of Sociology*, vol. I, p. 584.
36. Ibid., pp. 585–6.
37. Ibid., vol. 2, p. 321.
38. Here is to be found a confirmation of the proposition already enunciated earlier (p. 76), which shows governmental power to be an emanation of the life inhering in the collective consciousness.

Chapter VII

Organic Solidarity and Contractual Solidarity

It is true that in the industrial societies of Spencer, just as in organised societies, social harmony derives essentially from the division of labour.[1] Its characteristic feature is that it consists of a co-operation that is automatically produced by the fact that each person follows his own interest. It is enough for every individual to devote himself to one special function to discover that inevitably he is solidly linked to other people. Is not this the distinguishing mark of organised societies?

But if Spencer quite rightly pointed out what was, in the higher forms of society, the principal cause of social solidarity, he was mistaken about the way in which this cause produces its effect and, in consequence, about the nature of the latter.

Indeed, for him, industrial solidarity, as he terms it, displays the two following characteristics:

Since it is spontaneous, there is no need for any coercive apparatus either to produce it or to maintain it. Society has therefore no need to interfere in order to effect a harmony that is established of its own accord. 'Each man may maintain himself by labour, may exchange his products for the products of others, may give aid and receive payment, may enter into this or that combination for carrying on an undertaking, small or great, without the direction of society as a whole.'[2]

The sphere of social action would therefore continue to grow increasingly smaller, for it would no longer have any purpose save to prevent individuals from encroaching upon one another and from doing one another mutual harm, that is, that it would no longer be a regulating mechanism save in a negative way.

In these conditions the sole link remaining between men would be that of absolutely free exchange. 'All trading transactions . . . are effected by free exchange. . . . This relation becomes the predominant relation throughout society in proportion as the individual activities predominate.'[3]

Now the normal form of exchange is contract. This is why, with the decline of militarism and the ascendancy of industrialism, the power as well as the extent of authority diminishes, and as freedom of action increases, so does the relationship of contract become general. Finally, in the fully industrialised type of society, this relationship becomes universal.[4]

By this Spencer does not mean that society ever rests upon an implicit or formal contract. The hypothesis of a social contract is, on the contrary, irreconcilable with the principle of the division of labour. The greater the importance one ascribes to the latter, the more completely must one abandon Rousseau's postulate. This is because for such a contract to be feasible, at any given time all individual wills should be in agreement regarding the common foundations of the social organisation and consequently every individual consciousness should pose to itself the political problem in all its generality. But in order to do this each individual must step out from his own sphere; all should equally play the same role, that of the statesman and the constituent member of society. Imagine to yourself the moment when society is making the contract: if assent is unanimous the thoughts of every consciousness are identical. Thus, in so far as social solidarity arises from such a cause, it has no connection with the division of labour.

Above all, nothing resembles less that automatic and spontaneous solidarity which, according to Spencer, is the distinguishing mark of industrial societies, for, on the contrary, he sees in this conscious pursuit of social ends the characteristic of military societies.[5] Such a contract assumes that all individuals can represent to themselves what are the general conditions for collective life, so that they are able to make an informed choice. Now Spencer knows very well that such a representation goes beyond science in its present state of knowledge, and consequently beyond consciousness. He is so convinced of the futility of reflective thinking when applied to such matters that he wishes even to remove them from the ambit of the legislator, far from submitting them to public opinion. He esteems that social life, like all life in general, cannot be organised naturally save by an unconscious and spontaneous adaptation, under the immediate pressure of necessity and not according to some plan thought out by the reflective intelligence. Thus he does not believe that higher societies can be constructed according to some programme that has been solemnly debated.

The conception of the social contract is today therefore very difficult to defend, because it bears no relation to the facts. The observer does not, so to speak, meet with it in his path. Not only are there no societies that have had such an origin, but there are none whose present structure bears the slightest trace of a contractual organisation. Thus it is neither a fact derived from history nor a trend that emerges from historical development. Consequently in order to instil new life into this doctrine and to give it fresh credibility, it has been necessary to term the contract the acceptance on the part of each individual, once he has become an adult, of the society into which he is born, by the mere fact that he continues to live in it. But then one must term contractual any step taken by men that is not determined by constraint.[6] On this reckoning there is no society, whether present or past, which is not, or has not been, contractual, for there is not one that can continue to exist through constraint alone. We have stated the reason for this earlier. If it has occasionally been believed that constraint was once greater than it is today, it is by virtue of the illusion that the small importance accorded to individual liberty in lower societies has been attributed to a coercive regime. In reality social life, where it is normal, is spontaneous; if it is abnormal, it cannot last. The individual abdicates spontaneously, and it is not even fair to talk of abdication when there is nothing to be abdicated. If therefore we give the word this wide and somewhat distorted meaning, there is no distinction to be made between the different social types. And if we only mean by this the well-defined legal bond that this expression designates, we may be assured that no link of this kind has ever existed between individuals and society.

But if higher societies do not rest upon a basic contract which has a bearing on the general principles of political life, they would have – or tend to have – according to Spencer, as their sole basis the vast system of special contracts that link individuals with one another. Individuals would only be dependent upon the group to the extent that they depended upon one another, and they would not depend upon one another save within the limits drawn by private agreements freely arrived at. Thus social solidarity would be nothing more than the spontaneous agreement between individual interests, an agreement of which contracts are the natural expression. The type of social relations would be the economic relationship, freed from all regulation, and as it emerges from the entirely free initiative of the parties concerned. In short, society would be no more than the establishment of relationships between individuals exchanging the products of their labour, and without any social action, properly so termed, intervening to regulate that exchange.

Is this indeed the nature of societies whose unity is brought about by the division of labour? If this were so, one might reasonably doubt their stability. For if mutual interest draws men closer, it is never more than for a few moments. It can only create between them an external bond. In the fact of exchange the various agents involved remain apart from one another and once the operation is over, each one finds himself again 'reassuming his self' in its entirety. The different consciousnesses are only superficially in contact: they neither interpenetrate nor do they cleave closely to one another. Indeed, if we look to the heart of the matter we shall see that every harmony of interests conceals a latent conflict, or one that is simply deferred. For where interest alone reigns, as nothing arises to check the egoisms confronting one another, each self finds itself in relation to the other on a war footing, and any truce in this perpetual antagonism cannot be of long duration. Self-interest is, in fact, the least constant thing in the world. Today it is useful for me to unite with you; tomorrow the same reason will make me your enemy. Thus such a cause can give rise only to transitory links and associations of a fleeting kind. We see how necessary it is to examine whether such is effectively the nature of organic solidarity.

Nowhere, as Spencer admits, does industrial society exist in a pure state: it is a type that is partly ideal, one that develops more and more in the course of evolution, but which has not yet been completely realised. Consequently, in order to have the right of attributing to it the traits we have just set out, we should establish methodically that societies exhibit them the more completely the more evolved they are, with the exception of those cases where regression has occurred.

In the first place it is asserted that the sphere of social activity continues to diminish more and more in favour of that of the individual. But in order to demonstrate this proposition by a valid experiment it is not enough to do as Spencer does and cite some cases where the individual has effectively emancipated himself from collective influence. No matter how numerous such examples are, they can only serve as illustrations and in themselves lack any power of proof. It is very possible that in one respect social action has regressed whilst in others it has been enlarged, so that in the end we mistake transformation for disappearance. The sole way of proving this objectively is not to quote a few facts as they occur to one, but to follow the history from its origins down to most recent times of the mechanism through which social action is essentially exerted, and to see whether over time it has grown or diminished in volume. We know what is the legal position. The obligations that society imposes upon its members, however slight in importance and duration, take on a legal form. Consequently the relative dimensions of this mechanism allow one to measure precisely the relative extent of social action.

It is abundantly clear that, far from decreasing, this mechanism is continuing to grow, becoming more complex. The more primitive a legal code is, the smaller it is in size. On the other hand, the more recent it is, the more considerable it becomes. Of this there is no possible doubt. But it assuredly does not follow that the sphere of individual activity is growing smaller. We must indeed not forget that if life is more regulated it is also generally more abundant. This is nevertheless adequate proof that social discipline is not continually growing more lax. One of the forms that it assumes tends, it is true, to regress, as we have ourselves established. But other forms, much richer and more complex, are developing in its place. If repressive law is losing ground, restitutory law, which in the beginning did not exist at all, is continually growing. If social intervention has no longer the effect of imposing certain uniform practices upon everybody, it consists more in defining and regulating the special relationship between the different social functions, and this is not less because it is different.

Spencer will answer that he did not assert that every kind of control had decreased, but only positive control. Let us accept this distinction. Whether positive or negative, this control is nevertheless social, and the main question is to know whether it is extended or contracted. But whether it is for decreeing something to happen or for prohibiting it, for saying *Do this* or *Do not do that*, if society intervenes more we have no right to say that individual spontaneity is increasingly adequate for all purposes. If the rules that determine conduct are multiplied, whether their commands are positive or negative, it is not true to say that they spring more and more completely from private initiative.

But is the distinction itself well-founded? By positive control Spencer means one that constrains a person to act, whilst negative control constrains him only to abstain from action. For example, a man has a piece of land; I cultivate it for him either wholly or in part, or I impose upon him, either partially or entirely, the mode of cultivation he must employ: this is a positive control. On the other hand, I give him no help or advice about his farming; I merely prevent him from touching his neighbour's crop or from tipping his rubbish there: this is negative control. The difference is fairly clear-cut between taking it upon oneself to pursue in the place of another citizen some goal which is properly his or to intervene concerning the means that this citizen employs to pursue it, and on the other hand to prevent him harassing another citizen who is pursuing his own chosen goal.[7] If this is the meaning of the terms, positive control is far from disappearing.

In fact we know that restitutory law is continually growing. In the vast majority of cases it either indicates to the citizen the aim that he should pursue or it intervenes in the means that this citizen is employing to attain his chosen goal. For each juridical relationship it resolves the two following questions: (1) In what conditions and in what form does the relationship normally exist? (2) What are the obligations to which it gives rise? The determination of the form and conditions is essentially positive, since this forces the individual to follow a certain procedure in order to attain his goal. As for obligations, if in principle they came down to a prohibition not to disturb another in the exercise of his functions, Spencer's thesis would be true, at least in part. But more often than not these obligations consist in the performance of services of a positive nature.

But let us go into the detail.

II

It is absolutely true that contractual relationships that originally were rare or completely missing are multiplied as labour in society is divided up. But what Spencer seems to have failed to perceive is that non-contractual relationships are developing at the same time.

Let us first examine that section of the law that is wrongly termed private and that, in reality, regulates the relationships between diffused social functions or, to put it differently, the innermost life of the social organism.

In the first place we know that domestic law, from being originally simple, has become increasingly complex, that is, the different species of legal relationships that give rise to family life are much more numerous than formerly. On the one hand, the relationships that result from them are pre-eminently of a positive kind; it is a reciprocity of rights and duties. On the other hand, they are not contractual, at least in their typical form. The conditions upon which they depend are related to our personal status, which itself depends upon our birth, our blood-relationships, and consequently upon facts independent of our will.

However, marriage and adoption are sources of domestic relationships and these are contracts. Yet it so happens that the closer we come to the highest types of society, the more these two legal relationships also lose their strictly contractual character.

Not only in lower societies, but in Rome itself right up to the end of the Empire, marriage remained an entirely private matter. It was generally a type of sale, a real one among primitive peoples, a fictitious one later, but which was valid only by sole consent of the parties, duly attested. Neither solemn forms of ceremony of any kind, nor the intervention of any authority whatsoever were then necessary. It is only with Christianity that marriage took on a different character. Early on, Christians got into the habit of having their union blessed by a priest. A law of the emperor Leo the Philosopher converted this usage into a law for the East; the Council of Trent did as much for the West. Henceforth marriage was no longer freely contracted, but only through the mediation of a public authority, that is, the Church. The role of the Church is not only that of a witness, but she it is and only she that forges the legal bond that up to then the will of private individuals had sufficed to establish. We know how at a later stage the civil authority became the substitute for the religious authority in fulfilling this function and how, at the same time, the role of social intervention and of the necessary formalities was extended.[8]

The history of the adoption contract is still more cogent.

We have already seen how easily and on how large a scale adoption was practised among the Indian clans of North America. It could give rise to every form of kinship. If the person adopted was of the same age as the person adopting him or her, they became brothers and sisters. If the former was a women who was already a mother, she became the mother of the person adopting her.

Among the Arabs, before Mahomet's time, adoption was often used to found real families.[9] It frequently happened that several persons adopted one another; they then became brothers and sisters, and the relationship that united them was as strong as if they were of common descent. The same kind of adoption is to be found among the Slavs. Very often members of different families took one another as brothers and sisters, and formed what is called a confraternity (*probatinstvo*). These associations were contracted freely and without formality: an agreement was sufficient to establish them. However, the bond that united these siblings by election was even stronger than that which springs from a natural sibling relationship.[10]

Among the Germans adoption was probably as easy and frequent. Very simple ceremonies sufficed to constitute it.[11] But in India, Greece or Rome it was already subject to conditions that were laid down. The person adopting had to be of a certain age, had not to be related to the person adopted in a degree that would not have allowed him to be the natural father. Finally this change of family became a very complex legal operation that necessitated the intervention of a magistrate. At the same time the number of those who enjoyed the right of adoption became more limited. Only the father of a family or a bachelor *sui juris* could undertake adoption, and the former could only do so if he had no legitimate children.

Under our present law restrictive conditions have multiplied. The person adopted must be of the age of majority, the person adopting must be over fifty and have treated the adopted person for a long time as his child. Even so we must add that within such limitations adoption has become a very rare event. Before the drawing-up of our legal code it had even fallen almost completely into disuse and still today certain lands such as Holland and Lower Canada do not allow it at all.

At the same time as adoption was becoming rarer, it was losing its effectiveness. In the beginning the adoptive parental relationship was in every respect similar to that of natural parenthood. In Rome the similarity was still very great, yet it was no longer perfectly identical.[12] In the sixteenth century it no longer gave any right to the inheritance *ab intestat* of the adoptive father.[13] Our legal code has re-established this right, but the kinship to which adoption gives a right does not extend beyond that of the adopting and the adopted persons.

We see how defective is the traditional explanation that attributes this custom of adoption among ancient societies to the need to ensure the perpetuation of the cult of one's ancestors. The peoples who have practised it most widely and freely, such as the American Indians, the Arabs and the Slavs, did not know of this cult. On the contrary, it is Rome and Athens, that is, in countries where the domestic type of religion was at its height, where this right was subjected for the first time to control and restrictions. Thus if it has been able to satisfy these needs, it was not because of them that it was established. Conversely, if it tends to disappear it is not because we are less eager to ensure the perpetuating of our name and race. It is in the structure of present-day societies and in the place that the family occupies in them that we must seek the cause that determined this change.

A further proof of this truth is that it has become even more impossible to leave a family by a private act of authority than to enter it. Just as the bond of kinship is not the outcome of a binding contractual relationship, it cannot be broken through an undertaking of a similar kind. Amongst the Iroquois we occasionally see part of the clan depart to swell the ranks of the neighbouring clan.[14] Among the Slavs a member of the Zadruga who is tired of the common life can separate himself from the rest of his family and become legally a stranger to it, as in the same way he can be excluded by it.[15] With the Germans a not very complicated ceremony allowed every Frank who so desired to free himself completely from the obligations of kinship.[16] In Rome a son could not renounce his family of his own volition, and from this trait we can recognise a higher social type. But the bond that the son could not break could be broken by the father. It was this operation that constituted emancipation. Today neither father nor son can modify the natural condition of domestic relationships: they remain as determined at birth.

To sum up: at the same time as domestic obligations are becoming more numerous they are taking on, so to speak, a public character. In principle they not only have no contractual origin, but the role played by contract is continually decreasing. On the other hand the social control over the way in which obligations are entered into and dissolved is modified, and is continually increasing. The reason for this lies in the progressive disappearance of the segmentary organisation. In fact the family was for a long while a true social segment. Originally it was mixed together in the clan. If it later became distinct from it, it was as a part of the whole. It is the product of a secondary segmentation of the clan, identical to that which gave rise to the clan itself. When the latter has disappeared it still retains that same capacity. But everything that is segmentary tends increasingly to be absorbed into the mass of society. This is why the family is obliged to transform itself. Instead of remaining an autonomous society within the larger one, it is drawn increasingly into the system of organs of society. It becomes one of these organs itself, invested with special functions. Consequently all that takes place within it is capable of having general repercussions. It is this that brings about the need for the regulatory organs of society to intervene, to exercise a moderating effect over the way in which the family functions or even, in certain cases, one that acts as a positive stimulus.[17]

But it is not only outside the sphere of contractual relationships, but also on the interplay between these relationships themselves that social action is to be felt. For in a contract not everything is contractual. The only undertakings worthy of the name are those that are desired by individuals, whose sole origin is this free act of the will. Conversely, any obligation that has not been agreed by both sides is not in any way contractual. Wherever a contract exists, it is submitted to a regulatory force that is imposed by society and not by individuals: it is a force that becomes ever more weighty and complex.

It is true that the contracting parties can agree to dispense in certain respects with the arrangements laid down in the law. But firstly, their rights in this respect are not unlimited. For example, an understanding between parties cannot validate a contract that does not satisfy the conditions for validity laid down by the law. It is certain that in the vast majority of cases the contract is no longer now constrained to employ set forms, but we must not forget that in our legal codes there still exist 'solemn contracts'. Yet if the law generally does not prescribe the formalist requirements that once it did, it subjects the contract to obligations of another kind. It denies any binding power to undertakings entered into by one incapacitated mentally, or those that lack a purpose, or whose reasons are illegal, or made by a person who has no right to sell, or relating to a thing that cannot be sold. Among the obligations that the law decrees must flow from the various forms of contract, there are some that cannot be changed by any stipulations whatsoever. Thus the seller cannot shirk the obligation to guarantee the buyer against any eviction which results from an action which is his (the seller's) responsibility (art. 1628), nor to reimburse the price of the sale in the case of an eviction, whatever the cause, providing that the buyer was unaware of the risk he was running (art. 1629) nor to explain clearly what the buyer is binding himself to do (art. 1602). Likewise, to a certain extent at least, he cannot be dispensed from giving a guarantee against hidden defects (arts. 1641 and 1643), particularly if he (the seller) was aware of them. If it concerns real estate, it is the buyer who has a duty not to profit from the situation by offering a price appreciably far below the real value of the thing, etc. (art. 1674). Moreover, concerning all matters of proof, the nature of the actions to which the contract assigns a right, the time scale within which they must be performed – these are all entirely removed from the sphere of individual negotiation.

In other cases the action of society is manifested not only in the refusal to recognise a contract drawn up in contravention of the law, but by positive intervention. Thus, regardless of the terms of the agreement, the judge in certain circumstances may grant the debtor a stay of execution (arts 1184, 1244, 1655, 1900), or oblige a borrower to return to the lender the latter's property before the date agreed upon, if he has pressing need of it (art. 1189). But what demonstrates even more clearly that contracts give rise to obligations that have not been contracted for is that 'they commit one not only to what is expressed in them, but also to all the consequences that equity, usage and the law impart to the obligation incurred, according to its nature' (art. 1135). By virtue of this principle there must be ascribed, in addition to the contract, 'the clauses which are customary to it, although not expressed' (art. 1160).

Yet even when social action is not stated in this express form, it does not cease to be real. Indeed this possibility of dispensing with the law, which seems to reduce contractual law to the role of a possible substitute for contracts proper, is in the vast majority of cases purely theoretical. To convince ourselves of this we have only to represent to ourselves what it consists of.

Undoubtedly when men bind one another by contract it is because, through the division of labour, whether this be simple or complex, they have need of one another. But for them to co-operate harmoniously it is not enough that they should enter into a relationship, nor even be aware of the state of mutual interdependence in which they find themselves. The conditions for their co-operation must also be fixed for the entire duration of their relationship. The duties and rights of each one must be defined, not only in the light of the situation as it presents itself at the moment when the contract is concluded, but in anticipation of circumstances that can arise and can modify it. Otherwise, at every moment there would be renewed conflicts and quarrels. Indeed we must not forget that if the division of labour joins interests solidly together, it does not mix them together: it leaves them distinct, and in competition with one another. Just as within the individual organism each organ is at odds with the others, whilst still acting in concert with them, each contracting party, whilst having need of the other, seeks to obtain at least cost what he needs, that is, to gain the widest possible rights in exchange for the least possible obligations.

Thus it is necessary for the allocation of both rights and obligations to be prescribed in advance, and yet this cannot take place according to some preconceived plan. There is nothing in the nature of things from which we can deduce that the obligations of either party should attain any particular limit. But every decision of this kind can only be the result of a compromise, one that steers a middle course between the interests that are in competition and their solidarity with one another. It is a position of equilibrium that can only be found by a more or less laborious process of trial and error. It is very clear that we cannot begin this process again, or restore after fresh effects this equilibrium, every time that we enter into a contractual relationship. We lack all the elements for doing this. It is not at the moment when difficulties arise that they should be resolved. Yet we cannot foresee the variety of possible circumstances that may arise during the period our contract will run, nor fix beforehand, by means of a simple mental calculation, what will be in every case the rights and duties of each person, save in matters of which we have very special practical experience. Moreover, the material conditions of life prevent a repetition of such operations.

For at every instant, and often unexpectedly, we find we bind ourselves in this way, either in what we buy or sell, or in travelling, hiring out our services, and putting up at a hotel, etc. Most of our relationships with others are of a contractual nature. If therefore we had each time to launch ourselves afresh into these conflicts and negotiations necessary to establish clearly all the conditions of the agreement, for the present and the future, our actions would be paralysed. For all these reasons, if we were only bound by the terms of our contract as they had been worked out, only a precarious solidarity would emerge.

But contractual law exists to determine the legal consequences of those of our acts that we have not settled beforehand. It expresses the normal conditions for attaining equilibrium, as they have evolved gradually from the average case. Epitomising numerous, varied experiences, it foresees what we could not do individually; what we could not regulate is regulated, and this regulation is mandatory upon us, although it is not our handiwork, but that of society and tradition. It constrains us to respect obligations for which we have not contracted, in the precise meaning of the term, since we have not deliberated upon them or, on occasions, even be aware of them beforehand. Undoubtedly the initial action is always a contractual one. But it entails consequences, even immediately, that more or less go beyond the limits of the contract itself. We co-operate because we have wished to do so, but our voluntary co-operation creates for us duties that we have not desired.

Viewed in this light, the law of contract appears very differently. It is no longer a useful supplement to individual agreements, but their basic norm. It imposes itself upon us with the traditional authority of experience, it constitutes the foundation of our contractual relationships. We can only depart from it in part, and by chance. The law confers rights and imposes duties upon us as if they derived from a certain act of our will. In particular cases we can renounce some rights and relieve ourselves of some duties. Both nevertheless represent the normal type of rights and duties that the circumstances entail, and deliberate action must be taken if we wish to modify them. Thus modifications are comparatively rare; in principle, it is the rule that is applied, and innovations are exceptional. The law of contract therefore exercises over us a regulatory action of the utmost importance, since it determines in advance what we should do and what we can demand. It is a law that can be changed only by the agreement of the parties concerned. Yet so long as it has not been repealed or replaced, it retains an entire authority. Moreover, we can only act in the capacity of legislator very periodically. Thus only a difference in degree marks the law that regulates the obligations arising from contract and those that prescribe the other duties of citizens.

Finally, beyond this organised, precise pressure exerted by the law, there is another that arises from morals. In the way in which we conclude and carry out contracts, we are forced to conform to rules which, although not sanctioned, either directly or indirectly, by any legal code, are none the less mandatory. There are professional obligations that are purely moral but that are nevertheless very strict. They are particularly apparent in the so-called liberal professions. If perhaps they are less numerous in other occupations, we may, as we shall see, have grounds for asking whether this is not the result of some unhealthy state. Although this kind of action is more diffuse than the legal one, it is just as much a social matter. Moreover, it is necessarily more extensive the more contractual relationships are developed, for like contracts its action has many ramifications.

Summing up, therefore, the contract is not sufficient by itself, but is only possible because of the regulation of contracts, which is of social origin. This is implicit, firstly because the function of contract is less to create new rules than to diversify pre-established rules in particular cases; secondly, because it has not, and cannot have, any power to bind save under certain conditions that need to be defined. If in principle society confers upon it a power of obligation it is because generally the agreement of individual wills is sufficient to ensure – excepting the reservations made above – harmonious collaboration between the diffused social functions. But if it runs contrary to its own purpose, if it is such as to disturb the regular working of the social organs, if, as has been said, it is not fair, then, since it lacks social value, it must needs be stripped of all authority. Thus in any case the role of society cannot be reduced to a passive one of seeing that contracts are carried out. It has also to determine in what conditions they are capable of being executed and, if the need arise, restore them to their normal form. Agreement between the parties concerned cannot make a clause fair which of itself is unfair. There are rules of justice that social justice must prevent being violated, even if a clause has been agreed by the parties concerned.

Thus some regulation is necessary, but its extent cannot be delimited in advance. A contract, states Spencer, has the purpose of ensuring for the workman expenditure on his behalf equivalent to what his labour has caused him.[18] If this is really the role of contract, it can never fulfil it unless it is regulated much more meticulously than it is today. For it would indeed be a miracle if it sufficed to guarantee to produce such equivalents. In fact, sometimes gain outweighs the outlay, sometimes the opposite – and the disproportionality is often glaring. Yet – and this is the retort of a whole school of thought – if the gains are too low, the function will be abandoned for other functions; if they are too high, the function will be much sought after and competition will reduce the gain. They forget that a whole section of the population cannot abandon their function in this way, since no other is available to them. Even those possessing more freedom of mobility cannot immediately take advantage of it. Such revolutions are always long drawn-out before being accomplished. Meanwhile unfair contracts, unsocial by definition, have been executed with the co-operation of society, and when equilibrium has been established in one respect there is no reason for it to be upset in another.

We need not demonstrate that this intervention, in its various forms, is of an eminently positive kind, since its effect is to determine the manner in which we should co-operate together. It is true that it is not the act of intervention that sets off the functions that co-operate with one another. Yet it regulates their co-operation once it has begun. As soon as we have taken the first step towards co-operation, we are committed and the regulatory action of society exerts itself upon us. If Spencer termed this action negative it is because for him contract consists solely in exchange. Yet even from this standpoint the expression he employs is inexact. Undoubtedly, after having taken delivery of an article or had a service performed for me, when I refuse to provide the agreed equivalent I am taking from another what belongs to him, and it may be said that society, in obliging me to keep my promise, is merely preventing the occurrence of some prejudice or indirect act of aggression. But if I have merely promised a service without having received in advance the recompense for it, I am nonetheless bound to fulfil my undertaking. However, in that case I am not enriching myself at the expense of others. I am merely refusing to be of service to them. Moreover, exchange, as we have seen, is not the whole of contract; there is also the harmonious working of the functions that are co-operating. These are not only in contact in the brief time when things pass from one person to another. More extensive relationships necessarily result from them, in the course of which it is important that their solidarity should not be disturbed.

Even the biological comparisons with which Spencer likes to support his theory of the free contract, however, rather serve to refute it. He compares, as we have done, economic functions to the visceral activity within the individual organism, and remarks that the latter does not directly depend upon the cerebro-spinal system, but upon a special mechanism whose main branches are the great sympathetic nerve system, and the pneumo-gastric nerve. Yet if from this comparison it is legitimate to induce, with some degree of probability, that economic functions are not of a kind to be placed under the immediate influence of the social 'brain', it does not follow that they can be isolated from all regulatory influence. For although the sympathetic nerve system is to a certain extent independent of the brain, it dominates the movements of the viscera just as the brain does those of the muscles. Thus if there is in society a mechanism of the same kind, there must be organs that are subject to a similar effect.

According to Spencer, what corresponds to this is that exchange of information that takes place continually from one market-place to another regarding the state of supply and demand and which, in consequence, halts or stimulates production.[19] But nothing in this resembles any kind of regulatory action. To transmit information is not to be in command of movement. This function is indeed that of the afferent nerves, but has nothing in common with the nerve ganglions. It is the latter that exercise the domination we have just referred to. Stationed on the pathway of the sensations, it is wholly through their mediation that the sensations can be manifested in movement. Very probably, if research on this were more advanced, we would see that their role, whether central or not, is to ensure harmonious co-operation between the functions they govern. This would be constantly disorganised if it were to vary with every fluctation in stimulatory impressions. The sympathetic nerve system of society must therefore include, apart from a system of transmission paths, truly regulatory organs which, entrusted with the task of combining the action of the intestines just as the cerebral ganglion combines action from outside, would have the power to halt, amplify or moderate stimuli according to need.

This comparision induces us even to think that the regulatory action to which economic life is at present subject is not what it should be normally. It is undoubtedly not non-existent, as we have just shown. But either it is diffuse or it emanates directly from the state. It will be difficult to find in our present-day societies regulatory centres analogous to the ganglions of the great sympathetic nerve system. Certainly if this uncertainty had no basis other than this lack of symmetry between the individual and society, it would not merit our attention dwelling upon it. Yet we must not forget that up to very recent times such mediating organs did exist: these were the trade guilds. We need not discuss here their advantages and disadvantages. Moreover, such discussion cannot easily be objective, for we can hardly decide these questions of practical utility save according to our personal feelings. But the mere fact that an institution has been necessary to societies for centuries would make it seem rather improbable that societies have suddenly found themselves able to do without it. Undoubtedly they have changed, but it is legitimate to presume *a priori* that the changes undergone demanded far less radical a destruction of that organisation than its transformation. In any case they have existed for far too short a time under these conditions for us to be able to decide whether such a state is normal and definitive or simply one of sickness that has occurred by chance. Even the disturbances in this sphere of social life that have been felt since do not appear to prejudice a favourable answer. Later in this study we shall find other facts which confirm this assertion.[20]

III

Finally, there remains administrative law. This is what we call the set of rules that firstly determine the functions of the central organ and their relationships, and then the functions of the organs directly subordinate to the central organ, their relationships with one another and with those of the central organ, and with the diffused functions of society. If we again borrow from biology a terminology which, although metaphorical, is none the less convenient, we would say that the rules regulate the way in which the cerebro-spinal system of the social organism functions. It is this system that in common parlance is given the name of the state.

That the social action expressed in this form is of a positive kind is not disputed. Indeed its object is to fix how these special functions should co-operate. In certain respects it even imposes co-operation, for these various organs cannot be maintained except through taxes exacted obligatorily from every citizen. Yet according to Spencer this regulatory apparatus is on the decline as the industrial type of society emerges from the military type, and in the end the functions of the state may be destined to be limited solely to the administration of justice.

However, the reasons advanced to support this proposition are remarkably weak. It is almost wholly by a short comparison between England and France, and between the England of former times and England today that Spencer believes he can induce this general law of historical development.[21] But conditions for proof are no different in sociology from what they are in the other sciences. To prove a hypothesis is not to show that it accounts fairly satisfactorily for some facts that are conveniently recalled; it means to set up methodical experiments. It is to show that the phenomena between which a relationship is established are either universally in harmony or do not exist save together, or vary in the same direction and in the same relationship. But a few examples expounded in any order do not constitute proof.

What is more, these facts taken by themselves in the event prove nothing, for all that they demonstrate is that the place of the individual is becoming greater and governmental power *less absolute*. But there need be no contradiction in the fact that the scope of individual action is growing at the same time as that of the state, or that the functions not directly placed in a state of dependence *vis-à-vis* the central regulatory mechanism develop at the same time as the latter. Moreover, a power can be both absolute and very simple. Nothing is less complex than the despotic government of a barbaric chief, where the functions it fulfils are rudimentary and few in number. This is because the organ directing social life may have absorbed all that life within itself, so to speak, nevertheless without being very developed, if social life itself is not very developed. It merely enjoys an exceptional supremacy over the rest of society, because nothing is capable of containing or neutralising it. But it may well be that it assumes greater size as other organs begin to form that act as a countervailing force to it. For it is enough that the total volume of the organism should have increased. Doubtless the action it exerts in these conditions is no longer of the same nature. Yet the points at which it is exerted have multiplied in number. If the action is less violent, it does not cease from exercising constraint in no less formal a way. Acts of disobedience to the orders of authority are no longer treated as sacrilege, nor are they consequently repressed with the same superabundance of severity. But they are not more tolerated, and such orders are more numerous and relate to more different species. Now the problem posed is to not to know whether the coercive power which this regulatory apparatus has at its command is more or less intense, but whether that mechanism itself has become greater or less in size.

Once the problem has been formulated in this way the solution is sure. History indeed shows that administrative law is regularly more developed the more societies belong to a higher type. On the other hand, the more we go back to their origins, the more rudimentary it is. The state that Spencer holds up as an ideal is in reality the state in its primitive form. Indeed, according to the English philosopher, the sole functions peculiar to it are those of justice and war, at least in so far as war is necessary. In lower societies it has in fact no other role. Doubtless these functions are not understood in the same way as they are nowadays, but they are no different because of that. That entirely tyrannical intervention that Spencer points to is only one of the ways in which judicial power is exercised. By repressing attacks on religion, etiquette, or traditions of every kind the state fulfils the same office as do our judges today when they protect the life or property of individuals. On the other hand, the state's attributions become ever more numerous and diverse as one approaches the higher types of society. The organ of justice itself, which in the beginning is very simple, begins increasingly to become differentiated. Different law-courts are instituted as well as distinctive magistratures, and the respective roles of both are determined, as well as the relationships between them. A host of functions that were diffuse become more concentrated. The task of watching over the education of the young, protecting health generally, presiding over the functioning of the public assistance system or managing the transport and communications systems gradually falls within the province of the central body. As a result that body develops. At the same time it extends progressively over the whole area of its territory an ever more densely packed, complex network, with branches that are substituted for existing local bodies or that assimilate them. Statistical services keep it up to date with all that is happening in the innermost parts of the organism. The mechanism of international relations – by this is meant diplomacy – itself assumes still greater proportions. As institutions are formed, which like the great establishments providing financial credit are of general public interest by their size and the multiplicity of functions linked to them, the state exercises over them a moderating influence. Finally, even the military apparatus, which Spencer asserts is disappearing, seems on the contrary to develop, becoming ever more centralised.

This evolution emerges with so much clarity from the lessons of history that it does not seem necessary for us to enter into greater detail in order to demonstrate it. If we compare tribes that lack all central authority with tribes that are centralised, and the latter to the city, the city to feudal societies, feudal societies to those of the present day, we can follow step by step the principal stages in the development whose general progression we have just traced out. Thus it runs counter to all method to regard the present dimensions of the organ of government as a morbid phenomenon attributable to a chance concatenation of circumstances. Everything compels us to look upon it as a normal phenomenon, inherent in the very structure of higher societies, since it advances in a regular, continuous fashion, as societies evolve towards this type.

Moreover, we can show, at least in broad outline, how it is the outcome of the progress of the division of labour itself and of the process of transformation, whose effect is to facilitate the passage of societies of a segmentary type to the organised type.

So long as each segment has a life peculiarly its own, it forms a small society within the larger one and consequently has its own special regulatory organs, just as does the larger one. But their vigour is necessarily proportional to the intensity of this more local activity. Thus they cannot fail to grow weaker when that activity itself grows weaker. We know that this weakening process occurs with the progressive disappearance of the segmentary organisation. The central organ, finding itself faced with less resistance, since the forces that held it in check have lost some of their strength, develops, attracting to itself these functions, similar to those it exercises already, but that can no longer be retained by those entities that held them up to then. The local organs, instead of preserving their individuality and remaining diffuse, therefore come to merge into the central mechanism, which in consequence is enlarged, and this the more society becomes extensive and the fusion complete. This signifies that it is all the more voluminous the more societies belong to a higher species.

This phenomenon occurs with a kind of mechanical necessity and is moreover useful, because it corresponds to the new state of affairs. In so far as society ceases to be formed by a replication of similar segments, the regulatory mechanism must itself cease to be composed of a replication of autonomous segmentary organs. However, we do not mean that normally the state absorbs into itself all the regulatory organs of society of whatever kind, but only those that are of the same nature as its own, that is, those that govern life generally. As for those that control special functions, such as economic functions, they lie outside its zone of attraction. Among these there can certainly be effected a coalescence of the same kind, but not between them and the state – or at least if they are subject to the action of the higher centres they remain distinct from them. With vertebrates the cerebro-spinal system is very developed and it does have influence on the sympathetic nervous system, although it also leaves it great autonomy.

In the second place, so long as society is made up of segments what occurs in one of these has less chance of having any repercussion upon the others, the stronger the segmentary organisation. The alveolar system naturally lends itself to the localisation of social phenomena and their effects. Thus in a colony of polyps one may be sick without the others feeling any ill effect. This is no longer the case when society is made up of a system of organs. As a result of their mutual dependence, what infects one infects the others, and thus any serious change assumes a general interest.

This generalisation is more easily arrived at because of two other circumstances. The more labour is divided up, the less each organ of society consists of distinctive parts. As large-scale is substituted for small-scale industry, the number of separate undertakings grows less. Each undertaking acquires relatively more importance, because it represents a larger fraction of the whole. All that happens in it has therefore social repercussions that are much more extensive. The closing of a small workshop gives rise to only very limited disturbances, which are not felt beyond a small circle. On the contrary, the failure of a large industrial company entails a great public upheaval. Moreover, as the progress of the division of labour determines a greater concentration in the mass of society, between different parts of the same tissue, organ or mechanism there exists a closer contact which renders easier the chances of infection. Motion originating at one point is rapidly passed on to others. We have only to observe, for example, the rapidity with which a strike today becomes general throughout the same trade. A disturbance of a somewhat general character cannot occur without having repercussions upon the higher centres. Since these are painfully affected, they are obliged to intervene, and this intervention occurs all the more frequently the higher the type of society. But consequently they must be organised to do so. They must extend their ramifications in all directions, so as to keep in touch with the different areas of the organism and to maintain in a more immediate state of dependence certain organs whose action could occasionally give rise to exceptionally grave repercussions. In short, since their functions become more numerous and complex, the organ serving as their substratum needs to develop, just as does the body of legal rules determining these functions.

To the complaint often levelled against him of contradicting his own theories by admitting that the development of the higher centres occurs in an inverse direction in societies and organisms, Spencer has answered that these different variations in the organ follow corresponding variations in the function. According to him, the role of the cerebro-spinal system consists essentially in regulating the relationships of the individual with the outside world, to combine movements so that he may seize his prey or escape from his enemy.[22] As a mechanism of attack and defence, the system is naturally very large in the highest organisms, where these external relationships are themselves very developed. This is the case in military societies, which live in a state of perpetual hostility with their neighbours. In contrast, among industrial peoples war is the exception. Social interests mainly concern the inner order. The external regulatory mechanism, having no longer any reason to exist, thus necessarily declines.

But this explanation is based on a double error.

Firstly, any organism, whether or not it has any depredatory instincts, lives in an environment with which, the more complex it is, the larger the number of its relationships. Thus if hostile relationships diminish as societies become more pacific, they are replaced by others. Industrial peoples have mutual connections that have developed differently from those that the lower tribes maintain with one another, no matter how warlike they may be. We are talking not of the connection established directly between one individual and another, but of that which unites social bodies among themselves. Every society has general interests to defend against others, if not by taking up arms, at least through negotiations, coalitions and treaties.

Moreover, it is not the case that the brain does no more than govern relationships outside it. On occasion not only does it seemingly modify the state of the organs by wholly internal channels, but even when it acts from the outside it exerts an effect on what is internal. Indeed, even the innermost intestinal viscera can function only with the help of substances that come to them from the outside; as the brain has absolute command over these, it has at every single moment an influence in this way over the whole organism. It is said that the stomach does not function at its command, but the presence of foodstuffs is enough to stimulate peristaltic action. If food is available, it is because the brain has willed it to be so, and it is there in the quantity the brain planned and of the quality it has chosen. It is not the brain that governs the heart beat, but it can by appropriate action slow it down or speed it up. There are scarcely any body tissues that do not undergo one or other of the disciplined treatments it decrees, and the control that it exercises in this way is more extensive and profound the higher the type to which the animal belongs. This is because the brain's real role is to assume charge not only of relationships merely external to it, but of the whole of life. This function is therefore the more complex the richer and more concentrated life itself is. The same holds good for societies. What renders the organ of government more important or less so is not because people are more pacific or less so. But it grows through the progress of the division of labour, as societies include a greater number of different organs which are more closely linked to one another.

IV

The following propositions sum up this first part of our work.

Social life is derived from a dual source, the similarity of individual consciousnesses and the social division of labour. In the first case the individual is socialised because, lacking any individuality of his own, he is mixed up with his fellows in the same collective type. In the second case it is because, whilst his physionomy and his activities are personal to him, distinguishing him from others, he depends upon them to the very extent that he is distinguished from them, and consequently upon the society that is the result of their combining together.

The similarity of consciousnesses gives rise to legal rules which, under the threat of repressive measures, impose upon everybody uniform beliefs and practices. The more pronounced the similarity, the more completely social life is mixed up with religious life, and the closer economic institutions are to communism.

The division of labour gives rise to legal rules that determine the nature and relationships of the function thus divided up, but the infringement of the rules entails only measures of reparation lacking any expiatory character.

Each set of legal rules moreover is accompanied by a set of rules that are purely moral. Where penal law is very voluminous common morality is very extensive. This means that there are a host of collective practices placed under the protection of public opinion. Where restitutory law is very developed, for each profession a professional morality exists. Within the same group of workers a public opinion exists, diffused throughout this limited body, which despite the lack of any legal sanctions, is nevertheless obeyed. There are customs and usages common to the same group of functionaries which none can infringe without incurring the reprimand of the corporation.[23] Yet this morality is distinguished from the previous one by differences analogous to those that separate the two corresponding species of laws. This morality is in fact localised within a limited area of society. Moreover, the repressive character of the sanctions attached to it is appreciably less severe. Professional faults give rise to a disapproval much weaker than attacks upon public morality.

However, the rules of professional morality and law are categorical, like the others. They force the individual to act in accordance with ends that are not for his own, to make concessions, to agree to compromises, to take into account interests superior to his own. Consequently even where society rests wholly upon the division of labour, it does not resolve itself into a myriad of atoms juxtaposed together, between which only external and transitory contact can be established. The members are linked by ties that extend well beyond the very brief moment when the act of exchange is being accomplished. Each one of the functions that the members exercise is constantly dependent upon others and constitutes with them a solidly linked system. Consequently the nature of the task selected derives from duties that are permanent. Because we fulfil this or that domestic or social function we are caught up in a network of obligations from which we have no right to disengage ourselves. There is above all one organ in regard to which our state of dependence continues to grow: this is the state. The points where we come into contact with it are multiplied, as well as the occasions when it is charged with reminding us of the sentiment of our common solidarity.

Thus altruism is not destined to become, as Spencer would wish, a kind of pleasant ornament of our social life, but one that will always be its fundamental basis. How indeed could we ever do without it? Men cannot live together without agreeing, and consequently without making mutual sacrifices, joining themselves to one another in a strong and enduring fashion. Every society is a moral society. In certain respects this feature is even more pronounced in organised societies. Because no individual is sufficient unto himself, it is from society that he receives all that is needful, just as it is for society that he labours. Thus there is formed a very strong feeling of the state of dependence in which he finds himself: he grows accustomed to valuing himself at his true worth, viz., to look upon himself only as a part of the whole, the organ of an organism. Such sentiments are of a kind not only to inspire those daily sacrifices that ensure the regular development of everyday social life but even on occasion acts of utter renunciation and unbounded abnegation. For its part society learns to look upon its constituent members no longer as things over which it has rights, but as co-operating members with whom it cannot do without and towards whom it has duties. Thus it is wrong to oppose a society that derives from a community of beliefs to one whose foundation is co-operation, by granting only the first a moral character and seeing in the latter only an economic grouping. In reality, co-operation has also its intrinsic morality. There is only reason to believe, as we shall later see more clearly, that in our present-day societies this morality has still not developed to the extent which from now onwards is necessary for them.

But this morality is not of the same nature as the other. The latter is strong only if the individual is weak. Made up of rules practised by all without distinction, it receives from this universal, uniform practice an authority that makes it something superhuman, removing it more or less from argument. The other, by contrast, develops as the individual personality grows stronger. However regulated a function may be, it always leaves plenty of room for individual initiative. Even many of the obligations that are subject to penalties in this way have their origin in a choice by the will. It is we who choose our profession and even certain of our domestic functions. Doubtless once our resolve has ceased to be internal and been translated externally into social consequences, we are bound by it: duties are imposed upon us that we have not expressly wished. Yet it is through a voluntary act that they arose. Finally, because these rules of conduct relate not to the conditions of ordinary life but to different forms of professional activity, they have for this reason a more temporal character which, so to speak, whilst retaining all their obligatory force, makes them more accessible to the actions of men.

There are thus two great currents in social life, to which correspond two types of structure that are no less different.

Of these currents, the one that has its origin in social similarities flows at first alone, and has no competition. At that time it mingles with the very life of society. Then gradually it becomes channelled and becomes less apparent, whilst the second continues to grow bigger. Likewise the segmentary structure is more and more overshadowed by the other, but without ever disappearing completely.

We have just established the reality of this relationship of inverse variation. We shall discover its causes in the following book.

Notes

1. H. Spencer, *Principles of Sociology* (London, 1855) vol. II, p. 245.
2. Ibid., vol. II, p. 697.
3. Ibid., vol. I, p. 589.
4. Ibid., vol. II, p. 701.
5. Ibid., vol. II, p. 246. Cf. also H. Spencer, *The Man versus the State* (London, 1884).
6. This is what Fouillée does when he opposes contract to pressure. Cf. *Science sociale*, p. 8.
7. Spencer. Source not identified.
8. Naturally the same holds good for the dissolution of the marriage tie.
9. Smith, *Marriage and Kinship in early Arabia* (Cambridge, 1885) p. 135.
10. Krauss, *Sitte und Brauch der Südslaven*, ch. 31.
11. Viollet, *Précis de l'histoire du droit français*, p. 402.
12. Accarias, *Précis de droit romain*, vol. I, pp. 240 ff.
13. Viollet, *Précis de l'histoire*, p. 406.
14. L. H. Morgan, *Ancient Society* (London, 1877) p. 81.
15. Krauss, *Sitte und Brauch*, pp. 113 ff.
16. Salic Law, title LX.
17. For example, in the cases of guardianship and interdict, where the public authority sometimes intervenes by virtue of its office. The progress of this regulatory action does not contradict the regression, as stated above, of the collective sentiments concerning the family. On the contrary, the first phenomenon presumes the latter. For these sentiments to have diminished or grown weaker, it was necessary for the family to cease to be confused with society, and to have constituted a sphere of personal action withdrawn from the common consciousness. Such a transformation was needed for it later to become an organ of society, for an organ is an individualised part of society.
18. Spencer. Source not identified.
19. Spencer. Source not identified.
20. Cf. Book III, Chapter I. Cf. particularly the Preface, where we express ourselves more explicitly on this point.
21. Spencer, *Principles of Sociology*, vol. II, pp. 710–18.
22. Spencer. Source not identified.
23. Moreover, this rebuke, like any moral punishment, is translated into external action (disciplinary punishments, dismissal of employees, loss of relationships, etc.).

Book II

The Causes and Conditions

Chapter I

The Progress of the Division of Labour and of Happiness

What are the causes of the division of labour?

Undoubtedly there can be no question of finding one single formula to account for all the possible forms of the division of labour. Such a formula does not exist. Each particular case depends upon special causes that can only be determined by a special investigation. The problem that we are posing is less wide. If we leave out of account the various forms that the division of labour assumes according to the conditions of time and space, the general fact remains that the division develops regularly as history proceeds. This fact certainly depends on causes that are likewise constant, causes that we shall investigate.

This cause could not consist of a mental representation beforehand of the effects that the division of labour produces by contributing to the maintenance of the equilibrium of societies. This is a side-effect too remote to be understood by everybody and most minds have no consciousness of it. In any case it could only begin to become apparent when the division of labour was already very advanced.

According to the most widely held theory it may have had no other origin than the constant desire man has of increasing his happiness. Indeed we know that the more work is divided up, the higher the production. The resources that it places at our disposal are more abundant; they are also of better quality. Science is carried out better and more quickly; works of art are more plentiful and more delicate; industry produces more and its products are more finished. Now, man needs all these things. Thus it seems that he must be the happier the more of them that he possesses, and consequently be naturally induced to seek after them.

179

Having postulated this, the regularity with which the division of labour has increased can be easily explained. It has been said that a combination of circumstances, very easy to envisage, has alerted men to some of these advantages, so that they have sought to extend the division of labour ever farther, in order to derive the maximum benefit from it. Thus its progress, it is alleged, has been influenced entirely by individual and psychological causes. To construct a theory regarding this, it would not be necessary to observe societies and their structure: the simplest and most basic instinct of the human heart would suffice to account for it. It is the need for happiness that may impel the individual to specialise more and more. Doubtless, since every specialisation presumes the simultaneous presence of several individuals and their mutual co-operation, it would not be possible without the existence of society. But instead of being the determining cause, society might be merely the means by which specialisation is realised, the material necessary for the organisation of divided labour tasks. It might even be an effect of the phenomenon rather than its cause. Is it not repeatedly stated that it is the need for co-operation that has given rise to societies? Might societies therefore not have been constituted so that work can be divided up, far from work being divided up for social reasons?

This is a classical explanation of political economy. Moreover, it appears so simple and self-evident that it is accepted unconsciously by a host of thinkers whose conceptions are changed by it. This is why we need first of all to examine it.

I

Nothing has been so little proved as the alleged axiom upon which it rests. No rational limits can be assigned to the productive power of labour. It doubtless depends upon the state of technology, the capital available, etc. But these obstacles are never anything other than provisional, as experience demonstrates, and each generation pushes back farther the frontier at which the previous generation halted. Even if one day a maximum should be arrived at beyond which it could not go – and this is a purely gratuitous conjecture – it is at least certain that even now it has behind it an immense field of development. If, therefore, as is supposed, happiness has increased regularly with it, it would have to be able to increase indefinitely, or at least the stages of growth that are feasible for it should be proportionate to those that have gone before. If happiness increased as pleasant stimuli became more frequent and more intense, it would be entirely natural for man to seek to produce more so as to have still greater enjoyment. Yet in reality our capacity for happiness is very restricted.

Indeed it is a truth generally recognised today that pleasure does not accompany states of consciousness that are either too intense or are too weak. There is pain when functional activity is insufficient, but excessive activity produces the same effect.[1] Certain physiologists even believe that pain is linked to an over-intense form of nervous stimulation.[2] Pleasure is therefore situated between these two extremes. This proposition is moreover a corollary of the law of Weber and Fechner. If the mathematical formula that these experimenters have given to it may be of questionable accuracy, they have at least placed one point beyond dispute. This is that the variations in intensity through which a sensation can pass extend between two limits. If the stimulus is too weak it is not felt. But if it goes beyond a certain level, the increments it receives produce less and less effect, until they cease entirely to be noticed. Now this law is equally true of that quality of sensation called pleasure. The law was even formulated for pleasure and pain long before it was for other elements of sensation. Bernoulli applied it directly to the most complex sentiments, and Laplace, interpreting it in the same way, gave it the form of a relationship existing between physical fortune and moral fortune.[3] The gamut of variability through which the intensity of a single pleasure may move is thus restricted.

What is more, if states of consciousness of moderate intensity are generally pleasant, they do not all present conditions equally favourable to the production of pleasure. Around the lower limit the changes through which the agreeable activity passes are too small, in absolute value, to arouse feelings of pleasure of great strength. Conversely, when it is close to the point of indifference, that is, near its maximum, the orders of magnitude in which it increases have too weak a relative value. A man possessing a very small capital cannot easily increase it in proportions that are sufficient appreciably to change his condition. This is why the initial economies that he makes bring so little enjoyment. They are too small to better his situation. The insignificant advantages they procure do not compensate for the privations that they have cost. Likewise a man whose fortune is excessive finds no longer any pleasure save in exceptional profits, for he measures their importance against what he already possesses. The state of affairs is completely different in the case of moderate fortunes. Here both the absolute size and the relative size of the variations occur under the best conditions for pleasure to arise from them, for they are easily important enough, and yet they need not be outstanding to be valued at their worth. The standard that serves to measure their value is not so high for a big depreciation in it to occur. The intensity of a pleasant stimulus cannot therefore *usefully* increase save between limits even narrower than we stated at the outset, for it produces its complete effect only in the space that corresponds to the average area of the pleasant activity. Below this and beyond this pleasure still continues, but it is not in proportion to the cause that produces it, whilst in that more temperate zone the slightest variations are savoured and appreciated. Nothing is lost of the force of the stimulus, which is converted wholly into pleasure.[4]

What we have just said about the intensity of each stimulus could be repeated about their number. They cease to be pleasant when they are too many or too few, just as when they exceed or do not reach a certain degree of intensity. Not without reason does human experience see the *aurea mediocritas* as the condition of happiness.

Thus if the division of labour had in reality only made progress in order to increase our happiness, it would have arrived at its extreme limit long ago, just as would have the civilisation that has arisen from it, and both would have come to a halt. In order to put man in a position to lead that modest existence that is the most favourable to pleasure it was not necessary to go on accumulating indefinitely stimuli of all kinds. A moderate development of them would have sufficed to ensure that individuals had reached the sum total of enjoyment of which they were capable. Humanity would therefore have arrived at a state of immobility from which it would never have emerged. This is what happened to the animals: the majority have not changed for centuries because they have arrived at that state of equilibrium.

Other considerations lead to the same conclusion.

We cannot state categorically that every pleasurable state is useful, nor that pleasure and utility always vary in the same direction and in the same relationship. Yet an organism that in principle might take pleasure in things that were harmful to it could plainly not sustain itself. Thus we can accept as a very general truth that pleasure is not linked to harmful states, that is, on the whole, happiness coincides with a state of health. Only creatures afflicted with some kind of physiological or psychological abnormality find pleasure in states of sickness. Now health consists in a moderate degree of activity. In fact it implies the harmonious development of all functions and these cannot develop harmoniously unless they moderate one another, that is, contain one another mutually within certain bounds, beyond which sickness begins and pleasure ceases. As for the simultaneous growth of all faculties, this is not possible for any given creature, save to a very restricted extent that is determined by the congenital state of the individual.

In this way we understand what limits human happiness: it is the constitution of man itself, taken at every moment in his history. Given his temperament, the degree of physical and moral develop- ment that he has attained, there is a maximum degree of happiness, just as there is a maximum degree of activity, that he cannot exceed. This proposition is hardly disputed, so long as it is only the organism in question: everyone recognises that the needs of the body are limited and that in consequence physical pleasure cannot increase indefinitely. But it has been claimed that spiritual functions were the exception. 'No pain to discipline and repress . . . the most energetic impulsions to devotion to others and charity, the passion- ate search for the true and the beautiful. One's hunger is assuaged with a certain quantity of food; one's reason is not satisfied by a certain quantity of learning.'[5]

This is to forget that the consciousness, like the organism, is a system of functions that balance one another and that moreover the consciousness is joined to an organic substratum of the state on which it depends. It is said that although there is a level of brightness that the eyes cannot bear there is never enough brightness for the reason. However, too much knowledge can only be acquired by an exaggerated development of the higher nervous centres, which itself cannot come about without being accompanied by painful distress. Thus there is a *maximum* limit that cannot be exceeded with impunity, and as this varies in accordance with the average brain, it was especially low at the dawn of humanity. Consequently it would have been quickly reached. Moreover, the understanding is only one of our faculties. Thus it cannot increase beyond a certain point without detriment to our practical faculties, by undermining the sentiments, beliefs and habits by which we live, and such a breakdown in equilibrium cannot occur without some distress. Sectarians of the most rudimentary religion find pleasure in the elementary cosmogony and philosophy taught them, a pleasure that we would deprive them of without any possible compensation if we succeeded in abruptly initiating them into our scientific theories, however indisputable their superiority may be. At every moment in history and in the consciousness of each individual, for clear ideas and well-conceived views, in short, for science, there is a precise limit beyond which one normally cannot go.

The same holds good for morality. Every people has its moral code that is determined by the conditions under which it is living. Thus another morality cannot be inculcated, no matter how lofty it may be, without disorganising it, and such disturbances cannot fail to have a painful effect upon individuals. Yet does not the morality of each society, taken on its own, imply the indefinite development of the virtues it recommends? This is not the case at all. To act morally is to do one's duty, and all duty is of a finite nature. It is limited by other duties. We cannot give ourselves over to other people, absolutely and utterly, without an abandonment of ourselves. Nor can we develop too much our personality without falling into a state of egoism. Moreover, the sum total of our duties is itself limited by other needs of our nature. If it is necessary for certain forms of behaviour to be subjected to that categorical domination characteristic of morality, there are other forms of it, on the other hand, which are by nature unamenable to it and yet that are none the less essential. Morality cannot direct unduly the industrial and commercial functions, etc., without paralysing them, and yet these functions are vital. Therefore to consider wealth as immoral is an error no less pernicious than to see in it the supreme good. Thus there can be excesses in morality, excesses from which, moreover, morality itself is the first to suffer. This is because, since its immediate purpose is to regulate our temporal existence, it cannot turn us away from that existence without itself extinguishing the matter to which it applies.

It is true that aesthetic and moral activity, because it is not regulated, appears to be free of any constraint or limitation. Yet in reality it is closely circumscribed by activity that is properly of a moral kind. This is because it cannot go beyond a certain limit without having an adverse effect upon morality. If we expend too much of our strength upon what is superfluous, we have not enough left to do what is needful. When too large a share is given to the imagination in morality, obligatory tasks are necessarily neglected. Any discipline must needs appear intolerable when one has grown over-accustomed to acting without any rules save those imposed by oneself. An excess of idealism and too lofty a morality often make men no longer inclined to carry out their daily duties.

Much the same may be said generally about aesthetic activity; it is only healthy if engaged in with moderation. The need to play, to indulge in acting without any purpose and for the pleasure of so doing cannot be developed beyond a certain point without detaching oneself from the serious business of life. Too much artistic sensibility is a sign of sickness that cannot be generalised without danger to society. The limit beyond which excess begins is moreover a variable one according to different peoples and the social environment. Such a limit is lower the less advanced the society is or the less cultured the environment. The ploughman, if he is at one with the conditions of his existence, is and must remain, shut off from aesthetic pleasures which are normal with the man of letters, and the same is true for the savage as compared with the civilised person.

If this is true for the luxuries of the mind, it is even more so for material luxuries. Thus there is a normal degree of intensity for all our needs, intellectual and moral as well as physical, which cannot be exceeded. At any moment in history our yearning for science, art and material wellbeing is defined, as are our appetites, and everything exceeding this amount leaves us indifferent or causes us to suffer. This is too easily forgotten when we compare the happiness of our forefathers with our own. We reason as if all our pleasures must have been theirs also. Then, as we think of all those refinements of civilisation we enjoy and that they did not know, we feel inclined to pity their lot. We forget that they had no capacity to enjoy them. Thus if they underwent so much agony so as to increase the productive capacity of labour it was not to acquire possessions of no value to them. To appreciate them they would first have had to contract tastes and habits that they did not have, that is, to change their nature.

This is in fact what they did, as is shown by the history of the transformations through which humanity has passed. For the need for greater happiness to be able to account for the development of the division of labour, it would therefore be necessary for it also to be the cause of changes that have come about progressively in human nature, and for men to have changed as well, in order to become happier.

But even if we assume that these transformations have finally produced such a result, they cannot possibly have occurred for this purpose and consequently must depend upon a different cause.

Indeed any change in human existence, whether sudden or prepared in advance, always constitutes a painful crisis, for it does violence to acquired instincts, which offer it resistance. All the past holds us back, even when the brightest prospects tempt us to go forward. It is always a laborious operation to uproot habits that time has fixed and organised within us. It is possible that a sedentary life offers greater chances of happiness than a nomad life. But when one has led for centuries no other existence than that of the nomad, one cannot easily free oneself from it. Thus if such transformations are far-reaching, the lifetime of one individual is not sufficient to bring them about. One generation does not suffice to cast off the work of generations and install the new man in the place of the old. In the present state of our societies work is not only useful, but necessary: indeed everyone feels this to be the case, and this necessity has for long been felt. However, those who find their pleasure in regular and persistent labour are rare. For most men it is still an unbearable servitude. For them the idleness of primitive times has not lost its old attraction. Such metamorphoses thus cost a great deal, without bringing in any return for a long while. The generations that initiate them do not garner the fruits, if there are any, because these come too late. They have only to provide the labour for them. Consequently it is not the expectation of very great happiness that tempts them in such undertakings.

But is it true that the happiness of men increases in proportion as men progress? Nothing is more doubtful.

II

There are certainly many pleasures open to us today that more simple natures are unaware of. Yet on the other hand we are prone to much suffering that is spared them, and it is by no means sure that the balance is in our favour. Thought is undoubtedly a source of enjoyment, one that can be very acute. On the other hand, however, how many joys are disturbed by it! For one problem resolved, how many questions are raised to which there is no answer! For one doubt cleared up, how many mysteries do we perceive that disconcert us! Likewise, although the savage does not know the pleasures that a very active life procures for us, his compensation is that he is not a prey to boredom, that torment of the cultured mind. He lets his life flow gently by without continually feeling the need to fill its too fleeting moments with great but hasty activity. Moreover, let us not forget that work is still only for the majority of men a toil and a burden.

The objection will be made that among civilised peoples life is more varied, and that variety is necessary for pleasure. But accompanying a greater mobility, civilisation brings in its train greater uniformity, for it has imposed upon mankind monotonous and unceasing labour. The savage goes from one occupation to another, according to the circumstances and the needs that impel him. Civilised man gives himself entirely over to his task, always the same, and one that offers less variety the more restricted it is. Organisation necessarily implies an absolute regularity in habits, for a change cannot occur in the mode of functioning of an organ without its having repercussions upon the whole organism. In this sense our life offers us a lesser share of the unexpected, whilst at the same time, by its greater instability, it takes away from enjoyment some of the security that it needs.

It is true that our nervous system, which has become more delicate, is open to feeble stimuli that did not affect our forefathers, because they were of a coarser grain. Yet also many stimuli that were agreeable have become too strong for us, and are in consequence painful. If we are sensitive to more pleasures, we are also sensitive to more sorrows. Moreover, if it is true that, other things being equal, suffering produces in the organism greater repercussions than does joy,[6] that an unpleasant stimulus has a more painful effect upon us than a pleasant stimulus of the same intensity causes us pleasure, this greater sensibility might well be more contrary than favourable to happiness. In fact, very highly strung nervous systems live in pain and even end up by becoming attached to it. Is it not very remarkable that the fundamental cult of the most civilised religions is that of human suffering? Doubtless, for life to continue today, as in former times, on average the amount of pleasure should exceed the sorrow. Yet it is not certain that this excess of pleasure is very considerable.

Finally, above all it is not proved that this excess ever gives the measure of happiness. Doubtless such obscure questions as yet have hardly been studied, and nothing can be affirmed with certainty. However, it does really seem that happiness is something different from the sum total of pleasure. It is a general and constant state that accompanies the regular activity of all our organic and psychological functions. Thus continuous activities such as respiration and circulation procure no positive enjoyment. Yet it is above all upon these that depend our good humour and vitality. Every pleasure is a sort of crisis; it is born, lasts for a moment, and dies. Life, on the other hand, goes on. What causes its basic charm must be continuous, just as it is. Pleasure is local; it is an affective sentiment limited to one spot in the organism or the consciousness. Life resides in neither, but is everywhere present. Our attachment to it must therefore depend on some cause that is likewise of a general nature. In short, what happiness expresses is not the momentary state of this or that particular function, but the healthiness of physical and moral life as a whole. As pleasure accompanies the normal exercise of intermittent functions, it is indeed an element in happiness, and the greater place these functions have in one's life the more important it is. But it is not happiness. Pleasure cannot vary the level of happiness save within restricted limits, for it relates to ephemeral causes, whereas happiness consists of permanent attitudes. For local events to be able to affect profoundly this fundamental basis of our sensibility, they must be repeated with exceptional frequency and have exceptional consequences. Most often, on the contrary, it is pleasure that depends upon happiness: according to whether we are happy or unhappy, everything appears to smile upon us or make us sad. It has been very rightly asserted that we carry our happiness within ourselves.

But if this is true there is no need to ask oneself whether happiness increases with civilisation. It is the index of the state of health. Now the health of a species is no more fuller because that species is of a higher type. A healthy mammal does not feel better than an equally healthy protozoa. The same must be true of happiness. It does not increase because activity becomes richer, but it is the same wherever it is healthy. The most simple creature and the most complex one experience the same happiness if they both equally realise their own nature. The average savage can be just as happy as the normal civilised person.

Thus the savages are just as content with their lot as we can be with our own. This perfect contentment is even one of the distinctive traits of their character. They desire nothing more than what they have and have no longing to change their condition:

> The inhabitant of the North [states Waitz] does not seek out the South in order to better his situation, and the inhabitant of a hot, unhealthy country no more aspires to leave it for a more favourable climate. In spite of the numerous illnesses and afflictions of every kind to which the inhabitant of Darfour is exposed, he loves his native land, and not only can he not emigrate, but he yearns to return home if he is abroad. . . . As a general rule, whatever may be the material misery in which a people is living, it continues to consider its country as the best in the world, its way of living the most fertile in pleasure that there could be, and it looks upon itself as the first among all peoples. This conviction appears generally to reign among the black peoples.[7] Thus in those countries which, like so many lands in America, have been exploited by the Europeans, the natives firmly believe that the Whites have only left their own countries in order to come seeking happiness in America. It is true that the example is quoted of a few young savages whose unhealthy anxiety led them to seek happiness outside their own country. But these are very rare exceptions.

It is true that observers have sometimes depicted the life of lower societies in a completely different light. But this is because they have taken their own impressions to be those of the natives. Now an existence that appears to be intolerable for us can be pleasant for men of a different physical and moral constitution. For example, when from infancy one is accustomed to exposing one's life at every moment and, in consequence, to set it at naught, what is death? In order to feel pity at the fate of primitive peoples, it does not therefore suffice for us to establish that hygiene rules are hardly respected and that peoples are badly policed. Only the individual is in a position to appreciate his own happiness; he is happy if he feels happy. Now, 'From the inhabitant of Tierra del Fuego to the Hottentot, man in his natural state lives satisfied with himself and with his lot.'[8] How much rarer is this state of contentment in Europe! These facts explain what a man of experience has been able to state: Cowper Rose declares that there are situations where the man who thinks feels himself inferior to the one whom nature alone has nurtured, where he asks whether the most solid convictions are of greater worth than narrow prejudices that are nevertheless pleasing to the heart.[9]

But here is a more objective proof.

The sole fact of experience that demonstrates that life is generally good is that the overwhelming majority of men prefer it to death. For this to be so it must be that in the average existence happiness triumphs over unhappiness. If the relationship were reversed one would not understand either whence arose the attachment of men to life, nor above all how it could continue, threatened as it is at every moment by the facts. It is true that pessimists explain the persistence of this phenomenon by the illusions of hope. According to them if, in spite of the disappointments of experience, we still cling to life, it is because we hope vainly that the future will redeem the past. But even admitting that hope suffices to explain the love for life, it does not explain itself. It has not miraculously fallen from heaven into our hearts, but must have, like all the sentiments, been formed under the influence of the facts. Thus if men have learnt to hope, if under the blows of misfortune, they have grown accustomed to turn their gaze towards the future and to expect from it compensation for their present suffering, it is because they have perceived that such compensation occurred frequently, that the human organism was both too flexible and too resisting to be easily brought down, that the moments when misfortune gained the day were exceptional and that generally the balance ended up by being re-established. Consequently, whatever the role of hope in the genesis of the instinct of self-preservation, that instinct is a convincing testimony to the relative goodness of life. For the same reason, where that instinct loses its power or generality we may be sure that life itself loses its attractiveness, that misfortune increases, either because the causes of suffering multiply or because the capacity for resistance on the part of the individual diminishes. Thus, if we possessed an objective and measurable yardstick to translate the variations in intensity through which this sentiment passes in different societies, we could at the same time measure the variation in unhappiness that on average exists in these same environments. This yardstick is the number of suicides. Just as the scarceness originally of voluntary homicides is the best proof of the power and universality of this instinct, the fact that the number is increasing shows that it is losing ground.

Now suicide hardly exists before the arrival of civilisation. At least the sole kind observed in lower societies of a chronic nature presents very special features that make it a special type whose value as a symptom is not the same. It is an act not of despair but of abnegation. If among the primitive Danes, the Celts and the Thracians, an old man who has arrived at a great age puts an end to his days, this is because it is his duty to rid his companions of a useless mouth to feed. If the widow in India does not survive her husband or the Gaul the chief of his clan, if the Buddhist allows himself to be crushed under the wheels of the chariot bearing his idol, it is because religious and moral prescriptions oblige them to do so. In all such cases man kills himself not because he esteems life evil, but because the ideal to which he clings requires this sacrifice. Such voluntary deaths are therefore no longer suicides, in the common meaning of the term, any more than the death of the soldier or the doctor who exposes himself knowingly to danger in order to perform his duty.

On the contrary the true suicide, the suicide of sadness, is an endemic state among civilised peoples. It is even geographically distributed according to the level of civilisation. On the maps of suicide it can be seen that the central region of Europe is occupied by a huge dark patch which extends between the 47th and 57th degree of latitude and between the 20th and 40th degree of longitude. This area is the favourite spot for suicide. According to the expression of Morselli, this is the 'suicidogenic' zone of Europe. There also are to be found the countries where scientific, artistic and economic activity is carried to the highest level: Germany and France. On the contrary, Spain, Portugal, Russia and the Slavonic peoples of the south are comparatively free from it. Italy, born only yesterday, is still somewhat protected from it, but is losing its immunity as it develops. England alone proves to be the exception, although we are still ill-informed as to the exact tendency to suicide in that country.

Within each country the same kind of relationship is to be seen. Everywhere suicide is more prevalent in towns than in the countryside. Civilisation is concentrated in the large towns, as is suicide. Occasionally we have seen a kind of contagious illness whose centres of propagation are alleged to be the national capitals and important towns. From these the sickness spreads out over the whole country. Finally, in the whole of Europe with the exception of Norway, the number of suicides has regularly increased for a century.[10] According to one calculation it may have trebled between 1821 and 1880.[11] The onward march of civilisation cannot be measured with the same exactness, but we know how rapid it has been over this period.

We could multiply these proofs. Classes in the population provide a number of suicide cases in proportion to their level of civilisation. Everywhere it is the liberal professions that are the most afflicted and agriculture that is most spared. The same is true for the sexes. Woman is less concerned than man in the civilising process; she participates less in it and draws less benefit from it. She more recalls certain characteristics to be found in primitive natures.[12] Thus the homicide rate among women is four times less than among men. But it will be objected that, if the upward climb in the number of suicides points to the fact that unhappiness is advancing on certain fronts, might it not be that at the same time happiness is increasing on others? In that case this positive benefit might perhaps be sufficient to compensate for the adverse balance suffered elsewhere. Thus in certain societies the number of the poor increases without the public coffers diminishing. It is only concentrated in a fewer number of hands.

But this hypothesis itself is hardly more favourable for our civilisation. For, if we assume that such compensations exist, we could not arrive at any conclusion save that the average level of happiness has remained more or less stationary. Or indeed if it had increased, it would only have been to a very slight extent which, since it was out of all proportion to the strenuousness of the efforts that progress has expended, could not account for it. But the hypothesis itself lacks any foundation.

In fact when we say of a society that it is more, or less, happy than another one, it is an average happiness that we are talking of, namely that enjoyed by the average members of that society. As they are placed in similar conditions of existence, in so far as they are subject to the effects of the same physical and social environment, there is necessarily a certain mode of existence and consequently a certain mode of happiness that is common to them. If we remove from the happiness of individuals everything that is due to personal or local causes, retaining only what results from general and common causes, the residue so obtained exactly constitutes what we call average happiness. Its order of size is therefore abstract, but one that is absolute and cannot vary in two opposing directions at the same time. It can increase or decrease, but it is impossible for it to increase and decrease at the same time. It has the same unity and same reality as the average type of society and of Quételet's average man, for it represents the happiness this ideal creature is presumed to enjoy. Consequently, as it cannot become at one and the same time larger and smaller, more moral and less moral, it cannot either become at the same time more happy and more unhappy.

Now the causes on which depend the advance of suicide among civilised peoples have undoubtedly a general character. Indeed suicide does not occur at isolated points, in certain parts of society to the exclusion of others: it can be observed everywhere. According to areas, the upward trend in suicide numbers is more rapid or more slow, but there is no exception. Agriculture is less prone than industry, but its share in the number of suicides is continually growing. We are therefore faced with a phenomenon not linked to any special local circumstance but to the general atmosphere of the social environment. This condition is reflected differently in special environments (provinces, professions, religious denominations, etc.). This is why its effect is not felt everywhere with the same intensity, but this does not change its nature.

This means that the decreasing happiness that the progression in the number of suicides demonstrates is the average happiness. What the mounting tide of self-inflicted deaths proves is not only that there is a greater number of individuals who are too unhappy to bear going on living – and this would in no way affect the rest, who nevertheless form the majority – but it is because the general happiness of society is on the decrease. Consequently, since this happiness cannot increase and decrease at the same time, it is impossible for it to increase, in any way at all, when suicide is on the increase. In other words, the growing deficiency revealed by the number of suicides is not being compensated for in any way. The causes on which they depend exhaust only a part of their effect in the form of suicide; the influence that they exert is much more extensive. Where they do not impel a man to commit suicide,

194 The Causes and Conditions

thereby destroying utterly his happiness, at least they reduce, in varying proportions, the normal excess of pleasure over pain. Undoubtedly in certain cases it can happen, through a combination of particular circumstances, that their effect is neutralised so as even to make possible an increase in happiness. But these chance individual and private variations have no effect upon *social happiness.* What statistician, moreover, would hesitate to see in an increase in mortality generally within a given society an assured symptom of a decline in public health?

Does this mean that we should attribute these sorry results to progress itself, and to the division of labour which is its necessary condition? This discouraging conclusion does not necessarily follow from the facts we have set out. On the contrary, it is very probable that these two orders of facts are merely concomitant. But their simultaneous occurrence suffices to prove that progress does not increase our happiness very much, since this decreases, and in very alarming proportions, at the very moment when the division of labour is developing with a vitality and speed that we have never previously known. If we have no reason to admit that it has effectively diminished our capacity for enjoyment, it is still more impossible to believe that it has perceptibly increased it.

All in all, everything that we have just said is only a particular application of that general truth that pleasure, like pain, is essentially a relative matter. There is no absolute happiness, objectively determinable, that men come nearer to as they progress. But just as, according to Pascal's maxim, the happiness of man is not that of woman, that of lower societies cannot be ours, and *vice versa*. Yet one is not greater than the other. For we cannot measure their relative intensity save by the strength with which they bind us to life in general, and to our style of life in particular. Now primitive peoples cling just as much to existence, and to their own particular existence, as we do to ours. They even give it up less easily.[13] Thus there is no connection between the variations in happiness and the progress of the division of labour.

This is an extremely important proposition. The upshot is that, in order to explain the transformations through which society has passed, we should not investigate what influence they exert upon men's happiness, since it is not that influence which has brought them about. Social science must resolutely renounce the utilitarian comparisons to which it has too often assented. Moreover, such considerations are necessarily subjective, for every time that we compare pleasures or interests, since all objective criteria are lacking, we cannot help throwing into the scales our own ideas and preferences, and we proclaim as scientific truth what is only personal opinion. This is a principle that Comte formulated very clearly. 'The essentially relative spirit,' he states, 'in which must necessarily be conceived any kind of ideas for positive policy, must firstly make us dismiss as both equally vain and useless the vague metaphysical controversy about the increase in man's happiness at the various stages of civilization. . . . Since the happiness of each individual requires an adequate harmony between the overall development of his various faculties and the set of local circumstances of whatever kind which dominate his life, and since, moreover, such an equilibrium always tends spontaneously towards a certain level, we are not in a position to compare positively, either by direct feeling or any rational means, in relation to individual happiness, social situations, where complete comparison is absolutely ruled out.'[14]

But the desire to become happier is the sole individual motivation that could account for progress. Once this is ruled out, nothing else remains. Why should the individual institute changes of his own accord that always cost him some trouble, unless he drew greater happiness from them? Thus it is outside himself, that is, in the environment that surrounds him, that are to be found the determining causes of social evolution. If societies change and he changes, it is because that environment changes. Moreover, as the physical environment remains comparatively constant it cannot explain that uninterrupted sucession of changes. Consequently it is in the social environment that we must begin to seek the original conditions for change. It is the variations produced in it that spark off those through which societies and individuals pass. This is a methodological rule that we shall later have occasion to apply and confirm.

III

We might ask, however, whether certain variations that pleasure undergoes, by the mere fact that it is lasting, have not the effect of spontaneously inciting men to vary, and whether, as a result, the progress of the division of labour cannot be explained in this way. This is how we might conceive such an explanation.

If pleasure is not happiness, it is none the less an element in it. Yet. it decreases in intensity if it is repeated. Indeed if it becomes too continuous it disappears completely. Time suffices to break the equilibrium that tends to be established, and to create new conditions of existence to which men may adapt only by changing themselves. As we become accustomed to a certain happiness it slips from our grasp and we are obliged to embark upon new enterprises to find it again. We must rekindle a pleasure that grows dim by means of more powerful stimuli, multiply or make more intense those stimuli we have at our command. But this is only possible if work becomes more productive and consequently more divided up. Thus every progress registered in art, science and industry would oblige us to make yet more progress, solely in order not to lose the fruits of what has gone before. So we would again explain the development of the division of labour by a set of entirely individual motivations without adducing the intervention of any social cause. Doubtless, it might be said, if we specialise, it is not to acquire new pleasures but to redress, as it occurs, the corrosive influence that time exerts over the pleasures we have already acquired.

But however real these variations in pleasure may be, they cannot play the role attributed to them. Indeed they occur everywhere pleasure exists, viz., everywhere man is. There is no society in which this psychological law does not apply. Yet there are some societies where the division of labour makes no headway. Indeed we have seen that a very great number of primitive peoples live in a static condition from which they have no thought of emerging. They aspire to nothing new. Yet their happiness is subject to the universal law. The same is true in rural areas among civilised peoples. The division of labour progresses in them only very slowly and the inclination to change is only very weakly felt. Finally, within the same society the division of labour develops at differing speeds according to the particular century. But the influence of time on pleasure is always the same. Thus it is not time that determines that development.

Indeed we cannot see how this influence might have such an effect. One cannot re-establish a balance that time destroys and maintain happiness at a constant level without effort which is all the more arduous the more we approach the upper limit of pleasure. For in the zone near the maximum the increments it receives are for ever smaller than those of the corresponding stimuli. One must put forth more effort for the same result. What one gains on the one hand one loses on the other, and one avoids a loss only by expending greater effort. Consequently, for the operation to be more beneficial this loss must at the very least be considerable and the need to make it good strongly felt.

Now in fact the need is only very moderately felt, because mere repetition takes nothing essential away from pleasure. We must not confuse the charm of variety with that of novelty. Variety is a necessary condition for pleasure, since an uninterrupted joy disappears or is changed into pain. But time alone does not abolish variety; continuity must be added. A state often repeated, but only discontinuously, can remain pleasurable, for if continuity destroys pleasure, it is either because it makes us unaware of it or because the exercise of any function requires the expenditure of effort which, if prolonged without interruption, eventually becomes painful and exhausting. Thus if the action, although it becomes habitual, recurs only at fairly well spaced out intervals, it will continue to be felt and the expenditure of effort can in the meantime be made good. This is why a healthy adult always feels the same pleasure in drinking, eating and sleeping, although he does all these every day. The same holds good for the needs of the mind, which are also periodical, like the psychological functions to which they correspond. The pleasures procured from music, the fine arts and science are sustained in their entirety, provided they are alternated.

Even if continuity can effect what repetition cannot, because of this it does not inspire in us a need for fresh and unexpected stimuli. For if continuity eliminates entirely an awareness of an agreeable state, we cannot perceive that the accompanying pleasure has vanished at the same time. Moreover, it is replaced by that general feeling of wellbeing that accompanies the regular exercise of normally continuous functions, and which has no less worth.

Thus we have no regrets about anything. Who amongst us has never had the desire to feel his heart beating or his lungs functioning? If, on the other hand, there is pain, we simply aspire to a state that will be different from the one that has become tiring to us. Yet in order to put a stop to this suffering there is no need for us to cudgel our brains. Some object we know, which normally leaves us unresponsive, can in this case even cause us great pleasure if it contrasts with what is wearisome to us. Thus there is nothing about the way in which time affects the basic ingredient in pleasure that can stimulate us to make any sort of progress. It is true that with novelty, whose attraction is not lasting, it is different. Yet if it imparts a greater freshness to pleasure, it does not constitute pleasure in itself. It is only a secondary and ancillary quality of it, without which pleasure can indeed exist, although it runs the risk of our relishing it less. Thus when the novelty wears off the vacuum that follows is not greatly felt, nor is the need to fill it very intense.

What diminishes the intensity of pleasure still more is that it is neutralised by an opposing sentiment that is much stronger and more deeply rooted within us. This is the need for stability in our enjoyment and regularity in our pleasure. Whilst we like change, we grow attached to what we like and cannot separate ourselves from it without being upset. Moreover, this state of affairs is necessary for us to carry on our lives. For if life is not possible without change, if it is even more flexible the more complex it is, yet it is above all a system of stable and regular functions. It is true that individuals exist for whom the need for novelty reaches an exceptional level of intensity. Nothing already existing satisfies them; they yearn for the impossible and would like to substitute a different reality for the one that has been imposed upon them. But these incorrigibly dissatisfied people are sick, and the pathological character of their case only confirms what we have just stated.

Finally we must not lose sight of the fact that this need of novelty is of a very indeterminate nature. It binds us to nothing precise, since it is a need for something that does not exist. Thus it is only half formulated, for a complete need includes two elements: a tension of the will and an assured object. Since the object is not present externally it can have no other reality than that which imagination imparts to it. This process is half 'representation'. It rather consists of combinations of images, in a kind of intimate poetry, than in an effective act of the will. It does not cause us to step outside ourselves. It is hardly more than an inner disturbance that seeks a path to the outside world, one that it has not yet found. We dream of new sensations, but this is a half-formulated aspiration that dissolves without taking on substance. Consequently even where it is most powerful it cannot have the strength of needs that are firmly defined, ones which, continually directing the will in the same

. direction along paths already traced out, stimulate it the more categorically because they leave no room for trial and error or deliberation.

In short, we cannot admit that progress is only the effect of boredom.[15] That periodical remoulding of human nature, which in certain respects is even continuous, has been a laborious task, one carried on with suffering. Humanity cannot have imposed such travail upon itself solely in order to vary slightly its pleasures and retain their virgin freshness.

Notes

1. H. Spencer, *Principles of Psychology* (London, 1855) vol. I, pp. 280–1. Cf. Wundt, *Psychologie Physiologique*, vol. I, ch. 10, § 1.
2. Richet. Cf. his article 'Douleur' in the *Dictionnaire encyclopédique des Sciences médicales.*
3. Laplace, *Théorie analytique des probabilités* (Paris, 1847) pp. 187 and 432; Fechner, *Psychophysik*, vol. I, p. 236.
4. Cf. Wundt, *Psychologie Physiologique, loc. cit.*
5. Rabier, *Leçons de philosophie*, vol. I, p. 479.
6. Cf. Hartmann, *Philosophie de l'Inconscient*, vol. II.
7. Waitz, *Anthropologie*, vol. I, p. 346.
8. Ibid., p. 347.
9. Cowper Rose, *Four Years in Southern Africa* (1829) p. 173.
10. Cf. the Tables of Morselli.
11. Oettingen, *Moralstatistik* (Erlangen, 1882) p. 742.
12. Tarde, *Criminalité comparée*, p. 48.
13. Except for cases where the instinct of self-preservation is neutralised by sentiments that are religious or patriotic, etc., without it being thereby weakened.
14. A. Comte, *Cours de philosophie positive*, 2nd edn, vol. IV, p. 273.
15. This was the theory of Georges Leroy. We only know it through what Comte says about it in his *Cours de philosophie positive*, vol. IV, p. 449.

Chapter II

The Causes

Thus it is in certain variations of the social environment that we must seek the cause that explains the progress of the division of labour. The results outlined in the preceding book allow us to induce immediately what these variations consist of.

In fact we have seen that the organised structure, and consequently the division of labour, develops regularly as the segmentary structure vanishes. It is therefore this disappearance that is the cause of this development; alternatively, the latter may be the cause of the former. This last hypothesis is not acceptable, for we know that the segmentary arrangement is an insurmountable obstacle to the division of labour and that the arrangement must have disappeared, at least in part, for the division of labour to be able to appear. It can only do so when that arrangement no longer exists. Undoubtedly once the division of labour exists it can contribute to speeding up its disappearance, but it only becomes apparent after the segmentary arrangement has partly receded. The effect reacts upon the cause, but does not in consequence cease to be an effect. Thus the reaction that it exerts is a secondary one. The increase in the division of labour is therefore due to the fact that the social segments lose their individuality, that the partitions dividing them become more permeable. In short, there occurs between them a coalescence that renders the social substance free to enter upon new combinations.

But the disappearance of this type can only bring about this result for the following reason. It is because there occurs a drawing together of individuals who were separated from one another, or at least they draw more closely together than they had been. Hence movements take place between the parts of the social mass which up

200

to then had no reciprocal effect upon one another. The more the alveolar system is developed, the more the relationships in which each one of us is involved become enclosed within the limits of the alveola to which we belong. There are, as it were, moral vacuums between the various segments. On the other hand these vacuums fill up as the system levels off. Social life, instead of concentrating itself in innumerable small foci that are distinct but alike, becomes general. Social relationships – more exactly we should say intrasocial relationships – consequently become more numerous, since they push out beyond their original boundaries on all sides. Thus the division of labour progresses the more individuals there are who are sufficiently in contact with one another to be able mutually to act and react upon one another. If we agree to call dynamic or moral density this drawing together and the active exchanges that result from it, we can say that the progress of the division of labour is in direct proportion to the moral or dynamic density of society.

But this act of drawing together morally can only bear fruit if the real distance between individuals has itself diminished, in whatever manner. Moral density cannot therefore increase without physical density increasing at the same time, and the latter can serve to measure the extent of the former. Moreover, it is useless to investigate which of the two has influenced the other; it suffices to realise that they are inseparable.

The progressive increase in density of societies in the course of their historical development occurs in three main ways:
(1) Whilst lower societies spread themselves over areas that are relatively vast in comparison with the number of individuals that constitute them, amongst more advanced peoples the population is continually becoming more concentrated. Spencer says: 'If we contrast the populousness of regions inhabited by wild tribes with the populousness of equal regions in Europe; or if we contrast the density of population in England under the Heptarchy with its present density; we see that besides the growth produced by union of groups there has gone an interstitial growth.'[1]

The changes wrought successively in the industrial life of nations demonstrate how general this transformation is. The activity of nomadic tribes, whether hunters or shepherds, entails in fact the absence of any kind of concentration and dispersion over as wide an area as possible. Agriculture, because it is of necessity a settled existence, already presumes a certain drawing together of the social tissues, but one still very incomplete, since between each family tracts of land are interposed.[2] In the city, although the condensation process was greater, yet houses did not adjoin one another, for joined building was not known in Roman law.[3] This was invented on our own soil and demonstrates that the social ties have become tighter.[4] Moreover, from their origins European societies have seen their density increase continuously in spite of a few cases of temporary regression.[5]

(2) The formation and development of towns are a further symptom, even more characteristic, of the same phenomenon. The increase in average density can be due solely to the physical increase in the birth rate and can consequently be reconciled with a very weak concentration of people, and the very marked maintenance of the segmentary type of society. But towns always result from the need that drives individuals to keep constantly in the closest possible contact with one another. They are like so many points where the social mass is contracting more strongly than elsewhere. They cannot therefore multiply and spread out unless the moral density increases. Moreover, we shall see that towns recruit their numbers through migration to them, which is only possible to the extent that the fusion of social segments is far advanced.

So long as the social organisation is essentially segmentary, towns do not exist. There are none in lower societies; they are not met with among the Iroquois, nor among the primitive German tribes.[6] The same was true for the primitive populations of Italy. 'The peoples of Italy,' states Marquardt, 'originally used not to live in towns, but in family or village communities (*pagi*), over which farms (*vici*, οἴχοί) were scattered.'[7] Yet after a fairly short period of time the town made its appearance. Athens and Rome were or became towns, and the same transformation was accomplished throughout Italy. In our Christian societies the town appears from the very beginning, for those that the Roman Empire had left behind did not disappear with it. Since then, they have not ceased to grow and multiply. The tendency of country dwellers to flow into the towns, so general in the civilised world,[8] is only a consequence of this movement. But this phenomenon does not date from the present day: from the seventeenth century onwards it preoccupied statesmen.[9]

Because societies generally start with an agricultural period we have occasionally been tempted to regard the development of urban centres as a sign of old age and decadence.[10] But we must not lose sight of the fact that this agricultural phase is the shorter the more societies belong to a higher type. Whilst in Germany, among the American Indians and among all primitive peoples, it lasts as long as do'these peoples themselves, in Rome or Athens it ceases fairly early on, and in France we may say that this agricultural state has never existed in a pure form. Conversely, urban life begins very early on, and consequently extends itself more. The regularly quicker acceleration of this development demonstrates that, far from constituting a kind of pathological phenomenon, it derives from the very nature of the higher social species. Even supposing therefore that today this movement has reached threatening proportions for our societies, which perhaps have no longer sufficient flexibility to adapt to it, it will not cease to continue, either through them, or after them, and the social types to be formed after our own will probably be distinguished by a more rapid and more complete regression of agricultural society.

(3) Finally, there is the number and speed of the means of communication and transmission. By abolishing or lessening the vacuums separating social segments, these means increase the density of society. Moreover, there is no need to demonstrate that they are the more numerous and perfect the higher the type of society.

Since this visible and measurable symbol reflects the variations in what we have termed moral density,[11] we can substitute this symbol for the latter in the formula that we have put forward. We must, moreover, repeat here what we were saying earlier. If society, in concentrating itself, determines the development of the division of labour, the latter in its turn increases the concentration of society. But this is of no consequence, for the division of labour remains the derived action, and consequently the advances it makes are due to a parallel progress in social density, whatever may be the cause of this progress. This all we wished to establish.

But this factor is not the only one.

If the concentration of society produces this result, it is because it multiplies intra-social relationships. But these will be even more numerous if the total number of members in a society also becomes larger. If it includes more individuals, as well as their being in closer contact, the effect will necessarily be reinforced. Social volume has therefore the same influence over the division of labour as density.

In fact, societies are generally more voluminous the more

advanced they are and consequently labour is more divided up in them. Spencer says that, 'Societies, like living bodies, begin as germs – originate from masses which are extremely minute in comparison with the masses some of them eventually reach. That out of small wandering hordes such as the lowest races now form, have arisen the largest societies, is a conclusion not to be contested.'[12]

What we have said about the segmentary constitution makes this unquestionably true. We know in fact that societies are formed by a certain number of segments of unequal size that overlap with one another. These moulds are not artificial creations, particularly in the beginning. Even when they have become conventional they imitate and reproduce so far as possible the forms of natural arrangement that preceded them. Many ancient societies are maintained in this form. The largest among these subdivisions, those that include the others, correspond to the nearest lower social type. Likewise, among the segments of which they in turn are made up, the most extensive are the remains of the type that comes directly below the preceding one, and so on. Among the most advanced peoples we find traces of the most primitive social organisation.[13] Thus the tribe is made up of an aggregate of hordes or clans; the nation (the Jewish nation, for example) and the city, of an aggregate of tribes; the city, in its turn, with the villages that are subordinate to it, is one element that enters into the most complex societies, etc. The social volume therefore cannot fail to grow, since each species is made up of a replication of societies of the immediately preceding species.

Yet there are exceptions. The Jewish nation, before the conquest, was probably more voluminous than the Roman city of the fourth century; yet it was of a lower species. China and Russia are much more populous than the most civilised nations of Europe. Consequently among these same peoples the division of labour did not develop in proportion to the social volume. This is because the growth in volume is not necessarily a mark of superiority if the density does not grow at the same time and in the same proportion. A society can reach very large dimensions because it contains a very large number of segments, whatever may be the nature of these. If therefore the largest of them only reproduces societies of a very inferior type, the segmentary structure will remain very pronounced, and in consequence the social organisation will be little advanced. An aggregate of clans, even if immense, ranks below the smallest society that is organised, since the latter has already gone through those stages of evolution below which the aggregate has remained. Likewise if the number of social units has some influence over the division of labour, it is not through itself and of necessity, but because the number of social relationships increases generally with the number of individuals. To obtain this result it is not enough for the society to comprise a large number of persons, but they must be in fairly intimate contact so as to act and react upon one another. If on the other hand they are separated by environments that are mutually impenetrable, only very rarely, and with difficulty, can they establish relationships, and everything occurs as if the number of people was small. An increase in social volume therefore does not always speed up the progress of the division of labour, but only when the mass condenses at the same time and to the same degree. Consequently it is, one may say, only an additional factor. Yet, when joined to the first factor, it extends the effects by an action peculiarly its own, and thus requires to be distinguished from it.

We can therefore formulate the following proposition:

The division of labour varies in direct proportion to the volume and density of societies and if it progresses in a continuous manner over the course of social development it is because societies become regularly more dense and generally more voluminous.

At all times, it is true, it has been clearly understood that there was a relationship between these two orders of facts. This is because, for functions to specialise even more, there must be additional co-operating elements, which must be grouped close enough together to be able to co-operate. Yet in societies in this condition we usually see hardly more than the means by which the division of labour is developed, and not the cause of this development. The cause is made to depend upon individual aspirations towards wellbeing and happiness, which can be the better satisfied when societies are more extensive and more condensed. The law we have just established is completely different. We state, not that the growth and condensation of societies *permit* a greater division of labour, but that they *necessitate* it. It is not the instrument whereby that division is brought about; but it is its determining cause.[14]

Yet how can we represent to ourselves the way in which this dual cause produces its effect?

II

According to Spencer, if the growth in social volume has an influence on the progress of the division of labour, it is not that this growth determines it; it merely speeds it up. It is simply a facilitating condition for the phenomenon. Unstable by nature, any homogeneous mass necessarily becomes heterogeneous, whatever its dimensions. Only it becomes differentiated more completely and speedily when it is more extensive. Since this heterogeneity springs from the fact that the different parts of the mass are exposed to the action of different forces, it is all the greater when more parts are located in various places. This is the case in societies: Spencer says:

> A community which, growing populous, has overspread a large tract, and has become so far settled that its members live and die in their respective districts, keeps its several sections in different physical circumstances; and then they no longer remain alike in their occupations. Those who live dispersed continue to hunt or cultivate the earth; those who spread to the sea-shore fall into maritime occupations; while the inhabitants of some spot chosen for its centrality, as one of periodic assemblage, become traders, and a town springs up. . . . A result of differences in soil and climate, is that the rural inhabitants in different parts of the kingdom have their occupations partially specialized; and become respectively distinguished as chiefly producing cattle, or sheep, or wheat.[15]

In short, the variety of environments in which individuals are placed gives rise among them to different aptitudes that determine their specialisation along different paths, and if this specialisation increases with the dimensions of societies, it is because these internal differences increase at the same time.

It is beyond question that the external conditions in which individuals live leave their mark upon them and that, since these conditions are diverse, they cause this differentiation. But we need to know whether this diversity, which doubtless is not without its links with the division of labour, is sufficient to bring it about. Certainly the properties of the soil and the climatic conditions may explain that in this spot the inhabitants produce corn, elsewhere sheep or cattle. But functional differences are not always reducible, as in the two examples, to mere nuances. They are sometimes so clear-cut that the individuals among whom the work is divided up form so many distinct and even opposing species. It might be said that they conspire to place as great a distance as possible between one another. What resemblance is there between the brain that thinks and the stomach that digests? In the same way, what is there in common between the poet entirely given over to his dreaming, the scientist totally absorbed in his research, the workman who spends his life in making pinheads, the ploughman who steers his plough, the shopkeeper behind his counter? However great the variety of external conditions, nowhere do they present differences proportionate to such strongly drawn contrasts and that consequently could account for them. Even when we compare, not functions very remote from one another, but only various branches of the same function, it is often completely impossible to perceive to what external dissimilarities their separation from one another can be ascribed. Scientific work is continually being more divided up. What are the climatic, geological or even social conditions that can have given rise to those very different talents possessed by the mathematician, the chemist, the naturalist, the psychologist, etc.?

Yet even where external circumstances are most strongly favourable for individuals to specialise along a clearly defined path, they are not sufficient to determine what that specialisation will be. Constitutionally a woman is predisposed to lead a life different from that of a man. Yet there are societies where the occupations of both sexes are appreciably the same. By his age and the blood relationship that he sustains with his children, the father appears the proper person to exercise in the family those functions of control that constitute paternal powers as a whole, and yet in the maternal family it is not upon him that this authority devolves. It appears quite natural that the different members of the family should have attributes, that is, different functions, according to their degree of kinship and that father and uncle, brother and cousin should not possess the same rights or duties. There are, however, family types where all the adults fulfil the same role and are on an equal footing, regardless of blood relationship. The lower status that the prisoner of war occupies in a victorious tribe seems to condemn him, at least if his life is preserved, to the lowliest social functions. We have however seen that he is often assimilated to his conquerors and becomes their equal.

This is because, if such differences make the division of labour possible, they do not impose that division. Because such differences are given, it does not necessarily follow that they are used. All in all, they are of small account beside the resemblances that men continue to display between one another. A slight distinction exists only in embryo. For specialisation of activity to result, the differences must be developed and organised, and this development clearly depends upon causes other than the variation in external conditions. But, states Spencer, such a development will occur of its own accord, because it follows the line of least resistance and all the forces of nature are borne invincibly in this direction. Undoubtedly *if men specialise* it will be on the lines traced out by these natural differences, because in this way they will have less difficulty and receive the most benefit. But why do they specialise? What determines that they should come down in favour of distinguishing themselves from one another? Spencer explains fairly satisfactorily how this evolution will occur if it takes place, but does not tell us what is the trigger that sets it off. To tell the truth, for him the question does not even arise. He admits in fact that happiness grows with the productive power of labour. Each time therefore when a new means is provided of dividing labour yet further it appears inconceivable to him that we should not grasp it. Yet we know that things do not happen like that. In reality such a tool has only value for us if we have need of it and, as primitive man has no need of all those products that civilised man has learnt to desire and that the more complex organisation of labour has precisely the effect of providing for him, we cannot understand the source of the increasing specialisation of tasks unless we know how these new needs have been constituted.

III

If labour becomes increasingly divided as societies become more voluminous and concentrated, it is not because the external circumstances are more varied, it is because the struggle for existence becomes more strenuous.

Darwin very aptly remarked that two organisms vie with each other more keenly the more alike they are. Having the same needs and pursuing the same purposes, they are everywhere to be found in a state of rivalry. So long as they possess more resources than each needs, they can still live cheek by jowl. But if each happens to increase in number in such proportions that all appetites can no longer be sufficiently assuaged, war breaks out and it is the more violent the more striking the shortfall, that is, the numbers vying with one another are greater. The situation is totally different if the individuals coexisting together are of different species or varieties. As they do not feed in the same way or lead the same kind of life, they do not impede one another. What causes some to flourish lacks value for others. The occasions for conflict are therefore less, as are the occasions of meeting, and this is all the more the case when these species or varieties are more distant from one another. Darwin states that:

> In an extremely small area, especially if freely open to immigration, and where the contest between individual and individual must be very severe, we always find great diversity in its inhabitants. For instance, I found that a piece of turf, three foot by four in size, which had been exposed for many years to exactly the same conditions, supported twenty species of plants, and these belonged to eighteen genera and to eight orders, which shows how much these plants differed from each other.[16]

Moreover, everyone has noticed that in the same field, beside cereal crops there can grow a very great number of weeds. The animals likewise do better in the struggle the more they differ from one another. On an oak tree are to be found up to two hundred species of insects that have no contacts with one another save those of good neighbourliness. Some feed on the fruits of the tree, others on leaves, yet more on bark and roots. 'It would be absolutely impossible,' states Haeckel, 'for such a number of creatures to live on that tree if all belonged to the same species, if all, for example, lived on bark or only on leaves.'[17] Again, in the same way, within an organism what lessens the rivalry between the different tissues is the fact that they feed on different substances.

Men are subject to the same law. In the same town different occupations can coexist without being forced into a position where they harm one another, for they are pursuing different objectives. The soldier seeks military glory, the priest moral authority, the statesman power, the industrialist wealth, the scientist professional fame. Each one of them can therefore reach his goal without preventing others from reaching theirs. This is the case even when the functions are less remote from one another. The medical eye specialist does not compete with the one who cares for the mentally ill, the shoemaker does not compete with the hatter, the mason with the cabinet-maker, the physician with the chemist, etc. As they perform different services they can perform them in harmony.

However, the closer the functions are to one another, the more points of contact there are between them, and, as a result, the more they tend to conflict. As in this case they satisfy similar needs by different means, it is inevitable that they should seek, more or less, to encroach upon others. The magistrate is never in competition with the industrialist. But the brewer and the winegrower, the draper and the maker of silks, the poet and the musician often attempt mutually to supplant each other. As for those that discharge exactly the same function, they cannot prosper save to the detriment of their fellows. If therefore one represents these different functions in the form of a cluster of branches springing from a common root, the struggle is least between the extreme points, whilst it increases steadily as it approaches the centre. This is the case not only within each town but over society as a whole. Similar occupations located at different sites over an area enter into fiercer rivalry the more alike they are, provided that difficulties of communications and transport do not constrain their sphere of action.

This having been said, it is easy to understand that any concentration in the social mass, particularly if accompanied by a growth in population, necessarily determines the progress of the division of labour.

In fact, let us imagine an industrial centre that supplies a certain area of the country with a special product. The development that it is capable of reaching is restricted in two ways: firstly by the extent of the needs that have to be satisfied, or the so-called size of the market, and secondly, by the capacity of the means of production at its command. Normally it does not produce more than is necessary, even less does it produce more than it can. But if it is impossible for it to exceed these limits, as set out, it strives to reach them, for it is in the nature of a force to deploy all its energy so long as nothing brings it to a halt. Once it has arrived at this point, it has adapted to the conditions of its existence; it finds itself in a position of equilibrium that cannot change if nothing changes.

But there may be some region, until then independent of the

centre, that becomes linked to it by a means of communication which partly does away with distance. At a single stroke one of the barriers that prevented its upward ascent is broken down or at least is lowered. The market becomes more extensive, there are now more needs to be satisfied. Undoubtedly if all the individual undertakings that it includes had already reached their possible peak of production, as they could not expand further, things would stay as they were. However, such a situation is wholly an ideal one. In reality there is always a certain number of undertakings that have not reached their limit and which, so to speak, consequently have sufficient speed in reserve to go further. As an empty space has opened up for them, their needs must seek to spread over it and fill it. If they meet with similar undertakings that are capable of resisting them, these latter contain them, they impose mutual limits upon one another, and consequently their mutual relationships remain unchanged. To be sure, there are more competitors, but as they share a larger market, the share of each one on the two sides remains the same. Yet if there are some that manifest some kind of inferiority, they will have to yield ground that they occupied up to then, where they can no longer sustain themselves in the new conditions in which the struggle is fought out. They then have no longer any option but either to disappear or to transform themselves, and this transformation must necessarily result in a fresh specialisation. For if instead of creating at once yet another speciality, the weakest preferred to adopt a different kind of business, but which existed already, they would have to enter into competition with those who had been engaged in it up to then. The struggle would therefore no longer be over, but simply change its location, producing its consequences in a different place. Finally, somewhere there would certainly have to be either an elimination or a fresh differentiation. It would be pointless to add that if a society in fact comprises more members, and at the same time they have drawn closer to one another, the struggle is even fiercer and the specialisation that emerges from it more rapid and more complete.

In other words, to the extent that the social constitution is a segmentary one, each segment has its own organs that are, so to speak, protected and kept at a distance from similar organs by the partitions separating the different segments. But, as these partitions disappear, it is inevitable that organs similar to one another come into contact, embark upon a struggle and try to substitute themselves for one another. However, in whatever way this substitution occurs, some advance along the road to specialisation cannot fail to be the outcome. For on the one hand, the segmentary organ that triumphs, if we may speak in those terms, cannot be sufficient to undertake the larger task that now falls to it in the future save by a greater division of labour. On the other hand, the vanquished can only continue to exist by concentrating upon one part only of the total function that they fulfilled up to that time. The small employer becomes a foreman, the small shopkeeper an employee, etc. This share can moreover be of greater or lesser size depending on whether their inferiority is more or less glaring. It can even happen that the original function simply becomes split into two parts of equal importance. Instead of entering into competition, or remaining so, two similar undertakings find their equilibrium again by sharing their common task: instead of one becoming subordinate to the other, they co-ordinate their activities. But in every case new specialities appear.

Although the above examples are especially taken from economic life, this explanation is applicable to all social functions without distinction. Work, whether scientific, artistic, or otherwise, does not divide up in any other way or for any other reasons. It is still because of these same causes that, as we have seen, the central regulatory mechanism absorbs to itself the local regulatory organs, reducing them to the role of specialised auxiliary ones.

Does an increase in the average level of happiness emerge from all these changes? We cannot see to what cause it might be ascribed. The greater intensity of the struggle implies new and painful efforts that are not of a kind to make men any happier. Everything occurs mechanically. A break in the equilibrium of the social mass gives rise to conflicts that can only be resolved by a more developed form of the division of labour: this is the driving force for progress. As for external circumstances and the various combinations of heredity, just as the contours of the land determine the direction of a watercourse but do not create it, they indicate the direction in which specialisation is occurring in cases where it is needed, but they do not impose any obligation. The individual differences that they produce would remain in a state of virtuality if, in order to face up to new difficulties, we were not forced to give them prominence and to develop them.

The division of labour is therefore one result of the struggle for existence: but it is a gentle dénouement. Thanks to it, rivals are not obliged to eliminate one another completely, but can coexist side by side. Moreover, as it develops, it provides a greater number of individuals, who in more homogeneous societies would be condemned to extinction, with the means of sustaining themselves and surviving. Among many lower peoples, any ill-formed organism was fatally doomed to perish, for it was not usable for any function at all. Sometimes the law, anticipating and in some way sanctioning the results of natural selection, condemned to death the sickly and weak newborn babies, and Aristotle himself[18] found this practice natural. Things are completely different in more advanced societies. A puny individual can find within the complex cadres of our social organisation a niche in which he can render a service. If he is only weak bodily and his mind is healthy, he will devote himself to the labour of the study, to the speculative functions. If it is his brain that is defective 'he will undoubtedly have to renounce taking on great intellectual competition; but society has, in the secondary cells of the hive, places small enough which will prevent him from being eliminated'.[19] Likewise, among primitive tribes the conquered enemy is put to death; where industrial functions are separated from military functions, he continues to exist beside the conqueror as a slave.

There are certainly some circumstances where different functions compete with one another. Thus in the individual organism, as a result of a prolonged fast, the nervous system nourishes itself at the expense of other organs, and the same phenomenon occurs if brain activity is overtaxed. The same is true for society. In times of famine or economic crisis, in order to maintain themselves, the vital functions are obliged to draw their nourishment from less essential functions. Luxury industries decline, and those parts of the people's wealth that served to maintain them are absorbed by the food industries or by objects of prime necessity. Or indeed it may happen that an organism attains an abnormal level of activity that is out of all proportion to the need, and, to meet the expense occasioned by this exaggerated development, it must take away from the share of others. For example, there are societies where there are too many public officials, too many soldiers, too many middlemen, too many priests, etc. The other professions suffer from this hypertrophying effect. However, all such cases are pathological; they are due to the fact that the nourishment of the organism does not take place regularly or the fact that the functional equilibrium is broken.

However, an objection presents itself:

An industry can only live if it corresponds to some necessity. A function can only become specialised if that specialisation corresponds to some need in society. Every new specialisation has as a result an increase and improvement in production. If this advantage is not the reason for the existence of the division of labour, it is its necessary consequence. As a result, lasting progress cannot be established unless individuals really feel the need for more abundant or better-quality products. So long as a transport industry had not been set up, each individual journeyed about by any means at this disposal, and we were accustomed to this state of affairs. Yet for it to become a specialised industry, men had to cease to be content with what had been adequate for them until then, and to become more demanding. Yet from where may such new demands spring?

They are an effect of the same cause that determines the progress of the division of labour. Indeed we have just seen that progress is due to the greater fierceness of the struggle. Now a more violent struggle does not occur without a greater deployment of forces, and consequently not without greater fatigue. Yet in order for life to continue the reward must always be proportionate to the effort; this is why the nourishment that until then was sufficient to restore the organic equilibrium is henceforth insufficient. The food must be more abundant and choicer. Thus the peasant, whose labour is less exhausting than that of the town worker, nourishes himself equally well, although on a poorer type of food. The latter cannot content himself with a vegetable diet and again, in these conditions has great difficulty in making up the deficiency that intense and continuous work causes each day in the economy of his organism.[20]

Moreover, it is above all the central nervous system that bears the whole brunt of this.[21] This is because one must be inventive in finding the means of sustaining the struggle, to create new specialities, and make them known. Generally the more the environment is subject to change, the greater the part played by intelligence in life. It alone can discover the new conditions necessary for an equilibrium which is constantly being broken, and can restore it. Thus the activity of the brain develops at the same time as competition becomes fiercer, and to the same extent. This parallel advance can be noted not only among the elite, but in all classes of society. On this point we need only compare once more the industrial worker with the agricultural worker. It is an acknowledged fact that the former is much the more intelligent, in spite of the mechanical character of the tasks to which he is often tied. Moreover, it is not without reason that mental illnesses go hand in hand with civilisation, nor that they break out in towns rather than the countryside, and in large rather than small towns.[22] Now a more capacious and delicate brain has different needs from an encephalon which is of a coarser nature. Troubles and privations that the latter would not even feel wrack the former with pain. For the same reason more complex stimuli are necessary to give pleasure to the brain organ, once it has become refined, and more are needed because at the same time it has developed. Finally, more than all other needs, specifically intellectual needs increase.[23] Vulgar explanations can no longer satisfy more practised minds. New enlightenment is sought, and science nurtures these aspirations at the same time as it assuages them.

All these changes are therefore wrought automatically by necessary causes. If our intelligence and sensibility develop, becoming more acute, it is because we exercise them more. And if we do so, it is because we are constrained by the greater violence of the struggle we have to sustain. This is how, without having willed it, humanity finds itself prepared to accept a more intense and varied culture.

However, if another factor did not intervene, this mere predisposition could not of itself arouse the means of satisfaction, for it constitutes only an aptitude to enjoy and, according to a remark of Bain, 'Mere capabilities of pleasure do not evoke desire; we may be so constituted as to take pleasure in music, in pictures, in science, but, if we have been utterly debarred from the slightest taste of such things, desire does not arise.'[24] Even when we are drawn towards an object because of a very strong inherited disposition towards it, we can only desire it after having come into contact with it. The adolescent who has never heard of sexual relationships nor the enjoyment they procure can indeed feel a vague and indefinable sense of restlessness. He can have the feeling that he is missing something, but he does not know what and consequently strictly speaking he has no sexual desires. Thus these vague aspirations can fairly easily be diverted from their natural ends and their normal course. But at the very moment when man is in a position to taste these new joys and summons them up even unconsciously, he finds them within his grasp, because the division of labour has at the same time developed and has provided them for him. Without there being the slightest pre-established harmony in this, the two orders of facts meet, quite simply because they are effects of the same cause.

This is how we might conceive such an encounter to come about. The attraction of novelty would already be enough to induce man to taste these pleasures. He is even more naturally inclined to do so because the greater richness and complexity of these stimuli make him esteem to be of a more mediocre quality those with which he had contented himself up to that point. He can moreover adapt himself mentally to them before he has ever tried them out. As in reality they correspond to changes that have taken place in his constitution, he feels in advance that he will find them agreeable. Experience then comes to confirm this presentiment. Needs that were dormant are awakened, become precise, acquire an awareness of themselves and begin to be organised. However this does not signify that in each case this adjustment is equally perfect, or that every new product that is due to further advances in the division of labour, always corresponds to some real need in our nature. On the contrary, it is very likely that fairly often the needs take shape because we have acquired a habit for the object to which they relate. This object was neither necessary nor useful. Yet we have happened to experience it several times and have grown so accustomed to it that we can no longer do without it. Harmonies arising from wholly automatic causes can never be other than imperfect and approximate, but they are sufficient to maintain order generally. This is what happens with the division of labour. The progress that it makes is generally – but not in all cases – in harmony with the changes that occur in man, and this it is that makes them lasting.

But once again we are not on this account any the happier. Doubtless once our needs are stimulated, they cannot remain in a state of limbo without pain occurring. But our happiness is none the greater because they are stimulated. The point of reference in relationship to which we were measuring the relative intensity of our pleasures is displaced. The result is a disturbance over the whole gradation of enjoyment. But this regrading of pleasures does not imply an increase. Since the environment is no longer the same, we have had to change, and these changes have determined others in our manner of happiness. But changes do not necessarily signify progress.

We see how different our view of the division of labour appears from that of the economists. For them it consists essentially in producing more. For us this greater productivity is merely a necessary consequence, a side-effect of the phenomenon. If we specialise it is not so as to produce more, but to enable us to live in the new conditions of existence created for us.

IV

A corollary of everything that has gone before is that the division of labour cannot be carried out save between the members of a society already constituted.

Indeed when competition opposes isolated individuals not known to one another, it can only separate them still more. If they have ample space at their disposal, they will flee from one another. If they cannot go beyond set limits, they will begin to differentiate, but in a way so that they become still more independent of one another. We can cite no case where relationships of open hostility have been transformed into social relationships, without the intervention of any other factor. Thus, as there is generally no bond between individuals or creatures of the same vegetable or animal species, the war they wage upon one another serves only to diversify them, to give rise to dissimilar varieties that increasingly grow further apart. It is this progressive disjunction that Darwin has called the law of the divergence of characteristics. Yet the division of labour unites at the same time as it sets at odds; it causes the activities that it differentiates to converge; it brings closer those that it separates. Since competition cannot have determined their coming together, it must indeed have already pre-existed. The individuals between whom the conflict is joined must already be solidly linked to one another and feel so, that is, they belong to the same society. This is why, where this sentiment of solidarity is too weak to resist the centrifugal influence of competition, the latter produces completely different effects from the division of labour. In countries where existence is too difficult because of the extreme density of the population, the inhabitants, instead of specialising, withdraw permanently or provisionally from society by emigrating to other areas.

Moreover, it is enough to represent to ourselves what the division of labour is to make us understand that things cannot be otherwise.

It consists in the sharing out of functions that up till then were common to all. But such an allocation cannot be effected according to any preconceived plan. We cannot say beforehand where the line of demarcation is drawn between tasks, once they have been separated. In the nature of things that line is not marked out so self-evidently, but on the contrary depends upon a great number of circumstances. The division must therefore come about of itself, and progressively. Consequently, in these conditions for a function to be capable of being shared out in two exactly complementary fractions, as the nature of the division of labour requires, it is indispensable that the two parties specialising should be in constant communication over the whole period that this dissociation is occurring. There is no other way for one part to take over from the other the whole operation that the latter is surrendering, and for them to adapt to each other. Now, just as an animal colony, the tissue of whose members is a continuum, constitutes an individual, so every aggregate of individuals in continuous contact forms a society. The division of labour can therefore only occur within the framework of an already existing society. By this we do not just simply mean that individuals must cling materially to one another, but moral ties must also exist between them. Firstly, material continuity alone gives rise to links of this kind, provided that it is lasting. Moreover, they are directly necessary. If the relationships beginning to be established during the period of uncertainty were not subject to any rule, if no power moderated the clash of individual interests, chaos would ensue from which no new order could emerge. It is true that we imagine that everything occurs by means of private agreements freely argued over. All social action therefore seems to be absent. But we forget that contracts are only possible where a legal form of regulation, and consequently a society, already exists.

Thus it has been wrong sometimes to see in the division of labour the basic fact of all social life. Work is not shared out between independent individuals who are already differentiated from one another, who meet and associate together in order to pool their different abilities. It would be a miracle if these differences, arising from chance circumstances, could be so accurately harmonised as to form a coherent whole. Far from their preceding collective life, they derive from it. They can only occur within a society, under the pressure of social sentiments and needs. This is what makes them essentially capable of being harmonised. Thus there is a social life outside of any division of labour, but one that the latter assumes. This is in fact what we have directly established by demonstrating that there are societies whose cohesion is due essentially to a community of beliefs and sentiments, and that it is from these societies that others have emerged whose unity is ensured by the division of labour. The conclusions of the preceding book and those at which we have just arrived can therefore serve as a check, mutually confirming each other. In physiology the division of labour is itself subject to this law: it never occurs save with polycellular masses that are already endowed with a certain cohesion.

For a number of theorists, it is a self-evident truth that any society consists essentially in co-operation. Spencer states that 'a society, in the sociological sense, is formed only when, beside juxtaposition there is co-operation'.[25] We have just seen that this alleged axiom is the opposite of the truth. On the contrary, it is evident, as Auguste Comte says, 'that co-operation, far from being able to produce a society, supposes necessarily its spontaneous establishment beforehand'.[26] What draws men together are mechanical forces and instinctive forces such as the affinity of blood, attachment to the same soil, the cult of their ancestors, a commonality of habits, etc. It is only when the group has been formed on these bases that co-operation becomes organised.

Even so, the sole co-operation possible in the beginning is so intermittent and weak that social life, if it lacked any other source, would itself lack strength or continuity. *A fortiori*, the complex co-operation that results from the division of labour is a later, derived phenomenon. It results from the internal movements that develop within the mass of people, when this mass has been constituted. It is true that once co-operation has made its appearance, it tightens social bonds and imparts to society a more complete individuality. But this integration supposes another sort that it replaces. For social units to be able to differentiate from one another, they must first be attracted or grouped together through the similarities that they display. This process of formation is observed, not only at the origins, but at every stage of evolution. We know in fact that higher societies are the result of the coming together of lower societies of the same type. First of all, these latter must be blended together in the sense of a single and identical common consciousness so that the process of differentiation can begin or begin again. It is in this way that more complex organisms are formed by the replication of more simple organisms, similar to one another, which only differentiate after they have been associated together. In short, association and co-operation are two distinct events, and if the second, once it has been developed, reacts upon the first and transforms, if human societies consist increasingly of groups co-operating together, the dual nature of the two phenomena does not in consequence disappear.

If this important truth failed to be realised by the Utilitarians, it is an error springing from the manner in which they conceived the genesis of society. They supposed that originally there were isolated and independent individuals who thus could only enter into relationships with one another in order to co-operate, for they had no other reason to bridge the empty gap separating them, and to associate together. But this theory, which is so widely held, postulates a veritable creation *ex nihilo*.

It consists, in fact, of deducing society from the individual. But we possess no knowledge that gives grounds for believing in the possibility of such a spontaneous generation. On Spencer's admission, for society to be able to be formed on such an hypothesis, 'the units [must] pass from the state of perfect independence to that of mutual dependence'.[27] But what can have determined them to make so complete a transformation? The prospect of the advantages that social life offers? But these are balanced, and even unduly so, by the loss of independence, because for creatures destined by nature for a free and solitary life, such a sacrifice is the most intolerable of all. In addition, in the first social types, the sacrifice was as absolute as possible, because nowhere is the individual more completely absorbed within the group. How could man, if he were born an individualist, as we suppose, have resigned himself to an existence that goes so violently against his most fundamental inclination? How very pallid the problematic utility of co-operation must have appeared to him in comparison with such a surrender! From autonomous individualities, like those we imagine, nothing can therefore emerge save what is individual; consequently co-operation itself, which is a social fact, subject to social rules, cannot arise. It is in this way that the psychologist who begins to shut himself up within his own self can no longer emerge from it, to find again the non-self.

Collective life did not arise from individual life; on the contrary, it

is the latter that emerged from the former. On this condition alone
can we explain how the personal individuality of social units was
able to form and grow without causing society to disintegrate.
Indeed, since in this case it developed from within a pre-existing
social environment, it necessarily bears its stamp. It is constituted in
such a way as not to ruin that collective order to which it is solidly
linked. It remains adapted to it, whilst detaching itself from it. There
is nothing antisocial about it, because it is a product of society. It is
not the absolute personality of the monad, sufficient unto itself, and
able to do without the rest of the world, but that of an organ or part
of an organ that has its own definite function, but that cannot,
without running a mortal risk, separate itself from the rest of the
organism. In these conditions co-operation not only becomes
possible, but necessary. The Utilitarians therefore reverse the
natural order of events, and there is nothing less surprising than this
reversal. It is a particular illustration of the general truth that what is
first to be known is last in reality. Precisely because co-operation is
the most recent fact, this it is that strikes one's gaze first. If therefore
we look only to appearances, as does common sense, inevitably we
see it as the primary fact of moral and social life.

But if co-operation is not the whole of morality, we must not place
it outside the ambit of morality either, as do certain moralists. Just
like the Utilitarians, such idealists make it out to consist exclusively
of a system of economic relationships, of private arrangements that
are sparked off solely by egoism. In reality moral life permeates all
the relationships that go to make up co-operation, since it would not
be possible if social sentiments, and consequently moral ones, did
not preside over its elaboration.

The argument concerning the international division of labour will
be adduced. It seems clear, in this case at least, that the individuals
who share the work do not belong to the same society. But we
should remember that a group, whilst it retains its individuality, can
be enveloped within another larger one, which comprises others of
the same kind. We may even affirm that a function, whether of an
economic or any other kind, can only be divided up between two
societies if these share in some respects in the same common life
and, consequently, belong to the same society. Let us indeed
suppose that these two collective consciousnesses are not in some
respects intermingled together. Then we would not be able to see
how the two aggregates might have the continuous contact that is

necessary nor, in consequence, how one of them could abandon one of its functions to the other. For a people to allow itself to be penetrated by another, it must have ceased to shut itself up in an exclusive form of patriotism, and must have learned another that is more all-embracing.

However, we can observe directly this relationship of fact in the most striking example of the international division of labour that history offers us. We may indeed say that it has never really occurred save in Europe and in our own day. It was at the end of the last century and the beginning of our own that a common consciousness began to form in European societies:

> There is [says Sorel] a prejudice which we must rid ourselves of. It is to represent the Europe of the *ancien régime* as a society consisting of regularly constituted states in which each one made its conduct conform to principles universally recognized, where the respect for established law governed transactions and dictated treaties, where good faith controlled their implementation, where a sentiment of solidarity existing between monarchies ensured, with the maintenance of public order, the lasting character of the undertakings entered into by princes. . . . A Europe where the rights of each arise from the duties of all was something so foreign to the statesmen of the *ancien régime* that a war lasting a quarter of a century was needed, the most formidable seen up to then, in order to impose this notion upon them and to show them the necessity for it. The attempt made at the Congress of Vienna and in the ensuing congresses to give Europe some elementary form of organisation was a step forward and not a return to the past.[28]

Conversely, any reversion to a narrow nationalism has always resulted in the development of a protectionist spirit, that is, a tendency for peoples to isolate themselves, economically and morally, from one another.

If however, in certain cases, peoples lacking any common link, who sometimes even look upon one another as enemies,[29] exchange their products in more or less regular fashion, we should only see in these facts mere relationships of 'mutualism' which have nothing in common with the division of labour.[30] This is because, if two organisms that are different find they have properties that fit in usefully with each other, it does not follow that there is any sharing out of functions between them.[31]

Notes

1. H. Spencer, *Principles of Sociology* (London, 1855) vol. I, p 487.
2. 'Colunt diversi ac discreti,' says Tacitus of the Germans; 'suam quisque domum spatio circumdat' (*Germania*, vol. XVI).
3. Cf. in Accarias, *Précis*, vol. I, p. 640, the list of urban charges. Cf. Fustel de Coulanges, *La cité antique*, p. 65.
4. By reasoning in this way we do not mean that the increase in density is the result of economic changes. The two facts have a mutual conditioning effect upon each other, and this suffices for the presence of the one to attest to the presence of the other.
5. Cf. Levasseur, *La population française, passim*.
6. Tacitus, *Germania*, vol. XVI; Sohm, *Über die Entstehung der Städte*.
7. Marquardt, *Römische Altertümer*, vol. IV, p. 3.
8. Cf. on this point, Dumont, *Dépopulation et civilisation* (Paris, 1890) ch. 8; and Oettingen, *Moralstatistik*, pp. 273 ff.
9. Cf. Levasseur, *La population française*, p. 200.
10. This seems to us to be the opinion of Tarde in his *Lois de l'Imitation*.
11. However, there are special cases of an exceptional kind, where material density and moral density are perhaps not entirely in proportion. Cf. note 31 below.
12. Spencer, *Principles of Sociology*, vol. I, p. 481.
13. The village, which originally was only a clan whose abode was fixed.
14. On this point we can again rely upon the authority of Comte. 'I need only,' he says, 'point now to the progressive increase in density of our species as an ultimate general factor helping to regulate the effective rapidity of social movement. First, therefore, one may freely recognise that this influence contributes a great deal, above all at the beginning, in determining for human labour as a whole its increasingly specialised division, which is necessarily incompatible with a small number of people co-operating together. *Moreover, by a more intimate and less well-known property, although of even greater importance, such a densifying process directly and very powerfully stimulates the swifter development in social evolution*, either by stimulating individuals to put forth fresh efforts using refined methods, in order to ensure for themselves an existence which otherwise would become more difficult, or by obliging society also to react with greater energy and persistence, and in more concerted fashion, struggling against the increasedly powerful upsurge of particular divergences. On both counts we see that here it is not a question of the absolute increase in the number of individuals, but above all of the more intense competition between them in a given area' (*Cours de philosophie positive*, vol. IV, p. 455).

15. H. Spencer, *First Principles* (London, 1862) p. 382.
16. C. Darwin, *The Origin of Species* (London, 1891) pp. 82–3.
17. Haeckel, *Histoire de la création naturelle*, p. 240.
18. Aristotle, *Politics*, vol. IV(VII), 16, 1335b, pp. 20 ff.
19. Bordier, *Vie des sociétés*, p. 45.
20. Cf. ibid., pp. 166 ff.
21. Féré, *Dégérescence et criminalité*, p. 88.
22. Cf. article on 'Aliénation mentale' in *Dictionnaire encyclopédique des sciences médicales*.
23. This development of intellectual or scientific life proper has yet another cause, as we shall see in the next chapter.
24. Bain, *The Emotions and the Will*, p. 433.
25. Spencer, *Principles of Sociology*, vol. II, p. 244.
26. Comte, *Cours de philosophie positive*, vol. IV, p. 421.
27. Spencer, *Principles of Sociology*, vol. II, p. 244.
28. Sorel, *L'Europe et la Révolution française*, vol. I, pp. 9–10.
29. Cf. Kulischer, 'Der Handel auf den primitiven Kulturstufen', *Zeitschrift für Völkerpsychologie*, vol. X (1877) p. 378; also Schrader, *Linguistisch-historische Forschungen zur Handelsgeschichte* (Jena, 1886).
30. It is true that 'mutualism' generally occurs between individual creatures of different species, but the phenomenon remains the same, even where it takes place between individual creatures of the same species. (On 'mutualism', cf. Espinas, *Sociétés animales*, and Giraud, *Les Sociétés chez les animaux*.)
31. Finally we remind readers that in this chapter we have only studied how it comes about that generally the division of labour still goes on increasing, and we have stated the causes that determine this development. Yet it may well be that in any given society a certain division of labour, and in particular the economic division of labour, is very developed, although the segmentary social type is still very strongly pronounced. Indeed, this seems to be the case in England. Large-scale industry and commerce appear to be as developed there as on the Continent, although the 'alveolar' system is still very marked, as is demonstrated both by the autonomy of local life and the authority preserved by tradition. (The symptomatic value of this last fact will be addressed in the following chapter.)

It is because the division of labour, being a derived and secondary phenomenon, as we have just seen, occurs on the surface of social life, and this is particularly true for the economic division of labour. It skims the surface. Now, in the whole organism, superficial phenomena, by their very location, are more susceptible to the effect of external causes, even when the internal causes upon which they depend generally are not modified. Thus some circumstance or another stimulates a people to feel a stronger need for material wellbeing so that the economic division of labour develops without any appreciable change in the social structure. The spirit of imitation, the contact with a more refined civilisation, can bring about this result. Thus the understanding, being at the culminating point and consequently the most superficial area of the consciousness, can be easily modified by external influences such as education, without the foundations of psychological life being touched. Thus intelligences are created that are amply sufficient to ensure success, but that lack any deep roots. Hence this kind of talent is not transmitted by heredity.

This comparison shows that we must not judge the appropriate place for a society on the social scale according to the state of its civilisation, especially of its economic civilisation. The latter may be a mere imitation or copy, and conceal a social structure of an inferior species. It is true that such a case is exceptional, but it does occur.

It is only in such occurrences that the material density of a society does not express accurately the state of moral density. The principle we have enunciated is therefore true very generally, and this is adequate enough for our proof.

Chapter III

Secondary Factors

The Progressive Indeterminacy of the Common Consciousness and its Causes

We saw in the first part of this work that the collective consciousness weakened and became vaguer as the division of labour developed. It is even because of this progressive indeterminacy that the division of labour becomes the main cause of solidarity. Since these two phenomena are linked to such an extent, it is not unhelpful to investigate the causes of this regression. Undoubtedly, by demonstrating the regularity with which it occurs, we have directly established that it assuredly depends upon some basic conditions of social evolution. But this conclusion of the preceding book would be even more indisputable if we could discover what these conditions are.

This question, moreover, is closely linked to the one we are dealing with at present. We have just shown that the progress of the division of labour is due to the stronger pressure exerted by social units upon one another, which forces them to develop in more or less divergent directions. But at every moment this pressure is neutralised by a reverse pressure that the common consciousness exerts upon every individual consciousness. Whilst the one impels us to create for ourselves a distinctive personality, the other, by contrast, requires us to resemble everybody else. Whilst the former induces us to follow our personal inclinations, the latter checks us, preventing us from deviating from the collective type. In other words for the division of labour to be able to arise, and to increase, it is not enough for individuals to have within them the seeds of special aptitudes, nor for them to be stimulated to veer towards these aptitudes, but individual variations must also be possible. Such variations cannot occur when they are opposed to some strong, well-defined state of the collective consciousness. For the stronger

226

such a state, the more resistant it is to anything that might weaken it. The better defined it is, the less room it leaves for changes. Thus we can foresee that the division of labour will be more difficult and slower, the more vigour and precision the collective consciousness possesses. Conversely, the more swift that progress becomes, the more easily the individual can establish a harmony with his personal environment. Yet for this it is not enough for this environment to exist; he also needs to be free to adapt to it, that is, to be capable of moving independently within it, even when the group as a whole does not move with him nor in the same direction. Yet we know that particular movements of individuals are rarer the more mechanical solidarity is developed.

Examples are numerous where one can observe directly this countervailing influence of the common consciousness on the division of labour. So long as law and morals make the inalienable and indivisible nature of immovable property a strict obligation, the conditions necessary for the division of labour cannot yet exist. Every family forms a compact mass, and all devote themselves to the same occupation, the cultivation of the ancestral inheritance. Among the Slavs, the *Zadruga* often grow so much in number that there is great misery among them. However, as the home spirit is very strong, they generally continue to live together, instead of leaving and taking up specialised professions such as those of seafarer or merchant. In other societies, where the division of labour is more advanced, each class has functions that are prescribed, unvarying and protected from all innovations. Elsewhere there are whole categories of occupations whose access is more or less formally prohibited to citizens. In Greece,[1] in Rome,[2] industry and commerce were careers that were looked down upon; among the Kabyle tribes certain trades like those of butcher, shoemaker, etc., are despised by public opinion.[3] Specialisation cannot therefore occur in these various directions. Finally, even among peoples whose economic life has already reached a certain stage of development, as with our own in the days of the old corporations, functions were regulated in such a way that the division of labour could make no headway. Where everyone was obliged to manufacture goods in the same way any individual variation was impossible.[4]

The same phenomenon occurs in the representative life of societies. Religion, that outstanding form of the common consciousness, originally subsumed all the functions of representation with the practical functions. The former were only dissociated from the latter when philosophy came on the scene. Philosophy is only possible when religion has lost some of its sway. This new way of representing things shocks collective opinion, which resists it. It has occasionally been said that free investigation has caused the decline in religious beliefs. But this in turn assumes an earlier decline in those beliefs. This cannot happen unless the common faith allows it.

The same antagonism breaks out whenever a new science is established. Christianity itself, although it immediately assigned a larger place to individual reflection than any other religion, was not able to escape from this rule. Doubtless opposition was less fierce so long as scientists limited their studies to the material world, since in principle this had been abandoned to the disputations of men. Even so, since this act of abandonment was never total because the Christian God is not wholly a stranger to the things of this world, it necessarily turned out that in more than one respect the natural sciences found faith to be an obstacle. But it was above all when man himself became an object of scientific study that resistance became powerful. In fact the believer cannot help being repelled by the idea that man should be studied as a natural being, analogous to other beings, and moral facts studied just as are the facts of nature. We know to what extent these collective feelings, in the different guises they have assumed, have hampered the development of psychology and sociology.

Thus the progress made by the division of labour has not been entirely explained when we have demonstrated that it was necessitated by the changes that have occurred in the social environment. That progress still depends upon secondary factors that may facilitate or hamper it, or even stop it completely in its tracks. We must indeed not forget that specialisation is not the sole possible solution to the struggle for existence: there are also integration, colonisation, resignation to a precarious and more contested existence and, finally, the complete elimination of the weakest through suicide or other means. Since the outcome is to a certain degree contingent upon circumstances and the protagonists are not necessarily drawn towards any one of these solutions to the exclusion of all others, they strive towards the one nearest within their grasp. It is true that if nothing stands in the way of the development of the division of labour, they become specialised. But if this solution is rendered impossible or too difficult because of circumstances, they must needs resort to another.

The first of these secondary factors consists in a greater independence of individuals in relation to the group, which allows them to vary at will. The physiological division of labour is subject to this same condition. 'Even when they are drawn closer to one another,' states Perrier, 'the parts of the anatomy each preserve their complete individuality. Whatever their number, in the highest organism as in the humblest, they feed, grow and reproduce paying no heed of their neighbours. This is what constitutes *the law of independence of anatomical elements*, which has become so fertile a tool in the hands of the physiologists. This independence must be considered as a necessary condition among plastides for the free exercise of a more general faculty, their variability under the influence of external circumstances or even of certain forces immanent in protoplasms. Thanks to this ability to vary, and to their mutual independence, elements deriving from one another which were once all similar have been able to modify in different directions, assume various forms and acquire new functions and properties.'[5]

Contrary to what occurs in organisms, this independence was not a primitive fact in societies, since originally the individual was swallowed up in the group. Yet we have seen that independence appears later and progresses steadily with the division of labour, as a sequel to the regression of the collective consciousness. What remains to be studied is how this condition useful for the social division of labour is realised as it becomes necessary. Undoubtedly it is because it depends itself on causes that have determined the advance of specialisation. Yet how can the growth in the volume and density of societies bring about this result?

I

In a small society, since everybody is roughly placed in the same conditions of existence, the collective environment is essentially concrete. It is made up of human beings of every kind who people the social horizon. The states of consciousness that represent it are therefore of the same character. At first they relate to precise objects, such as a particular animal, tree, plant, or natural force, etc. Then, since everyone is similarly placed in relation to these things, they affect every individual consciousness in the same way. The whole tribe, provided it is not too extensive, enjoys or suffers equally the advantages and inconveniences of sun and rain, heat and cold, or of a particular river or spring, etc. The collective impressions resulting from the fusion of all these individual impressions are thus determinate in their form as in their objects. Consequently the common consciousness has a definite character. But this consciousness alters in nature as societies grow more immense. Because they are spread over a much vaster area, the common consciousness is itself forced to rise above all local diversities, to dominate more the space available, and consequently to become more abstract. For few save general things can be common to all these various environments. There is no longer question of such and such an animal, but of such and such a species; not this spring, but these springs; not this forest, but forest *in abstracto*.

Moreover, because living conditions are not the same everywhere, these common objects, whatever they may be, can no longer determine everywhere feelings so completely identical. The results for the collectivity thus lack the same distinctness, and this is even more the case because the component elements are more dissimilar. The more differences between the individual portraits that have served to make a composite portrait, the more imprecise the latter is. It is true that local collective consciousness can retain their individuality within the general collective consciousness and that, since they encompass narrower horizons, they can more easily remain concrete. But we know that gradually they vanish into the general consciousness as the different social segments to which they correspond fade away.

Perhaps the fact that best demonstrates this increasing tendency of the common consciousness is the parallel transcendence of the most vital of all its elements – I refer to the notion of divinity. Originally the gods were not apart from the universe, or rather there were no gods, but only sacred beings, without the sacred character with which they were invested being related to some external entity as its source. The animals or plants of the species that serve as the clan totem are the object of worship. But this is not because a principle *sui generis* coming from outside communicates to them their divine nature. This nature is intrinsic within them. They are divine in themselves. But gradually the religious forces become detached from the things of which they were at first only the attributes, and are reified. In this way is formed the notion of spirits or gods who, whilst preferring this or that location, nevertheless exist outside the particular objects to which they are more especially attached.[6] This fact alone renders them less concrete. However, whether they are many or have been reduced to a certain unity, they are still immanent in the world. Partly separated from things, they still exist in space. Thus they remain very close to us, continually intermingling with our life. Greco-Roman polytheism, which is a higher and better organised form of animism, marks a new step towards transcendence. The dwelling-place of the gods becomes more clearly distinct from that of man. Having withdrawn to the mysterious heights of Olympus or to the depths of the earth, except intermittently they no longer intervene personally in human affairs. But it is only with Christianity that God finally goes beyond space; His Kingdom is no longer of this world. The dissociation of nature and the divine becomes so complete that it even degenerates into hostility. At the same time the notion of divinity becomes more general and abstract, for it is formed not from sensations, as it was in the beginning, but from ideas. The God of humanity is necessarily not so comprehensible as those of a city or clan.

Moreover, at the same time as religion, legal rules become universalised, as do those of morality. First bound to local circumstances, to racial or climatic peculiarities, etc., they gradually free themselves from these and simultaneously become more general. What makes this increase in generality more apparent is the unbroken decline in formalism. In lower societies the form of behaviour – even its external form – is predetermined even down to the detail. The way in which men must take food or dress in every situation, the gestures they must perform, the formulas they must pronounce, are precisely laid down. On the other hand, the more distant the point of departure, the more moral and legal prescriptions lose clarity and preciseness. They no longer regulate any save the most general forms of behaviour, and these only in a very general way, stating what should be done, but not how it should be done. Now everything definite is expressed in a definite form. If collective sentiments were as determinate as once they were, they would be expressed in no less determinate a fashion. If the concrete details of action and thought were as uniform, they would be as obligatory.

The fact has often been remarked upon that civilisation has

tended to become more rational and logical. We can now see the cause of this. That alone is rational that is universal. What defies the understanding is the particular and the concrete. We can only ponder effectively upon the general. Consequently, the closer the common consciousness is to particular things, the more exactly it bears their imprint, and thus the more unintelligible it is. This is whence derives the effect that primitive civilisations have upon us. Not being able to reduce them to logical principles, we are inclined to view them only as bizarre, strange and fortuitous combinations of heterogeneous elements. In reality, there is nothing artificial about them. But we must look for their determining causes in sensations and impulsions of the sensibility, and not in concepts. If this is so, it is because the social environment for which they have been made is not sufficiently extensive. On the other hand, when civilisation is developed over a vaster field of action, when it relates to more people and things, general ideas necessarily appear and there become paramount. The notion of mankind, for example, replaces in law, morality and religion that of the Romans which, being more concrete, is more difficult to understand. Thus it is the growth in the size of societies and their greater density that explains this great transformation.

The more general the common consciousness becomes, the more scope it leaves for individual variations. When God is remote from things and men, His action does not extend to every moment of time and to every thing. Only abstract rules are fixed, and these can be freely applied in very different ways. Even then they have neither the same ascendancy nor the same strength of resistance. Indeed, if usages and formulas, when they are precise, determine thought and action with a compulsion analogous to that of the reflexes, by contrast these general principles can only be translated into facts with the assistance of the intelligence. Yet once reflective thinking has been stimulated, it is not easy to set bounds to it. When it has gathered strength, it spontaneously develops beyond the limits assigned to it. At the beginning certain articles of faith are stipulated to be beyond discussion, but later the discussion extends to them. There is a desire to account for them, the reason for their existence is questioned, and however they fare in this examination, they relinquish some part of their strength. For ideas arising from reflection have never the same constraining power as instincts. Thus actions that have been deliberated upon have not the instant immediacy of involuntary acts. Because the collective consciousness becomes more rational, it therefore becomes less categorical and, for this reason again, is less irksome to the free development of individual variations.

II

But this cause is not the one that contributes most to bringing about this result.

What constitutes the strength of the collective states of consciousness is not only that they are common to the present generation, but particularly that they are for the most part a legacy of generations that have gone before. The common consciousness is in fact formed only very slowly and modified in the same way. Time is needed for a form of behaviour or a belief to attain that degree of generality and crystallisation, and time also for it to lose it. Thus it is almost entirely a product of the past. But what springs from the past is generally an object of very special respect. A practice to which everyone unanimously conforms has without doubt great prestige. But if it is also strong because it bears the mark of ancestral approval, one dares even less to depart from it. The authority of the collective consciousness is therefore made up in large part of the authority of tradition. We shall see that this authority necessarily decreases as the segmentary type of society vanishes.

Indeed, when it is very marked, the segments form so many small societies more or less partitioned off from one another. Where they are based upon the family, it is as difficult to change them as to change the family. If, when they remain merely on a territorial basis, the barriers dividing them are less insurmountable, they nevertheless persist. In the Middle Ages it was still difficult for a workman to find work in a town other than his own.[7] Internal customs authorities, moreover, formed around each social compartment a protective belt against the infiltration of foreign elements. In these conditions the individual is fixed to his native heath by bonds that attach him to it, and also because he is rejected elsewhere. The scarcity of the means of communication and transmission is a proof of this occlusion of each segment. One repercussion is that the causes that retain a man in his native environment bind him to his domestic environment also. Originally the two were linked together. If at a later date a distinction is made between them, a person could not remove himself far from the domestic environment when he could not either go outside his native environment. The force of attraction that results from blood kinship acts with maximum intensity, since throughout his whole life each person is placed close to the very source of that force. Indeed that law admits of no exception which states that the more segmentary the social structure the more families form large, compact masses, indivisible, and turned in on themselves.[8]

On the other hand, as the demarcation lines separating the different segments disappear, this equilibrium is inevitably broken. Since individuals are no longer restricted to their place of origin and free space is opened up, attracting them, they cannot fail to spread out over it. Children no longer remain irrevocably attached to the locality of their parents, but set off in all directions to seek their fortune. Populations mingle together, and this it is that finally causes their original differences to disappear. Unfortunately statistics do not permit us to follow the historical course of these interior migrations. But there is one fact sufficient to establish their growing importance: the formation and development of towns. Towns are certainly not formed by a sort of spontaneous growth, but by immigration. To state that they owe their existence and progress to a normal excess of births over deaths is far from the truth; there is in fact from this viewpoint an overall deficit. Thus it is from external sources that they receive those elements that cause their population to grow day by day. According to Dunant,[9] the annual increment of the entire population of thirty-one great cities of Europe, amounting to a rate of 784.6 per thousand, is due to immigration. In France the 1881 census revealed, as compared with that of 1876, an increase of 766,000 inhabitants. The *département* of the Seine and the forty-five towns of more than 30,000 inhabitants 'absorbed for the five-yearly figure of growth more than 661,000 inhabitants, leaving only 105,000 to be spread out over average and small towns, and over the countryside'.[10] Nor do these great migratory movements only install themselves in the large towns; they also spread out over the adjoining areas. Bertillon has calculated that during the year 1886, whilst on an average in France, out of 100 inhabitants, 11.25 only were born outside the *département*, in the *département* of the Seine the figure was 34.67. The proportion of strangers to the *département* is higher the more populous the towns within it. In the

Rhône *département* it is 31.47; in Bouches-du-Rhône 26.29, in Seine-et-Oise 26.41,[11] in the Nord 19.46, in the Gironde 17.62.[12] This phenomenon is not peculiar to large towns; it also occurs, although less intensely, in the small towns and the 'bourgs'. 'All such built-up areas are constantly increasing at the expense of smaller communes, so that at every census we can see the number of towns in each category growing by a number of units.'[13]

The greater mobility of social units that these phenomena of migration assume effects a weakening of all traditions.

What constitutes the strength of tradition is the character of those who hand it on and inculcate it, that is, the older generation. They are its living expression; they alone have witnessed what our predecessors were wont to do. They are the unique mediator between the present and the past. Moreover, they enjoy among the generations brought up under their supervision and control a prestige that nothing can supplant. The child is certainly conscious of his inferiority in relation to the older persons around him, feeling dependent upon them. The reverential respect he has for older persons is naturally communicated to everything that proceeds from them, all that they say and do. Thus it is the authority of age that mainly constitutes that of tradition. Consequently all that can contribute to prolonging that influence beyond childhood can only strengthen traditional beliefs and practices. This is what happens when the grown man continues to live in the environment where he was brought up, for he then remains in touch with those who have known him as a child, and subject to their influence. The feelings he has for them continue to exist, and consequently encompass the same effect, which means that they restrain the will to innovate. For innovations to occur in social life, it is not enough for new generations to see the light of day. They must also not be too strongly inclined to follow in their predecessors' footsteps. The more profound the latter's influence – and it is all the more so the longer it lasts – the more the obstacles to change. Auguste Comte rightly declared that if the span of human life was vastly increased, without any modification in the proportions of the age groups, there would occur 'an inevitable slowing-up in our social development, although this would be impossible to measure'.[14]

Yet the opposite occurs if a man, when he leaves adolescence behind, is transplanted into a new environment. He will doubtless find there men older than himself, but they are not the same ones whose influence he has undergone in childhood. His respect for them is therefore less, and of a more conventional nature, for it corresponds to no reality, whether present or past. He does not depend upon them and has never done so. He can therefore only respect them by analogy. It is moreover a well-known fact that the worship of age grows weaker as civilisation progresses. Once so highly developed, it is today reduced to a few polite usages, inspired by a kind of pity. Old men are pitied rather than feared. Age differences are levelled out. All men, once they have arrived at the age of maturity, treat one another as approximate equals. As a result of this levelling-out, the customs of one's forefathers lose their ascendancy, since for adults they lack anyone to represent them with authority. One is freer in regard to them, because one is freer with those who embody them. The solidarity that time imparts is less appreciable because it no longer has material expression in the unbroken contact of successive generations. Undoubtedly the effects of one's early education continue to be felt, but with less force, because they are no longer sustained.

That moment of the fullness of youth is moreover the one when men are most impatient at any restraint placed upon them, and when they are most eager for change. The life flowing within them has not had time to coagulate, to assume definitively a determined form, and is too intense to submit to any discipline without resistance. This imperative will thus be all the more easily satisfied if it is less restrained from outside, and it can only be satisfied at the expense of tradition. But tradition is breached at the very moment when its strength is ebbing away. Once implanted, this enfeebling germ can only continue to develop with each succeeding generation, for principles whose authority is more weakly felt will be handed down with weaker authority still.

One experience, which is characteristic, shows this influence of age upon the force of tradition.

Precisely because the population of large towns is principally added to by immigration, it is essentially made up of people who, once they had come of age, have left their homes and removed themselves from the influence of the older generation. Thus the number of old people in these towns is very few, whilst by contrast that of men in the prime of life is very high. Cheysson has shown that the population curves for each age cohort, for Paris and the provinces, only meet at the ages of 15–20 and 50–55. Between 20 and 50 the curve for Paris is very much higher, beyond that age it is lower.[15] In 1881 there were in Paris 1,118 people aged between 20 and 25 as compared with 874 in the rest of the country.[16] For the *departement* of the Seine as a whole, of 1,000 inhabitants, 731 are aged between 15 and 60, whereas only 76 are over that age, whilst in the provinces the corresponding figures are 618 and 106. In Norway, according to Jacques Bertillon, the proportions for 1,000 inhabitants are as follows:

Age	Towns	Rural areas
15–30	278	239
30–45	205	183
45–60	110	120
60 and over	59	87

It is therefore in the large towns that the moderating influence of age is at its lowest. At the same time it is notable that nowhere do traditions hold less sway over people's minds. Indeed the large towns are indisputably centres of progress. It is in them that ideas, fashions, morals and new needs take shape, to spread out afterwards over the rest of the country. When society changes it is following upon the towns and in imitation of them. The mood is so fluctuating in them that everything springing from the past is a little suspect. On the contrary, novelty, whatever kind it consists of, enjoys a prestige almost equal to that once enjoyed by the customs of our ancestors. Minds are naturally turned towards the future. Thus life is transformed with extraordinary speed: beliefs, taste, passions are in a state of perpetual evolution. There is no more favourable soil for developments of every kind. This is because collective life can have no continuity where the different strata of social units, called upon to replace one another, so lack continuity.

After observing that, during the youthful period of societies and particularly at the time of their maturity, the respect for traditions is much greater than in their old age, Tarde thought he could present the decline of traditionalism as merely a transitory phase, a passing crisis in all social evolution. 'Man,' he declares, 'only escapes the yoke of custom in order to fall back into it, that is, to fix and consolidate by falling back into it the conquests due to his temporary emancipation.'[17] This error derives, we believe, from the method of comparison followed by the author, the disadvantages of which we have pointed out several times before. Doubtless, if we compare the final days of one society with the beginnings of the one that follows it, we perceive a return to traditionalism. Only this phase, by which every social type begins, is always much less violent than it had been in the immediately preceding type. With us ancestral customs have never been the object of superstitious worship such as that devoted to them at Rome. There was never in Rome an institution similar to the γραφὴ παρανόμων of Athenian law, which was hostile to every kind of innovation.[18] Even in Aristotle's time it was still a question in Greece of knowing whether it was good to change established laws in order to improve them, and the philosopher only gives his assent with the greatest circumspection.[19] Finally, with the Jews any deviation from the traditional rule was even more utterly ruled out, since it constituted an act of impiety. In order to judge the course of social events, we must not place end-on to one another successive societies, but compare them only at the corresponding period in the career of each one. If therefore it is true that all social life tends to crystallise in form, becoming customary, the form that it assumes becomes ever less resistant and more accessible to change. In other words the authority of custom is continually diminishing. Moreover, it cannot be otherwise, since this weakening depends upon the very conditions that dominate historical development.

In addition, since common beliefs and practices draw their strength for the most part from the force of tradition, they are clearly less and less in a position to hinder the free flourishing of individual variations.

III

Finally as society spreads out and becomes denser, it envelops the individual less tightly, and in consequence can restrain less efficiently the diverging tendencies that appear.

To confirm that this is the case it is sufficient to compare large and small towns. With the latter, the person who seeks to emancipate himself from accepted customs comes up against resistances that are on occasion very fierce. Any bid for independence is a subject of public scandal, and the general opprobrium attached to it is such as to discourage imitators. On the contrary, in large towns the individual is much more liberated from the yoke of the collectivity;

this is indisputably a fact of experience. It is because we depend more closely upon public opinion the more narrowly it supervises all our activities. When everyone's attention is constantly fixed upon what everyone else is doing, the slightest deviation is remarked upon and immediately repressed. Conversely, the greater freedom each individual has to follow his own bent, the easier it is for him to escape surveillance. Now, as the proverb has it, one is nowhere so well hidden as in the crowd. The more the group is spread out, although densely concentrated, the more the collective attention, dissipated over a wide area, becomes incapable of following the movements of each individual, because attention does not become more intense as the number of individuals increases. It must oversee too many points at one time to be able to concentrate on any single one. The surveillance is less careful, because there are too many people and things to watch.

Moreover, the great motivator of attention, interest, is more or less completely lacking. We only desire to know the doings and actions of a person if his image stirs up in us memories and emotions that are linked to it. This desire is all the more active when the states of consciousness awakened in this way are greater in number and stronger.[20] If, on the other hand, the person in question is someone whom we only perceive at a distance and in passing, what his concerns are, since they arouse no echo within ourselves, leave us indifferent. Consequently we have no inducement to inform ourselves about what is happening to him nor to observe what he is doing. Collective curiosity is therefore stronger when personal relations between individuals are more continuous and frequent. On the other hand, it is evident that they are rarer and briefer when each separate individual is in contact with a larger number of other people.

This is why the pressure of opinion is felt with less force in large population centres. It is because the attention of each individual is distracted in too many different directions. Moreover, we do not know one another so well. Even neighbours and members of the same family are in contact less often and less regularly, separated as they are at every moment by a host of matters and other people who come between them. Undoubtedly if the population is larger in number than it is concentrated in density, it can happen that the business of living, scattered over a wider area, is less intense at any and every point. The large town then splits up into a certain number of smaller ones and consequently the preceding remarks do not apply exactly.[21] Yet wherever the density of the conurbation is proportionate to its volume, personal ties are few and weak. We lose sight of others more easily, even those very close to us physically. And to the same extent we lose interest in them. Since this mutual indifference has the effect of relaxing the supervision of the collectivity, the range of freedom of individual action is enlarged *de facto*, and gradually this situation of fact becomes one *de jure*. Indeed we know that the common consciousness only retains its strength if it countenances no contradiction. As a result of this decrease in social control, acts are committed daily that infringe it, without however its reacting. If therefore some acts are repeated sufficiently frequently and consistently, they end up by enfeebling the collective sentiment that they offend. A rule no longer appears as respectable when it ceases to be respected, and this without incurring punishment. One does not find so self-evident an article of faith that has been allowed to be challenged unduly. Moreover, once we have enjoyed a liberty, we acquire a need for it. It becomes as necessary and as sacred to us as all the others. We deem intolerable a control we are no longer accustomed to. An acquired right to a greater autonomy is set up. Thus encroachments committed by the individual personality, when that personality is less forcibly constrained externally, end up by receiving the consecration of custom.

If this fact is more apparent in large towns, it is not peculiar to them. It happens also in the others, depending upon their importance. Thus since the disappearance of the segmentary type of society entails an ever-increasing development of urban centres, this is a prime reason for causing this phenomenon to become more general. But, in addition, as the moral density of a society is raised, so it becomes itself like a large city, which would contain within its walls the whole population.

Indeed, as the material and moral distance between different regions tends to vanish, they are placed in relation to one another in a situation still more analogous to that of different quarters of the same city. The cause that in large towns determines the weakening of the common consciousness must therefore produce its effect over the whole expanse of society. So long as the various segments, retaining their individuality, remain sealed off from one another, each narrowly restricts the social horizon of individuals. Separated from the rest of society by barriers more or less difficult to surmount, there is nothing to turn us away from the life of the neighbourhood, and in consequence our entire activity is concentrated upon it. But as the fusion of segments becomes more complete, perspectives broaden out – all the more because at the same time society itself becomes generally more extensive. From then onwards even the inhabitant of a small town lives less exclusively upon the life of the small group immediately around him. He enters into relationships with distant localities that are all the more numerous as the movement towards concentration advances. His more frequent journeys, the more active communications that he exchanges, the affairs with which he busies himself outside his own locality, etc., divert his gaze from what is taking place around him. The centre of his life and concerns is no longer to be found wholly in the place where he lives. Thus he takes less interest in his neighbours, because they occupy a more minor place in his life. Moreover, the small town has less hold upon him, by the very fact that his life has broken out beyond its narrow framework and his interests and affections stretch well beyond it. For all these reasons local opinion weighs less heavily with each one of us, and as public opinion in society generally is not capable of replacing it, because it cannot supervise closely the behaviour of all its citizens, collective surveillance is irrevocably relaxed, the common consciousness loses its authority, and individual variability increases. In short, for social control to be rigorous and for the common consciousness to be maintained, society must be split up into moderately small compartments that enclose completely the individual. By contrast, both social control and the common consciousness grow weaker as such divisions fade.[22]

Yet it will be objected that the crimes and offences to which are attached organised punishments never leave indifferent the organs charged with their repression. Whether the town be large or small, or the density of society be concentrated or not, the magistrates do not let go unpunished the criminal and the delinquent. It would therefore appear that the particular process of weakening, the cause of which we have just indicated, must be located in that part of the collective consciousness that determines only diffuse reactions and is incapable of extending further. Yet in reality so specific a location is impossible, for the two areas are so closely linked to each other that the one cannot be affected without the other being disturbed also. The actions that morality alone represses are no different in nature from those the law punishes; they are merely less serious. Thus if one action loses its serious character, the corresponding graduation in seriousness of the others is upset at the same time. They diminish in gravity by one or several degrees and appear less abhorrent. If one is no longer sensitive to small failings, one is even less so to major ones. When no great importance any longer attaches to simple neglect of religious observances, blasphemous or sacrilegious acts are no longer inveighed against with such indignation. When we have grown accustomed to suffering free unions complacently, adultery becomes less scandalous. When the weakest sentiments lose their potency the stronger ones of the same kind, which serve the same purpose, cannot retain intact their own potency. Thus the disturbance is gradually transmitted to the common consciousness in its entirety.

IV

Now we can explain how it happens that mechanical solidarity is linked to the existence of the segmentary type of society, as we established in the preceding book. It is because this particular structure enables society to hold the individual more tightly in its grip, making him more strongly attached to his domestic environment, and consequently to tradition. Finally, by helping to limit his social horizon, the structure also[23] helps in making the latter concrete and definite. Thus it is entirely mechanical causes which ensure that the individual personality is absorbed into the collective personality, and it is causes of the same nature which ensure that the same individual personality can free itself. Undoubtedly this emancipation is useful, or at least is used. It makes advances in the division of labour possible. More generally, it imparts more flexibility and elasticity to the social organism. Yet it is not because it is useful that it occurs. It is because things cannot be otherwise. The experience of the services that it renders can only consolidate it once it exists.

However, we may ask if, within organised societies, the organ does not play the same role as the segment, and whether the corporate and professional spirit does not bid fair to replace local parochialism and exert the same pressure upon individuals. In that case individuals would have gained nothing from the change. This doubt is all the more legitimate, since the class ethos has certainly had this effect, and class is a social organ. We know also how greatly the organisation of trade guilds for a long time impeded the development of individual variations. We have cited some examples of this above.

It is certain that organised societies are not possible without a developed system of rules laying down in advance the functioning of each organ. As work becomes divided up many professional moralities and legal prescriptions are constituted.[24] Yet this regulatory process does not leave the individual with a scope for action any less enlarged.

Firstly, the professional spirit can only have influence upon professional life. Beyond this sphere the individual enjoys that larger liberty whose origin we have just demonstrated. It is true that social class enlarges its action ever further, but it is not properly an organ. It is a segment transformed into an organ.[25] It therefore partakes of the nature of both. At the same time as it is entrusted with special functions, it constitutes a distinctive society within the total aggregate. It is a 'society-cum-organ', analogous to those 'individuals-cum-organ' observable within certain organisms.[26] It is this that allows class to embrace the individual in a way more exclusive than do the ordinary corporations.

In the second place, as these rules have roots only in a small number of consciousnesses, leaving society as a whole indifferent, their authority is less because of this lesser universality. Thus they offer less resistance to change. It is for this reason that in general faults that may properly be termed professional are not of the same degree of seriousness as the others.

On the other hand, the same causes that in general lighten the collective yoke produce their liberating effect within the corporation as they do outside it. To the extent that the segmentary organs fuse together each social organ becomes larger in volume, and this all the more so because in principle the overall volume of society increases simultaneously. Practices common to the professional group thus become more general and abstract, as do those common to society as a whole, and consequently leave the field more open for particular divergences. Likewise the greater independence enjoyed by the later generations in comparison with their elders cannot fail to weaken the traditionalism of the profession, and this makes the individual still freer to innovate.

Thus not only does professional regulation, by its very nature, hinder less than any other form of regulation the free development of individual variation, but moreover it hinders it less and less.

Notes

1. Büsschenschütz, *Besitz und Erwerb*.
2. According to Denis of Halicarnassus (vol. IX, p. 25), during the first years of the Republic no Roman could become a merchant or artisan. Cicero still talks of any mercenary labour as a degrading occupation (*De officiis*, vol. I, p. 42).
3. Hanoteau and Letourneux, *La Kabylie*, vol. II, p. 23.
4. Cf. Levasseur, *Les Classes ouvrières en France jusqu'à la Révolution*, *passim*.
5. Perrier, *Colonies animales*, p. 702.
6. Cf. Réville, *Religions des peuples non-civilisés*, vol. I, pp. 67 ff.; vol. II, pp. 230 ff.
7. Levasseur, *Les Classes*, vol. I, p. 239.
8. The reader can perceive for himself the facts that verify this law, express proof of which we cannot give here. It results from research we have carried out on the family and that we wish to publish shortly.
9. Quoted by Layet, *Hygiène des peuples*, last chapter.
10. Dumont, *Dépopulation et civilisation*, p. 175.
11. This high figure reflects the proximity of Paris.
12. *Dictionnaire encyclopédique des sciences médicales*. Article on: 'Migration'.
13. Dumont, *Dépopulation*.
14. A. Comte, *Cours de philosophie positive*, vol. IV, p. 451.
15. 'La question de la population', *Annales d'Hygiène* (1884).
16. *Annales de la ville de Paris*.
17. Tarde, *Lois de l'Imitation*, p. 271.
18. Cf. concerning this γραφή, Meier and Schönmann, *Der attische Prozess*.
19. Aristotle, *Politics*, vol. II, 8, 1268b, 26.
20. It is true that in a small town the foreigner or stranger is no less subject to surveillance than the inhabitants. But this is because the image that represents him is made very striking by the effect of contrast, because he is the exception. The same is not true in a large town, where he is the rule, since, so to speak, everyone is a stranger.
21. This is a question to be studied. We believe we have already remarked that in populous towns, but where the density is not great, collective opinion retains its strength.

22. To this basic cause we must add the contagious influence that spreads from large towns to small ones, and from small ones to rural areas. But this influence is only secondary and, moreover, only assumes importance as social density increases.

23. This third effect is only partially a result of the segmentary nature. Its principal cause is in the growth of social volume. It would remain to be ascertained why, in general, density grows at the same time as volume. This is a question we ask ourself.

24. Cf. *supra*, Book I, Chapter V, particularly pp. 162 ff.

25. Cf. *supra*, p.132.

26. Cf. Perrier, *Colonies animales*, p. 764.

Chapter IV

Secondary Factors (cont.)

Heredity

In what has gone before we have reasoned as if the division of labour depended only on social causes. However, it is also linked to organic and psychological conditions. The individual receives at birth tastes and aptitudes that predispose him to certain functions more than others, and these predispositions have certainly an influence upon the way in which tasks are distributed. According to the most commonly held opinion, we should even see in this diversity of human nature the prime condition for the division of labour, whose main reason for existence would be to classify individuals according to their abilities.[1] Thus it is of interest to determine precisely the part played by this factor, even more so because it constitutes another obstacle to the capacity for variation of each individual, and consequently an obstacle to the division of labour.

Indeed, as these innate aptitudes are handed down to us by our ancestors, they refer not to the present conditions in which an individual is placed, but to those in which our forefathers lived. Thus they join us to our race, just as the collective consciousness joined us to our group, and they have the effect of fettering our freedom of movement. As this part of ourselves is wholly turned towards the past, and towards a past that is not personal to ourselves, it deflects us from our own proper sphere of interest and the changes that are occurring within it. The more developed this part is, the more it restricts our movements. The race and the individual are two opposing forces that vary in inverse proportion to each other. In so far as we merely reproduce and continue our ancestors, we tend to live as they lived, unreceptive to all innovation.

246

A creature whose legacy from heredity was too considerable and too burdensome would be almost incapable of change. This is the case for animals, which can only advance with extreme slowness.

The obstacle that progress encounters in this respect is even more difficult to surmount than that which derives from a community of beliefs and practices. These latter are only imposed upon the individual from the outside, by means of a moral action, whilst hereditary tendencies are congenital, and have an anatomical basis. Thus the greater the role of heredity in the distribution of tasks, the more invariable that distribution is. Consequently, the more the development of the division of labour becomes difficult, even when it would be useful. This is what happens within the organism. The function of each cell is determined through its birth. According to Spencer:

> In a living animal . . . the progress of organisation implies, not only that the units composing each differentiated part severally maintain their position, but also that their progeny succeed to those positions. Bile-cells which, while performing the functions, grow and give origin to new bile-cells, are, when they decay and disappear, replaced by these: the cells descending from them do not migrate to the kidneys, or the muscles, or the nervous centres, to join in the performance of their duties.[2]

Thus, however, the changes that occur in the physiological organisation of labour are very rare, limited and slow.

Now, many facts tend to demonstrate that originally heredity had very considerable influence over the distribution of social functions.

Undoubtedly, among extremely primitive peoples from this viewpoint heredity plays no part at all. The few functions that begin to specialise are elective ones, but they are still not entirely constituted. The chief or chiefs are hardly distinguishable from the masses they lead. Their power is as limited as it is ephemeral. All members of the group are on an equal footing. But as soon as the division of labour appears in any marked fashion it is fixed in a form that is passed on by heredity. It is in this way that castes arise. India offers us the most perfect model of this organisation of labour, but it is to be found elsewhere. Among the Jews the sole functions that were sharply separated from others were those of the priesthood, which were strictly hereditary. The same was true in Rome for all public functions, which carried with them religious functions, and which were the privilege of the patricians alone. In Assyria, Persia and Egypt society was divided up in the same way. Where castes tended to disappear they were replaced by social classes which, although they were less hermetically closed to the outsider, nevertheless rest upon the same principle.

Certainly this institution is not the mere consequence of the fact of hereditary transmission. Many causes have contributed to bring it about. Yet it would not have been able to become so generalised, nor to have persisted so long if, *in general*, it had not had the effect of installing each individual in the place for which he was most suitable. If the caste system had gone counter to individual aspirations and the interests of society, no expedient could have ensured that it was maintained. If, in the average case, individuals had not been born capable of really fulfilling the function assigned to them by custom or law, this traditional classification of citizens would quickly have been overtoppled. This is proved by the fact that such a collapse indeed occurs as soon as such a mismatch arises. Thus the rigidity of the social framework merely expresses the immutable way in which abilities were distributed at that time, and this immutability itself can only be due to the action exerted by the laws of heredity. Doubtless, education reinforced their influence, since it was carried on entirely within the family circle and prolonged to a late age for reasons we have already stated. But education could not have produced such results by itself, for it only has utility and effectiveness if its action is in conformity with heredity. In short, heredity was only able to become a social institution where it played an effective social role. We know in fact that ancient peoples had a very keen feeling as to what it was. We not only find traces of it in the customs about which we have just spoken, and in similar ones, but it is voiced directly in more than one literary record.[3] It is impossible for so general an error to be a mere illusion, corresponding to nothing real. 'All peoples,' declares Ribot, 'have at least a vague faith in hereditary transmission. One might even maintain that this faith was stronger in primitive times than in civilised times. Institutional heredity arose from such a natural faith. Certainly social and political reasons, or even prejudices, must have contributed to the development of this faith, strengthening it, but it would be absurd to believe that it was pure invention.'[4]

Moreover, the heredity of professions was very often the rule, even when the law did not insist upon it. Thus medicine among the Greeks was first of all cultivated by a small number of families. 'The Asclepiads, or priests of Aesculphasus, claimed that they were the offspring of that god. . . . Hippocrates was the seventeenth doctor in his family. The art of divination, the gift of prophecy, that lofty sign of the gods' favour, was esteemed by the Greeks to be transmitted most frequently from father to son.'[5] 'In Greece,' states Hermann, 'heredity of function was only prescribed by law for certain conditions and functions which appertained very closely to religious life, such as in Sparta for cooks and flute-players. But custom had also made it more generally the rule for artisan professions than is commonly believed.'[6] Even today, in many lower societies functions are distributed according to race. In a large number of African tribes the blacksmiths are descendants of a different race than the rest of the population. The same was true for the Jews in the time of Saul:

> In Abyssinia almost all artisans are of a foreign race; the mason is a Jew, the tanner and the weaver are Moslems, the armourer and the goldsmith are Greeks and Copts. In India many of the differences between castes which indicate differences in occupations still coincide today with differences in race. In all countries with a mixed population the descendants of the same family customarily devote themselves to certain professions. Thus in Eastern Germany for centuries the fishermen were Slavs.[7]

These facts give great credence to Lucas's view, according to which 'the heredity of professions is the primitive type, the elementary form of all those institutions founded upon the principle of the heredity of the moral nature'.

But we also know how much in these societies any progress is slow and difficult. For centuries work remains organised in the same way, with no thought of any innovation. 'Heredity displays itself to us with its usual characteristics: conservation and stability.'[8] Consequently, for the division of labour to develop, men needed to succeed in throwing off the yoke of heredity and progress to be made by breaking up castes and classes. Their progressive disappearance goes indeed to prove that this emancipation became a reality, for one cannot see how, if heredity had lost none of its rights over the individual, it could have grown weaker as an institution. If statistics stretched far enough back into the past, and particularly if they provided firmer data on this, they would very probably inform us that cases of professions by inheritance became increasingly less frequent. What is certain is that the once so strong faith in heredity is today replaced by a faith that is almost its opposite. We tend to believe that the individual is for the most part what his works have made him, and we even fail to recognise the links that bind him to his race and cause his dependence upon it. At least this view is very widespread and is one that causes the psychologists of heredity almost to complain. It is also a somewhat curious fact that heredity did not come into the purview of science until the moment when it had almost vanished from that of belief. Yet there is no contradiction here. For what, finally, the common consciousness affirms is not that heredity does not exist, but that its importance is less great, and science, as we shall see, reveals nothing that contradicts this view.

But it is important to establish this fact directly, and particularly to demonstrate the causes.

I

Firstly, heredity loses its sway over the course of evolution because simultaneously new modes of activity were constituted that did not depend upon its influence.

A first proof of the static state of heredity is the static state of the main human races. From the most distant times, no new races have arisen. If at least this same term is applied, as de Quatrefages[9] applies it, to the different types that have sprung from the three or four main basic types, then we must add that the more they move away from their point of origin, the less these types present those characteristics that constitute a race. Indeed everyone agrees in recognising that what is the characteristic of race is the existence of hereditary similarities. Thus anthropologists make physical characteristics the basis for their classifications, because these are the most hereditary of all. But the more limited anthropological types are, the more difficult it becomes to define them as a function of exclusively organic properties, because these are no longer numerous or distinctive enough. Wholly moral resemblances, established with the help of linguistics, archaeology and comparative law, become preponderant, although there is no reason to concede that these are hereditary. They serve to demarcate civilisations rather than races. As progress takes place, the human variations that form therefore become less hereditary and are less and less races. The continual powerlessness of our species to produce new races even stands in most vivid contrast with the opposite fecundity of the animal species. What does this signify, if not that human culture, as it develops, is increasingly unamenable to this kind of transmission? What men have added, and continue daily to add, to the primitive basis that has been fixed for centuries in the structure of the first races, thus increasingly eludes the action of heredity. But if this is true for the main stream of civilisation it is all the more so for each of the special tributaries that go to make it up, that is, each functional activity and its products.

The facts that follow confirm this inductive statement.

It is an established truth that the degree of simplicity of psychological facts provides the yardstick for their transmissibility. Indeed the more complex such conditions are, the more easily they break up, because their greater complexity maintains them in a state of unstable equilibrium. They resemble those skilful constructions whose architecture is so delicate that some small event is enough to disturb their structure so that, at the slightest tremor, the edifice is undermined and crumbles apart, laying bare the area of ground it covered. Thus in cases of general paralysis the self dissolves slowly until, so to speak, nothing else remains than the organic basis upon which it rested. Normally it is under the shock of illness that such disruptive acts occur. But we can see that seminal transmission can have analogous consequences. Indeed, in the act of fertilisation strictly individual characteristics tend mutually to cancel one another out. This is because, since those that are specific to one parent can only be transmitted to the detriment of the other parent, a kind of conflict is set up between them from which they cannot possibly emerge unscathed. But the more complex the state of consciousness, the more personal it is, the more it bears the stamp of the special circumstances in which we have lived, and of our sex and temperament. We resemble one another much more by the lower and basic depths of our being than by these higher reaches. On the other hand, it is by the latter we are distinguished from one another. Thus if they do not disappear completely in hereditary transmission at least they can only survive in a withdrawn, enfeebled state.

The more specific the aptitudes, the more complex they are. It is indeed mistaken to believe that our activity grows simpler as our tasks become more delimited. On the contrary, it is when these are dissipated over a multitude of objects that our activity is simple. Since the activity then neglects what is personal and distinctive in order to concentrate on what they have in common, it is reduced to a few very general operations appropriate to very many different circumstances. But when it is a matter of adapting ourselves to particular and specific objects, so as to take account of the subtle distinctions between them, we can only succeed by combining a very large number of states of consciousness, differentiated according to the image of the very things to which they relate. Once these are articulated together and established, these systems undoubtedly function with greater ease and rapidity, but they are still very complex. What a prodigious assembly of ideas, images and habits are to be observed when a printer sets up a page of type, a mathematician combines together a host of isolated theorems and causes in order to derive a new theorem, a doctor who, from some imperceptible sign, recognises instantly the illness and at the same time foresees how it will develop! Compare the extraordinarily elementary technique of the ancient philosopher and sage who, by the sheer power of thought, sets out to explain the world, with that of the scientist of today who only succeeds in solving a very specific problem by an extremely complex combination of observations and experiments, thanks to the reading of works written in every language, to correspondence and discussion, etc. It is the dilettante who preserves intact his primitive simplicity. The complexity of his nature is only superficial. As he tackles the job of interesting himself in everything, he seems to have a thousand different tastes and aptitudes. This is pure illusion! Look into the heart of things and you will see that everything boils down to a very small number of general, simple faculties, ones which, however, having lost none of their primal indeterminateness, relinquish easily their grasp upon the objects to which they are attached in order to snatch at others. Viewed from the outside, one perceives an uninterrupted succession of varied events, but it is the same actor playing all the parts in slightly different costume. That surface resplendent with so many finely shaded colours skilfully blended together, in the end covers a lamentable monotone. The dilettante has loosened up and refined the potentialities within him, but has not been able to transform them and blend them differently so as to draw from them some new and definite work. He has raised up nothing individual and lasting upon the ground that nature has bequeathed him.

Consequently, the more specific the faculties, the more difficult it is to pass them on. Or, if one succeeds in passing them on from one generation to another, they cannot fail to lose some of their strength and precision. They are less resistant, more malleable. Through their greater lack of determinacy they can the more easily change under the influence of family circumstances, fortune and education, etc. In short, the more the forms of activity are specialised, the more they elude the effect of heredity.

Yet cases have nevertheless been cited where professional abilities seem to be hereditary. Tables drawn up by Galton seem to demonstrate that occasionally there are veritable dynasties of scientists, poets and musicians. De Candolle, for his part, has established that the sons of scientists 'have often been engaged in science'.[10] In the event, these observations have no value as proof. Of course we would not dream of maintaining that the transmission of special abilities is fundamentally impossible. We merely say that in general it does not occur, because it cannot be effected save by a miracle of equilibrium that cannot often be repeated. It is therefore valueless to quote this or that special case where it has occurred or appears to have occurred. But we should still see what part such cases play in the overall total of scientific vocations. Only then can we judge whether they really do demonstrate that heredity has a gréat influence on the way in which social functions are divided up.

Although this comparison cannot be made methodically, one fact established by de Candolle tends to prove how limited is the effect of heredity on these careers. Of 100 foreign associate members of the Académie de Paris whose genealogy de Candolle has been able to trace, 14 descend from Protestant clergymen and 5 only from physicians, surgeons and pharmacologists. Of 48 members of the Royal Society of London in 1829, 8 were the sons of clergymen and only 4 had fathers in the same [scientific] type of activity. Yet the total number of the latter:

> in countries not including France, must be very much greater than the number of Protestant clerics. Indeed among Protestant populations, considered separately, physicians, surgeons, pharmacologists and veterinary surgeons are roughly as numerous as

clergymen. When there is added those from countries which are purely Catholic, omitting France, they constitute a much more considerable number than the total of Protestant pastors or ministers. The studies that medical men have undertaken and the work to which they must habitually devote themselves in their profession lie much more in the realm of science than do the studies and work of a Protestant clergyman. If success in the sciences were solely a matter of heredity there would be many more sons of doctors, pharmacologists, etc., on our list than sons of the manse.[11]

Even then it is not at all certain that the scientific vocations of the sons of scientists are really due to heredity. To be correct in ascribing them to heredity it is not enough to discover a similarity of aptitude in parents and children. The latter would still have needed to have demonstrated their abilities after having been brought up from earliest childhood outside their own family and in an environment completely devoid of any scientific culture. In fact all the sons of scientists who were observed were brought up in their own families, where they naturally found more intellectual support and encouragement than their fathers had received. There are also the matters of advice and example, the desire to follow their father's example, to use his books, his scientific collections, his research, his laboratory: all of these are for a well-disposed and alert mind powerful stimulants. Finally, in the institutions where they complete their studies, scientists' sons come into contact with cultured minds, or ones ready to imbibe the high culture. The effect of this new environment is only to strengthen the previous one. Doubtless in societies where it is the rule for the child to follow the father's profession, such regularity cannot be explained by a mere coincidence of external circumstances, for it would be a miracle if in every case it occurred with such perfect congruence. Yet the situation is not the same with those isolated and almost exceptional chance meetings of circumstances that are to be observed today.

It is true that several of the English scientists to whom Galton addressed himself[12] have insisted upon a special and innate aptitude that they allegedly felt from childhood for the science that they were to study later. But, as de Candolle remarks, it is very difficult to know whether these aptitudes

arise from birth or from the vivid impressions of youth, and the influences which have aroused and directed them. Moreover, these tastes change, and the sole ones important for a career are those which persist. In that case, the individual who distinguishes himself in a science or who continues to cultivate it with pleasure unerringly declares that with him it was an innate taste. On the contrary, those who have had special aptitudes in childhood and who have thought no more about them, do not speak of them. Let us consider the innumerable children who hunt butterflies or form a collection of shells or insects, etc., who do not become naturalists. I also know a fair number of examples of scientists who in their youth had a passion for writing poetry or plays, and who later on have had an entirely different occupation.[13]

Another observation by the same author shows how great is the effect of the social environment upon the genesis of these aptitudes. If they were due to heredity, they would be equally hereditary in every country. Scientists springing from scientists would be in the same proportion among all peoples of the same type.

Now the facts reveal an entirely different state of affairs. In Switzerland for two centuries there have been more scientists grouped by family than isolated cases of scientists. In France and Italy, on the other hand, the number of scientists who are the sole representatives in their family constitute the overwhelming majority. Yet physiological laws are the same for all men. Thus in each family education, the example and the advice given must have exercised a more considerable influence than heredity on the particular career of young scientists. It is moreover easy to understand why this influence has been stronger in Switzerland than in most countries. Education continues up to the age of eighteen or twenty in each town, and in conditions such that pupils live at home with their father. This was particularly true during the last century and the first half of the present one, especially in Geneva and Bâle, i.e. in those two cities which have provided the largest proportion of scientists linked by family ties. Elsewhere, and especially in France and Italy, it has always been common for the young to be brought up in colleges where they board, and where consequently they find themselves removed from family influence.[14]

Thus there are no grounds for admitting 'the existence of innate, compelling vocations for special purposes'.[15] At least, if they exist they are not the rule. Bain likewise remarks that 'The son of a great philologist does not inherit a single vocable the son of a great traveller may be surpassed, at school, in his geography by the son of a coal-miner'.[16] This is not to say that heredity has no influence, but what it transmits are very general faculties and not a special aptitude for this or that science. What the child receives from his parents is some force of attention, a certain degree of perseverance, a sound judgement, imagination, etc. But each one of these faculties can be appropriate for a host of different specialisms and ensure his success in them. Take the case of a child endowed with a fairly lively imagination. From an early age he is in contact with artists: he will become a painter or a poet. If he lives in an industrial environment he will become an engineer with an inventive mind. If chance places him in the business world he will perhaps one day become the daring financier. Naturally he will take with him everywhere his own nature, his need to create and imagine, his passion for innovation. But the careers where he will be able to use his talents and satisfy his bent are very many. Moreover, this is what de Candolle established by direct observation. He noted the qualities useful in the sciences that his father got from his grandfather. Here is the list: willpower, a sense of order, sound judgement, a certain power of attention, distaste for metaphysical abstractions, and independence of views. It is undoubtedly a fine legacy, but one with which he might equally have become an administrator, a statesman, an historian, an economist, a great industrialist, an excellent doctor, or indeed a naturalist, as did de Candolle. It is therefore clear that circumstances played a large part in his choice of a career, and indeed it is from his own son that we learn this.[17] Only a mathematical mind and musical feeling may well be tendencies that fairly frequently stem from birth, due to direct inheritance from the parents. This apparent anomaly will come as no surprise, if we recall that these two talents developed very early on in the history of humanity. Music is the first of the arts and mathematics the first of the sciences that men have cultivated. This double faculty must therefore be more general and less complex than is believed, and it is this that would explain its transmissibility.

Much the same may be said about another vocation, that of crime. According to the very true remark of Tarde, the different varieties of crime and of offences relate to professions, despite the fact that they are harmful. Occasionally the technique they employ is very complex. The swindler, the counterfeiter and the forger are forced to display more science and more art in their occupation than are many normal workers. It has been maintained that not only moral perversity generally, but also the specific forms of criminality are a product of heredity. People have believed it was possible to put at over 40 per cent 'the rate of born criminals'.[18] If this proportion were proved correct, we would have to conclude from it that heredity has occasionally a great influence upon the way in which the professions, even special ones, are distributed.

To demonstrate this, two different methods have been tried. Often we have contented ourselves with quoting the case of families who have devoted themselves entirely to wrongdoing over several generations. But apart from the fact that we cannot determine the relative contribution of heredity among all criminal vocations, such observations, however numerous, do not constitute demonstrations of proof from experience. Because the son of a thief becomes a thief himself it does not follow that his immoral nature is a legacy bequeathed him by his father. To interpret the facts in this way we would have to be able to isolate the effects of heredity from those of circumstances, education, etc. If the child manifested his aptitude for thieving after having been brought up in a perfectly sound family, we would then have good grounds for citing the influence of heredity. Yet we possess very few observations of this nature that have been systematically undertaken. This objection cannot be met by noting that the families who are dragged into wrongdoing in this way are occasionally very numerous. Numbers do not enter into it, for the home environment, which is the same for the whole family, no matter how extensive it may be, suffices to explain this endemic criminality.

The method followed by Lombroso would prove more conclusive if it gave the results that its author anticipated. Instead of enumerating for us a certain number of particular cases, he builds up the criminal type, from both the anatomical and physiological viewpoint. As anatomical and physiological characteristics – particularly the first – are congenital, that is, determined by heredity, it would suffice to establish the proportion of offenders who represent the type defined in these terms, so as to measure exactly the influence of heredity upon this particular form of activity.

As we have seen, according to Lombroso this proportion would be considerable. But the figure quoted only expresses the relative frequency of the criminal type in general. Consequently all we can conclude from it is that the propensity to wrongdoing in general is often hereditary. Yet nothing can be deduced from it relating to the particular forms of crimes and of offences. Moreover, nowadays we know that this alleged criminal type really consists of nothing specific. Many traits that go to make it up are to be found elsewhere. All we can perceive is that it resembles the type of the degenerate and neurasthenic.[19] If this fact proves that among criminals there are many neurasthenics it does not always follow that neurasthenia leads inevitably to crime. There are at least as many neurasthenics who are honest, and they may even be men of talent or genius.

Thus if abilities are the less transmissible the more specific they are, the importance of heredity in the social organisation of labour is all the greater when that labour is less divided up. In lower societies, where the functions are very general, these demand only aptitudes that are likewise general and that can more easily pass as a whole from one generation to another. Each person receives at birth all that is essential to sustain his personality; what he must acquire for himself is of little consequence compared with what he derives from heredity. In the Middle Ages the noble, in order to carry out his duty, had no need of any very intricate knowledge or practices, but above all had need of courage, which came to him by virtue of blood. The Levite and Brahmin, in order to carry on their occupations, had no need of very extensive knowledge – we can measure its extent from the books that contained it – but required an inborn intellectual superiority that made them open to ideas and sentiments that were closed to the common people. To be a good doctor in Aesculapius' time, there was no need to receive a very extensive education. It sufficed to have a natural taste for observation and concrete things and, as this taste is general enough to be easily transmissible, it was inevitable that it was perpetuated in certain families and, in consequence, the medical profession was hereditary.

Under these conditions we can very easily explain how heredity becomes a social institution. Doubtless, it was not these wholly psychological causes that may have inspired the organisation of castes. Yet once that organisation was created under the aegis of other causes it lasted because it happened to be perfectly in accord with the taste of individuals and the interests of society. Since professional ability was a quality of the race rather than the individual, it was quite natural that the same held good for the function. Since the functions were allocated invariably in the same way, it could only be beneficial for the law to put the seal of its approval on the principle of this distribution. When the individual has only a small share in the training of his mind and character, he can have no greater say in the choice of his career and, if greater freedom were allowed him, generally he would not know what to do with it. If only the same general ability could serve different professions! But precisely because the work is so little specialised, only a small number of functions exist that are separated from one another by clear-cut differences. Consequently one can hardly succeed in more than one of them. Thus in this respect the margin left to individual combinations is limited. In the end, inheritance of functions is like that of property inheritance. In lower societies the heritage handed down by one's ancestors, most usually consisting of landed estate, represents the most considerable portion of inheritance of each individual family. The individual, because the economic functions are scarcely active at that time, cannot add much to that inheritance. Thus it is not he who is the owner, but the family, the collective entity, made up not only of all the members of the present generation, but of the whole succession of generations. This is why family property is inalienable. No transient representative of the domestic unit can dispose of it, for it is not his. It belongs to the family, just as the function belongs to the caste. Even when the law modifies its initial prohibitions, alienation of the patrimony is considered a breach of faith. It is for every class of the population what an ill-matched marriage is for the aristocracy. It is an act of treason to the race, a defection. Thus, whilst tolerating it, for a long while the law put all kinds of obstacles in its way. It is from this that the right of repossession springs.

This is not the case in societies of more considerable size, in which work is more divided up. As functions are more diversified, the same faculty can be of service in different professions. Courage is as necessary to the miner, the balloonist, the doctor or the engineer as it is to the soldier. A liking for observation can equally turn a man into a novelist, a playwright, a chemist, a naturalist or a sociologist. In short, the direction in which an individual goes is less essentially predetermined by heredity.

But above all what diminishes the relative importance of heredity is the fact that the share of individual acquisitions becomes more considerable. To exploit the hereditary legacy much more must be added to it than formerly. Indeed, as functions became more specialised, merely general abilities were no longer adequate. It was necessary to subject them to a process of active development, to acquire a whole world of ideas, actions and habits, co-ordinating and systematising them, reshaping their nature and giving it new form and contour. If we only compare – and we are taking points of comparison very close to one another – the 'honourable man' of the seventeenth century with his open but sparsely furnished mind, with the modern scientist, armed with all the procedures and knowledge needful for the science that he professes; or let us compare the nobleman of former times, with his natural courage and pride, with the officer of today, with his laborious and complicated techniques: then we are able to judge the importance and variety of the combinations that have been gradually superimposed upon the original foundation.

Yet because they are very complex, such skilful combinations are fragile. They are in a state of unstable equilibrium that cannot resist any powerful shock. If indeed they were found to be identical in both parents, they might perhaps survive the crisis of the generations. But such a state of identity is wholly exceptional. Firstly, these combinations are specific to each sex; then, as societies spread out while becoming denser, cross-matchings are made over a broader area, bringing together individuals more different in temperament. All this superb flowering of states of consciousness thus dies with us, and we hand on to our descendants only some indeterminate germ of it. It is for them to fertilise it afresh, and consequently they can, if necessary, the more easily modify its development. They are no longer constrained to replicate so closely what their fathers did. It would doubtless be mistaken to believe that each generation begins with new effort, and in its entirety, the work of centuries, as this would make all progress impossible. If the past is no longer transmitted through inheritance by blood, it does not follow that it is wiped out: it remains fixed in the records, the traditions of every kind, and in the habits imparted by education. But tradition is a much weaker bond than heredity; it predetermines in a con-siderably less rigorous way, and less clearly, our thought and conduct. Moreover, we have seen how tradition becomes more flexible as societies become more densely concentrated. A wider field is thus opened up for individual variations, one that broadens out still more as labour is increasingly divided up.

In short, civilisation can only be fixed in the organism through the most general bases upon which it rests. The more it raises itself up, the more in consequence does it free itself from the body: it becomes less and less an organic thing, more and more a social thing. But then it is no longer through the mediation of the body that it can perpetuate itself, viz., heredity is increasingly incapable of ensuring its continuity. Thus heredity loses its dominance, not because it has ceased to be a law of our nature, but because in order to live we must have weapons that it cannot provide for us. To be sure, we can draw nothing from nothing, and the raw materials which it alone furnishes us are of capital importance. But those that are added to them are no less important. The hereditary patrimony retains great value, but it no longer represents more than an increasingly restricted part of the individual fortune. In these conditions we can already explain how heredity has disappeared from social institutions and how the mass of the people, no longer discerning the initial hereditary capital because of the additions overlaying it, no longer feel so much its importance.

II

But there is something else: there is every reason to think that the hereditary component decreases not only in relative, but also in absolute value. Heredity becomes a lesser value in human development, not only because there is an ever-increasing multitude of new acquisitions that it cannot pass on, but also because those that it does pass on do not impede to such an extent individual variations. This conjecture makes the following facts very likely to be correct.

One can measure the importance of the hereditary legacy for any given species by the number and strength of the instincts. Now it is already very remarkable how the life of the instincts grows weaker as one rises in the animal scale. Instinct is in fact a definite way of acting, attuned to an end that is narrowly determined. It impels the individual to undertake acts that are invariably the same and that are reproduced automatically when the necessary conditions are given. It is fixed in form. Doubtless *in extremis* instincts can be made to deviate from these acts. But, in addition to the fact that such deviations, in order to remain stable, demand a long process of development, their effect is none other than to substitute one instinct for another one, one special mechanism for another of the same kind. On the other hand, the more the animal belongs to a higher species, the more the use of the instinct becomes optional. 'It is no longer,' states Perrier, 'an unconscious ability to form a combination of indeterminate actions; it is the ability to act differently according to the circumstances.'[20] To state that the influence of heredity is more general, vaguer, less categorical, is to declare that it has grown less. It no longer imprisons the animal inside a rigid framework, but leaves it more free play. As Perrier also states, 'With the animal, as intelligence increases, the conditions of heredity are profoundly modified.'

When we pass from animals to man, this regression of heredity is even more striking. 'Man does everything that the animals do, and more; only he does it knowing what he is doing and why he is doing it. This simple consciousness of his actions seems to liberate him from all the instincts which would necessarily impel him to carry out these same acts'.[21] It would take too long to enumerate here all those movements instinctive to the animal but that have ceased to be hereditary with man. Even where instinct survives, it has less power, and the will can more easily master it.

But then there is no reason to suppose that this regressive movement, which has continued uninterruptedly from the species of lower animals to the highest, and from these to man, ceases abruptly with the coming of the human race. Was man, from the very day that he entered historical times, totally freed from instinct? But we still feel the burden of it today. Can it be that the causes effecting this progressive liberation, whose continuity we have just seen, have suddenly lost their power? But clearly they become mixed up with the very causes that determine the general progress of the species, and as this progress does not cease, they cannot be halted either. Such an hypothesis runs counter to all analogies. It is even contrary to well-established facts. It is indeed proved that intelligence and instinct always vary in inverse proportion to each other. For the moment we have no need to investigate how this relationship arises; we are content to assert its existence. Yet from his origins man has not ceased to develop; instinct must therefore have followed the opposing course. Consequently, although this proposition cannot be established by a positive observation of the facts, we must believe that heredity has lost ground in the course of human evolution.

Another fact corroborates this. Not only has evolution not been the cause of new races arising since the dawn of history, but even the ancient races have always been in a state of regression. In fact a race is formed by a certain number of individuals who present, in relation to the same hereditary type, a sufficiently large degree of conformity for individual variations to be neglected. Yet the importance of these variations is continually increasing. Individual types become ever more prominent, to the detriment of the generic type. The characteristics from which the generic type is formed are dispersed in all directions, intermingled with a host of others, and infinitely diversified, so that they can no longer easily be brought together in a whole that has some semblance of unity. This dispersion and effacement moreover began even with peoples who were very little advanced. Through their isolation the Eskimos seem to be placed in very favourable conditions for the maintenance of the purity of their race. However, 'the variations in size exceed the permitted individual limits. . . . At Hotham's Inlet the Eskimo [N. Alaska] resembled exactly a negro; at Spafaryeva Promontory [Siberia], a Jew (Seeman). The oval face, assorted with a Roman nose, is not rare (King). Their complexion is sometimes very dark and sometimes very fair.'[22] If this is the case in so restricted societies, the same phenomenon must be replicated much more markedly in our great modern-day societies. In Central Europe are to be found side by side all the possible varieties of skull, all the possible forms of the face. The same is true for the complexion. According to observations carried out by Virchow, out of ten million children drawn from different social classes in Germany, the fair-headed type, which is characteristic of the German race, has been observed only between 43 to 33 times in a hundred in the North, 32 to 25 times in the Central region, and 24 to 18 times in the South.[23] In these conditions, which are constantly getting worse, one can see why the anthropologist is scarcely unable to draw up clearly defined types.

Galton's recent research confirms, as well as enabling us to explain, this weakening of the influence of heredity.[24]

According to this author, whose observations and calculations seem difficult to refute, the sole characteristics regularly and wholly transmitted by heredity in any given social group are those that when they occur together constitute the average type. Thus a son born of exceptionally tall parents will not be of their height, but will approximate more to the average height. Conversely, if they are too small, he will be taller than they. Galton was even able to measure, at least approximately, this relationship of deviation from the mean. If we agree to call the average parent a composite being who represents the average of two real parents (the characteristics of the woman are transposed in such a way as to be able to be compared with those of the father, added together and then divided), the deviation of the son in relation to this fixed standard, will be two-thirds that of the father.[25]

Galton has established this law not only for size, but also for eye colour and artistic abilities. It is true that he has only focused his observations upon quantitative deviations, and not upon the qualitative deviations that individuals represent in relation to the average type. But one cannot see why the law should apply to one category and not to the other. If the rule is that heredity only transmits well those attributes constituting this type, according to the degree of development in which they are to be found, it must also transmit well only those attributes found there. What is true for the abnormal extent of normal characteristics must *a fortiori* be true for the abnormal characteristics. They must in fact pass from one generation to another in only a weakened form and tend to vanish.

This law, moreover, can be explained without difficulty. A child does not inherit only from his parents, but from all his ancestors. Undoubtedly the effect of the parents is especially strong, because it is immediate, but the effect of the previous generations is liable to be cumulative when it is all exerted in the same direction. Thanks to this accumulation, which makes up for the effects of remoteness in time, it can reach a degree of effectiveness sufficient to neutralise or weaken that of the parents. The average type *of a natural group* is that which corresponds to the conditions of average life, and consequently to the most ordinary conditions. It expresses the way in which individuals have adapted to what we may term the average environment, both physical and social, that is, the environment in which the largest number live. These average conditions were more frequent in the past, for the same reason that makes them the most general conditions in the present day. They are therefore the conditions in which most of our ancestors were placed. It is true that over time they may have changed, but generally they are modified only slowly. The average type thus remains appreciably the same for a long time. It is consequently this type that is most frequently and most uniformly replicated in the series of past generations, at least in those generations that are recent enough to bring their influence effectively to bear. It is because of this consistency that the average type becomes fixed, making it the gravitational centre for hereditary influence. The characteristics that go to make it up are those that are the most resistant, and that tend to be transmitted most powerfully and precisely. On the other hand, those that deviate from this gravitational centre survive only in an indeterminate state, all the more indeterminate the more considerable their degree of deviation. This is why the deviations that occur are never other than temporary and never even succeed in lasting for any time, save in very imperfect fashion.

However, this very explanation, which is moreover slightly different from that which Galton himself proposed, permits us to speculate whether his law, to be perfectly exact, may need some slight rectification. Indeed the average type of our ancestors is never merged with that of our generation save in so far as that average life has not changed. Yet in fact variations occur from one generation to another that entail changes in the constitution of the average type. If the facts gathered by Dalton nevertheless appear to confirm his law in the way that he has formulated it, it is because he has scarcely verified it save for physical characteristics, which are relatively unchangeable, such as size and eye colour. But if we carried out observations regarding other properties, using the same method, whether these properties were organic or psychological, it is certain that we should perceive the effects of evolution. Consequently, to speak with absolute accuracy, the characteristics whose transmissibility is of the highest order are not those the sum of which constitutes the average type for any given generation, but those we would obtain by taking the average among the average types of successive generations. Without this correction, moreover, one could not explain how the average of the group can improve. If we take Galton's proposition literally, societies would always and inevitably be brought back to the same level, since the average type of two generations, even distant from one another, would be identical. Yet far from this identity constituting the law, on the contrary, we see even physical characteristics as simple as average height or the average colour of eyes gradually change, although very slowly.[26] The truth is that if lasting changes occur in the environment, the organic and psychological modifications resulting from them end up by becoming fixed, integrating themselves in the average type that is evolving. The variations that occur on the way cannot therefore have the same degree of transmissibility as the elements that are constantly being replicated.

The average type results from the superposing of individual types and expresses what they most have in common. Consequently the characteristics that form it are the more defined the more identically they are repeated among the different members of the group. When this identity is complete they are to be found in their entirety, with all their characteristics, down to the last detail. On the other hand, when they vary from one individual to another, as the points at which they coincide are rarer, what subsists of them in the average type is reduced to a rudimentary outline which is even more general the greater the differences are. We know that individual dissimilarities continue to multiply, that is, that the elements that go to make up the average type become more diversified. The type itself therefore must comprise a lesser number of definite characteristics, and this is all the more so when society is more differentiated. The average man takes on an appearance increasingly less precise, less clearly defined – his physionomy is more sketchy. He is an abstraction that is increasingly difficult to fix and delimit. On the other hand, the more societies belong to a higher species, the more rapidly they evolve, since tradition becomes more flexible, as we have already established. Thus the average type changes from one generation to another. Consequently the type, which is a doubly composite one resulting from the superposing of all these average types, is even more abstract than each one of them, and becomes ever increasingly so. Since therefore it is heredity of this type that constitutes normal heredity, we see that, in Perrier's phrase, the conditions of normal heredity are profoundly modified. This undoubtedly does not mean that heredity passes on fewer characteristics in an absolute way. If individuals display more dissimilar characteristics, they nevertheless display more characteristics as a whole. But what heredity transmits consists more and more in indeterminate predispositions, general ways of feeling and thinking that can become specialised in a thousand different ways. There is no longer question, as once there was, of complete mechanisms, finely attuned for special purposes, but only of very vague tendencies that do not definitively bind the future. The inheritance has not become any the less rich, but no longer does it consist entirely of transmittable possessions. Most of the values of which it is composed are not yet realised, and everything depends upon the use to be made of them.

This greater flexibility in inherited characteristics is not due solely to their indeterminate state, but to the battering they have undergone because of the changes through which they have passed. In fact we know that a type is more unstable the more deviations it has already passed through. 'Sometimes,' says Quatrefages, 'the slightest causes swiftly transform these organisms which, so to speak, have become unstable. The Swiss bull, transported to Lombardy, becomes a Lombardy bull in two generations. Two generations also suffice for our Burgundian bees, which are small and brown, to turn into large, yellow ones in the Bresse region.' For all these reasons heredity always leaves the field open to fresh combinations. Not only is there an increasing number of things over which it has no hold, but the properties whose continuity it ensures become more plastic. Thus the individual is tied less strongly to his past; it is easier for him to adapt to new circumstances as they occur, and progress in the division of labour therefore becomes easier and swifter.[27]

Notes

1. J. S. Mill, *Principles of Political Economy* (London, 1852) p. 159.
2. H. Spencer, *Principles of Sociology* (London, 1855) vol. II, pp. 257–8.
3. Ribot, *L'hérédité*, 2nd edn, p. 360.
4. Ibid., p. 345.
5. Ibid., p. 365. Cf. Hermann, *Griechische Antiquitäten*, vol. IV, p. 353, note 3.
6. Hermann, *Griechische*, p. 395, note 2; ch. 1, p. 33. For the facts, cf. particularly Plato, *Eutyphr.*, 11C; *Alcibiades*, 121A; *Republic*, IV, 421D; above all, *Protag.*, 328A; Plutarch, *Apopth. Lacon.*, 208B.
7. Schmoller, 'La division du travail', *Revue d'économie politique* (1888) p. 590.
8. Ribot, *L'hérédité*, p. 360.
9. Cf. De Quatrefages, *L'espèce humaine*.
10. De Candolle, *Histoire des Sciences et des savants*, 2nd edn, p. 293.

11.   Ibid., p. 294.
12.   F. Galton, *English Men of Science* (1874) pp. 144 ff.
13.   De Candolle, *Histoire des Sciences*, p. 320.
14.   Ibid., p. 296.
15.   Ibid., p. 299.
16.   A. Bain, *The Emotions and the Will* (London, 1889) p. 53.
17.   De Candolle, *Histoire des Sciences*, p. 318.
18.   C. Lombroso, *L'homme criminel*, p. 669.
19.   Cf. Féré, *Dégénérescence et criminalité*.
20.   Perrier, *Anatomie et physiologie animales*, p. 201. Cf. the preface to Romanes, *L'Intelligence des animaux*, p. xxiii.
21.   Guyau, *Morale anglaise*, p. 330.
22.   Topinard, *Anthropologie*, p. 458.
23.   Wagner, 'Die Kulturzüchtung des Menschen', *Kosmos* (1886) p. 27.
24.   F. Galton, *Natural Inheritance* (London, 1889).
25.   Ibid., p. 101.
26.   Cf. Arréat, 'Récents travaux sur l'hérédité', *Revue philosophique* (April 1890) p. 414.
27.   What appears to be most substantial in Weismann's theories might serve to confirm the above. Doubtless it is not proved what that scientist affirms, viz., that individual variations are radically not transmissible by heredity. But it seems indeed well established that the type normally transmissible is not the individual type, but the generic one, which has in some way as its organic substratum the reproductive elements. It also appears that this type is not so easily affected by individual variations, as has on occasion been supposed. (Cf. Weismann, *Essais sur l'hérédité*, Fr. trans (Paris, 1892) particularly the third essay; cf. W. P. Ball, *Are the Effects of Use and Disuse Inherited?* (London, 1890).) The result is that the more indeterminate and plastic this type, the more also the individual factor gains ground.

      From another viewpoint also these theories are of interest to us. One of the conclusions of our work to which we attach the most importance is this idea that social phenomena derive from social and not psychological causes. Also, the collective type is not the mere generalisation of an individual type, but on the contrary the latter arises from the collective type. For a different order of facts Weismann likewise shows that the race is not a mere prolongation of the individual; that the specific type, from the physiological and anatomical viewpoint, is not an individual type that has perpetuated itself over time, but that has its own course of evolution. Also the individual type has detached itself from the collective type, far from being its source. His views are, like ours, it seems, a protest against the simplistic theories that reduce the composite to the simple, the whole to the part, the society or the race to the individual.

Chapter V

Consequences of the Foregoing

I

What has been said above allows us better to understand how the division of labour functions in society.

From this viewpoint the social division of labour is distinguished by one essential feature from the physiological division of labour. In the organism each cell has its definite role which it cannot change. In society tasks have never been allocated so immutably. Even where the organisational framework is most rigid, the individual has room to manoeuvre with a certain freedom within the area destiny has apportioned to him. In ancient Rome the plebeian could freely undertake all the functions not exclusively reserved for the patricians. Even in India the careers allocated to each caste were sufficiently general in nature to leave room for a certain choice.[1] In all countries, if the enemy has gained possession of the capital city, that is, the very brain of the nation, social life is not on that account suspended. After a relatively short period another town is capable of fulfilling that complex function, which, however, it has not been prepared for in any way.

As labour splits up even more, this flexibility and freedom become greater. We can see the same individual rise from the most humble occupations to the most important ones. The principle whereby all jobs are equally accessible to all citizens would not have become so general if it were not constantly being applied. What is even more frequent is for a worker to abandon one career in order to take up a similar one. So long as scientific activity was not specialised, the scientist, who included in his purview almost the whole of science, could hardly change his function because he would have had to give up science itself. Nowadays it often happens that he devotes himself to different sciences in succession, passing from

269

chemistry to biology, from physiology to psychology, from psychology to sociology. This ability to adopt successively very diverse forms of occupation is nowhere so clearly evident as in the economic world. As nothing is more variable than the tastes and needs to which these functions correspond, commerce and industry must remain in a perpetually unstable state, so as to be able to adapt to all the chances occurring in demand. Whilst immobility was formerly the almost natural state of capital, and the law even prevented it being mobilised too easily, today we can hardly follow it through all the metamorphoses it undergoes, so great is the speed with which it is applied in a business undertaking, and then withdrawn to be deposited elsewhere, where it remains only for a few moments. Thus the workers must be ready to follow it, and consequently to serve it in different forms of employment.

The nature of the causes on which the social division of labour depends explains this characteristic. If the role of each cell is fixed almost immutably, it is because it has been imposed upon it at birth. It is imprisoned within a hereditary system of habits that put their stamp upon its life and from which it cannot rid itself. It cannot even modify these habits to any appreciable extent, because they have affected too profoundly the substance from which the cell is formed. Its structure predetermines its life. We have just seen that the same does not hold good for society. The individual is not doomed by his origins to a special kind of career. His innate constitution does not necessarily destine him for one single role, making him incapable of performing any other, but he receives from hereditary only very general predispositions, which are furthermore very flexible and can assume different forms.

It is true that he determines the forms himself by the use that he makes of them. As he must involve his faculties in special functions and cause them to specialise, he is obliged to subject to a more intense cultivation those more directly required for his employment and to let the others in part atrophy. Thus he cannot develop his brain beyond a certain point without its losing a part of its muscular force or reproductive powers. He cannot overstimulate his faculties of analysis and reflection without weakening the force of his will and the keenness of his feelings, nor acquire the habit of observation without losing that of the dialectic. Moreover, by the very nature of things, the faculty that he intensifies to the detriment of others is obliged to take on definite forms, of which it gradually becomes a prisoner. It contracts the habit of certain practices, of a determinate way of functioning, which it becomes all the more difficult to change the longer it lasts. But this specialisation is the result of a purely individual effort, and has neither the stability nor the rigidity that long heredity alone can produce. The practices are more flexible because they are of more recent origin. As it is the individual who is involved in them, he can free himself from them and mobilise his energies to acquire new practices. He can even awaken faculties that are paralysed because they have long remained dormant, restore their vitality, and bring them into prominence once more, although assuredly this kind of resurrection is already more difficult.

At first sight one is tempted to see in these facts phenomena of regression, or proof of a certain inferiority; or at the very least the transitional state of an incomplete being in the process of development. Indeed, it is especially among the lower animals that the different parts of the whole can as easily change their function and be substituted for one another. On the other hand, as social organisation is perfected, it becomes more and more impossible for them to move out of the role assigned to them. Thus one is led to ask whether the day will not dawn when society will take on a more stable form, in which each organ and individual will have a definite function and will not change it any more. This was, it would appear, the thinking of Comte,[2] and is certainly that of Spencer.[3] However, such an induction is precipitous. The phenomen of substitution is not peculiar to very simple creatures, but is also observed in the highest levels of the hierarchy, notably in the higher organs of the higher organisms. Thus:

the disturbances that follow upon the removal of certain areas of the cerebral cortex very often disappear after a somewhat lengthy lapse of time. This phenomenon can only be explained by the following assumption: other elements act as surrogates in the function of the elements that have been removed. This implies that these surrogate elements are trained to perform new functions. . . . An element which, under normal relationships of transmission, activates a visual sensation becomes, thanks to this change in conditions, a factor in the sense of touch, in a muscular sensation, or in the motor distribution of the nerves. What is much more, we are almost forced to suppose that if the central

272 The Causes and Conditions

network of the nervous tracts has the power to transmit phenomena of various kinds to one and the same element, this element will be capable of assembling internally a number of different functions.[4]

In this way the motor nerves can become centripetal and the sense nerves be transformed into centrifugal ones.[5] Finally, if a redistribution of all these functions can be carried out when the conditions of transmission are modified, there is reason to suppose, according to Wundt, that 'even in the normal state, oscillations or variations occur which depend upon the variable development of individuals'.[6]

This indeed shows that rigorous specialisation is not necessarily a mark of superiority. Far from specialisation being good in all circumstances, there is often an advantage in the organ not being fixed in its role. Doubtless stability, even to a very great extent, is useful when the environment itself is fixed. This is the case, for example, for the nutritional functions in the individual organism. They are not subject to great changes for the same organic type. Consequently there is no disadvantage, but every advantage, in their assuming a clear and definitive form. This is why the polypus, whose internal and external tissues replace each other with so great ease, is less armed for the struggle than higher animals for whom this substitution is always incomplete and almost impossible. But it is completely different when the circumstances upon which the organ depends change frequently. Then it is a case of change or perish. This is what happens to complex functions, which cause creatures to adapt to complex environments. In fact these environments, because of their complexity, are essentially unstable. Some break in the equilibrium constantly occurs, or some new circumstance. To stay adapted the function must therefore also be always ready to change, accommodating to new situations. Now of all the environments that exist, there is none more complex than the social environment. It is therefore quite natural that the specialisation of social functions is not definitive like that of the biological functions, and since this complexity increases as labour is divided up more, this elasticity becomes ever greater. Doubtless it is still confined within determinate limits, but these are for ever receding.

In the final analysis, what this relative flexibility, which is always increasing, attests to is the fact that the function becomes more and more independent of the organ. In fact, nothing paralyses a function so much as to be tied to a structure that is too closely defined, for of all arrangements there is none more stable or more opposed to change. A structure is not only a certain mode of acting, it is a mode of being that necessitates a certain mode of acting. It implies not only a certain mode of vibration peculiar to molecules, but an arrangement of them that makes any other mode of vibration almost impossible. Thus if a function acquires more flexibility it is because it sustains a less restricted relationship with the form of the organ. It is because the bond between these two elements becomes more relaxed.

We certainly observe this slackening occurring as societies and their functions become more complex. In lower societies, where tasks are general and simple, the different categories that are entrusted with them are distinguished from one another by morphological characteristics; in other words, each organ is distinguished from the others anatomically. Like each caste, each stratum of the population has its own way of feeding and clothing itself, etc., and these differences in the way of living entail physical differences:

> Of the Fijians we read that 'the chiefs are tall, well made, and muscular; while the lower orders manifest the meagreness arising from laborious service and scanty nourishment'. The chiefs among the Sandwich Islands 'are tall and stout, and their personal appearance is so much superior to that of the common people, that some have imagined them a distinct race'. Ellis, verifying Cook, says of the Tahitian, that the chiefs are, 'almost without exception, as much superior to the peasantry . . . in physical strength as they are in rank and circumstances'; and Erskine notes a parallel contrast among the Tongans.[7]

On the contrary, in higher societies these contrasts disappear. Many facts go to show that men performing different social functions are distinguished less from one another than once they were, by body shape, features or build. Pride is even taken in not having the appearance of one's occupation. If, in accordance with Tarde's wishes, statistics and anthropometrics were applied to determine with greater exactness the constituent characteristics of various professional types, we should probably find that they differ less than they did in the past, particularly if we take into consideration the greater differentiation in functions.

One fact that confirms this assumption is that the observance of professional customs is falling more and more into disuse. Indeed, although modes of dress have certainly served to highlight differences in function, we cannot see this role as their sole reason for existing, since they are disappearing as social functions are becoming more and more differentiated. They must therefore correspond to dissimilarities of another kind. If, moreover, before this practice of dress was instituted, men of different classes had not already exhibited bodily differences that were apparent, one cannot see how it would have occurred to them to distinguish themselves from others in this way. These external marks of conventional origin must therefore have been invented only in imitation of external marks of natural origin. Dress does not seem to us anything more than the mark of one's occupation which, so as to be apparent even in one's clothes, puts its stamp on them and differentiates between them according to its own image. It is, so to speak, an extension of it. It is above all apparent in those distinctions that play the same role as does dress and certainly spring from the same causes, such as the habit of wearing one's beard trimmed in this or that particular fashion, or not to wear one at all, or to have one's hair shaved off or left long, etc. These are the very characteristics of the professional type which, after having sprung up and been constituted spontaneously, reproduced themselves by imitation and artificially. The diversity of dress thus symbolises above all morphological differences. Consequently, if they disappear, it means that these differences are also vanishing. If the members of the various professions no longer feel the need to distinguish themselves from one another by visible marks, it is because that distinction no longer corresponds to any reality. Yet the functional dissimilarities continue to grow in number, becoming more pronounced. This means therefore that the morphological types are being evened out. But it certainly does not signify that every kind of brain is capable of every kind of function without distinction, but that their functional lack of differentiation, whilst remaining subject to limits, is nevertheless increasing.

Now this liberation of the function, far from being a mark of inferiority, only proves that it is becoming more complex. For if it is more difficult for the constituent elements in the tissues to be arranged so as to embody it and, in consequence, to retain and imprison it, it is because it is made up of mechanisms too intricate and delicate. We may even ask whether, after a certain level of complexity, the function does not definitively escape these elements, ending up by saturating the organ to such a degree that it is impossible for the latter to absorb it completely. That in fact the function is independent of the form of the substratum is a truth long established by naturalists. Yet, when it is general and simple, it cannot remain for long in that state of freedom, because the organ assimilates it easily, and at the same time enslaves it. However, we have no reason to suppose that this power of assimilation is indefinite. Everything gives rise to the presumption, on the contrary, that from a certain moment onwards the gap continues to increase between the simplicity of the molecular arrangements and the complexity of the functional arrangements. The bond between the latter and the former thus continues to slacken. Doubtless it does not follow that the function can exist outside any organ, nor even that there can ever be an absence of any kind of relationship between the two elements. But the relationship becomes less direct.

Progress may therefore have the effect of increasingly detaching the function from the organ – without separating it entirely, however – and life from matter, consequently 'spiritualising' it, rendering it more flexible and freer by making it more complex. It is because 'spiritualism' gives rise to the feeling that it is the characteristic of the higher forms of existence that one has always shrunk from regarding psychological life as a mere consequence of the molecular constitution of the brain. In fact, we know that the lack of functional difference in the various areas of the encephalon, if not absolute, is nevertheless large. Thus the cerebral functions are the last to take on an immutable character. They are malleable longer than other functions and retain their malleability the more complex they are. Thus their evolution continues much longer with the scientist than it does with the uneducated man. If therefore social functions display this same characteristic even more markedly, it is not because they constitute an exception without precedent, but because they correspond to a still higher stage in the development of nature.

II

By determining the main cause of the progress of the division of labour we have at the same time determined the essential factor in what is called civilisation.

It is itself a necessary consequence of the changes occurring in the volume and density of societies. If science, art and economic activity develop, it is as the result of a necessity imposed upon men. It is because for them there is no other way to live, in the new condition in which they are placed. As soon as the number of individuals between whom social relationships are established is greater, men can only maintain their position by specialising more, working harder, and stimulating their faculties to excess. From this general stimulation there inevitably arises a higher level of culture. Viewed in this light civilisation thus appears not as a goal that motivates people through the attraction it exerts upon them, nor as some good they dimly perceive and desire beforehand, of which they seek by every means to possess the largest possible share. Rather is it the effect of a cause, the necessary resultant of a given state. It is not the pole to which historical development is orientated, and to which men seek to draw closer in order to become happier or better, for neither happiness nor morality necessarily increase with the intensity with which life is lived. Men go forward because they must. What determines the speed of their advance is the more or less strong pressure they exert upon one another, depending upon their number.

This is not to signify that civilisation serves no purpose, but it is not the services that it renders that cause it to progress. It develops because it cannot but develop. Once this development has been accomplished it is generally found to be useful, or at least it is used. It corresponds to needs that have been formed at the same time, because these needs depend upon the same causes. But this is an adjustment after the event. Even so we must add that the benefits it renders in this respect are not a positive enrichment, an increase in our capital stock of happiness, but only serve to make good the losses that civilisation itself has caused. It is because this hyperactivity of general life is wearisome, tensing up our nervous system, that it finds itself needing compensation proportionate to the effort that has been expended, that is, more varied, more complex satisfactions. Here we see even more clearly how incorrect it is to make civilisation the function of the division of labour. It is only an after-effect. It cannot explain the existence or progress of that division, since of itself it has no intrinsic or absolute value; on the contrary, it has no reason for existence except in so far as the division of labour itself is found necessary.

There will be no surprise at the importance that is thereby given to the question of numbers, if we note that this plays just as capital a role in the history of organisms. In fact, what defines a living creature is its dual property of being able to feed and reproduce itself, and reproduction is itself only a consequence of nutrition. It follows that the intensity of organic life is proportionate, all things being equal, to the activity of the feeding process, that is, to the number of elements that the organism is capable of absorbing. Furthermore, what has not only made possible but also necessitated the appearance of complex organisms is the fact that, in certain conditions, the simpler ones remain grouped together in such a way as to form entities of greater size. As the constituent parts of the animal are then more numerous their relationships are no longer the same, the conditions of social life have changed, and it is these changes in turn that determine both the division of labour and polymorphism, and the concentration and greater strength of the vital forces. The growth of organic substance is therefore the fact dominating all zoological development. It is not surprising that social development is subject to the same law.

Moreover, without resorting to this reasoning by analogy, the fundamental role of this factor is easily explained. All social life is made up of a system of facts deriving from positive and durable relationships that are established between a number of individuals. That life is thus the more intense the more the reactions exchanged between its component units are themselves more frequent and energetic. But on what do this frequency and energy depend? From the nature of the elements present, on the degree of vitality they possess? But we shall see later in this chapter that individuals are much more a product of common life than a determining factor in it. If we remove from each one of them everything due to the action of society, the residue thus obtained, apart from the fact that it is reduced to very little, is incapable of presenting a very great variety. Without the diversity of social conditions on which individuals depend, the differences dividing them would be inexplicable. Thus it is not in the unequal abilities of men that we must look for the unequal development of societies. Might it be in the unequal length of time these relationships last? But time, by itself, produces nothing. It is only necessary for the latent forces to come to the light of day. Thus no other variable remains than the number of individuals who have entered into relationships, and their moral and physical proximity, that is, the volume and density of society. The more numerous they are and the more closely they exert their action upon one another, the more strongly and rapidly do they react together. Thus, as a result, the more intense social life becomes. It is this intensification that constitutes civilisation.[8]

But whilst it is an effect of necessary causes, civilisation can become an end, a desirable object – in short, an ideal. Indeed, for a society at every moment in its history a certain intensity of collective life exists that is normal, given the number and distribution of social units. Certainly if everything happens normally, this state will arise automatically. But the point is that one cannot propose to act in such a way that everything occurs normally. If health exists in nature, so also does sickness. Health, in societies as in individual organisms, is a mere ideal type that is nowhere realised absolutely. Every healthy individual displays characteristics of that type, which may be few or many; but no one combines them all. Thus it is an end worth pursuing to seek to raise society as nearly as possible to this level of perfection.

Moreover, the path indicated to attain this goal can be shortened. If, instead of our letting causes produce their effects at random, according to the forces impelling them, reflective thinking intervenes to direct their path, this can spare us many a painful ordeal. The development of the individual only replicates that of the species in abridged form. It does not repeat all the phases that the species has passed through. Some it omits, others it goes through more swiftly, because what the race has already experienced allows the individual to speed up his own experiences. Yet reflective thinking can produce similar results, for it is likewise a use of previous experience in order to make future experience easier. Furthermore, by reflection we should not understand solely the scientific knowledge of the goal and means. Sociology, at its present stage, is hardly capable of guiding us effectively towards the solution of these practical problems. But, beyond the clear ideas within which the scientist operates, there are others that are obscure, and to them trends are linked. For necessity to stimulate the will, it need not be illuminated by science. Mere vague trial and error suffices to teach men that something is missing, to awaken their aspirations and at the same time cause them to perceive in what direction they should bend their efforts.

Thus a mechanistic conception of society does not exclude the ideal; the conception is wrongly blamed for reducing man to be a mere inactive spectator of his own history. What indeed is an ideal, if not the anticipated representation of a result that is desired, and whose realisation is only possible through that very act of anticipation? Just because everything happens according to laws it does not follow that we have to do nothing. Perhaps such a purpose will seem to be ignoble, because after all its aim is merely one of helping us to live in a state of health. But this is to forget that for the educated man, health consists in satisfying regularly his highest needs just as much as the others, for the former no less than the latter are deeply rooted in man's nature. It is true that such an ideal is proximate, and that the horizons it opens up for us are in no way boundless. In no circumstances could such an ideal consist in unduly exalting the forces of society, but only in developing them within the limits marked out by the defined state of the social environment. All excess is an evil, as is every insufficiency. But what other ideal can we put forward for ourselves? To seek to realise a higher civilisation than that demanded by the nature of the prevailing conditions is to desire to let sickness loose upon the society of which one forms a part. It is not possible to stimulate collective activity excessively, beyond the level determined by the state of the social organism, without compromising its health. In fact, in every age a certain refinement of civilisation occurs whose unhealthy character is demonstrated by the anxiety and restlessness that always accompany it. And sickness is never desirable.

But if the ideal is always defined, it is never definitive. Since progress is a consequence of the changes taking place in the social environment, there is no reason to suppose that it must ever end. For it to be able to come to a stop, at a given moment the environment would have to remain static. But such a hypothesis runs counter to the most legitimate inductions. So long as distinct societies exist, the number of social units in each one will necessarily vary. Even supposing that the number of births ever succeeds in being held at a constant level, movements of population will always occur from one country to another, either through violent conquests or through a slow and silent infiltration. Indeed the strongest peoples cannot but tend to swallow up the weakest, just as those with the greatest population density pour into those countries where it is less dense. This is a mechanical law of social equilibrium no less necessary than that which regulates the equilibrium of liquids. For it to be otherwise, all human societies would have to possess the same vitality and be of the same density – which is inconceivable, if only because of the diversity of habitats in which they live.

It is true that this source of variation would dry up if the whole of humanity formed one and the same society. But, leaving aside the fact that we do not know whether such an ideal is realisable, for progress to be halted within that gigantic society the relationships between the social units would themselves have to be shielded from any changes. They would have to stay distributed in the same manner. Not only the total aggregate, but each of the primary aggregates from which it was formed, would have to retain the same dimensions. Yet such uniformity is impossible, by the mere fact that these sub-groups are not the same in area, nor do they possess equal vitality. The population cannot be concentrated at every point in the same way. Inevitably the largest centres, where life is most intense, exercise a power of attraction over the others commensurate with their importance. The migrations occurring in this way have the effect of concentrating social units more in certain regions and consequently determining further progress, which gradually radiates out over the rest of the country from the base where it originated. Moreover, these changes entail others occurring in the communications network, which set off in turn still more, without it being possible to say where such repercussions cease. In fact, far from societies approaching a static state as they develop, they become on the contrary more mobile and malleable.

Nevertheless, if Spencer was able to concede that social evolution has limits that cannot be extended,[9] it is, according to him, because progress has as its sole reason for existence to assist the individual in adapting to the cosmic environment around him. For this philosopher perfection consists in growth in the life of the individual, that is, in a more absolute congruence of the organism with its physical conditions. As for society, it is one means whereby this congruence is established, rather than the end point in a special congruence. Because the individual is not alone in this world, but is surrounded by rivals who quarrel with him over the means of existence, he has every interest in establishing between his fellows and himself relationships with them that serve rather than impede him. Thus society is born, and the whole of social progress consists in improving these relationships in such a way as to cause them to accomplish more completely the effect for which they were established. Thus in spite of the biological analogies on which he has so insistently dwelt, Spencer does not see in societies a true reality, existing by itself by virtue of specific and necessary causes, one that consequently bears down upon man, imposing upon him its own nature and to which he is forced to adapt in order to continue living, just as he does to his physical environment. For Spencer it is rather an arrangement instituted by individuals so as to extend the length and scope of human life.[10] It consists wholly in co-operation, either positive or negative, and both kinds have no other purpose than to adapt the individual to his physical environment. In this sense it is indeed a secondary condition for such an adaptation. According to how it is organised, it can bring man closer, or draw him further away from the state of perfect equilibrium, but itself is not a factor contributing to the determination of the nature of that equilibrium. Moreover, since the cosmic environment is endued with a state of relative constancy, with changes being endlessly prolonged or infrequent, a development whose purpose is to attune us to that environment must needs be limited in scope. Inevitably the time will come when no external relationships that correspond to internal ones any longer exist. The social progress will unerringly come to a halt, since it will have arrived at the goal towards which it was striving, and which was the reason for its existence: it will have beeen completed.

Yet in these conditions the progress of the individual itself becomes inexplicable.

Indeed, why should that progress aim at a more perfect congruence with the physical environment? For greater happiness? We have already set out our position on this point. We cannot even say of any particular form of congruence that it is any more complete than another, by the mere fact that it is more complex. It is alleged that an organism is in a state of equilibrium when it responds appropriately, not to all external forces, but only to those that have an impact upon it. If some do not affect it, for the organism they are as if they did not exist, and consequently it has no need to adapt to them. Whatever may be their physical proximity, they lie outside the sphere within which it must adapt, since it in turn lies outside the sphere of their effect. Thus if the object is constituted simply and homogeneously, there will only be a few external circumstances of a kind that require its attention; consequently it will be capable of responding to these demands, that is, of arriving at an impeccable state of equilibrium, with very little effort. If, by contrast, the object is very complex, the conditions for adaptation will be more numerous and complicated, but nevertheless the adaptation itself will be no less complete. Since there are so many stimuli affecting us that left untouched the more rudimentary nervous system of men of past times, we are forced to embark on a more considerable development in order to adjust to it. But the product of that development, that is, the resulting adjustment, is no more perfect in one case than in the other. It is only different because the organisms adjusting to one another are different also. The savage whose skin does not feel variations in temperature strongly is as well adapted as the civilised person who protects himself by the use of clothes.

Thus if man does not depend upon a variable environment, one cannot see what reason he would have to vary it. Society is not therefore the secondary condition for progress, but the determining factor. It is a reality that is no more our handiwork than the external world, one to which in consequence we must bow in order to go on living. It is because society changes that we must change. For progress to be halted the social environment would have to achieve at one moment a static state, and we have just established that such an hypothesis is against all the postulates of science.

A mechanistic theory of progress then not only does not deprive us of an ideal, but allows us to have faith that we shall never be without one. Precisely because the ideal depends upon the social environment, which is essentially dynamic, it is constantly changing. Thus we have no reason to fear that we will ever be constricted, that our activity will have run its course, and that we shall see the horizon close up before it. Yet, although we may never pursue any ends that are not limited and definite, there is, and always will be, between the extreme point at which we arrive and the goal towards which we strive, vacant ground available for our efforts.

III

At the same time as societies, individuals are transformed through the changes occurring in the number of social units and their relationships.

Firstly, they free themselves increasingly from the dominance of the organism. An animal is placed almost exclusively in a state of dependence on its physical environment; its biological make-up predetermines its existence. Man, on the other hand, is dependent on social causes. Doubtless the animal also forms societies, but as they are very limited collective life in them is very simple. It is at the same time static, because the equilibrium of such small societies is necessarily stable. For these two reasons collective life is easily rooted in the organism: not only are its roots there, but it incorporates itself into it so fully that it loses its own characteristics. It functions thanks to a system of instincts or reflexes that are not essentially different from those ensuring the functioning of organic life. These instincts certainly exhibit one peculiar feature: they adapt the individual to the social and not the physical environment and their causes have arisen from happenings in the common life. However, they are no different in nature from those which in certain instances determine, without any preliminary training, the motions necessary for flying or walking. With man it is completely different, because the societies he creates are much larger; even the smallest we know of are more extensive than most animal societies. Being more complex, they are also more changeable, and the conjuncture of these two causes results in social life among human beings not becoming fixed in a biological form. Even where it is most simple, it retains its specificity. There are always beliefs and practices that are common to men but that are not innate in them. But this characteristic becomes accentuated as social elements and social density increase. The greater the number of people associated together, the more they react upon one another; the more also the product of these reactions flows out beyond the organism. Man is thus subjected to causes *sui generis*, whose relative share in the constitution of human nature becomes ever more important.

Something else must be added: the influence of this factor not only increases relatively, but also absolutely. The same cause that increases the importance of the collective environment disturbs the organic environment in such a way as to make it more open to the action of social causes and to subordinate it to them. Because there are more individuals living together, common life is richer and more varied. Yet, for such variety to be possible, the organic type must be less well-defined, so that it can diversify. In fact we saw that the tendencies and abilities transmitted by heredity became ever more general and indeterminate, and consequently less capable of being conceived of in the form of instincts. Thus a phenomenon occurs that is precisely the opposite of that observed at the beginning of evolution. With animals it is the organism that assimilates social facts to itself and, stripping them of their special nature, transforms them into biological facts. Social life takes on material shape. With human beings, on the other hand, and above all in higher societies, it is social causes that are substituted for organic causes. It is the organism that takes on 'spiritual' shape.

Through this change in dependence the individual is transformed. As this activity, which stimulates to excess the special effect of social causes, cannot take root in the organism, a new life, also *sui generis*, is added on to that of the body. Freer, more complex and more independent of the organs that maintain it, its distinguishing characteristics become increasingly more marked, as it progresses and is consolidated. From this description may be recognised the essential features of psychological life. It would doubtless be extravagant to state that psychological life begins only with societies, but it certainly only becomes more widespread when societies develop. This is why, as has often been remarked, the advance of the consciousness is inversely proportional to that of the instinct. Whatever may have been stated, it is not a case of the former absorbing the latter. The instinct, the product of experience accumulated over generations, has too great powers of resistance to vanish by the mere fact that it has arrived at consciousness. The truth is that the consciousness only invades those areas that instinct has ceased to occupy or those where it cannot establish itself. It is not the consciousness that causes instinct to retreat. Consciousness only fills the space that instinct leaves free. Moreover, if instinct regresses instead of extending as general life becomes more widespread, the cause lies in the greater importance of the social factor. Thus the great difference that separates man from the animals, viz., the greater development of his psychological life, comes down to this: his greater sociability. To understand why the psychological functions, from the very first steps that the human race took, have been carried to a level of perfection unknown in the animal species, we need firstly to know why men, instead of living as solitary creatures or in small bands, began to form larger societies. If, to repeat the classic definition, man is a reasonable animal, it is because he is a sociable animal, or at least infinitely more sociable than the other animals.[11]

Nor is this all. So long as societies do not attain a certain size or a certain level of concentration, the sole psychological life that is really developed is one common to all the members of the group, one that is identical in each individual. But as societies grow larger and above all more densely populated, a psychological life of a new kind makes its appearance. Individual differences, at first lost, mixed up in the mass of social similarities, begin to emerge, take shape and multiply. A host of things that remained outside the individual consciousness because they did not affect the collectivity become the object of representations. Whereas individuals acted only because they were urged on by one another, except in cases where their behaviour was determined by physical needs, each one of them becomes a spontaneous source of activity. Individual personalities are formed and become conscious of themselves. Yet this growth in the psychological life of the individual does not weaken that of society, but merely transforms it. It becomes freer and more extensive, and since in the end it has no other substrata than the consciousnesses of individuals, these latter grow, becoming more complex and incidentally more flexible.

Thus the cause that provoked the differences separating man from the animals is also that which has constrained him to rise above himself. The ever-increasing distance arising between the savage and the civilised man has no other origin. If from the sensibility, originally in a state of confusion, the capacity for the generation of ideas has gradually emerged, if man has learnt to form concepts and to formulate laws, his mind has embraced ever more extensive areas of space and time. If, not satisfied with clinging to the past, he has encroached more and more upon the future, if his emotions and inclinations, at first simple and few in number, have multiplied and diversified, it is because the social environment has constantly been changing. Indeed, unless these transformations have stemmed from nothing, they can only have as their cause corresponding transformations in the environment around them. Man depends upon only three kinds of environment: the organism, the external world and society. If we set aside chance variations due to the combinations of heredity – and their role in human progress is certainly not very considerable – the organism is not modified spontaneously; it must be constrained to do so by some external cause. As for the physical world, from the very dawn of history this has remained appreciably unchanged, if at least we take no account of innovations of a social origin.[12] Consequently there is only society that has changed enough to be able to explain the parallel changes in the nature of the individual.

It is therefore not foolhardy to affirm straightaway that, whatever progress takes place in the psycho-physiological field, it can only ever represent a fraction of psychology, since most psychological phenomena do not derive from organic causes. This is what the spiritualist philosophers have understood, and the great service they have rendered to science has been to combat all those doctrines that reduce psychological life to being a mere efflorescence of physical life. Such philosophers were very rightly aware that psychological life, in its highest manifestations, is much too free and complex to be the mere prolongation of physical life. But, since the former is partly independent of the organism, it does not follow that it is independent of any natural cause or that it should be placed outside the realm of nature. Yet all these facts, whose explanation cannot be found in the make-up of physical elements, derive from properties of the social environment. This hypothesis is at least one that is very feasible from what has been stated above. The social kingdom is no less natural than the organic kingdom. Consequently from the fact that a vast area of consciousness exists whose genesis is incomprehensible by psycho-physiological causes alone, we should not conclude that it developed of its own accord and that, as a result, it is not amenable to scientific investigation, but rather that it is dependent on another positive science that might be called socio-psychology. The phenomena that constitute its subject-matter are indeed of a mixed nature. They have the same essential traits as other psychological facts, but they derive from social causes.

Thus we should not, as does Spencer, present social life as the mere resultant of individual natures alone, since, on the contrary, it is rather the latter that emerge from the former. Social facts are not the mere development of psychological facts, which are for the most part only the prolongation of social facts within the individual consciousness. This proposition is very important, for to uphold the opposite viewpoint exposes the sociologist at every moment to risk taking the cause for the effect, and vice versa. For example, if, as has often happened, we see in the organisation of the family the necessarily logical expression of human sentiments inherent in every consciousness, we reverse the real order of facts. Quite the opposite is true: it is the social organisation of kinship relationships that has determined respectively the sentiments between parents and children. These sentiments would have been completely different if the social structure had been different. Proof of this lies in the fact that paternal love is unknown in a large number of societies.[13] We could cite many other examples of the same fallacy.[14] It is doubtless a self-evident truth that there is nothing in social life that is not in the consciousness of individuals. Yet everything to be found in the latter comes from society. Most of our states of consciousness would not have occurred among men isolated from one another and would have occurred completely differently among people grouped together in a different way. Thus they derive not from the psychological nature of man generally, but from the way in which men, once they associate together, exert a reciprocal effect upon one another, according to their number and proximity. Products of the life of the group, it is the nature of the group alone that can explain the states of consciousness. Naturally they would not be possible unless the individual constitution favoured them. But such constitutions are only remote conditions and not determining causes. Somewhere Spencer[15] compares the work of the sociologist to the calculations of the mathematician who, from the shape of a certain number of balls, deduces the way in which they must be combined together to hold them in equilibrium. The comparison is inexact and does not apply to social facts. Here it is indeed rather the form of the whole that determines that of the parts. Society does not find ready-made in individual consciousnesses the bases on which it rests; it makes them for itself.[16]

Notes

1. *Laws of Manou*, vol. I, pp. 87–91.
2. A. Comte, *Cours de philosophie positive*, vol. VI, p. 505.
3. H. Spencer, *Principles of Sociology* (London, 1855) vol. I, p. 508.

4. Wundt, *Psychologie physiologique*, Fr. trans., vol. I, p. 234.
5. Cf. the experiment by Kühne and Paul Bert, reported in ibid., p. 233.
6. Ibid., vol. I, p. 239.
7. Spencer, *Principles of Sociology*, vol. II, p. 301.
8. Here we need not go into the question as to whether the fact that determines the progress of the division of labour and civilisation, that is, the growth in social mass and density, is itself to be explained mechanistically; or whether it is a necessary outcome of effective causes; or a means imagined towards a desired end, towards a greater good that is dimly perceived. We shall content ourselves with postulating this law of gravitation of the social world, without going back any farther. Yet it does not appear that a teleological explanation is essential here any more than it is elsewhere. The partitions that shut off the different parts of society are more and more disappearing, by the very nature of things, as a result of a kind of natural erosion, whose effect can moreover be reinforced by the action of violent causes. Population shifts thus become more numerous and more rapid, and migratory paths are channelled out as these movements occur. These form the network of communications. Such movements are more especially active where several of these paths intersect: these are the towns. Thus social density increases. As for the growth in volume, it is due to causes of the same kind. The barriers that divide peoples are similar to those that separate the various alveola within the same society and disappear in like manner.
9. H. Spencer, *First Principles* (London, 1862) pp. 465–71.
10. Spencer. Source not identified.
11. The definition of Quatrefages which makes man a religious animal is a special case of the preceding definition, for the religiosity of man is a consequence of his eminent sociability. Cf. *supra*, pp. 118 ff.
12. Transformation of the soil, the waterways, by the skill of farmers, engineers, etc.
13. This is the case in societies where the maternal family is paramount.
14. To quote only one example, this is the case of religion, which has been explained by motions of the individual sensibility, whereas these motions are only the extension in the individual of social states that give rise to religions. We have developed this point further in an article: 'Etudes de science sociale', *Revue philosophique* (June 1886). Cf. also *Année sociologique*, vol. II, pp. 1–28.
15. Spencer. Source not identified.
16. We believe this is sufficient to answer those who think they can prove that in social life everything is individual, because society is made up only of individuals. Undoubtedly no other substratum exists. But because individuals form a society, new phenomena occur whose cause is association, and which, reacting upon the consciousness of individuals, for the most part shapes them. This is why, although society is nothing without individuals, each one of them is much more a product of society than he is the author.

Book III

The Abnormal Forms

Chapter I

The Anomic Division of Labour

Up to now we have studied the division of labour only as a normal phenomenon. Yet, like all social facts, and more generally, like all biological ones, it manifests pathological forms that we must analyse. If normally the division of labour produces social solidarity, it can happen, however, that it has entirely different or even opposite results. It is important that we should investigate what makes it deviate in this way from its natural course, for so long as it has not been established that these cases are exceptional, the division of labour might be suspected of logically implying them. Moreover, the study of deviant forms will allow us to determine better the conditions for the existence of the normal state. When we know the circumstances in which the division of labour ceases to engender solidarity, we shall know better what is necessary for it to have its full effect. Here as elsewhere pathology is a precious ancillary to physiology.

We might be tempted to range among the irregular forms of the division of labour the criminal profession and other harmful professions. They are the very negation of solidarity and yet they are made up of just as many specialised activities. But, precisely speaking, here there is no division of labour, but differentiation pure and simple, and the two terms should not be confused. In the same way cancer and tuberculosis increase the diversity of the organic tissues without it being possible to see in this a fresh specialisation of the biological functions.[1] In all these cases there is no allocation of a common function, but within the organism, whether it is individual or social is formed another one that seeks to live at the expense of the first one. There is even no function at all, for a way of acting does not deserve that term unless it concerts with others to maintain life generally. This question does not therefore enter into the scope of our investigation.

We shall reduce to three types the exceptional forms of the phenomenon that we are studying. This is not because there cannot be others, but those that we shall discuss are the most general and the most serious.

I

A first case of this nature is provided for us by industrial or commercial crises, and by the bankruptcies that are so many partial breaks in organic solidarity. They demonstrate in fact that at certain points of the organism certain social functions are not adjusted to one another. As labour becomes increasingly divided up these phenomena seem to become more frequent, at least in certain cases. From 1845 to 1869 bankruptcies increased by 70 per cent.[2] However, this fact cannot be ascribed to the growth of economic life, for business undertakings have become more concentrated rather than increasing in number.

Hostility between labour and capital is another example, a more striking one, of the same phenomenon. As industrial functions specialise more the struggle becomes more fierce, far from solidarity increasing. In the Middle Ages the workman everywhere lived side by side with his master, sharing in his work 'in the same shop, on the same bench'.[3] Both formed part of the same corporation and led the same existence. 'Both were almost equal to each other; he who had completed his apprenticeship could, at least in many trades, set up on his own, if he had the wherewithal.'[4] Thus conflicts were completely exceptional. From the fifteenth century onwards things began to change. 'The trade guild is no longer a common refuge for all; it is the exclusive possession of the masters who decide everything on their own. . . . From then onwards a deep gulf was established between masters and journeymen. The latter formed, so to speak, a separate order; they had their habits, their rules, their independent associations.'[5] Once this separation had been carried out quarrels became frequent. 'As soon as the journeymen thought they had something to complain about, they went on strike or boycotted a town or an employer, and all were forced to obey the call. . . . The power of association gave the workers the means to struggle with equal weapons against their employers.'[6] However, matters were far from having reached then the 'point where we see them at present. The journeymen rebelled in order to obtain a higher salary or some change in working conditions, but they did not consider their employer to be a perpetual enemy to be obeyed under constraint. They wanted him to give way on one point and they applied themselves to this energetically, but the struggle did not last for ever. The workshops did not contain two enemy races; our socialist doctrines were unknown.'[7] Finally, in the seventeenth century there began the third phase of this history of the working classes: the coming of large-scale industry. The workman became even more separated from his boss. 'To some extent he is regimented. Each individual has his function, and the system of the division of labour makes some progress. In the factory of the Van Robais, which employed 1,692 workmen, there were special workshops for the cartwright's craft, for cutlery, washing, dyeing, and warping cloth, and the weaving mills themselves included several kinds of workers whose work was completely distinct.'[8] At the same time as specialisation becomes greater, revolts become more frequent. 'The slightest cause of discontent was enough to cause a firm to be boycotted, and woe to the journeyman who did not respect the decision of his community.'[9] We know well enough that since then the war has become increasingly more violent

We shall certainly see in the following chapter that this tension in social relationships is due in part to the fact that the working classes do not really desire the status assigned to them and too often accept it only under constraint and force, not having any means of gaining any other status. Yet this constraint alone would not by itself account for the phenomenon. Indeed it weighs down no less heavily upon all who are generally bereft of fortune, and yet this state of permanent hostility is absolutely peculiar to the industrial world. Then, within that world, it is the same for all workers without exception. Now small-scale industry, where work is less divided up, affords the spectacle of a relative harmony existing between employer and worker;[10] it is only within large-scale industry that these upheavals are acute. It is therefore because they depend in part upon a different cause.

In the history of science another illustration of the same phenomenon has often been pointed out. Up to very recent times, science, not being very much divided, could be studied almost in its entirety by one and the same person. Thus there was a very strong feeling of unity about it. The particular truths of which it was made up were neither so numerous nor so heterogeneous that the link that united them in one and the same system could not be easily discerned. The methods, being themselves very general, differed very little from one another, and one could perceive the common trunk from which they imperceptibly began to diverge. But as specialisation was introduced into scientific work each scientist shut himself off increasingly, not only within a particular science, but within a particular kind of problem. Already Comte had complained that in his time there were in the scientific world 'very few intelligences who in their conceptions included even the totality of one science, which in its turn is however only one part of a great whole. The majority,' he said, 'already limit themselves to the isolated consideration of a more or less extensive field within a given science, without bothering overmuch about the relationship of these special studies to the general system of positive knowledge.'[11] Yet then science, carved up into a host of detailed studies that have no link with one another, no longer forms a solid whole. What perhaps best demonstrates this absence of harmony and unity is the theory, so widespread, that each special science has an absolute value, and that the scientist must devote himself to his special research without caring about whether it serves any purpose or leads anywhere. 'This division of intellectual labour,' states Schaeffle, 'gives serious grounds for fearing that this return to a new Alexandrian philosophy will lead once again to the ruination of all science.'[12]

II

What makes these facts serious is that sometimes they have been seen to be a necessary consequence of the division of labour, as soon as it has passed a certain stage in its development. In that case, it has been said, the individual, bent low over his task, will isolate himself in his own special activity. He will no longer be aware of the collaborators who work at his side on the same task, he has even no longer any idea at all of what that common task consists. The division of labour cannot therefore be pushed too far without being a source of disintegration.

Every decomposition of any kind [asserts Auguste Comte] necessarily tending to set off a corresponding dispersion, the basic distribution of human labour cannot avoid creating individual divergences, both intellectual and moral, in proportion, whose combined influence must require to the same extent a permanent discipline, capable of constantly forestalling or containing their discordant upsurge. If on the one hand the separation of social functions allows a spirit of attention to detail to develop happily, in a way that would otherwise be impossible, on the other hand it tends spontaneously to stifle a spirit of attention to the whole, or at least to hamper it profoundly. Likewise, from the moral angle, just at the time when each individual is thus placed in a state of close dependence upon the mass of other people, he is also naturally turned away from them by working at his own special activity, which constantly reminds him of his own private interest, whose true relationship to the public interest he only vaguely perceives. . . . Thus the same principle which alone permitted the development and extension of society in general threatens, in another form, to split it up into a host of incohesive corporations which seem hardly, or not at all, to belong to the same species.[13]

Espinas expresses himself roughly in the same terms: 'Division,' he says, 'means dispersion.'[14]

The division of labour, by its very nature, may therefore exert a dissolving influence, which above all may be appreciable where its functions are very specialised. Comte, however, did not conclude from his principle that we should return societies to what he himself calls the age of generality, viz., that state of indistinctiveness and homogeneity that was their point of departure. The diversity of functions is both useful and necessary. But, as unity, which is no less indispensable, does not arise from it spontaneously, the task of realising and maintaining it will have to constitute a special function of the social organism, represented by an independent organ. That organ is the state or the government:

The social purpose towards which government tends [asserts Comte] appears to me to consist especially in containing adequately and forestalling as far as possible that fatal trend to a fundamental dispersion of ideas, sentiments and interests, the inevitable result of the very principle of human development, which, if it were able to follow unimpeded its own natural course, would inevitably end by halting social progress in all important aspects. In my eyes this conception constitutes the prime positive and rational basis for the elementary and abstract theory of government proper, envisaged in its most noble and most complete scientific corollary, i.e. as characterized generally by the necessary universal reaction, at first spontaneous and then regulated, of the whole upon the parts. Indeed it is clear that the sole real means of avoiding such a dispersion consists in building up this indispensable reaction into a new special function, capable of intervening appropriately in the normal accomplishment of all the various functions of the management of society, in order constantly to remind us of the concept of the whole and the sentiment of common solidarity.[15]

What the government is to society in its entirety philosophy must be to the sciences. Since the diversity of the sciences tends to break up the unity of science, a new science must be entrusted with the task of reconstituting it. Since detailed studies cause us to lose sight of the totality of human knowledge, we must institute a special system of research to rediscover it and bring it into prominence. In other words:

We must make the study of scientific generalizations an extra principal specialization. Let a new category of scientists, suitably prepared by education, without devoting themselves to the special study of any particular branch of natural philosophy, and by considering the various positive sciences in their present state, busy themselves solely with determining the spirit of each one of them, discovering their relationships and linkages, summarizing, if possible, all the principles peculiar to each one into a smaller number of common principles . . . and the division of labour in the sciences will be extended, at no danger, so far as the development of the various orders of knowledge requires.[16]

We have ourselves undoubtedly shown[17] that the organ of government develops with the division of labour, not as a counterbalance to it, but by mechanical necessity. As the organs are closely linked where the functions are very widely distributed, what affects one has an impact upon the others, and social events more easily acquire a general interest. At the same time, because of the disappearance of the segmentary type, they spread more easily over the whole surface of the same tissue or the same apparatus. For these two sets of reasons, there are more such events impacting upon the controlling organ, whose functional activity, more frequently exercised, grows, as does the volume of events. But its sphere of action extends no further.

Now, beneath this general and superficial life, there is an internal one, a world of organs that, without being entirely independent of the controlling organ, functions however without any intervention on its part, without its even being conscious of it, at least in the normal state. These organs are outside its range of action because it is too distant from them. It is not the government that can at every moment regulate the conditions of the different economic markets, fix the prices of goods and services, regulate production to the needs of consumption, etc. All these practical problems throw up a mass of details, depend upon thousands of special circumstances that they alone are aware of who know them intimately. *A fortiori* the government cannot effect an adjustment between these functions and make them work harmoniously together if they themselves are not in harmony. Thus if the division of labour has the dispersive effect attributed to it, these effects must spread without resistance into that area of society, since there is nothing able to restrain them. However, what causes the unity of organised societies, as it does of any organism, is the spontaneous consensus of its parts, that internal solidarity that is not only just as indispensable as the regulatory action of society's higher centres, but that is indeed its necessary condition, since the centres only translate it into another language and, so to speak, bestow their blessing upon it. Thus it is not the brain that creates the unity of the organism, but it expresses it, setting its seal upon it. Some speak of the necessity for a reaction of the whole upon the parts, but the whole also needs to exist. This means that the parts must be already solidly linked to one another so that the whole may become conscious of itself and react accordingly. We should then see, as labour is divided up, a sort of progressive decomposition occurring, not at any particular points, but over the whole extent of society, instead of the ever-increasing concentration observed in reality.

But, it will be said, there is no need to go into details. It is sufficient to recall, wherever it is necessary, 'the spirit of the whole and the sentiment of common solidarity', and this action is one that the government alone is qualified to carry out. This is true, but it is much too general to ensure the co-operation of the social functions, if such co-operation is not realised spontaneously. Indeed, what is at stake? To make each individual feel that he is not sufficient unto himself, but forms part of a whole upon which he depends? But such a representation, abstract, vague and, moreover, sporadic, like all complex representations, is of no avail against the vivid, concrete impressions that are aroused at every moment in each one of us by his professional activity. Thus if this activity has the effect attributed to it, if the occupations that fill our daily lives tend to detach us from the social group to which we belong, such a conception, which only is awakened at a distance and never occupies more than a small part of our field of consciousness, will never be sufficient to hold us. For the feeling of our state of dependence to be effective, it should also be continuous, yet cannot be so unless it is linked to the operation of each special function. But then specialisation would no longer have the consequences that it is accused of producing. Or might the purpose of governmental action be to maintain between the professions a certain moral uniformity, to prevent 'the social dispositions gradually concentrated on individuals in the same profession from becoming more and more alien to other classes, through lack of sufficient similarity in habits and thought?'[18] But this uniformity cannot be maintained by force and despite the nature of things. Functional diversity entails a moral diversity that nothing cannot prevent, and it is inevitable that the one should grow at the same time as the other. Moreover, we know the reasons why these two phenomena develop side by side. The collective sentiments thus become more and more powerless to contain the centrifugal tendencies that the division of labour is alleged to bring about; for, on the one hand, these tendencies increase as labour becomes increasingly divided up, and at the same time the collective sentiments grow weaker.

For the same reason philosophy becomes more and more incapable of ensuring the unity of science. So long as one mind could cultivate all the different sciences at the same time, it was possible to acquire the necessary competence to restore their unity. But as they become more specialised, these great syntheses can hardly be anything other than premature generalisations, for it becomes increasingly impossible for the human intelligence to have sufficiently exact knowledge of that innumerable number of

phenomena, laws and hypotheses that the syntheses must epitomise. 'It would be interesting to ask,' states Ribot very aptly, 'what
philosophy, as a general conception of the world, may one day
become, when the individual sciences, because of their increasing
complexity, will become incapable of being tackled in detail, and
philosophers will be reduced to the knowledge of their most general
results, which will necessarily be superficial.'[19]

Doubtless there is some reason to judge excessive that pride of
the scientist who, enclosed within his own special research, refuses
to recognise any outside control. Yet it is certain that to have some
idea of science that is in any way exact one must have practised it
and, so to speak, have lived it. This is in fact because it is not wholly
contained in the few propositions that it has definitively demonstrated. Beside this present-day science, consisting of what has
already been acquired, there is another, which is concrete and
living, which is in part still unaware of itself and still seeking its way:
beside the results that have been obtained, there are the hopes,
habits, instincts, needs, and presentiments that are so vague that
they cannot be expressed in words, yet so powerful that occasionally
they dominate the whole life of the scientist. All this is still science:
it is even the best and major part of it, because the truths discovered
are very few in number beside those that remain to be discovered,
and, moreover, to master the whole meaning of the discovered
truths and to understand all that is summarised in them, one must
have looked closely at scientific life whilst it is still in a free state,
that is, before it has been crystallised in the form of definite
propositions. Otherwise one will only grasp the letter of it and not
the spirit. Each science has, so to speak, a soul that lives in the
consciousness of scientists. Only a part of that soul takes on
substance and palpable forms. The formulas that express it, being
general, are easily transmissible. But the same is not true for that
other part of science that no symbol translates externally. Here
everything is personal, having to be acquired by personal experience. To have a part in it, one must set to work and confront the
facts. According to Comte, for the unity of science to be assured, it
would be sufficient for these methods to be reduced to a unity.[20] But
it is precisely the methods that are the most difficult to unify. For, as
they are immanent in the sciences themselves, as it is impossible to
disentangle them completely from the body of established truths in
order to codify them separately, one cannot know them unless one

has practised them oneself. Yet even now it is impossible for the same man to practise a great number of sciences. These broad generalisations can therefore only rest upon a fairly cursory view of things. If, moreover, we reflect upon the slowness and with what patient precautions scientists normally proceed to the discovery of their truths, even the most specialised ones, one can explain how these improvised disciplines exercise only very weak authority over them.

Yet whatever may be the value of these philosophical generalisations, science would not be able to find in them the unity it needs. They clearly express what the sciences have in common, their laws, their special methods, but, besides these similarities, there are differences that require to be integrated. It is often stated that the general contains potentially within it the particular facts that it summarises, but the statement is not exact. It contains only what they have in common. There are no two phenomena in the world that resemble each other, however simple they may be. This is why any general proposition lets slip from its grasp a part of the subject-matter that it is attempting to master. It is impossible to blend together the concrete characteristics and the distinctive properties of things within one and the same impersonal homogeneous formula. Yet, so long as the resemblances exceed the differences, they are sufficient to integrate the representations brought together in this way. Discrepancies in detail vanish within the total harmony. On the contrary, as the differences become more numerous, the cohesion becomes more unstable, needing to be consolidated by other means. If we imagine the increasing multiplicity of special sciences with their theorems, laws, axioms, conjectures, procedures and methods, then we can understand that a short, simple, formula such as, for example, the law of evolution, cannot suffice to integrate such a prodigious complexity of phenomena. Even if these general conspectuses applied exactly to reality, the part of it that they explain is too insignificant compared with what they leave unexplained. Thus it is not by this means that we shall ever be able to tear the positive sciences loose from their isolation. There is too great a gap between the detailed research on which they are sustained and such syntheses. The bond linking to each other these two orders of knowledge is too slight and too loose; consequently, if the special sciences can only become conscious of their mutual dependence within a philosophy that encompasses them, the feeling they will have about their dependence will always be too vague to be effective.

Philosophy is, so to speak, the collective consciousness of science and here, as elsewhere, the role of the collective consciousness diminishes as labour become more divided up.

III

Although Auguste Comte recognised that the division of labour is a source of solidarity, he does not appear to have perceived that this solidarity is *sui generis* and is gradually substituted for that which social similarities engender. This is why, noticing that these similarities are very blurred where the functions are very specialised, he saw in this process of disappearance a morbid phenomenon, a threat to social cohesion, due to excessive specialisation. He explained in this way the fact of the lack of co-ordination which sometimes accompanies the development of the division of labour. Yet since we have established that the weakening of the collective consciousness is a normal phenomenon, we could not make it the cause of the abnormal phenomena we are at present studying. If in certain cases organic solidarity is not all that is needful, it is certainly not because mechanical solidarity has lost ground, but because all the conditions of existence for the former have not been realised.

Indeed we know that wherever it is to be observed, we meet at the same time a regulatory system sufficiently developed to determine the mutual relationships between functions.[21] For organic solidarity to exist it is not enough for there to be a system of organs necessary to one another that feel their solidarity in a general way. The manner in which they should co-operate, if not on every kind of occasion when they meet, at least in the most common circumstances, must be predetermined. Otherwise, a fresh struggle would be required each time in order to bring them into a state of equilibrium with one another, for the conditions for this equilibrium can only be found by a process of trial and error, in the course of which each party treats the other as an opponent as much as an auxiliary. Such conflicts would therefore break out continually, and in consequence solidarity would be hardly more than virtual, and the mutual obligations would have to be negotiated anew in their entirety for each individual case. It will be objected that contracts exist. But firstly, not every social relationship is capable of assuming this legal form. Moreover, we know that a contract is not sufficient in itself, but supposes a regulatory system that extends and grows more complicated just as does contractual life itself. Moreover, the ties originating in this way are always of short duration. The contract is only a truce, and a fairly precarious one at that; it suspends hostilities only for a while. Doubtless, however precise the regulatory system may be, it will always leave room for much dispute. But it is neither necessary nor even possible for social life to be without struggle. The role of solidarity is not to abolish competition but to moderate it.

Moreover, in the normal state, these rules emerge automatically from the division of labour; they are, so to speak, its prolongation. Certainly if the division of labour only brought together individuals who unite for a brief space of time with a view to the exchange of personal services, it could not give rise to any regulatory process. But what it evokes are functions, that is, definite ways of acting that are repeated identically in given circumstances, since they relate to the general, unchanging conditions of social life. The relationships entertained between these functions cannot therefore fail to arrive at the same level of stability and regularity. There are certain ways of reacting upon one another which, being more in accordance with the nature of things, are repeated more often and become habits. Then the habits, as they grow in strength, are transformed into rules of conduct. The past predetermines the future. In other words, there exists a certain allocation of rights and duties that is established by usage and that ends up by becoming obligatory. Thus the rule does not set up the state of mutual dependence in which the solidly linked organs are to be found, but only serves to express it in a perceptible, definite way, as a function of a given situation. Likewise the nervous system, far from dominating the evolution of the organism, as was once believed,[22] is a result of it. The nerve tracts are probably only the paths along which have passed the wave-like movements and stimuli exchanged between the various organs. They are the channels that life has dug for itself by always flowing in the same direction, and the ganglions would only be the place where several of these paths intersect.[23] It is because they have failed to recognise this aspect of the phenomenon that certain moralists have charged the division of labour with not producing real solidarity. They have seen in it only individual exchanges, ephemeral combinations, without a past, just as they also have no tomorrow, in which the individual is abandoned to his own devices. They have not perceived that slow task of consolidation, that network of ties that gradually becomes woven of its own accord and that makes organic solidarity something that is permanent.

Now, in all the cases we have described above, this regulatory process either does not exist or is not related to the degree of development of the division of labour. Nowadays there are no longer any rules that fix the number of economic undertakings, and in each branch of industry production is not regulated in such a way that it remains exactly at the level of consumption. Moreover, we do not wish to draw from this fact any practical conclusion. We do not maintain that restrictive legislation is necessary. We have not to weigh here the advantages and disadvantages. What is certain is that this lack of regulation does not allow the functions to perform regularly and harmoniously. The economists show, it is true, that harmony is re-established by itself when necessary, thanks to the increase or decrease in prices, which, according to the need, stimulates or slows production. But in any case it is not re-established in this way until after breaks in equilibrium and more or less prolonged disturbances have occurred. Moreover, such disturbances are naturally all the more frequent the more specialised the functions, for the more complex an organisation is, the more the necessity for extensive regulation is felt.

The relationships between capital and labour have up to now remained in the same legal state of indeterminacy. The contract for the hiring of services occupies in our legal codes a very small place, particularly when we consider the diversity and complexity of the relationships it is called upon to regulate. Moreover, we need emphasise no further the deficiencies that all peoples feel at the present time and that they are attempting to remedy.[24]

Methodological rules are to science what rules of law and morality are to conduct. They direct the thinking of the scientist just as the latter govern the actions of men. Yet if every science has its method, the order that is established is entirely an internal one. The method co-ordinates the procedures followed by scientists who are studying the same science, but not their relationships externally. There are hardly any disciplines that harmonise the efforts of the different sciences towards a common goal. This is especially true of the moral and social sciences, for the mathematical, physical, chemical and even biological sciences do not seem to such an extent foreign to one another. But the jurist, the psychologist, the anthropologist, the economist, the statistician, the linguist, the historian – all these go about their investigations as if the various orders of facts that they are studying formed so many independent worlds. Yet in reality these facts interlock with one another at every point. Consequently the same should occur for the corresponding sciences. This is how there has arisen the anarchy that has been pinpointed – moreover, not without some exaggeration – in science generally, but that is above all true for these special sciences. Indeed they afford the spectacle of an aggregate of disconnected parts that fail to co-operate with one another. If they therefore form a whole lacking in unity, it is not because there is no adequate view of their similarities, it is because they are not organised.

These various examples are therefore varieties of a same species. In all these cases, if the division of labour does not produce solidarity it is because the relationships betwen the organs are not regulated; it is because they are in a state of *anomie*.

But from where does this state spring?

Since a body of rules is the definite form taken over time by the relationships established spontaneously between the social functions, we may say *a priori* that a state of *anomie* is impossible wherever organs solidly linked to one another are in sufficient contact, and in sufficiently lengthy contact. Indeed, being adjacent to one another, they are easily alerted in every situation to the need for one another and consequently they experience a keen, continuous feeling of their mutual dependence. For the same reason, exchanges between them occur easily; being regular, they occur frequently; they regulate themselves and time gradually effects the task of consolidation. Finally, because the slightest reaction can be felt throughout, the rules formed in this way bear the mark of it, that is, they foresee and fix in some detail the conditions of equilibrium. Yet if, on the other hand, some blocking environment is interposed between them, only stimuli of a certain intensity can communicate from one organ to another. Contacts being rare, they are not repeated often enough to take on a determinate form. Each time the procedure is again one of trial and error. The paths along which pass the wave-like movements can no longer become definite channels because the waves themselves are too intermittent. If at least some rules are successfully constituted, these are general and vague, for in these conditions only the most general outlines of the phenomena can be fixed. The same is true of closeness of contact: whilst it is sufficient, it is too recent or has lasted too short a while.[25]

Very generally this condition of contiguity is realised by the nature of things. For a function cannot distribute itself between two or more parts of an organism unless these parts are more or less in contact. Moreover, once labour is divided up, as they have need of one another, they tend naturally to reduce the distance that separates them. This is why, as one rises in the animal scale, one sees organs growing closer together and, as Spencer puts it, insinuating themselves into one another's interstices. But a coincidence of exceptional circumstances can cause it to be otherwise.

This is what occurs in the cases with which we are dealing at present. So long as the segmentary type of society is strongly marked, there are roughly as many economic markets as there are different segments. In consequence, each one of them is very limited. The producers, being very close to the consumers, can easily estimate the extent of the needs that have to be satisfied. The equilibrium is therefore established without difficulty and production is regulated by itself. On the contrary, as the organised type of society develops, the fusion of the various segments entails the fusion of the markets into one single market, which embraces almost all of society. It even extends beyond and tends to become universal, for the barriers between peoples are lowered at the same time as those that separate the segments within each one of them. The result is that each industry produces for consumers who are dispersed over the length and breadth of the country, or even the whole world. The contact is therefore no longer sufficient. The producer can no longer keep the whole market within his purview, not even mentally. He can no longer figure out to himself its limits, since it is, so to speak, unlimited. Consequently production lacks any check or regulation. It can only proceed at random, and in the course of so doing it is inevitable that the yardstick is wrong, either in one way or the other. Hence the crises that periodically disturb economic functions. The increase in those local and limited crises represented by bankruptcies is likely to be an effect of the same cause.

As the market becomes more extensive, large-scale industry appears. The effect of it is to transform the relationship between employers and workers. The greater fatigue occasioned to the nervous system, linked to the contagious influence of large urban areas, causes the needs of the workers to increase. Machine work replaces that of the man, manufacturing that of the small workshop. The worker is regimented, removed for the whole day from his family. He lives ever more apart from the person who employs him, etc. These new conditions of industrial life naturally require a new organisation. Yet because these transformations have been accomplished with extreme rapidity the conflicting interests have not had time to strike an equilibrium.[26]

Finally, what explains why the moral and social sciences are in the state that we have depicted, is that they were the last to enter the group of positive sciences. In fact it is hardly a century ago since this new field of phenomena was opened up to scientific investigation. Scientists have installed themselves in them, some here, some there, according to their natural inclinations. Scattered over this vast surface, they have up to now remained too distant from one another to be aware of all the bonds that unite them. But the very fact that they will push their research ever farther from the point of departure means they will necessarily end up by coming into contact with one another and consequently become aware of their solidarity. The unity of science will thus be formed by itself, not by the abstract unity of a formula, one moreover that is too narrowly conceived for the host of things it must include, but by the living unity of an organic whole. For science to be one, there is no need for it to keep its gaze wholly fixed upon one single area of consciousness – which is moreover impossible – but it is enough for all those who study it to feel that they are collaborating in the same task.

The foregoing removes all grounds for one of the gravest reproaches that have been made against the division of labour.

It has often been accused of diminishing the individual by reducing him to the role of a machine. And indeed, if he is not aware of where the operations required of him are leading, if he does not link them to any aim, he can no longer perform them save out of routine. Every day he repeats the same movements with monotonous regularity, but without having any interest or understanding of them. He is no longer the living cell of a living organism, moved continually by contact with neighbouring cells, which acts upon them and responds in turn to their action, extends itself, contracts, yields and is transformed according to the needs and circumstances. He is no more than a lifeless cog, which an external force sets in motion and impels always in the same direction and in the same fashion. Plainly, no matter how one represents the moral ideal, one cannot remain indifferent to such a debasement of human nature. If the aim of morality is individual perfection, it cannot allow the individual to be so utterly ruined, and if it has society as its end, it cannot let the very source of social life dry up. The evil not only threatens economic functions, but all the social functions, no matter how elevated these may be. 'If,' says Comte, 'we have often rightly deplored on the material plane the fact of the worker exclusively occupied throughout his life in making knife handles or pinheads, a healthy philosophy must not, all in all, cause us to regret any the less on the intellectual plane the exclusive and continual use of the human brain to resolve a few equations or classify a few insects: the moral effect, in both cases, is unfortunately very similar.'[27]

Occasionally the remedy has been proposed for workers, that besides their technical and special knowledge, they should receive a general education. But even assuming that in this way some of the bad effects attributed to the division of labour can be redeemed, it is still not a means of preventing them. The division of labour does not change its nature because it has been preceded by a liberal education. It is undoubtedly good for the worker to be able to interest himself in artistic and literary matters, etc. But it remains none the less wrong that throughout the day he should be treated like a machine. Moreover, who can fail to see that these two types of existence are too opposing to be reconciled or to be able to be lived by the same man! If one acquires the habit of contemplating vast horizons, overall views, and fine generalisations, one can no longer without impatience allow oneself to be confined within the narrow limits of a special task. Such a remedy would therefore only make specialisation inoffensive by making it intolerable, and in consequence more or less impossible.

What resolves this contradiction is the fact that, contrary to what has been said, the division of labour does not produce these consequences through some imperative of its own nature, but only in exceptional and abnormal circumstances. For it to be able to develop without having so disastrous an influence on the human consciousness, there is no need to mitigate it by means of its opposite. It is necessary and sufficient for it to be itself, for nothing to come from outside to deform its nature. For normally the operation of each special function demands that the individual should not be too closely shut up in it, but should keep in constant contact with neighbouring functions, becoming aware of their needs and the changes that take place in them, etc. The division of labour supposes that the worker, far from remaining bent over his task, does not lose sight of those co-operating with him, but acts upon them and is acted upon by them. He is not therefore a machine who repeats movements the sense of which he does not perceive, but he knows that they are tending in a certain direction, towards a goal that he can conceive of more or less distinctly. He feels that he is of some use. For this he has no need to take in very vast areas of the social horizon; it is enough for him to perceive enough of it to understand that his actions have a goal beyond themselves. Thenceforth, however specialised, however uniform his activity may be, it is that of an intelligent being, for he knows that his activity has a meaning. The economists would not have left this essential characteristic of the division of labour unclarified and as a result would not have lain it open to this undeserved reproach, if they had not reduced it to being only a way of increasing the efficiency of the social forces, but had seen it above all as a source of solidarity.

Notes

1. This is a distinction that Spencer does not draw. For him the two terms are seemingly synonymous. Yet the differentiation that causes disintegration (cancer, microbe, criminal) is very different from that that concentrates the life forces (division of labour).
2. Cf. Block, *Statistique de la France.*
3. Levasseur, *Les classes ouvrières en France jusqu'à la Révolution,* pp. 311 and 315.
4. Ibid., vol. I, p. 496.
5. Ibid.
6. Ibid., vol. I, p. 504.
7. Hubert Valleroux, *Les corporations d'arts et de métiers,* p. 49.
8. Levasseur, *Les classes,* vol. II, p. 315.
9. Ibid., p. 319.
10. Cf. Cauwès, *Précis d'économie politique,* vol. II, p. 39.
11. A. Comte, *Cours de philosophie positive,* vol. I, p. 27.
12. Schaeffle, *Bau und Leben des sozialen Körpers,* vol. IV, p. 113.
13. Comte, *Cours de philosophie positive,* vol. IV, p 429.
14. Espinas, *Sociétés animales,* vol. IV, conclusion.
15. Comte, *Cours de philosophie positive,* vol. IV, pp. 430–1.

16. There is nothing that should be surprising about this comparison between government and philosophy, for in Comte's eyes, the two are inseparable from each other. Government, as he conceives it, is only possible when a positive philosophy has already been instituted.
17. Cf. *supra*, Book I, Chapter VII, ss. III, pp. 165–71.
18. Comte, *Cours de philosophie positive*, vol. IV, p. 42.
19. Ribot, *Psychologie allemande*, introduction, p. xxvii.
20. Comte, *Cours de philosophie positive*, vol. I, p. 45.
21. Cf. *supra*, Book I, Chapter VII.
22. Cf. Perrier, *Colonies animales*, p. 746.
23. Cf. H. Spencer, *Principles of Biology* (London, 1884) vol. I.
24. This was written in 1893. Since then industrial legislation has assumed a more important place in our law. This demonstrates how serious the gap was, and it is far from having been filled.
25. There is, however, one case where *anomie* can occur, although the contiguity is sufficient. This is when the necessary regulation can only be established at the expense of transformations that the social structure is no longer capable of carrying out, for the malleability of societies is not indefinite. When it has reached its limit, even necessary changes are impossible.
26. Let us nevertheless remember that, as we shall see in the next chapter, this antagonism is not due wholly to the speed of these transformations, but to a considerable extent to the still too great inequality in the external conditions of the struggle. Over this factor time has no effect.
27. Comte, *Cours de philosophie positive*, vol. IV, p. 430.

Chapter II

The Forced Division of Labour

I

However, it is not enough for rules to exist, for occasionally it is these very rules that are the cause of evil. This is what happens in the class war. The institution of classes or castes constitutes one organisation of the division of labour, one that is closely regulated. Yet it is often a source of dissension. Since the lower classes are not, or no longer are, satisfied with the role that has fallen to them by custom or law, they aspire to functions that are prohibited to them and seek to dispossess those who exercise them. Hence civil wars, which arise from the way in which labour is shared out.

No similar phenomenon is to be observed within the organism. Doubtless in moments of crisis its different elements war with one another, feeding at the expense of one another. But a cell or an organ never attempts to usurp any role other than that which is rightfully its own. The reason for this being the case is that each anatomical element proceeds mechanically towards its goal. Its constitution and place in the organism determine its vocation; its task is a consequence of its nature. It can perform it badly, but it cannot assume that of another, unless the latter abandons it, as happens in the rare cases of substitution about which we have spoken. The same does not hold good for societies. Here the chance factor is greater. There is a larger gap between the hereditary tendencies of the individual and the social function he will fulfil. Hereditary tendencies do not signify with such direct necessity any set function. The field is open to trial and error and discussion, as well as being open to the free play of a host of causes that may make the individual nature deviate from its normal path, thus creating a pathological state. Since the organisation is more flexible, it is also more delicate and amenable to change. We are certainly not

310

predestined from birth to any particular form of employment, but we nevertheless possess tastes and aptitudes that limit our choice. If no account is taken of them, if they are constantly frustrated in our daily occupation, we suffer, and seek the means of bringing that suffering to an end. There is no solution other than to change the established order and create a new one. For the division of labour to engender solidarity, it is thus not sufficient for everyone to have his task: it must also be agreeable to him.

This condition is not realised in the instance we are examining. Indeed, if the institution of class or caste sometimes gives rise to miserable squabbling instead of producing solidarity, it is because the distribution of social functions on which it rests does not correspond, or rather no longer corresponds, to the distribution of natural abilities. For, whatever may have been asserted,[1] it is not solely the spirit of imitation that makes the lower classes end up by having ambitions for an upper-class life. To tell the truth, imitation of itself cannot even explain anything, for it supposes something other than itself. Imitation is only possible between creatures who already resemble one another, and according also to the degree of resemblance. It does not occur between different species or varieties. The same is true for moral contagion as is true for physical contagion: it only manifests itself in fields favourable to it. For needs to spread from one class to another, the differences originally separating these classes must have disappeared or grown less. As a result of the changes that have occurred in society, one group must have become capable of carrying out functions that were originally beyond its capacity, at the same time as another group was losing its original superiority. When the plebeians began to dispute with the patricians the honour of performing religious and administrative functions, it was not merely to imitate them, but it was because they [the plebeians] had become more intelligent, more wealthy and more numerous, and their tastes and ambitions had in consequence been modified. Through these transformations the congruence in a whole sector of society was broken between the aptitudes of individuals and the kind of activity allocated to them. Constraint alone, more or less violent, more or less direct, henceforth binds them to these functions. In consequence only an imperfect, troubled form of solidarity can exist.

Such an outcome is therefore not a necessary sequel to the division of labour. It only occurs in very special circumstances, that is, when it is the result of some external constraint. Matters are very different when it is established through some purely internal and spontaneous action, without anything arising to hinder individual initiatives. On this condition, in fact, a harmony between individual natures and social functions cannot fail to occur, at least over the average number of cases. If nothing hampers or favours unduly rivals who are disputing the tasks they perform, inevitably only those most fitted for each type of activity will succeed in obtaining it. The sole cause then determining how labour is divided up is the diversity of abilities. In the nature of things this allocation is made according to aptitude, since there is no reason for it to happen otherwise. Thus a harmony is automatically realised between the constitution of each individual and his condition. It will be argued that this is not always sufficient to satisfy men, for there are some whose desires overreach their abilities. This is true, but these are exceptional cases and may be termed of a morbid kind. Normally a man finds happiness in fulfilling his nature; his needs are proportionate to his means. Thus in the organism each organ claims only that quantity of food consistent with its position.

The forced division of labour is thus a second morbid type that we can distinguish. But we must not mistake the meaning of the term. What causes constraint is not any kind of regulation, since on the contrary the division of labour, as we have just seen, cannot do without this. Even when functions are allocated in accordance with set rules, the distribution is not necessarily the result of constraint. This is what takes place even under a caste regime, so long as it is based upon the nature of society. Indeed the institution of caste is not at all times and places an arbitrary one. When it functions regularly in a society, meeting with no opposition, it is because it at least approximately expresses the immutable way in which professional abilities are distributed throughout society. This is why, although tasks are to a certain extent allocated by law, each organ performs its own spontaneously. Constraint begins only when regulation, no longer corresponding to the true state of affairs and consequently without any moral foundation, is only maintained by force.

Conversely, we may therefore state that the division of labour only produces solidarity if it is spontaneous, and to the degree that it *is* spontaneous. But spontaneity must mean not simply the absence of any deliberate, formal type of violence, but of anything that may hamper, even indirectly, the free unfolding of the social force each individual contains within himself. It not only supposes that individuals are not consigned forcibly to performing certain determined functions, but also that no obstacle whatsoever prevents them from occupying within the ranks of society a position commensurate to their abilities. In short, labour only divides up spontaneously if society is constituted in such a way that social inequalities express precisely natural inequalities. It is a necessary and sufficient condition for these inequalities neither to be emphasised nor played down through some external cause. Perfect spontaneity is therefore only a sequel to, and another form of, this further fact: absolute equality in the external conditions of the struggle. It does not consist of a state of anarchy which would allow men to satisfy freely every inclination they have, good or bad. It rather comprises a finely articulated organisation in which each social value, neither distorted in one direction or the other by anything outside it, is appreciated at its true worth. It will be objected that even under these conditions, struggle still occurs, because of the fact that there must be victors and vanquished, with the latter accepting their defeat only under constraint. But this constraint does not resemble the other form; it has nothing in common with it save the term. What constitutes real constraint is when even struggle becomes impossible, and one is not even allowed to fight.

It is true that this perfect spontaneity is nowhere encountered as a fact realised in practice. There is no society where it exists in an unalloyed form. If the institution of castes corresponds to the natural distribution of abilities, it nevertheless does so only approximately – in short, in a rough and ready way. Indeed, heredity never acts with such precise accuracy that even where it meets with conditions most favourable for its influence, children are the exact replicas of their parents. There are always exceptions to the rule. Consequently cases occur where the individual is not attuned to the functions that are attributed to him. Such disharmonies become more frequent as society develops, until the time when the bounds burst, having become too constricting. When the caste regime has disappeared by law, it survives in morality. Thanks to the persistence of certain prejudices, a certain favouritism is attached to some individuals, and the converse, unrelated to their merits, obtains for others. Finally, even when, so to speak, no trace of all these past vestiges remains, the hereditary transmission of wealth suffices to render very unequal the external conditions for the struggle, since it gives to some the benefit of advantages that do not necessarily correspond to their personal value. Even today, among the most cultured peoples, careers exist that are totally closed, or more difficult to enter for those ill-blessed by fortune. It might then appear that we have no right to consider as normal a characteristic that the division of labour never manifests in its pure state, if on the other hand, we did not observe that the higher the elevation in the social scale, the more the segmentary type of society is submerged beneath the organised type, and the more also these inequalities tend to be evened out completely.

In fact the progressive decline of castes from the time when the division of labour was instituted is a law of history, for, being linked to the politico-family organisation, they necessarily regress with that form of organisation. The prejudices to which they gave rise and that they leave behind do not survive indefinitely, but are gradually extinguished. Employment in the public sector is increasingly thrown open freely to everybody, with no stipulation as to wealth. Lastly, even this ultimate inequality, which springs from the fact that rich and poor exist by birth, without disappearing completely, is at least somewhat mitigated. Society strives to reduce it as much as possible, by helping in various ways those placed in too disadvantageous a situation, and by assisting them to move out of it. It demonstrates in this way that it feels itself obliged to make room for all the deserving, and that it recognises as unjust an inferiority that is personally not merited. But what manifests even more clearly this tendency is the belief, nowadays very widespread, that equality between citizens is becoming ever greater, and that it is right that this should continue to grow. So general a sentiment cannot be a pure illusion, but must express, in some obscure way, an aspect of reality. Moreover, as the progress of the division of labour implies on the contrary an ever-increasing inequality, the equality for which the public consciousness affirms in this way the necessity cannot be that which we are discussing, that is, equality in the external conditions of struggle.

Moreover, it is easy to understand what necessitates this levelling process. We have just seen that any external inequality compromises organic solidarity. This effect is not very harmful to lower societies, where solidarity is above all ensured by a community of beliefs and sentiments. Indeed, however strained may be the ties deriving from the division of labour, as it is not they that bind the individual most strongly to society, social cohesion is not threatened.The dissatisfaction arising from thwarted aspirations is not sufficient to turn those who suffer from it against the social order that is its cause, for they continue to adhere to it. This is not because they find in it the necessary field for the development of their professional activity, but because it epitomises in their eyes a host of beliefs and practices by which they live. They cling to it because the whole of their inner life is bound up with it, because all their convictions assume its existence, and because, serving as a basis for the moral and religious order, it appears sacred to them. Private frustrations that are of a temporal kind are plainly too slight to undermine the states of consciousness deriving from such an origin, which retain an exceptional power. Moreover, as professional life is little developed, these frustrations are only intermittent. For all these reasons they are only weakly felt. Thus one grows accustomed to them without difficulty. Such inequalities are not only even found to be tolerable, but also natural.

This is exactly the opposite to what occurs when organic solidarity becomes predominant, for then everything that causes it to weaken touches the social bond in its most vital spot. Firstly, since in these conditions specialised activities are exercised almost continuously, they cannot be disturbed without some suffering occurring at every moment. Then, as the collective consciousness grows weaker, the contestation that arises cannot be so completely neutralised. The sentiments held in common no longer possess the same strength, so as to keep the individual, in spite of everything, bound to the group. Subversive tendencies, lacking in future any countervailing force, emerge more readily. Losing increasingly the transcendency that placed it, as it were, above human interests, the social organisation no longer has the same power to resist. Yet at the same time it is more strongly under attack. As the work of wholly human hands, it can no longer so effectively oppose human demands. At the very moment when the flood tide grows more violent, the dyke that contained it is breached. Thus the situation becomes much more dangerous. This is why in organised societies it is indispensable for the division of labour to attain more nearly that ideal of spontaneity we have just defined. If societies attempt – and they should attempt – to eliminate external inequalities as much as possible, it is not only because the undertaking is a noble one, but because in solving this problem their very existence is at stake. For they cannot continue to be sustained unless all their constituent parts are solidly linked, and solidarity is only possible on this condition. Thus we may predict that this matter of doing justice will become still more absolute as the organised type of society develops. However considerable the progress already realised in this domain may be, it probably gives only a very slight idea of what will be accomplished later.

II

Equality in the external conditions of the struggle is not only needed to secure each individual to his function, but also to link these functions with one another.

Indeed, contractual relationships necessarily develop with the division of labour, since the latter is not possible without exchange, of which contract is the legal form. In other words, one of the important varieties of organic solidarity is what might be termed contractual solidarity. It is undoubtedly incorrect to believe that all social relationships can be reduced to a contract, all the more so because a contract assumes the existence of something other than itself. However, there are special ties that originate in the will of individuals. There is a *consensus* of a certain kind that is expressed in contracts and that, in the higher species, represents an important factor in the general *consensus*. Thus it is necessary in higher societies for contractual solidarity to be shielded so far as possible from anything that might disturb it. For if, in less advanced societies, it can remain unstable without much difficulty arising, for the reasons we have stated, in a position where it is one of the pre-eminent forms of social solidarity it cannot come under threat without the unity of the body social being threatened at the same time. The conflicts that arise from contracts therefore assume greater seriousness the more importance the contract itself assumes in general life. What is more, whilst there exist primitive societies that do not even intervene to resolve these conflicts,[2] the law of contract in civilised peoples becomes ever more voluminous. This law's sole purpose is to ensure the regular co-operation of functions that enter into relationships in this way.

But in order to achieve this result, it is not enough for the public authority to ensure that undertakings entered into are kept. It must also, at least in roughly the average number of cases, see that they are spontaneously kept. If contracts were observed only by force or the fear of force, contractual solidarity would be in an extremely parlous state. A wholly external order would ill conceal a state of contestation too general to be contained indefinitely. Yet it may be argued that for this danger not to be feared, it is enough that contracts should be freely agreed. This may be true, but the difficulty is not resolved by this, for what constitutes free consent? Verbal or written acquiescence is not sufficient proof of it – it is possible to acquiesce only under duress. All constraint must therefore be absent. But where does constraint begin? It does not consist only in the direct use of violence, for indirect violence suppresses freedom equally effectively. If the undertaking that I have forced from someone by threatening him with death is morally and legally null and void, how could it be valid if, in order to obtain it, I have profited from a situation that, it is true, I had not caused, but that put someone else in a situation where he had either to give way to me or die?

In any given society, every object of exchange has, at any moment, a fixed value that might be called its social value. It represents the amount of useful work intrinsic to it. By this must be understood not the total labour that it may have cost, but the part of that effort capable of producing socially useful effects, that is, effects that correspond to normal needs. Although such a quantum cannot be calculated mathematically, it is none the less real. The principal conditions as a function of which it varies can even be grasped without difficulty. These are, especially, the sum total of effort needed for the production of the object, the intensity of the needs that it satisfies, and finally the extent of the satisfaction that it affords. Moreover, in fact it is around this level that the average value fluctuates. It only diverges from it under the influence of abnormal factors. In that case the public consciousness generally more or less perceives this deviation. That consciousness finds unfair any exchange where the price of the article bears no relationship to the effort expended and the services it renders.

Having enunciated this definition, we assert that the contract is not fully agreed to unless the services exchanged are equivalent in social value. In these conditions each person will receive the object that he desires and hand over what he gives in return – what both are worth. This equilibrium of wants that the contract proclaims and embodies therefore happens and is maintained of its own accord, since it is only a consequence and a different form of the very equilibrium of things. It is truly spontaneous. It is occasionally the case that we desire to receive more for the product that we are surrendering than it is worth. Our ambitions are boundless and are consequently only moderated when they are mutually held in check by one another. But this constraint, which prevents us from satisfying freely even our most inordinate wants, cannot be confused with that which removes from us the means of obtaining a just reward for our labour. The first type of constraint does not exist for the healthy person. The second type alone merits that appellation; it alone changes consent. But it does not exist in the cases we have just cited. If, on the contrary, the values exchanged do not produce an equilibrium when balanced against one another, they could only do so if some external force were thrown into the scales. There is injury done to both sides. Wills have consequently only been able to arrive at an agreement through one of them suffering some direct or indirect pressure, and this pressure constitutes a violent act. In short, for the obligatory force of the contract to be entire, it is not sufficient for it to have been an object of express assent. It must also be fair, and it is not fair by the mere fact that it has been agreed verbally. A mere statement cannot of itself engender that power to bind that inheres in agreements. For the consent to possess this power, it must itself at least rest upon some objective basis.

The necessary and sufficient condition for this equivalence to be the rule governing contracts is that the contracting parties should be placed externally under equal conditions. As the assessment of matters cannot be determined *a priori*, but arises from the exchange itself, in order to have their labour appraised at its precise worth the individuals involved in the exchange must dispose of no other force than that which they draw from their social merit. In this way the value of objects corresponds exactly to the services that they render and the toil that has been expended. For any other factor capable of causing the value to vary is ruled out by hypothesis. Doubtless their unequal merit will always leave men unequally placed in society. But these inequalities are only apparently external, for they merely interpret internal inequalities from the outside. Thus their only influence over the determination of values is to establish between them a gradation that runs parallel to the hierarchy of social functions. It is no longer the same if some receive additional power from some other source. That power must needs result in displacing the point of equilibrium, and it is clear that such a displacement is independent of the social value of things. Every form of superiority has repercussions on the way in which contracts are arrived at. If therefore it does not depend upon the person of individuals and their services to society, it invalidates the moral conditions of the exchange. If one class in society is obliged, in order to live, to secure the acceptance by others of its services, whilst another class can do without them, because of the resources already at its disposal, resources that, however, are not necessarily the result of some social superiority, the latter group can lord it over the former. In other words, there can be no rich and poor by birth without their being unjust contracts. This was the more true when the social condition was itself hereditary and the law sanctioned all kinds of inequalities.

Nevertheless, such injustices are only strongly felt so long as contractual relationships are little developed, and the collective consciousness is strong. Because of the rarity of contracts, less opportunities occur for injustices to arise, and the common beliefs particularly neutralise their effects. Society does not suffer, because it is not endangered. But, as labour becomes more divided up and social doctrine weakens, these injustices become more unbearable, because the circumstances that give rise to them recur more frequently, and also because the sentiments they arouse can no longer be tempered so completely by countervailing ones. To this the history of contract bears witness, for it tends increasingly to declare invalid those agreements where the contracting parties are too unequally placed.

Originally any contract, concluded in due form, had the force of obligation, no matter how it had been obtained. Consent was not the prime factor in it. A consensus of wills was not sufficient to bind, and the bonds formed did not result directly from this consensus. For the contract to exist a necessary and sufficient condition was that certain ceremonies should have been carried out, certain words pronounced, and the nature of the undertakings entered into was determined not by the intentions of the parties, but by the formulas employed.[3] The consensual contract only appears at a comparatively recent date.[4] It is a first step along the path of justice, yet for a long time the consent that was sufficient to validate agreements could be very imperfect in nature, that is, extorted by force or fraud. It was at a fairly late period that the Roman praetor granted to victims of ruse and violence the right to action *de dolo* or *quod metus causa*.[5] Even the plea of violence did not exist legally unless there had been a threat of death or bodily injury.[6] Our law has become more stringent on this point. At the same time prejudice suffered and duly established was admitted among the causes which can in certain cases render contracts null and void.[7] It is not moreover for this reason that all civilised peoples refuse to recognise a contract of usury? It is because it supposes that one of the contracting parties is placed too absolutely at the mercy of the other. Finally, common morality condemns more severely still any kind of contract where one party gets the lion's share, where one is exploited by the other because he is the weaker, so that he does not receive the fair price for his pains. The public consciousness ever more insistently demands exact reciprocity in the services exchanged and, recognising only a very reduced form of obligation for those agreements that do not fulfil this basic condition of all justice, it shows itself much more indulgent than the law for those who break them.

It is to the economists that the credit goes for having first pointed out the spontaneous character of social life, showing that constraint can only cause it to deviate from its natural course and that normally it arises not from arrangements imposed from without, but from its free internal nature. In this respect they have rendered a signal service to the science of morality, but have erred regarding the nature of that freedom. Since they see it as a constituent attribute in men and deduce it logically from the concept of the individual *per se*, such a freedom appears to them to be absolute even from the state of nature, leaving out of account any kind of society. According to them, social action has therefore nothing to add to it; all that it can, and must, do, is to regulate its external functioning in such a way that the liberties vying with one another do not do injury to one another. But if social action does not confine itself strictly within these limits, it encroaches upon their legitimate domain and diminishes it.

Yet, apart from the fact that it is incorrect to say that any form of regulation is the product of constraint, it so happens that liberty itself is the product of regulation. Far from being a type of antagonist to social action, it is the resultant. It is so little a property inherent in the state of nature that it is, on the contrary, a conquest by society over nature. Men are naturally unequal in physical strength; they are placed in external conditions that give unequal advantages. Domestic life itself, with the property inheritance that it implies and the inequalities that flow from this, is, of all forms of social life, the one that most narrowly depends upon natural causes. We have just seen that all these inequalities are the very negation of liberty. In the final analysis what constitutes liberty is the subordination of external to social forces, for it is only on this condition that the latter can develop freely. Yet such a subordination is rather an utter reversal of the natural order.[8] Thus it can only be realised progressively, as man raises himself above things so as to regulate them as he wishes, stripping them of their fortuitous, absurd and amoral character, that is, to the extent that he becomes a social being. For he cannot escape from nature save by creating another world in which he dominates it. That world is society.[9]

The task of the most advanced societies may therefore be said to be a mission for justice. That in fact they feel the need to tread this path we have already demonstrated, and this is proved also by everyday experience. Just as the ideal of lower societies was to create or maintain a common life as intense as possible, in which the individual was engulfed, ours is to inject an even greater equity into our social relationships, in order to ensure the free deployment of all those forces that are socially useful. However, when we consider that for centuries men have contented themselves with a justice that is much less than perfect, we may begin to ask whether such aspirations are not perhaps ascribable to impatient acts that lack any reason, whether they do not represent a deviation from the normal state rather than an anticipation of the normal state to come – whether, in brief, the way to cure the ill whose existence they lay bare is to satisfy these aspirations or to combat them. The propositions established in the preceding books allow us to answer with precision this question that preoccupies us. There are no better justified needs than these trends, for they are a necessary consequence of the changes that have taken place in the structure of societies. Because the segmentary type is vanishing and the organised type developing, because organic solidarity is gradually substituting itself for the solidarity that arises from similarities, it is indispensable that external conditions should be evened out. The harmony between functions, and consequently in existence, is at this price. Just as ancient peoples had above all need of a common faith to live by, we have need of justice. We can rest assured that this need will become ever more pressing if, as everything leads us to foresee, the conditions that dominate social evolution remain unchanged.

Notes

1. Tarde, *Lois de l'imitation*.
2. Cf. Strabonius, p. 702. Likewise in the Pentateuch no regulation of contract is to be found.
3. Cf. the contract *verbis, litteris et re* in Roman law. Cf. Esmein, *Etudes sur les contrats dans le très ancien droit français* (Paris, 1883).
4. Ulpian regards consensual contracts as being *juris gentium* (Book V, 7 pr., and § 1, *De Pactis*, vol. II, p. 14). Yet the whole *jus gentium* is certainly of a later origin than civil law. Cf. Voigt, *Jus gentium*.
5. The action *quod metus causa* is slightly earlier than the action *de dolo* but later than the dictatorship of Sulla. The date is put at 674.
6. Cf. Ulpian, book 3, § 1, and book 7, § 1.
7. Diocletian decided that a contract could be rescinded if the price was lower than half the real value. Our law allows rescindment for unfair dealing only in cases of the sale of 'real' property.
8. Naturally we do not mean that society is outside nature, if by this is signified the totality of phenomena subject to the law of causality. By natural order we understand only what might occur in what has been termed the state of nature, that is, under the sole influence of physical and organico-physical causes.
9. Cf. *supra*, Book II, Chapter V. We see once again that the free contract is not sufficient by itself, since it is only possible because of a very complex social organisation.

Chapter III

Another Abnormal Form

There remains one last abnormal form to describe.

It often happens in a commercial, industrial or any other kind of undertaking that functions are distributed in such a way that they fail to afford sufficient scope for individual activity. It is plain that there is a regrettable waste of effort, although we need not deal with the economic aspect of the phenomenon here. What should be of interest to us is another fact that always accompanies this wastage, that is, a more or less lack of co-ordination of these functions. We know that in a business where every employee has not enough work to occupy himself activities are badly co-ordinated and operations are carried out without concertation; in short, solidarity relaxes its hold, and incoherency and disorder appear. At the court of the Eastern Roman Empire functions were infinitely specialised, and yet the outcome was veritably a state of anarchy. Thus there are cases where the division of labour, although very highly developed, result in a very imperfect integration. From where does this arise? It would be tempting to reply that what is lacking is some kind of regulatory organ, a managing body. Such an explanation is hardly satisfying, for very often this state of sickness is the work of the controlling management itself. For the evil to vanish it does not therefore suffice to have some kind of regulatory mechanism; it needs to be exercised in a certain way. Consequently we must know how it will be exercised. The prime task of an intelligent and experienced leader will be to abolish useless jobs and distribute work in such a way that each individual will be kept sufficiently busy, thus increasing the functional activity of every worker. Then order will spontaneously arise once more, at the same time as the work is more economically arranged. How is this to be brought

323

about? At first sight this is very difficult to envisage. For if every operator has a clearly determined task and performs it with precision, he will necessarily require the co-operation of his neighbours and cannot fail to feel solidly linked to them. What does it matter whether this task is great or small, provided that it is specialised? What does it matter whether it absorbs his time and energy fully or not?

On the contrary, it matters a great deal. This is because solidarity in general depends very closely upon the functional activity of the specialised parts. These two terms vary with each other. Where functions are faltering, in vain may they be specialised, for they are badly co-ordinated with one another and are incompletely aware of their mutual dependence. A few examples will make this fact very apparent. In a man suffocation blocks the flow of blood through the capillaries, and this obstacle is followed by a congestion and the stopping of the heart; in a few seconds a great upheaval occurs throughout the organism, and after a minute or two life functions cease.[1] Life in its entirety therefore depends very closely upon the respiratory process. But with a frog respiration can be suspended for a long time without entailing any disturbance, either because the supply of air to the blood that is carried out through the skin is sufficient for it, or even because, being totally deprived of air to breathe in, it makes do with the oxygen stored up in its tissues. Thus there is a fairly large degree of independence and consequently an imperfect solidarity between the frog's respiratory function and the other functions of its organism, since the latter can subsist without the help of the former. This results from the fact that the frog's tissues, having a functional activity less than those of a man, have also less need to renew their oxygen and rid themselves of the carbonic acid produced by their combustion. Likewise a mammal needs to take in food very regularly; its breathing rhythm in a normal state remains appreciably the same; its rest periods are never very long. In other words its respiratory, nutritional and relational functions are continuously necessary to one another and to the whole organism, to such an extent that not one can remain suspended for any length of time without endangering the others and life in general. The snake, on the other hand, only takes in food at long intervals. Its periods of activity and drowsiness are very spaced out from one another. Its respiration, very visible at certain moments, is occasionally almost non-existent, that is, its functions are not closely knit together, but can be isolated from one another without ill-effect. The reason is that its functional activity is less than that of mammals. Since the exhalation process of the tissues is weaker, these have less need of oxygen. Since the rate of deterioration is less, the respiration required is necessary less frequently, as are the movements designed for pursuing and capturing its quarry. Spencer has moreover remarked that examples of the same phenomenon are to be found in unorganised nature. Look, he says, at a very complicated machine, whose parts are not very well adjusted or have become loose through wear; examine it when it is about to stop. You will observe certain irregularities in the movement just before it comes to a halt: some parts stop first, then start up again because others continue on, and then in their turn become the cause of the movement, restarting in other parts that had ceased to move. In other words, when the rhythmical changes in the machine are rapid, the actions and reactions they exert upon another are regular and all the movements are nicely integrated. But as the speed slows down, irregularities occur and the movements disintegrate.[2]

What causes every increase in the functional activity to determine an increase in solidarity is the fact that the functions of an organism can only become more active on condition that they also become more continuous. Let us consider one function in particular. As it can accomplish nothing without the co-operation of others, it cannot produce more unless the others produce more also. But the output of these functions cannot in turn increase unless the first function increases again as further after-effect. Any increase in the activity of a function, implying a corresponding increase in the functions that are solidly linked to it, implies a fresh increase in the first function. This is only possible if the activity becomes more continuous. Furthermore, these repercussions are naturally not produced indefinitely, for a moment arrives when equilibrium is once again established. If the muscles and nerves work harder they will need richer nourishment, which the stomach will provide on condition that it functions more actively. But for this it must receive more nutrients on which to work, and these cannot be obtained save by a fresh expenditure of nervous and muscular energy. Larger industrial production necessitates tying up a greater amount of capital in the form of machines. But this capital in turn, in order to be sustained, demands greater industrial production in order to make up for its losses, that is, to pay its rent. When the motion that works all parts of a machine is very rapid, it is uninterrupted because it passes incessantly from one part to another. They pull each other along, so to speak. If, moreover, it is not solely an isolated function but all functions at the same time that become more active, the continuity of each one of them will be increased still more.

Consequently they will be more solidly linked to one another. Indeed, being more continuous their relationships are more sequential, and are more continuously in need of one another. They are therefore more aware of their dependence. Under the regime of large-scale industry the entrepreneur is more dependent upon his workers, provided they know how to take concerted action, for by stopping production strikes prevent capital from earning its keep. But the worker also can less easily be idle, because his needs have increased with his work. When, on the contrary, activity is less, needs are more intermittent, and this is true for the relationships that link functions together. They feel their solidarity only sporadically, and for this reason it grows slacker.

Thus if the work provided is not only not of a large amount, but is even insufficient, that solidarity is itself naturally not only less than perfect, but may even be more or less completely missing. This is what happens in business enterprises where the tasks are distributed in such a way that each worker's activity is lower than what it should normally be. The different functions are therefore too discontinuous to be adjusted precisely to one another or to work harmoniously together. This is where their lack of cohesion is noticeable. ·

But exceptional circumstances must prevail for the division of labour to occur in this way. Normally it does not develop without functional activity increasing at the same time and in the same proportion. Indeed the same causes that force us to specialise more also force us to work harder. When the number of competitors increases generally throughout society, it increases also in each individual profession. The struggle within them becomes more fierce, and consequently greater effort must be put forward to be able to sustain it. Furthermore, the division of labour itself tends of its own accord to render functions more active and sustained. For a long time the economists have set out reasons for this phenomenon, the main ones being as follows:

(1) When tasks are not divided up one is constantly disturbed,

passing from one occupation to another. The division of labour economises all this lost time; according to Karl Marx's expression, it causes the pores of the working-day to contract.

(2) Functional activity increases with skill, the ability of the worker, which the division of labour develops. There is less time used up in vacillation and trial and error.

Carey, the American sociologist, has very clearly highlighted this characteristic of the division of labour. He states that there can be no continuity in the actions of the isolated settler. Depending for his subsistence upon his acquisitive ability and obliged to cover immense areas of ground, he is often in danger of perishing through lack of food. Even when he succeeds in obtaining it he is forced to suspend his operations and to think of how to accomplish the indispensable removal of his dwelling-place in order to transport at the same time his subsistence, his miserable home and himself. Once he has arrived, he is forced to become cook and tailor in turn. Deprived of the aid of artificial light, his nights are spent in complete idleness, and at the same time his ability to use the daylight in fruitful employment depends completely on the hazard of temperature. Finally, however, discovering he has a neighbour,[3] exchanges take place between them. But since both occupy different parts of the island, they are forced to move closer together, just like the stones with the help of which they grind their corn. Moreover, when they meet, difficulties arise in fixing the terms on which they trade, because of the irregularity of the supply of the various foodstuffs they wish to barter. The fisherman has had good luck and has caught a vast quantity of fish, but by chance the hunter has been able to get fish already and at this moment needs only fruit, and the fisherman does not have any. Differentiation being, as we know, indispensable for association, the absence of this condition would set up an obstacle to association, one difficult to overcome.

Yet, continues Carey, with time, wealth and population grow and, with this development there appears an increase in movements within society. From then onwards the husband exchanges services with his wife, parents with those of their children, and the children with one another. The one provides fish, the second meat, a third corn, whilst a fourth converts wool into cloth. At every step we perceive a growth in the speed of the exchanges, at the same time as an increase in strength on the part of man.[4]

Moreover, we can observe that work becomes more continuous

the more it is divided up. Animals and savages work in most capricious a fashion, when they are compelled by necessity to satisfy some immediate need. In exclusively agricultural or pastoral societies work is almost entirely suspended during bad weather. At Rome it was interrupted by a whole host of feast days or unpropitious days.[5] In the Middle Ages free time was still further increased.[6] Yet, as time passes, work becomes a permanent occupation, a habit, and even a necessity, if this habit has been sufficiently reinforced. But such a habit could not have grown up, and the corresponding need could not have arisen, if work had remained regular and intermittent, as once it was.

We are thus led to acknowledge another reason that makes the division of labour a source of social cohesion. Not only does it cause individuals to be solidly linked to one another, as we have maintained up to now, because it limits the activity of each one, but also because it increases that activity. It fosters the unity of the organism, by the very fact that it adds to its life. In the normal state, at least, it does not produce one effect without the other.

Notes

1. H. Spencer, *Principles of Biology* (London, 1884) vol. I.
2. Ibid.
3. Naturally this is only one way of setting out matters. Historically things did not occur in this way. Man did not discover one fine day that he had a neighbour.
4. C. H. Carey, *The Principles of Social Science*.
5. Cf. Marquardt, *Römische Staatsverwaltung*, vol. III, pp. 545 ff.
6. Cf. Levasseur, *Les classes ouvrières en France jusqu'à la Révolution*, vol. I, pp. 474 and 475.

Conclusion

I

We can now resolve the practical problem that we set ourselves at the beginning of this study.

If there is one rule of conduct whose moral character is undisputed, it is that which decrees that we should realise in ourselves the essential features of the collective type. It is among lower peoples that it attains the greatest inflexibility. There the first duty is to resemble everyone else, to have nothing that is personal, whether as regards beliefs or practices. In the more advanced societies, the similarities that are required are fewer in number. However, as we have seen, some exist, the absence of which constitutes for us a state of moral error. Doubtless crime comprises a lesser number of different categories. But today as formerly, if the criminal is the object of reprobation, it is because he is not like us. Likewise, on a lower plane, acts that are merely immoral and prohibited as such are those that display dissimilarities that are less profound, although still serious. Moreover, is it not this rule that common morality expresses, although in somewhat different language, when it ordains that a man should be a man in every sense of the word, that is, possess all the ideas and sentiments that constitute a human consciousness? Undoubtedly if one follows this formula to the letter, the man it prescribes for us would be man in general, and not one of this or that social species. But in reality that human consciousness that we must realise within ourselves in its entirety is nothing other than the collective consciousness of the group of which we form part. For of what can it be made up, if not of the ideas and sentiments to which we are most attached? Where should we turn to look for the characteristics of our model if it is not within ourselves and around us? If we believe that this collective ideal is

329

that of the whole of humanity, it is because it has become sufficiently abstract and general to appear to suit all men without distinction. Yet in fact every people forms regarding this alleged type of humanity a particular conception that derives from its personal temperament. Each one represents it in his own image. Even the moralist who believes he is able, by the power of thought, to withdraw himself from the influence of surrounding ideas, cannot succeed in doing so. For he is entirely permeated by them and, whatever he does, it is they that he discovers once more at the conclusion of his deductions. This is why every nation has a school of moral philosophy that is in harmony with its character.

On the other hand, we have shown that the function of this rule was to forestall any disturbance of the common consciousness and, consequently, of social solidarity. It cannot perform this role save on condition that it possesses a moral character. It is impossible for offences against the most fundamental of the collective sentiments to be tolerated without society disintegrating. But such offences must be combated with the aid of that particularly energetic reaction associated with moral rules.

Now the opposite rule, which decrees that we should specialise, has exactly the same function. It is also necessary for the cohesion of societies, at least from a certain time onwards in their evolution. Doubtless, the solidarity that it ensures differs from the former one. But if it is different, it is no less indispensable. Higher societies cannot maintain their equilibrium unless work is divided up. The attraction of like for like suffices less and less to produce this effect. If therefore the moral character of the first of these rules is necessary for it to be able to perform its role, this necessity is no less for the second rule. They both correspond to the same social need and satisfy it only in different ways because the conditions of existence within societies themselves differ. Consequently, without our needing to speculate on the prime foundation of ethics, we can induce the moral value of the one from the moral value of the other. If from certain viewpoints, there is truly antagonism between them, it is not because they serve different ends. On the contrary, it is because they lead to the same aim, but by opposing routes. Thus it is not necessary to choose between them once and for all, nor to condemn the one in the name of the other. What must be done is to give to each one, at each moment of history, the place that is fitting.

We may perhaps be able to generalise even more.

The necessities of our subject have in fact obliged us to classify moral rules and to review the main species among them. Thus we are better able than we were at the outset to perceive, or at the very least to conjecture, not merely the external signs but the internal character that is common to them all and that can serve to define them. We have split them into two kinds: rules with a repressive sanction, which is either diffuse or organised, and rules with a restitutory sanction. We have seen that the former express the conditions of that solidarity *sui generis* which derives from resemblances, and to which we have given the name mechanical solidarity. The latter, those of negative solidarity,[1] we have termed organic solidarity. Thus we may state generally that the characteristic of moral rules is that they enunciate the basic conditions of social solidarity. Law and morality represent the totality of bonds that bind us to one another and to society, which shape the mass of individuals into a cohesive aggregate. We may say that what is moral is everything that is a source of solidarity, everything that forces man to take account of other people, to regulate his actions by something other than the promptings of his own egoism, and the more numerous and strong these ties are, the more solid is the morality. We can see how inaccurate it is to define it, as has often been done, in terms of freedom. It rather consists much more in a state of dependence. Far from it serving to emancipate the individual, disengaging him from the surrounding environment, its essential function, on the contrary, is to be the integrating element in a whole, and in consequence it removes from the individual some of his freedom of movement. It is true that occasionally we meet souls who are not without nobility but who find this idea of dependence intolerable. Yet this is because they do not perceive the source from where flows their own morality, because that source is too deep. Conscience is a poor judge of what occurs in the depths of one's being, because it does not penetrate that far.

Thus society is not, as has often been believed, some happening that is a stranger to morality, or which has only secondary reprecussions upon it. It is not a mere juxtaposition of individuals who, upon entering into it, bring with them an intrinsic morality. Man is only a moral being because he lives in society, since morality consists in solidarity with the group, and varies according to that solidarity. Cause all social life to vanish, and moral life would vanish at the same time, having no object to cling to. The state of nature of the eighteenth-century Philosophes is, if not immoral, at least *amoral*, a fact that Rousseau himself recognised. For that reason, moreover, we do not fall back upon the formula that expresses morality as a function of social interest. Doubtless society cannot exist if its parts are not solidly bound to one another, but solidarity is only one of the conditions for its existence. There are many others no less necessary, which are not moral. Moreover, it can be that, within this network of the ties that go to make up morality, there are some that are not useful in themselves, or whose strength bears no relationship to their degree of usefulness. The idea of the useful does not therefore come into our definition as an essential element of it.

As for what is termed individual morality, if by this is meant a set of duties in relation to which the individual would be both subject and object, which would bind him only to himself and would consequently subsist even if he were alone, this is an abstract conception that has no foundation in reality. Morality, at all levels, is never met with save in the state of society and has never varied save as a function of social conditions. Thus to ask what morality might become if societies did not exist is to depart from the facts and to enter the realm of gratuitous hypothesis and unverifiable fantasy. In reality the duties of the individual to himself are duties to society. They correspond to certain collective sentiments which it is no more permissible to offend when the offended person and the offender are one and the same person than when they are two distinct individuals. For example, today there is in every healthy consciousness a very active feeling of respect for human dignity, to which we are obliged to make our behaviour conform both in our relationship with ourselves and in our relationship with others – this is indeed all that is essential in the kind of morality termed individual. Any action that offends it is blamed, even when the doer and the sufferer of the offence are one and the same person. This is why, in Kant's formula, we must respect human personality wherever we meet it, that is, within ourselves and within our fellow-beings. This is because the sentiment of which it is the object is no less offended in the one case than in the other.

Not only does the division of labour exhibit that character by which we define morality, but it increasingly tends to become the essential condition for social solidarity. As evolution advances, the bonds that attach the individual to his family, to his native heath, to the traditions that the past has bequeathed him, to the collective practices of the group – all these become loosened. Being more mobile, the individual changes his environment more easily, leaves his own people to go and live a more autonomous life elsewhere, works out for himself his ideas and sentiments. Doubtless all trace of common consciousness does not vanish because of this. At the very least there will always subsist that cult of the person and individual dignity about which we have just spoken, which today is already the unique rallying-point for so many minds. But how insignificant this is if we consider the ever-increasing scope of social life and, consequently, of the individual consciousness! As the latter becomes more expansive, as the intelligence becomes even better equipped, and activity more varied, for morality to remain unchanged, that is, for the individual to be bound to the group even so strongly as once he was, the ties that bind him must be reinforced, becoming more numerous. Thus if only those ties were forged that were based on similarities, the disappearance of the segmentary type of society would be accompanied by a steady decline in morality. Man would no longer be held adequately under control. He would no longer feel around him and above him that salutary pressure of society that moderates his egoism, making of him a moral creature. This it is that constitutes the moral value of the division of labour. Through it the individual is once more made aware of his dependent state *vis-à-vis* society. It is from society that proceed those forces that hold him in check and keep him within bounds. In short, since the division of labour becomes the predominant source of social solidarity, at the same time it becomes the foundation of the moral order.

We may thus state literally that in higher societies our duty lies not in extending the range of our activity but in concentrating it, in making it more specialised. We must limit our horizons, select a definite task, and involve ourselves utterly, instead of making ourselves, so to speak, a finished work of art, one that derives all its value from itself rather than from the services it renders. Finally, this specialisation must be carried the farther the more society is of a higher species. No other limits can be placed upon it.[2] Undoubtedly we must also work towards realising within ourselves the collective type, in so far as it exists. There are common sentiments and ideas without which, as one says, one is not a man. The rule prescribing that we should specialise remains limited by the opposite rule. We

334 *The Abnormal Forms*

conclude that it is not good to push specialisation as far as possible, but only as far as necessary. The weight to be given to these two opposing necessities is determined by experience and cannot be calculated *a priori*. It suffices for us to have shown that the latter is no different in nature from the former, but that it is also moral and that, moreover, this duty becomes ever more important and urgent, because the general qualities we have discussed suffice less and less to socialise the individual.

Thus it is not without reason that public sentiment is continually distancing itself even more markedly from the dilettante, and even from those who, too much absorbed with a culture that is exclusively general, shrink from allowing themselves to be wholly caught up with the professional organisation. This is in fact because they do not adhere closely enough to society or, if one likes, society does not hold on to them closely enough. They elude it, and precisely because they do not feel it with the sense of vividness and continuity needed, they are unaware of all the obligations laid upon them by their condition as social beings. The general idea to which they are attached being, for reasons we have given, formal and fluctuating, it cannot draw them very much outside themselves. Without a determinate goal one does not cling to very much, so that one can scarcely lift oneself out of a more or less refined egoism. On the other hand, he who has dedicated himself to a definite task is reminded at every moment of the common sentiment of solidarity through the thousand and one duties of professional morality.[3]

II

Yet does not the division of labour, by rendering each one of us an incomplete being, not entail some curtailment of the individual personality? This criticism has often been made.

Firstly, let us note that it is difficult to see why it might be more in accord with the logic of human nature to develop more superficially rather than in depth. Why should a more extensive activity, one that is more dispersed, be superior to one more concentrated and circumscribed? Why should more dignity attach to being complete and mediocre than in leading a more specialised kind of life but one more intense, particularly if we can recapture in this way what we have lost, through our association with others who possess what we lack and who make us complete beings? We start from the principle that man must realise his nature as man – as Aristotle said, accomplish his οἰχέιον ἔργον. But at different moments in history this nature does not remain constant; it is modified with societies. Among lower peoples, the act that connotes a man is to resemble his fellows, to realise within himself all the characteristics of the collective type which, even more than today, was then confused with the human type. In more advanced societies man's nature is mainly to be a part of society; consequently the act that connotes a man is for him to play his part as one organ of society.

There is something more: far from the progress of specialisation whittling away the individual personality, this develops with the division of labour.

Indeed to be a person means to be an autonomous source of action. Thus man only attains this state to the degree that there is something within him that is his and his alone, that makes him an individual, whereby he is more than the mere embodiment of the generic type of his race and group. It will in any case be objected that he is endowed with free will, and that this is sufficient upon which to base his personality. But whatever this freedom may consist of – and it is the subject of much argument – it is not this impersonal, invariable, metaphysical attribute that can serve as the sole basis for the empirical, variable and concrete personality of individuals. That personality cannot be formed by the entirely abstract capacity to choose between two opposites. This faculty must be exercised in relation to ends and motives that are peculiar to the person acting. In other words the stuff of which his consciousness is made up must have a personal character. Now we have seen in the second book of this study that is an outcome that occurs progressively as the division of labour itself progresses. The disappearance of the segmentary type of society, at the same time as it necessitates greater specialisation, frees the individual consciousness in part from the organic environment that supports it, as it does from the social environment that envelops it. This dual emancipation renders the individual more independent in his own behaviour. The division of labour itself contributes to this liberating effect. Individual natures become more complex through specialising; by this very fact they are partly shielded against the effects of the collectivity and the influences of heredity, which can scarcely enforce themselves except in simple, general matters.

Thus, as a consequence of a veritable illusion, one could

occasionally believe that the personality was more whole, so long as it had not been breached by the division of labour. Doubtless, viewing from the outside the variety of occupations that the individual embarks upon, it may seem that the personality then develops more freely and completely. But in reality the activity he displays is not his own. It is society, it is the race, which act in and through him; he is only the intermediary through which they are realised. His liberty is only apparent, his personality is borrowed. Since the life of societies is in certain respects less regular, we imagine that original talents can more easily come to light, that it is easier for each individual to follow his own tastes, that greater room is left for the free play of fantasy. Yet this is to forget that personal sentiments are then very rare. If the motives governing conduct do not occur with the same regularity as they do today, they do not cease to be collective, and consequently impersonal. The same is true for the actions they inspire. We have moreover shown above how the activity becomes richer and more intense the more specialised it becomes.[4]

Thus the advance of the individual personality and that of the division of labour depend on one and the same cause. Thus also it is impossible to will the one without willing the other. Nowadays no one questions the obligatory nature of the rule that ordains that we should exist as a person, and this increasingly so.

One final consideration will show to what extent the division of labour is linked to our whole moral life.

It has long been a dream cherished by men to succeed at last in achieving as a reality the ideal of human brotherhood. Peoples raise their voices to wish for a state of affairs where war would no longer govern international relations, where relationships between societies would be regulated peacefully as are already those between individuals, and where all men would co-operate in the common task and live the same life. Although these aspirations are partly neutralised by others that relate to the particular society of which we form part, they remain very strong and are continually gathering strength. However, they cannot be satisfied unless all men form part of one and the same society, subject to the same laws. For, just as private conflicts can only be contained by the regulatory action of a society that embraces all individuals, so inter-social conflicts can only be contained by the regulatory action of a society that embraces all societies. The only power that can serve to moderate individual egoism is that of the group; the only one that can serve to moderate the egoism of groups is that of another group that embraces them all.

Really, once the problem has been posed in these terms, we must acknowledge that this ideal is not on the verge of being realised in its entirety. Between the different types of society coexisting on earth there are too many intellectual and moral divergences to be able to live in a spirit of brotherhood in the same society. Yet what is possible is that societies of the same species should come together, and it is indeed in this direction that our society appears to be going. We have seen already that there is tending to form, above European peoples, in a spontaneous fashion, a European society that has even now some feeling of its own identity and the beginnings of an organisation.[5] If the formation of one single human society is for ever ruled out – and this has, however, not yet been demonstrated[6] – at least the formation of larger societies will draw us continually closer to that goal. Moreover, these facts do not at all contradict the definition we have given of morality. If we cling to humanity and ought to continue to do so, it is because it is a society in the process of realising itself in this way, one to which we are solidly bound.[7]

Yet we know that more extensive societies cannot be formed without the development of the division of labour. Without a greater specialisation of functions not only could they not sustain their equilibrium, but the increase in the number of elements in competition would also automatically suffice to bring about that state. Even more would this be the case, for an increase in volume does not generally occur without an increase in population density. Thus we may formulate the following proposition: the ideal of human brotherhood cannot be realised unless the division of labour progresses. We must choose: either we must abandon our dream, if we refuse to limit our individual activity any further; or we can pursue the consummation of our dream, but only on the condition just stated.

III

Yet if the division of labour produces solidarity, it is not only because it makes each individual an agent of exchange, to use the language of the economists.[8] It is because it creates between men a whole system of rights and duties joining them in a lasting way to one another. Just as social similarities give rise to a law and a morality that protect them, so the division of labour gives rise to rules ensuring peaceful and regular co-operation between the functions that have been divided up. If economists have believed that this would produce enough solidarity, however it came about, and in consequence have maintained that human societies could and should resolve themselves into purely economic associations, it is because they believed that only individual and temporary interests were at stake. Thus, in order to evaluate the interests that conflict and ascertain how they should be balanced, that is, to determine the conditions in which exchange should take place, individuals alone are competent. Moreover, since these interests are continually developing, there is no room for any permanent regulatory system. But from every viewpoint such a conception is inadequate and does not fit the facts. The division of labour does not present individuals to one another, but social functions. Society has an interest in the interplay of those functions: depending on whether they co-operate regularly or not, society will be healthy or sick. Its existence is therefore dependent upon them, all the more intimately bound up with them the more they are divided. This is why it cannot let them remain in an indeterminate state; moreover, they determine one another. It is like this that rules arise which increase in number the more labour is divided – rules whose absence makes organic solidarity either impossible or imperfect.

But the mere existence of rules is not sufficient: they must also be just. For this the external conditions of competition should be equal. If, on the other hand, we call to mind that the collective consciousness is increasingly reduced to the cult of the individual, we shall see that the characteristic of morality in organised societies, as compared to segmentary societies, is that it possesses something more human, and consequently more rational, about it. It does not cause our activity to depend upon ends that do not directly concern us. It does not make us the servants of some ideal powers completely different in nature from ourselves, powers who follow their own course without heeding the interests of men. It requires us only to be charitable and just towards our fellow-men, to fulfil our task well, to work towards a state where everyone is called to fulfil the function he performs best and will receive a just reward for his efforts. The rules constituting this morality have no constraining power preventing their being fully examined. Because they are better made for us and, in a certain sense, by us, we are freer in relation to them. We seek to understand them and are less afraid to change them. Moreover, we must be careful not to esteem such an ideal defective on the pretext that it is too down-to-earth, too easily within our grasp. An ideal is no more lofty because it is more transcendent, but because it opens up broader vistas to us. It is not important that such an ideal should soar high above us – to an extent that it becomes foreign to us. But it is important that it should open up for our activity a long-term perspective – and such an ideal is far from being on the point of realisation. We feel only too well how laborious a task it is to erect such a society, one in which each individual will have the place he merits and will be rewarded according to his deserts, where everyone will consequently co-operate spontaneously both for the common good and that of the individual. Likewise no morality is superior to all others because its imperatives are couched in a drier, more authoritarian manner, or because it is immune from reflective thinking. Doubtless it must be capable of linking us to something other than ourselves. But there is no need for it to fetter us to the point that it immobilises us.

It has been rightly stated[9] that morality – and this must include both theory and the practice of ethics – is in the throes of an appalling crisis. What we have expounded can help us to understand the causes and nature of this sickness. Over a very short space of time very profound changes have occurred in the structure of our societies. They have liberated themselves from the segmentary model with a speed and in proportions without precedent in history. Thus the morality corresponding to this type of society has lost influence, but without its successor developing quickly enough to occupy the space left vacant in our consciousness. Our beliefs have been disturbed. Tradition has lost its sway. Individual judgement has thrown off the yoke of the collective judgement. On the other hand, the functions that have been disrupted in this period of trial have had no time to adjust to one another. The new life that all of a sudden has arisen has not been able to organise itself thoroughly. Above all, it has not been organised so as to satisfy the need for justice that has been aroused even more passionately in our hearts. If this is so, the remedy for the ill is nevertheless not to seek to revive traditions and practices that no longer correspond to present-day social conditions, and that could only subsist in a life that would be artificial, one only of appearance. We need to put a stop to this anomie, and to find ways of harmonious co-operation between those organs that still clash discordantly together. We need to introduce into their relationships a greater justice by diminishing those external inequalities that are the source of our ills. Our disease is therefore not, as occasionally we appear to believe, of an intellectual order, but linked to deeper causes. We are not suffering because we no longer know on what theoretical idea should be sustained the morality we have practised up to now. The cause is that certain elements of this morality have been irretrievably undermined, and the morality we require is only in the process of taking shape. Our anxiety does not arise because the criticism of scientists has demolished the traditional explanation handed down to us regarding our duties. Consequently it is not a new philosophical system that will ever be capable of dispelling that anxiety. Rather is it because certain of these duties no longer being grounded on reality, a loosening of ties has occurred that can only stop when a new discipline has become established and consolidated itself. In short, our first duty at the present time is to fashion a morality for ourselves. Such a task cannot be improvised in the silence of the study. It can arise only of its own volition, gradually, and under the pressure of internal causes that render it necessary. What reflection can and must do is to prescribe the goal that must be attained. That is what we have striven to accomplish.

Notes

1. Cf. *supra*, Book I, Chapter III, § II.
2. However, there is perhaps another limit about which we need not speak, since it rather concerns individual hygiene. It might be maintained that, as a result of our organic and psychological make-up, the division of labour cannot go beyond a certain limit without disorders ensuing. Without going into the question, let us however note that the extreme specialisation that the biological functions have attained does not seem to substantiate this hypothesis. Furthermore, even in the domain of psychological and social functions, through historical development, has not the division of labour between man and woman been carried to its ultimate limit? Have not whole abilities been lost by the latter, and is the converse not also true? Why should the same phenomenon not occur between persons of the same sex?

Undoubtedly time is always needed for the organism to adapt to these changes, but we cannot see why a day should come when this adaptation will become impossible.

3. Among the practical consequences that could be drawn from the proposition we have just established, there is one that concerns pedagogy. As regards education one always reasons as if the moral foundation of man was made up of generalities. We have just seen that this is in no way true. Man is destined to fulfil a special function in the social organism, and consequently he must learn in advance how to play his part as one organ. An education is necessary for this, just as it is for him to learn to play his part as a man, as is said. Moreover, we do not mean that the child should be brought up prematurely for a particular occupation, but he should be induced to like limited tasks and well-defined horizons. This aptitude is very different from that of general matters and cannot be awakened by the same means.

4. Cf. *supra*, pp. 214 ff. and p. 252.

5. Cf. pp. 222–3.

6. There is nothing that demonstrates that the intellectual and moral diversity of societies is destined to continue. The ever greater expansion of higher societies, whereby the absorption or elimination of less advanced societies occurs, is tending in any case to lessen that diversity.

7. Thus the duties we have towards society do not take precedence over those we have towards our country. For the latter is the sole society that is at present realised of which we form part. The other is hardly more than a *desideratum*, whose realisation is not even certain.

8. The term is that of de Molinari, *La morale économique*, p. 248.

9. Cf. Beaussire, *Les principes de la morale*, introduction.

Index

DOL is often used as an abbreviation for 'Division of Labour'

343

348   *Index*